India

THE NORTH

VANESSA BETTS
VICTORIA McCULLOCH

D1011962

CONTENTS

THIS IS
NORTH INDIA

India captures the imagination like no other place on earth. It is many countries all rolled into one, and the diversity of landscape and culture is especially pronounced in the North. On one dream trip, you could be on a camel in Rajasthan riding out into the desert sunset. On another, find yourself on top of the world, feet in snow, as you trek to the source of the Ganges. Maybe your fantasy is to float on a houseboat in Kashmir or to venture deep into the jungle stalking tigers in Ranthambhore. You could be among the press of bodies at the Kumbh Mela, the biggest spiritual gathering on earth, or simply on a quest to find the perfect cup of tea in Darjeeling. The magic of North India is that you can experience all these things and more.

India is a place of pilgrimage. You may find inner peace at the Golden Temple in Amritsar or at the busy Krishna temple in Mathura, by following the Buddhist trail to Bodhgaya, or by drifting back in time on a boat along the Ganges at Varanasi. Or maybe you want to uncover the country's glorious past through its magnificent palaces and forts. Being a Maharani for a day is easy in northern India: stay in a jewel-like palace in the middle of a lake, ride an elephant to the top of Meherangarh fort, or perch on a bench like Princess Diana outside the Taj Mahal – a 'teardrop on the face of humanity'.

North India puts chaos theory to the test. It's a place of contrasts: chaotic but charming; challenging but colourful; delightfully overwhelming and stunningly beautiful. This assault on your senses includes being woken by bird calls at Chhatra Sagar reservoir, by clanging temple bells in Orchha, by the Muslim call to prayer in Lucknow, or by building works at five in the morning (almost anywhere). Meanwhile your eyes are confronted with a rich tapestry of colour: from the rainbow-painted hillside towns in Uttarkhand, to the pink, blue and golden cities of Rajasthan, and the rich ochre of Varanasi's timeless buildings. Even the camels, elephants and long-haul trucks are brightly decorated. And then there are the colourful people dressed in vivid, sweeping saris or flamboyant turbans. India has a population of 1.2 billion, and the northern states are the most populous: who might you meet along the way?

Vanessa Betts

Victoria McCulloch

Dal Lake, Srinagar

FIRST STEPS
PUTTING IT ALL TOGETHER

Late summer would be a good time to start with a trip through Kashmir and Ladakh.

North India covers a vast area encompassing many different terrains: the deserts in Rajasthan, the Gangetic plains of Uttar Pradesh and Bihar, subtropical forests in Meghalaya and, of course, the towering Himalaya and their foothills and valleys. The four suggested itineraries in this guide focus on the western state of Rajasthan, the far northern areas bordering Pakistan and China, a swathe of the central plains and the northeastern fringes of the subcontinent, where the culture becomes distinctly tribal. They offer comprehensive three-week tours, covering the highlights and must-sees of each area, but can be adapted to include specific interests, such as wildlife-watching, trekking or the Buddhist trail; for returning visitors, there are side-trips to more remote and less popular places.

If you have plenty of time, you could combine these routes into a grand tour of North India. Late summer would be a good time to start with a trip through Kashmir and Ladakh; Leh lies beyond the monsoon line, so, while the rains are sweeping across the lowland plains, here the days are clear and bright. Move on to Rajasthan, where you could easily spend a month or more. By October, the temperatures in Madhya Pradesh and Uttar Pradesh are much more tolerable, so you can explore Delhi, Lucknow, Agra and Varanasi, before moving east to Kolkata and the hills of North Bengal, Sikkim and Meghalaya before it gets too cool.

International arrivals will fly into Delhi, the starting point for three of the four itineraries. Domestic flights are relatively cheap, so it's worth using Delhi as a hub even if you don't wish to make repeat visits to the city itself. From Delhi, trains connect with all major Indian cities including Amritsar, Jaipur, Agra, Lucknow, Varanasi and Kolkata, and are preferable to taking the bus. An overnight train journey is an essential element of any trip to India and can be an entirely comfortable experience in first- or second-class air-conditioned carriages. However, train lines don't cover the northernmost areas of Himachal Pradesh, Kashmir and Ladakh, so by taking the occasional flight (such as between Leh and Delhi) you can save literally days of overland travel. For shorter journeys, buses come into their own: frequent state and private services link cities, towns and even tiny villages, meaning you can move on spontaneously without needing to book in advance. For some routes, including access to national parks, the best option is to hire a car and driver if you want to avoid inconvenient bus and train connections. In the mountainous north, jeeps are the fastest way to get around; shared jeeps cover the major destinations if you don't have the budget to hire a private vehicle.

→ DOING IT ALL

Delhi → Amritsar → Srinagar → Kargil → Leh → Delhi-Ranthambhore → Jaipur → Pushkar → Udaipur → Kumbhalgarh → Jodhpur → Nagaur → Jaisalmer → Agra → Gwalior → Orchha → Khujaraho → Bandhavgarh → Varanasi → Bodhgaya → Kolkata → Darjeeling → Sikkim → Guwahati → Shillong → Cherrapunji → Kaziranga → Jorhat → Sibsagar → Dibrugarh → Kolkata

1 Leh–Manali road 2 Camel fair, Pushkar 3 River Ganga, Varanasi 4 Buddhist prayer wheel, Ladakh

DREAM TRIP 1
DELHI → AGRA → RAJASTHAN → DELHI

Best time to visit
October to March is the best time to visit this area. After March you can expect high temperatures, even hitting 48°C, and the monsoon rains start in July and last until early October. There are usually pleasant temperatures around 30°C in October and November. Delhi is affected by the deserts and also by the Himalaya to the north, so January and February are much cooler in the city and can even drop to 5°C; fog can sometimes be an issue. Rajasthan is desert territory so expect warm days but chilly nights October through March.

This first itinerary takes you from the country's capital to the iconic Taj Mahal and then to the stunning desert forts and palaces of Rajasthan. Ideally you should allow for a three-week trip, although you could see the key sights in a shorter time. Delhi (page 35) deserves at least two days however tight your schedule. Don't miss Qutb Minar in the south, the first of Delhi's seven cities, where the Mughals used existing Hindu temples to make their 73-m minaret – the tallest in India. Then explore the Old City and the bustle of Chandni Chowk and Kinari Bazaar, where you'll find traditional craftsmen and *jalebi wallas* (sweetmakers). Hop on a cycle rickshaw through the labyrinthine streets to reach the Jama Masjid mosque and the Red Fort. One evening venture to Haus Khaz, a university district that is now a hub for designers and creative types with a great array of food and music.

From Delhi, head south by train to Agra (page 67), site of the unmissable Taj Mahal, and continue to the fascinating abandoned city of Fatehpur Sikri nearby. For a break from urban India, travel by road or rail to the jungles of Ranthambhore (page 84) to spend a couple of nights tiger-stalking, before continuing to the pink city of

1

Jaipur (page 89). During a two-day visit, you could see the beautiful city palace, the Jantar Mantar observatory and the vibrant markets, and enjoy the view from Nawalgarh (Tiger Fort) at sunset. From Jaipur, venture on to Pushkar (page 105), with its sacred lake circled by Hindu temples; walk to the hilltop Savitri temple to drink in the view. Within rural Rajasthan you will need to travel by bus (or with a private vehicle if you're short of time); the magic is often found

Spend a couple of nights tiger-stalking the jungles of Ranthambhore, before continuing to the pink city of Jaipur.

1 Taj Mahal, Agra 2 Ranthambhore National Park 3 Pushkar Lake

in the smaller places dotted along the way. Allow 24 hours to visit a desert palace like Deogarh or to go birdwatching and walking at Chhatra Sagar. Spend three nights in Udaipur (page 110), whose palaces are dotted in and around the lake and surrounding hills. Take a boat trip to Fateh Sagar, or simply sit at one of the many rooftop restaurants at sunset and watch the lights flickering on. Along the winding roads between Udaipur and Jodhpur are some beautiful retreats where it's worth spending a night: Kumbhalgarh has a wildlife sanctuary and Ranakpur is famed for its Jain temples. Closer to Jodhpur is Rohet Garh where William Dalrymple holed up to write *City of Djinns*. Rajasthan's most imposing fort, Meherangarh, rises above the blue city of Jodhpur (page 126), circled by birds of prey. Down in the town you will find a vibrant market famed for its spices and saffron lassi. After a couple of days here, head off the beaten track to stay at the recently renovated Nagaur fort, in the former residence of the King's many wives. Conclude your Rajasthan adventure with three days in and around Jaisalmer (page 135), including a night in the Thar desert on a camel safari. Fly from Jaisalmer back to Delhi to connect with your flight home.

1 Patna   2 Kumbhalgarh Fort   3 View of Jodhpur from Mehrangarh Fort   4 Bundi   5 Amber Fort, Jaipur

→ **GOING FURTHER**

From Ranthambhore, venture to **Bundi**, where Rudyard Kipling was inspired to write *Kim*. From Jaipur, visit the beautiful *haveli* mansions in the **Shekawati region**. → **page 87, page 101**

4

5

DELHI **1**

2

SHEKAWATI

10 Jaisalmer

9 Nagaur

8 Jodhpur

Rohet Sardar

7

Rawla Narlai

Kumbhalgarh

Udaipur

6

5 Jaipur

Samode

Pushkar

Chhatra Sagar

Deogarh

Bundi

Ranthambhore National Park

4

3 Agra

N

50 km
50 miles

1 Thar Desert, near Jaisalmer 2 Amber Fort, Jaipur 3 Bazar in Delhi

→ WISH LIST

1 See an alternative side of Delhi with a walking tour led by the inspirational street kids from Salaam Baalak Trust. **2** Visit happening Haus Khaz in south Delhi and find great restaurants, live music and DJs. **3** Be inspired by the inestimable Taj Mahal: it sums up India in one heartbeat. **4** Get the chance to spot tigers, leopards and sloths in stunning Ranthambhore National Park. **5** Don't miss the tiny atmospheric Shila Mata temple inside the hilltop fort of Amber. **6** Look down upon the beautiful lake city of Udaipur and its surrounding hills at sunset from the Monsoon Palace. **7** Drink chai from a clay cup at a roadside *dhaba* somewhere between Udaipur and Jodhpur. **8** Go up to Mehrangahr Fort in Jodhpur at night to see the lights of the city below. **9** Stay inside the atmospheric Nagaur Fort, north of Jodhpur. **10** Admire the fairytale 'sandcastle' fort at Jaisalmer before riding out into the sand dunes on a camel.

DREAM TRIP 2
DELHI → AMRITSAR → SRINAGAR → LEH → DELHI

Best time to visit June to September is tourist season in the mountain valleys of Ladakh, which lie beyond the monsoon line. Summer days can get searingly hot, while nights are pleasantly cool. In winter, temperatures can drop to -30°C and road access is made impossible by snowfall. The Srinagar–Leh road is usually open from April to November, however, so, if you aren't afraid of the cold, then the quieter months of May and October are also feasible. The monsoon comes to Kashmir from July to September, so the beginning and end of the season are best in order to miss the rains.

This itinerary takes you high up into the Himalaya: to the mountain plains of Ladakh and the stunning scenery of Kashmir. Your starting point, however, is Delhi (page 35). (For things to do in this overwhelming city, refer to Dream Trip 1, page 8.) Heading northwest by air, train or road from Delhi to Amritsar (page 145), you'll almost touch the Pakistani border. Amritsar is home to the Golden Temple, the holiest shrine of the Sikh faith. One of the best times to visit is at Amritvela (dawn of nectar), when the devotees gather for morning prayers and the light starts to reflect off the temple into the surrounding pool. You then fly into the beautiful Kashmir Valley (page 154) to enjoy the watery delights of Srinagar (page 154). Brightly painted *shikaras* paddle the waterways between Dal Lake, Nagin Lake and the River Jhelum, passing formal Mughal gardens, villages and islands.

1 Golden Temple, Amritsar 2 Dal Lake, Srinagar 3 Lamayuru Monastery, Leh

The Old City is crammed with Sufi shrines, curious mosques and little alleyways of artisans; set aside some time to browse the famed Kashmiri wares in shops by the Bund. After a day in the city, spend a couple of nights relaxing on one of the ornate wooden houseboats. The three-day road trip by jeep from Srinagar to Ladakh (page 170) is simply staggering, crossing mountain passes and plunging through river valleys dotted with monasteries and tiny villages. The moonscape setting of Lamayuru, with its gompa perched upon a crumbling crag, is the perfect spot for a lunch break and leg-stretch. Another must-see en route is the Alchi Monastery, where the interior murals represent the pinnacle of the region's Indo-Tibetan art.

After a day in the city, spend a couple of nights relaxing on one of the ornate wooden houseboats.

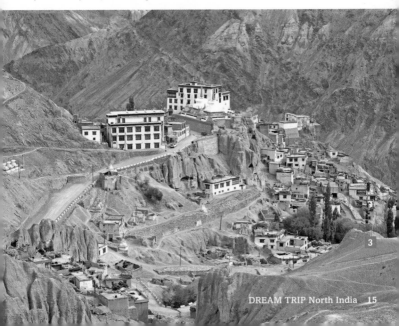

DREAM TRIP 2
DELHI → AMRITSAR → SRINAGAR → LEH → DELHI

Arrival at the mellow city of Leh (page 171) means a chance to kick-back for a day or two, sampling Ladakhi food in garden restaurants, and settling into a traditional family-run guesthouse. The pretty rural surroundings are peppered with stupas and orchards, while the Old Town bazar makes for a bustling contrast; the stern fortress of Leh Palace looms above it all. If you're the active type, there are a couple of treks in Ladakh that can be done over three days, or, instead, head north to the remote wilds of the Nubra Valley (page 178) to meet camels on the dunes. The high-altitude lake of Pangong-Tso lies half in Tibet and half in Ladakh; you can stay overnight by the turquoise waters for true isolation. From Leh, head back to Delhi by air.

1 Nubra Valley, Ladakh 2 Yuru Kabgyat festival, Lamayuru 3 Suru Valley, Ladakh

→ GOING FURTHER

From Delhi make a first foray into the Himalayan foothills to relax in the mellow Buddhist villages around **Dharamsala**. Make the long journey back to Delhi from Leh overland via **Manali** and the **Kullu Valley**, or explore the wildlife in **Corbett National Park**. **→ page 152, page 183, page 185**

→ ROUTE PLANNER

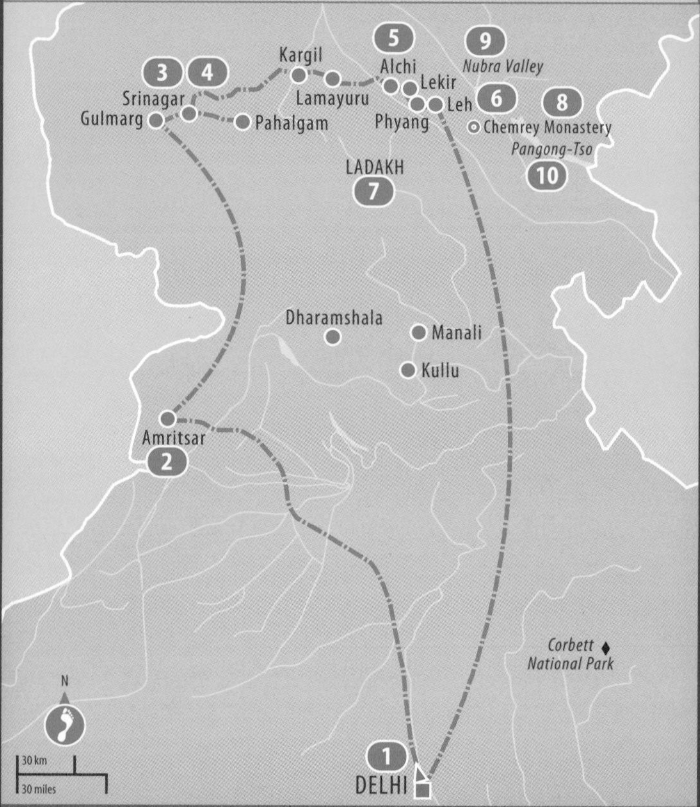

5
9
Kargil
Alchi
Nubra Valley
3
4
Lekir
Srinagar
Lamayuru
6
8
Leh
Gulmarg
Pahalgam
Phyang
Chemrey Monastery
Pangong-Tso
LADAKH
10
7
Dharamshala
Manali
Kullu
Amritsar
2
Corbett
National Park
N
1
30 km
30 miles
DELHI

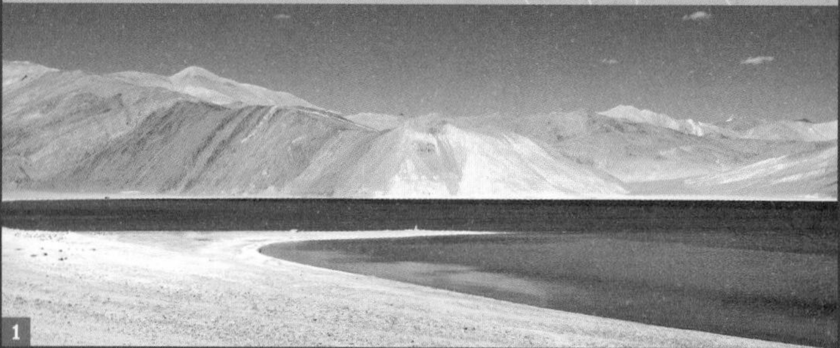

1

1 Pangong-Tso, Ladakh **2** Srinagar

1 Start with the first of Delhi's seven cities in the south at Qutb Minar, where a stunning minaret towers above the complex. **2** Listen to the chanting at the Golden Temple in Amritsar; time your visit to coincide with sunrise or sunset. **3** Get a *shikara* to paddle you along waterways lined with stilt homes in Srinagar, then stroll the gardens of the Mughal emperors around Dal Lake. **4** Delve into Srinagar's Old City alleyways to see mosques and Sufi shrines decorated with beautiful Kashmiri papier mâché. **5** Visit Alchi Monastery to admire its 1000-year-old wall paintings, some of the oldest surviving in Ladakh. **6** Climb up to Leh Palace to take in phenomenal views of the town and valley. Then take tiny pathways through barley fields to find hidden gompas, and enjoy a lingering lunch in one of Leh's garden restaurants. **7** Trek through one of Ladakh's unspoilt valleys; sleep in a village homestay, or camp under myriad stars. **8** Find peace and tranquillity at the spectacular Chemrey Monastery, just off the main tourist trail. **9** Take a camel ride through the dunes of the Nubra Valley: this is literally the end of the road in North India. **10** Brace yourself for the tough but unforgettable journey to Pangong-Tso, a shimmering lake that lies mainly in Tibet.

2

DREAM TRIP 3
DELHI → AGRA → VARANASI → LUCKNOW → DELHI

Best time to visit
October to March is the best time to visit this area. October and November enjoy particularly pleasant temperatures rarely exceeding 30°C. December and January are still a good time to visit, although Delhi and Agra can get quite chilly and temperatures are sometimes as low as 5°C. After March you can expect increasingly high temperatures, reaching 45°C in May and June. The monsoon rains start in July and sometimes cause flooding in Varanasi when the mighty River Ganga breaks its banks.

This route heads east from Delhi and Agra into the Ganges plains and takes in Islamic heritage, Hindu mythology and Buddhist wisdom. The majestic Ganga River, the central vein of Hindu mythology, sweeps through the state of Uttar Pradesh, which is also the cultural heartland of Islam in India, with Mughal architecture at its best in Agra, Gwalior and Lucknow. And, at Bodhgaya in Bihar, you reach the point where Buddha achieved enlightenment. To see the key sites in this area in three weeks involves travel by train and bus; occasionally, it makes sense to hire a car and driver.

As so much of this route takes in the rich spiritual history of India, why not start the exploration in Delhi (page 35), with the striking Hindu Lakshmi Narayan Birla Temple and the contemporary Lotus Temple of the Baha'i faith. You can go to Nizamuddin's tomb to enjoy the Sufi singing or walk around the beautiful pool surrounding the Sikh temple Gurudwara Bangla Sahib. (For other sights and experiences in the Indian capital, refer to Dream Trip 1, page 8.)

1 Gwalior Fort **2** Fatehpur Sikri **3** Sikh man **4** Lakshminarayan Temple, Orchha

Then it's a bus or train ride to India's teardrop, the Taj Mahal – a monument of love built for Mumtaz, the wife of Mughal emperor Shah Jahan. From Agra (page 67) you should also visit Akbar's mausoleum and the Mughal capital he built at Fathepur Sikri. It's a short hop by bus or train to the striking fort at Gwalior (page 189), which contains inspiring Jain and Hindu temples, and then a half-day journey moving off the beaten track to the sleepy town of Orchha (page 194), where the beautiful fort and palace of Jahangir Mahal nestle in a bend

of the Betwa river, blending Hindu and Muslim styles. From Orchha take a bus or taxi to get to Khajuraho (page 198), with its exquisitely worked erotic temple sculptures. It's best to take a driver from Khajuraho to Bandhavgarh National Park (page 206), home to tigers, leopards and a range of their prey. You can stay close to nature in a royal tent or a boutique tree house. From the national park, make your way to Katni or Umaria to catch the train to sacred Varanasi (page 210). Even in this bustling city, with its imposing riverside buildings, labyrinthine streets and burning ghats, peace and serenity can be found as you glide along the Ganga at dawn in a rowboat, or as you cast your flowers and prayers into the river at evening *puja*. Take the train from Varanasi (or better from Mughal Serai) to reach Gaya and the heart of Buddhism at Bodhgaya (page 221). Buddhists from all over the world gather here to visit the Bodhi tree where Buddha attained nirvana, so you will see examples of Japanese, Burmese, Tibetan, Chinese and Thai Buddhist temple architecture. And, finally, make your way back towards Delhi via Lucknow (page 225), a city filled with rich Islamic culture, decaying mansions and a vibrant craft market.

1 Khajuraho 2 Varanasi 3 Cycle-rickshaws in Lucknow 4 Kumbh Mela, Allahabad

3

4

→ GOING FURTHER

After visiting Bandhavgarh National Park, take a train from Katni to **Allahabad**, before continuing to Varanasi. **→ page 208**

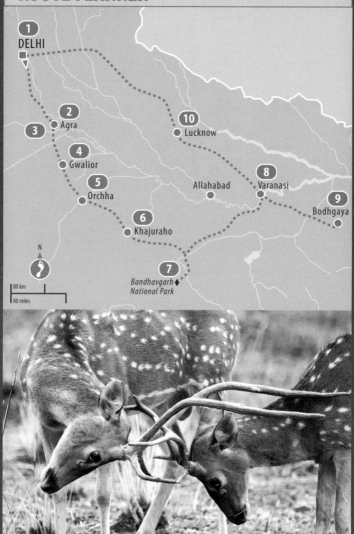

1 DELHI

2 Agra

3

4 Gwalior

5 Orchha

6 Khajuraho

7 Bandhavgarh National Park

8 Varanasi

9 Bodhgaya

10 Lucknow

Allahabad

N

80 km
80 miles

1 Bandhavgarh National Park 2 Jama Masjid, Delhi 3 Maha Sivaratri, Varanasi

1 Get into the heart of Old Delhi by cycle-rickshaw towards the majestic Jama Masjid, taking in the labyrinthine streets behind Chandni Chowk. **2** Gaze at the magnificent, Taj Mahal from the archways of Agra's Red Fort. **3** Explore the architecture of the Mughal Empire at the abandoned city of Fatehpur Sikri. **4** Visit the remains of the Teli Ka Mandir temple at Gwalior Fort, with its unusual stone and blue-tile façade. **5** Sleep inside the lovely Sheesh Mahal in the middle of Orchha fort; it really is like stepping back in time. **6** Don't miss the atmospheric Matangesvara at Khajuraho, a 1000-year-old Shiva temple that is still active for morning and evening *pujas*. **7** Go hunting for tigers with your camera in the rugged terrain of Bandhavgarh National Park. **8** Watch the sunrise and the early morning bathers as you are propelled by rowboat along the majestic Ganga river at Varanasi. **9** Soak up peace and prayers at the Mahabodi Temple in Bodhgaya at dusk. **10** Explore the historical monuments of Lucknow, where extravagant Mughal vies with best of classical European architecture.

Best time to visit The plains of West Bengal and Assam are most pleasant between October to March, when the days aren't too hot and the nights are cool. However, between December and February the Himalayan foothills in Darjeeling and Sikkim get extremely cold and night-time requires several layers. However, in November and December especially, air clarity is good and spectacular views are the benefit. Mid-June to September is monsoon season and best avoided, as are the very humid pre-monsoon months of April and May.

A trip to India's lesser-visited northeast begins in Kolkata (page 233) – the first capital of the Raj, and liberally sprinkled with iconic colonial buildings, churches, cemeteries and history. Each and every square foot in between is occupied by manic markets, streetfood stalls, pavement vendors, and life lived in public – at times a humbling sight. The mansions of north Calcutta still stand and the most re- markable is the Marble Palace, crammed with antiques and oodles of atmosphere. Be sure to try Bengali cuisine in either Kewpies or Oh! Calcutta, experience the *adda* (debate) in the legendary Indian Coffee House and a sip a beer in the garden at the Fairlawn Hotel. An overnight train takes you to the foothills of the Himalaya and the hill stations of Kurseong (page 251) and Darjeeling (page 252). Raj-era hotels enhance the colonial experience, and tea gardens and magnificent views surround. For the classic view of Kangchenjunga, you'll need to get up before dawn to see sunrise from Tiger Hill, but when the weather is clear Darjeeling itself gives an impressive aspect. Organize a permit for Sikkim when in Darjeeling, and take a jeep to Pelling to visit the 17th-century Pemayangste Monastery (page 262) with its stunning murals and *thangkas* in the Buddhist tradition. There's fantastic walking in the hills and forested valleys

around Pelling, Kecheopalri Lake and the attractive village of Yuksom (page 263) that you can undertake without guides and permits. This is also the starting point for the famed Gocha La trek which takes eight or nine days and ends with extraordinary close-up views of the eastern face of Kangchenjunga. The next stage of the journey can be done either by flying from Bagdogra or taking an overnight train to Guwahati (page 265) in Assam. The road then leads south to Shillong (page 269) in Meghalaya, to explore the largest market in the northeast where Khasi women trade mountains of betel nut, curious vegetables and sharp weapons, and hopefully you'll catch an archery competition in the afternoon. Moving on, Cherrapunji (page 271) is a short jeep ride away and set in wild moorlands reminiscent of Scotland. Distinctive not only for being the wettest

Yuksom is is also the starting point for the famed Gocha La trek which takes eight or nine days and ends with extraordinary close-up views of the eastern face of Kangchenjunga.

1 Kolkata 2 Bara Bazar, Shillong 3 Khasi hills between Shillong and Cherrapunji

place on earth, the forests and villages a few kilometres distant are also unique for their living root bridges, one of which is an impressive 'double-decker'.

Travel back to spend a night in Guwahati, on the Brahmaputra River, before delving deeper into Assam to see the great one-horned rhinoceros in Kaziranga National Park (page 272). Other fauna in this World Heritage Site include elephant, sambar, wild water buffalo and a wealth of birdlife attracting ornithologists from around the globe. Consider treating yourself to a stay in a fabulous lodge on the edge of the park, with the chance of glimpsing a rhino from the veranda as you enjoy a sundowner. A bus or taxi can cover the next leg, which takes you to the districts of either Jorhat (page 277) or Dibrugarh (page 278) for a spell of relaxation on a tea estate. Plantation bungalows offer the ideal retreat, among working tea gardens and near interesting little villages. Also worth a visit are the Hindu temples and Ahom monuments and palaces in Sibsagar, 'the ocean of Shiva', a couple of hours away. From Assam, you can fly, or take the long train ride, back to Kolkata.

1 Guwahati 2 Kaziranga National Park 3 Sela Pass 4 Tea harvest, Jorhat

→ GOING FURTHER

Murshidabad, trekking around Darjeeling and Tezpur to Tawang. → page 248, page 257, page 273

3

4

→ ROUTE PLANNER

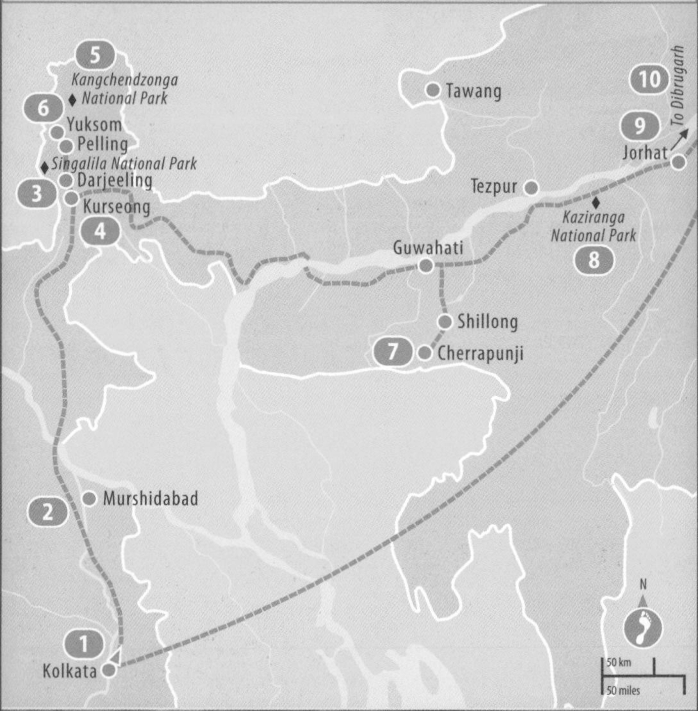
5
Kangchendzonga National Park
6
Yuksom
Pelling
Singalila National Park
3
Darjeeling
Kurseong
4
Tawang
10
9
To Dibrugarh
Jorhat
Tezpur
Kaziranga National Park
8
Guwahati
Shillong
7
Cherrapunji
2
Murshidabad
1
Kolkata
N
50 km
50 miles

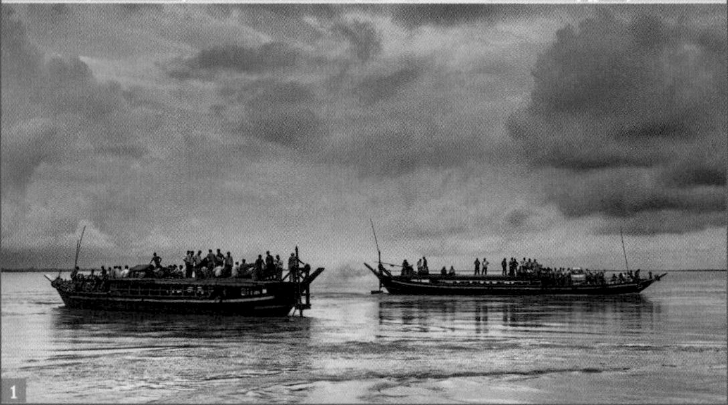
1

1 River Brahmaputra **2** Kaziranga National Park **3** Victoria Memorial, Kolkata **4** Buddhist monastery, Sikkim

→ WISH LIST

1 Stroll through Kolkata's expansive Maidan to the glorious white-marble Victoria Memorial, a Raj homage to the Empress of India, which houses a fascinating collection of paintings and a museum revealing the history of the city. **2** Experience rural life in sultry Murshidabad, the former capital of the Nawabs of Bengal. Monuments, palaces and mosques are sprinkled throughout the sleepy riverside town. It's worth the extra effort to get there. **3** Wind your way up to the hill stations of Kurseong and Darjeeling in the North Bengal hills, where tea estates, Tibetan communities and the colonial past intermingle. **4** Take a ride on the Toy Train to Ghoom, a World Heritage experience. **5** Marvel at the views of Kangchenjunga and the Himalaya — utterly breathtaking, when you get a break in the clouds. **6** Visit Sikkim's timeless Buddhist monasteries: Pemangyste, Rumtek and Tashiding all have memorable paintings, beautiful settings — and ancient rituals that are very much alive. **7** Head to mystical Meghalaya, the 'abode of the clouds', to discover the living root bridges that have connected villages in the forests around Cherrapunji for centuries. The matriarchal markets of the state are some of India's most fascinating. **8** Come face-to-face with one-horned rhinos in Kaziranga National Park, where 75% of the world's population of these magnificent beasts roam the jungle and plains. **9** Sit back and sip G'n'T on the veranda of a plantation bungalow, deep in the heart of Assam. Other more active pursuits might include horse-riding, tea tours, golf — or board games. **10** Treat yourself to a magical cruise on one of the Northeast's great rivers. Monsoon-time trips take in colonial and Islamic heritage along the Hooghly, or during the dry season visit the national parks and vast river islands of the Brahmaputra in Assam.

DREAM TRIP 1
Delhi→Agra→Rajasthan→Delhi 21 days

Delhi 2 nights, page 35

Agra 2 nights, page 67
Bus/train from Delhi (5-6 hrs/2½ hrs);
with a driver on Yamuna Expressway (3 hrs)

Ranthambhore 2 nights, page 84
Train/driver from Agra via Jaipur
(10 hrs/6 hrs)

Jaipur 2 nights (with option of 1 night
at Samode), page 89
Train/driver from Ranthambore (2 hrs/4 hrs)

Pushkar 1 night, page 105
From Jaipur, bus (4-5 hrs), train (4-5 hrs via
Ajmer with taxi on to Pushkar) or driver
(3½ hrs)

**Rural Rajasthan (Chhatra Sagar or
Deogarh Mahal)** 1 night, page 107
Bus/driver from Pushkar to Chhatra
Sagar (3 hrs/2 hrs) or to Deogarh Mahal
(4½ hrs/3½ hrs)

Udaipur 3 nights, page 110
Bus/driver from Chhatra Sagar (6½ hrs/
5 hrs) from Deogarh (5½ hrs/3½ hrs)

Kumbhalgarh 1 night, page 121
Bus/driver from Udaipur (2½ hrs/2 hrs)

**Rural retreat (Rawla Narlai or Rohet
Gahr)** 1 night, pages 123 or 124
Bus/driver from Kumbhalgarh to Rawla
Narlai (1 hr) and to Rohet Garh (3 hrs)

Jodhpur 2 nights, page 126
Bus/driver to Jodhpur from Rawla Narlai
(3½ hrs) and Rohet Garh (1½ hrs)

Nagaur 1 night, page 131
Bus/driver from Jodhpur (4 hrs/3 hrs)

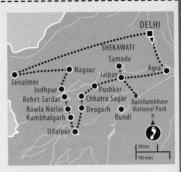

Jaisalmer 3 nights (including 1 night
desert safari), page 135
Bus/driver from Nagaur (7 hrs /5½ hrs)

Delhi page 35
Fly back to Delhi to connect with
international flight home

GOING FURTHER

Bundi page 87
3-hr drive from Jaipur

Shekhawati page 101
3-hr drive from Jaipur

DREAM TRIP 1
Delhi→Agra→Rajasthan→Delhi

The Golden Triangle of Delhi, Agra and Jaipur can be the window through which you see everything you had imagined India would be. It can be a window with ornate jali work, or an arch-shaped window, or one with bright stained-glass panels.

In Delhi, you might look out of your taxi window and see the rate of change: modern buildings vying for prominence with the colonial arches of Connaught Place and the Mughal architecture of Qutb Minar. From an ornate window in the Red Fort in Agra, you can gaze across the water to the Taj Mahal just as Shah Jahan must have done when he was imprisoned there – the view of the monument will take your breath away. From the windows of the ornate wind palace, the Hawa Mahal, you can look down onto the bustling streets of Tripolia Bazaar in Jaipur and see camel carts lope past, going head to head with cycle-rickshaws, cars and buses. This is where the ladies of the court used to sit to watch official processions. In Amber Fort you might look down on lines of elephants transporting people up to the imposing gateway of the fort, as they have for hundreds of years.

Beyond the Golden Triangle, lies the state of Rajasthan, which exceeds even the most far-fetched fantasies of what India might be: women dazzle in swathes of brilliant bright fabrics; luxuriously mustachioed men drive camels over dunes; tigers and leopards prowl through ancient forests; and princely forts and palaces loom up from the crushingly hot sweep of the Thar Desert. Despite its understandable popularity with tourists, this region is a sumptuous feast for the senses with many corners where you can still truly get away from it all.

DELHI

Delhi can take you aback with its vibrancy and growth. Less than 60 years ago the spacious, quiet and planned city of New Delhi was still the pride of late colonial British India, while to its north, the lanes of Old Delhi resonated with the sounds of a bustling medieval market. Today, both worlds have been overtaken by the rush of modernization. As Delhi's population surges, its tentacles have spread in all directions – from both the ancient core of Shahjahan's city in the north and the late British capital of New Delhi to its south.

Close to New Delhi Railway Station, the cheap hotels and guesthouses of Paharganj squeeze between cloth merchants and wholesalers. In Old Delhi, further north, with the Red Fort and Jama Masjid, the old city is still a dense network of narrow alleys and tightly packed markets and houses. Your senses are bombarded by noise, bustle, smells and apparent chaos. A 'third city' comprises the remorselessly growing squatter settlements (jhuggies), which provide shelter for more than a third of Delhi's population. To the south is another, newer, chrome-and-glass city, the city of the modern suburbs and urban 'farms', where the rural areas of Gurgaon have become the preserve of the prosperous, with shopping malls, banks and private housing-estates. Old and new, simple and sophisticated, traditional and modern, East and West are juxtaposed. Whatever India you are looking for, the capital has it all – getting lost in warrens of crowded streets, wandering through spice markets, eating kebabs by the beautiful Jama Masjid, lazing among Mogul ruins, listening to Sufi musicians by a shrine at dusk or shopping in giant shining malls, drinking cocktails in glitzy bars and travelling on the gleaming metro. But make no mistake, Delhi is developing at breakneck speed – visit soon before it changes beyond recognition (see box, page 41).

→ ARRIVING IN DELHI

GETTING THERE

Delhi is served by **Indira Gandhi International (IGI) Airport**, which handles both international and domestic traffic. The new T3 has one of the longest runways in Asia and is connected to the city centre by metro. It is about 23 km from the centre. During the day, it can take 30-45 minutes from the Domestic Terminal and 45 minutes to an hour from the International Terminal to get to the centre. With the metro, it should take 20 minutes. A free shuttle runs between the terminals. To get to town take a prepaid taxi or an airport coach or ask your hotel to collect you.

The **Inter State Bus Terminus (ISBT)** is at Kashmere Gate, near the Red Fort, about 30 minutes by bus from Connaught Place. Local buses connect it to the other ISBTs.

There are three main railway stations. The busy **New Delhi Station**, a 10-minute walk north of Connaught Place, can be maddeningly chaotic; you need to have all your wits about you. The quieter **Hazrat Nizamuddin** (which has some south-bound trains) is 5 km southeast of Connaught Place. The overpoweringly crowded **Old Delhi Station** (2 km north of Connaught Place) has a few important trains.

MOVING ON

Whether you are heading southeast to **Agra** (Dream Trips 1 and 3, see page 67, 2½ hours) or northwest to **Amritsar** (Dream Trip 2, see page 145, six hours), the train portal is New Delhi train station, north of Connaught Place. If you have minimal luggage you can get to

DELHI

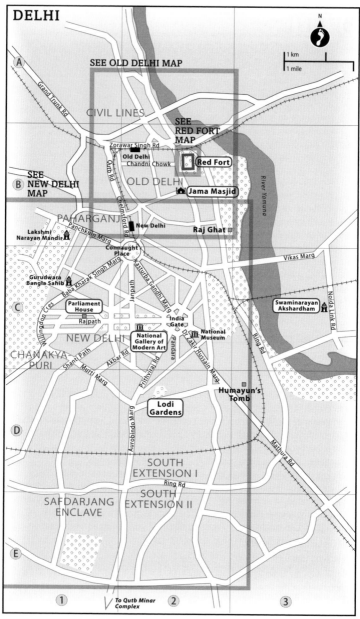

N

1 km
1 mile

SEE OLD DELHI MAP

CIVIL LINES

SEE RED FORT MAP

Grand Trunk Rd

Zorawar Singh Rd

Qutb Rd

Old Delhi
Chandni Chowk

Red Fort

SEE NEW DELHI MAP

OLD DELHI

Jama Masjid

River Yamuna

PAHARGANJ

Chelmsford Rd

Panchkuin Marg

New Delhi

Raj Ghat

Lakshmi Narayan Mandir

Connaught Place

Vikas Marg

Gurudwara Bangla Sahib

Baba Kharak Singh Marg

Kasturba Gandhi Marg

Swaminarayan Akshardham

Parliament House

Janpath

Willingdon Cres

Rajpath

India Gate

National Museum

Noida Link Rd

Ring Rd

NEW DELHI

National Gallery of Modern Art

Dr Zakir Hussain Marg

CHANAKYA PURI

Shanti Path

Akbar Rd

Pandara

Prithviraj Rd

Humayun's Tomb

Murti Marg

Aurobindo Marg

Lodi Gardens

Mathura Rd

SOUTH EXTENSION I

SOUTH EXTENSION II

Ring Rd

SAFDARJANG ENCLAVE

To Qutb Minar Complex

A
B
C
D
E

1
2
3

ON THE ROAD
Walking tours

One of the best ways to get to the heart of a city is to do a walking tour. It offers you a much more intimate view. With some walking tours, you get to see behind the big buildings and glimpse the real character of the city, its citizens, its craftsmen.

Salaam Baalak Trust (www.salaambaalaktrust.com) offer amazing and insightful walks around old Delhi and into the life of street kids. Set up over 20 years ago by Mira Nair and Dinaz Stafford who made the film *Salaam Bombay*, Salaam Baalak Trust have shelters, vocational training and education programmes for street kids. The walks are guided by the kids themselves and you get to visit the schools as well as meet the children.

Surekha Narain (www.delhimetrowalks) offers group and private walks which take you into the heart and soul of Old Delhi. But some of her favourite walks are around the Qutb Minar in South Delhi where you see the changes in architecture from ancient Hindu temple to Islamic minarets and more complex Mughal structures. Surekha also offers tours around the village of Mehrauli and Nizamuddin in South Delhi and further afield to Agra. She looks at everything with a historical and spiritual eye and most of all she has a passion for Delhi, which is infectious.

In Rajasthan, the great **Virasat Experiences** (www.virasatexperiences.com) offer insightful walks in Jaipur, Jodhpur and Udaipur. One of the most popular walks in Jaipur is the Temples and Havelis Tour; in the old pink city alone there are 500 temples generally not open to the public. Often the wives of the merchants who built the *havelis* did not want to leave their home to pray so private temples were built. They are stunning and intimate places: one example with 11 Shiva linga in the ground is a small temple but so beautiful and hidden behind an ordinary façade and a stall selling soft drinks, you would never know it was there.

the station via the metro yellow line. The best trains for both Agra and Amritsar are the *Shatabdi Express* trains. If you have a driver, opt for the excellent but underused Yamuna Expressway to Agra – there is a hefty toll of Rs 320 which puts many drivers off leaving smooth sailing and clear roads.

GETTING AROUND

The new metro is making the sprawling city very navigable: it's now possible to get from Connaught Place to Old Delhi in a cool five minutes; while Connaught Place to Qutb Minar is about 30 minutes and all the way down to the final stop in Gurgaon is about one hour. It is a strange experience to go from air-conditioned high tech to the bustling streets of Chandi Chowk. You can get to the airport from New Delhi train station in about 20 minutes. There is a women-only carriage at the front of each train, clearly marked inside and on the platform – this prevents women from having to succumb to the crush of the other carriages. There is a fine of Rs 250 for men ignoring all the signs in pink and in early 2011, a posse of women made men do sit-ups on the train for trespassing into the pink zone! Like any city metro service, try and avoid rush hour if you can. At each metro station you have to go through airport-like security and have your bag x-rayed, etc.

Auto-rickshaws and taxis are widely available, and a new initiative and new rate cards mean that drivers will now use their meters, even with foreigners. It's best to use prepaid stands at stations, airport terminals and at the junction of Radial Road 1 and

DELHI METRO

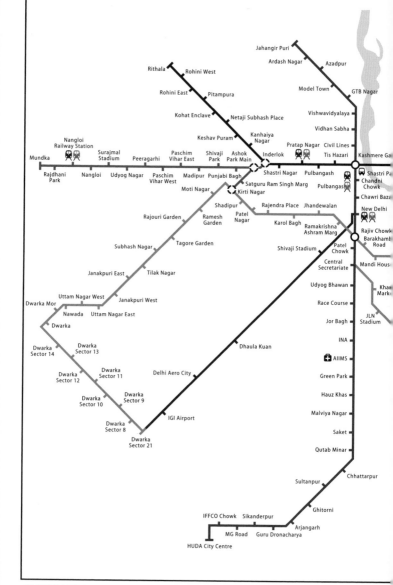

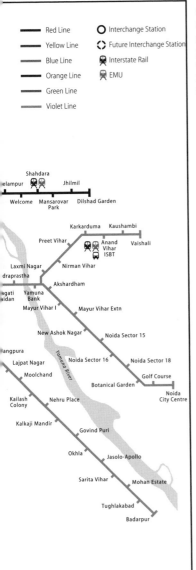

Red Line
Yellow Line
Blue Line
Orange Line
Green Line
Violet Line

○ Interchange Station
◇ Future Interchange Station
🚉 Interstate Rail
🚉 EMU

Shahdara
elampur   Jhilmil
Welcome   Mansarovar   Dilshad Garden
           Park

Karkarduma   Kaushambi
Preet Vihar   Anand   Vaishali
                   Vihar
                   ISBT
Laxmi Nagar   Nirman Vihar
draprastha
              Akshardham
agati   Yamuna
aidan   Bank
Mayur Vihar I   Mayur Vihar Extn

New Ashok Nagar   Noida Sector 15

langpura
Lajpat Nagar   Noida Sector 16   Noida Sector 18
Moolchand   Golf Course
              Botanical Garden
Kailash   Noida
Colony   Nehru Place   City Centre
Kalkaji Mandir
          Govind Puri
     Okhla   Jasolo-Apollo
       Sarita Vihar   Mohan Estate
          Tughlakabad
             Badarpur

Connaught Place if possible. The same applies to cycle-rickshaws, which ply the streets of Old Delhi. City buses are usually packed and have long queues. Be on your guard from thieves around New Delhi Station. State Entry Road runs from the southern end of Platform 1 to Connaught Place. This is a hassle-free alternative to the main Chelmsford Road during the day (gate closed at night). Also watch your change or cash interactions even at the prepaid booths – sometimes they do a switch of a Rs 100 note for a Rs 10, for example. Fleets of Radio Taxis are the newest additions to the city's transport options. These include: **Mega Cabs**, T011-4141 4141; **Delhi Cab**, T011-4433 3222; **Easy Cab**, T011-4343 4343; **Quick Cab**, T011-4533 3333.

ORIENTATION

The **Red Fort** and **Jama Masjid** are the focal point of Old Delhi, 2 km northeast of Connaught Place. Chandni Chowk, the main commercial area, heads west from the fort. Around this area are narrow lanes packed to the rafters with all different types of wares for sale. To the southeast are **New Delhi Railway Station** and the main backpackers' area, **Paharganj**, with **Connaught Place**, the notional 'centre' of New Delhi, about 1 km south. Running due south of Connaught Place is **Janpath** with small shops selling craft products, and hotels like the Imperial. Janpath is intersected by **Rajpath** with all the major state buildings at its western end. Immediately south is the diplomatic enclave, **Chanakyapuri**. Most of the upmarket hotels are scattered across the wide area between Connaught Place and the airport to the southwest. As Delhi's centre of gravity has shifted southwards, a series of new markets has grown up to serve extensive housing colonies such as **South Extension**, **Greater Kailash** and **Safdarjang Enclave**. This development has brought one of the major historic sites, the **Qutb Minar**, within the limits of the city; it's about half an hour by taxi south of Connaught Place. **Gurgaon**, which is strictly not in Delhi but in Haryana, is the new business hub with many shopping malls to boot.

TOURIST INFORMATION

Most tourist offices are open Monday-Friday 1000-1800 www.delhitourism.com. **Government of India Tourist Office** ① *88 Janpath, T011-332 0005, Mon-Sat 0900-1800*, is helpful and issues permits for visits to Rashtrapati Bhavan and gardens. There's also an office at the International Airport. **Delhi Tourism** ① *N-36 Connaught Pl, T011-2331 5322 (touts pester you to use one of many imposters; correct office is directly opposite 'Competent House');* **Coffee Home Annexe** ① *Baba Kharak Singh Marg, T011-336 5358; for hotel, transport and tour bookings T011-2462 3782, 0700-2100 (also at Airport Terminals and Inter-State Bus Terminal);* **New Delhi Railway Station** ① *T011-2373 2374;* **Nizamuddin Railway Station** ① *T011-2251 1083.* **India Tourism Development Corporation (ITDC)** ① *L-1 Connaught Circus, T011-2332 0331.*

BEST TIME TO VISIT

October to March are the best months to visit, but December and January can get quite cold and foggy at night. Pollution can affect asthma sufferers – in fact a lot of people develop respiratory problems and sore throats if they spend more than a few days in Delhi. Monsoon lasts from the end of June to mid-September. May and June are very hot and dry and with the whole city switching on its air-conditioning units, power cuts are suffered more frequently at this time. Even the malls in Saket were having to keep their air conditioning low in summer 2012.

→ BACKGROUND

In the modern period, Delhi has only been India's capital since 1911. It is a city of yo yo-ing fortunes and has been repeatedly reduced to rubble. There have been at least eight cities founded on the site of modern Delhi.

According to Hindu mythology, Delhi's first avatar was as the site of a dazzlingly wealthy city, Indraprastha, mentioned in the Mahabharata and founded around 2500 BC. The next five cities were to the south of today's Delhi. First was Lalkot, which, from 1206, became the capital of the Delhi Sultanate under the Slave Dynasty. The story of the first Sultan of Delhi, Qutb-ud-din Aybak, is a classic rags-to-riches story. A former slave, he rose through the ranks to become a general, a governor and then Sultan of Delhi. He is responsible for building Qutb Minar, but died before its completion.

The 1300s were a tumultuous time for Delhi, with five cities built during the century. Siri, the first of these, has gruesome roots. Legend has it that the city's founder, Ala-ud-din, buried the heads of infidels in the foundation of the fort. Siri derives its name from the Hindi word for 'head'. After Siri came Tughlaqabad, whose existence came to a sudden end when the Sultan of Delhi, Muhammad Tughlaq, got so angry about a perceived insult from residents, he destroyed the city. The cities of Jahanpanah and Ferozebad followed in quick succession. Delhi's centre of gravity began to move northwards. In the 1500s Dinpanah was constructed by Humayun, whose wonderful tomb (1564-1573) graces Hazrat Nizamuddin. Shahjahanabad, known today as Old Delhi, followed, becoming one of the richest and most populous cities in the world. The Persian emperor Nadir Shah invaded, killing as many as 120,000 residents in a single bloody night and stealing the Kohinoor Diamond (now part of the British royal family's crown jewels).

ON THE ROAD

A tale of two cities – anyone arriving in Delhi in the few months building up to the 2010 Commonwealth Games who got stuck in endless detours, had to dodge falling masonry in Connaught Place and negotiate piles of rubble while staring into the open fronts of buildings sliced off in Paharganj's Main Bazar would have to pinch themselves now as they arrive in the sparkly new T3 at Indira Gandhi Airport and jump on the metro into downtown Delhi.

The going did not look good at the start of the Commonwealth Games with the media reporting on the shoddy workmanship, collapsing flyovers and the words "filthy and unhygenic" imprinted in the memories of incoming travellers from all over the world. Chief Minister Sheila Dikshit announced plans to clear Delhi of 60,000 beggars in a move reminiscent of the 'beautification' dreamt up by Indira Gandhi during the state of emergency back in 1975. In the aftermath, there have been investigations into every backhander, kickback and dodgy dealing.

"When the world came visiting, we could've showcased how we manage poverty, instead of pretending it doesn't exist", says Shoma Chaudhury, managing editor of *Tehelka* magazine. "We could have showcased how we live in a proud, integrated city, instead of pretending it was a doll's house. Those who wish to turn Delhi into Dubai and Mumbai into Shanghai must remember: a great and unsustainable ugliness underpins their artificial beauty."

Nevertheless, Delhi is a new city post CWG. The games were a catalyst for improving the city's infrastructure. As well as T3 and the metro taking the pressure off the streets, three million new trees were planted, 1100 new low floorboard buses have taken to the avenues and the road network of Delhi has been widened and lengthened by about 25%.

But Delhi's population is expected to exceed 23 million by 2021. In a city that averages six power cuts a day during summer, where almost half the population still lacks access to an organized sewerage system, the recent wave of hectic growth is unlikely to prove sustainable.

The Delhi Development Authority (DDA) has released a marvellously quixotic Master Plan, which prescribes solutions to the problems of housing, land acquisition for industry and commercial developments, provision of green space, air and noise pollution, waste disposal and parking. But with 75% of Delhi already violating previous Master Plans, it is difficult to see how enforcing such a plan in the face of endemic corruption and vested interests will ever be possible.

The next destroyers of Delhi were the British, who ransacked the city in the wake of the Great Uprising/Mutiny of 1857. The resulting bloodbath left bodies piled so high that the victors' horses had to tread on them. For the next 50 years, while the port cities of Calcutta and Bombay thrived under the British, Delhi languished. Then, in 1911, King George, on a visit to India, announced that a new city should be built next to what remained of Delhi, and that this would be the new capital of India. The British architect Edwin Lutyens was brought in to design the city. You could argue that the building hasn't stopped since ...

The central part of New Delhi is an example of Britain's imperial pretensions. The government may have been rather more reticent about moving India's capital, if it had known that in less than 36 years time, the British would no longer be ruling India. Delhi's population swelled after the violence of partition, with refugees flooding to the city. In

10 years the population of Delhi doubled, and many well-known housing colonies were built during this period.

The economic boom that began in the 1990s has lead to an explosion of construction and soaring real estate prices. Delhi is voraciously eating into the surrounding countryside. It is a city changing at such breakneck speed that shops, homes and even airports seem to appear and disappear almost overnight. Go now and witness the changes as they happen.

PLACES IN DELHI

The sites of interest are grouped in three main areas. In the centre is the British-built capital of New Delhi, with its government buildings and wide avenues. The heart of Shahjahanabad (Old Delhi) is about 2 km north of Connaught Circus. Ten kilometres to the south is the Qutb Minar complex, with the old fortress city of Tughluqabad, 8 km to its east. Across the Yamuna River is the remarkable new Akshardham Temple. You can visit each separately, or link routes together into a day tour to include the most interesting sites.

→ OLD DELHI

Shah Jahan (ruled 1628-1658) decided to move back from Agra to Delhi in 1638. Within 10 years the huge city of **Shahjahanabad**, now known as Old Delhi, was built. The plan of Shah Jahan's new city symbolized the link between religious authority enshrined in the Jama Masjid to the west, and political authority represented by the Diwan-i-Am in the Fort, joined by Chandni Chowk, the route used by the emperor. The city was protected by rubble-built walls, some of which still survive. These walls were pierced by 14 main gates. The **Ajmeri Gate**, **Turkman Gate** (often referred to by auto-rickshaw wallahs as 'Truckman Gate'), **Kashmere Gate** and **Delhi Gate** still survive.

CHANDNI CHOWK

Shahjahanabad was laid out in blocks with wide roads, residential quarters, bazars and mosques. Its principal street, Chandni Chowk, had a tree-lined canal flowing down its centre which became renowned throughout Asia. The canal is long gone, but the jumble of shops, alleys crammed with craftsmen's workshops, food stalls, mosques and temples, cause it to retain some of its magic. A cycle-rickshaw ride gives you a good feel of the place. Make sure you visit Naughara Street, just off Kinari Bazar, one of the most atmospheric streets in Delhi, full of brightly painted and slowly crumbling *havelis*.

The impressive red sandstone façade of the **Digambar Jain Mandir** (temple) standing at the eastern end of Chandni Chowk, faces the Red Fort. Built in 1656, it contains an image of Adinath. The charitybird hospital within this compound releases the birds on recovery instead of returning them to their owners; many remain within the temple precincts (www.charity birdshospital.org). Beyond Shahjahanabad to its north lies Kashmiri Gate, Civil lines and the Northern Ridge. The siting of the railway line which effectively cut Delhi into two unequal parts was done deliberately. The line brought prosperity, yet it destroyed the unity of the walled city forever. The northern ridge was the British cantonment and Civil Lines housed the civilians. In this area the temporary capital of the British existed from 1911-1931 till New Delhi came. The Northern ridge is a paradise for birds and trees. Follow the **Mutiny Trail** by visiting Flagstaff Tower, Pir Ghaib, Chauburj, Mutiny Memorial. Around

Kashmire Gate and Civil Lines, you can discover the Old Residency, St James Church, Nicholson's cemetery and Qudsia Bagh.

RED FORT (LAL QILA)

🛈 *Tue-Sun sunrise to sunset, Rs 250 foreigners, Rs 10 Indians, allow 1 hr. The entrance is through the Lahore Gate (nearest the car park) with the admission kiosk opposite; keep your ticket as you will need to show it at the Drum House. There are new toilets inside, best to avoid ones in Chatta Chowk. You must remove shoes and cover all exposed flesh from your shoulders to your legs.*

Between the new city and the River Yamuna, Shah Jahan built a fort. Most of it was built out of red *lal* (sandstone), hence the name **Lal Qila** (Red Fort), the same as that at Agra on which the Delhi Fort is modelled. Begun in 1639 and completed in 1648, it is said to have cost Rs 10 million, much of which was spent on the opulent marble palaces within. In recent years much effort has been put into improving the fort and gardens, but visitors may be saddened by the neglected state of some of the buildings, and the gun-wielding soldiers lolling around do nothing to improve the ambience. However, despite the modern development of roads and shops and the never-ending traffic, it's an impressive site.

The approach The entrance is by the Lahore Gate. The defensive barbican that juts out in front of it was built by Aurangzeb. A common story suggests that Aurangzeb built the curtain wall to save his nobles and visiting dignitaries from having to walk – and bow – the whole length of Chandni Chowk, for no one was allowed to ride in the presence of the emperor. When the emperor sat in the Diwan-i-Am he could see all the way down the Chowk, so the addition must have been greatly welcomed by his courtiers. The new entrance arrangement also made an attacking army more vulnerable to the defenders on the walls.

Chatta Chowk and the Naubat Khana Inside is the **Covered Bazar**, which was quite exceptional in the 17th century. In Shah Jahan's time there were shops on both upper and lower levels. Originally they catered for the Imperial household and carried stocks of silks, brocades, velvets, gold and silverware, jewellery and gems. There were coffee shops too for nobles and courtiers.

The **Naubat Khana** (Naqqar Khana) (Drum House or music gallery) marked the entrance to the inner apartments of the fort. Here everyone except the princes of the royal family had to dismount and leave their horses or *hathi* (elephants), hence its other name of **Hathi Pol** (Elephant Gate). Five times a day ceremonial music was played on the kettle drum, *shahnais* (a kind of oboe) and cymbals, glorifying the emperor. In 1754 Emperor Ahmad Shah was murdered here. The gateway with four floors is decorated with floral designs. You can still see traces of the original panels painted in gold or other colours on the interior of the gateway.

Diwan-i-Am Between the first inner court and the royal palaces at the heart of the fort, stood the **Diwan-i-Am** (Hall of Public Audience), the furthest point the normal visitor would reach. It has seen many dramatic events, including the destructive whirlwind of the Persian Nadir Shah in 1739 and of Ahmad Shah the Afghan in 1756, and the trial of the last 'King of Delhi', **Bahadur Shah II** in 1858.

The well-proportioned hall was both a functional building and a showpiece intended to hint at the opulence of the palace itself. In Shah Jahan's time the sandstone was hidden behind a very thin layer of white polished plaster, *chunam*. This was decorated with floral

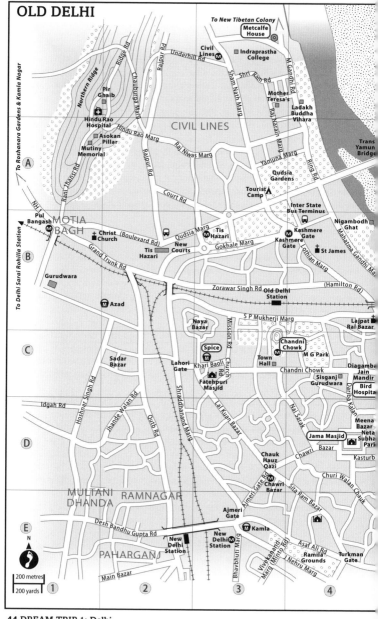

OLD DELHI

To New Tibetan Colony

Metcalfe House

To Roshanara Gardens & Kamla Nagar

Northern Ridge

Ridge Rd

Chauburja Marg

Raj Niwas Marg

Pir Ghaib

Hindu Rao Hospital

Asokan Pillar

Mutiny Memorial

Ram Thapa Rd

Hindu Rao Marg

Rajpur Rd

Court Rd

Underhill Rd

Civil Lines

Indraprastha College

Sham Nath Marg

Shri Ram Rd

M Gandhi Rd

Mother Teresa's

Ladakh Buddha Vihara

CIVIL LINES

Raj Narain Marg

Yamuna Marg

Qudsia Gardens

Tourist Camp

Ring Rd

Mahatma Gandhi Marg

Trans Yamun Bridge

NH

To Delhi Sarai Rohilla Station

Pul Bangash

MOTIA BAGH

Grand Trunk Rd

Christ Church

(Boulevard Rd)

Tis Hazari

Qudsia Marg

New Courts

Tis Hazari

Gokhale Marg

Inter State Bus Terminus

Kashmere Gate

Kashmere Gate

Lothian Marg

Nigambodh Ghat

St James

(Hamilton Rd)

Gurudwara

Azad

Zorawar Singh Rd

Old Delhi Station

Naya Bazar

Mission Rd

S P Mukherji Marg

Lajpat Rai Bazar

Sadar Bazar

Spice

Lahori Gate

Khari Baoli

Church Rd

Fatehpuri Masjid

Chandni Chowk

Town Hall

M G Park

Chandni Chowk

Diagamba Jain Mandir

Sisganj Gurudwara

Bird Hospita

Idgah Rd

Hoshiar Singh Rd

Jhande Walan Rd

Qutb Rd

Shraddhanand Marg

Lal Kuan Bazar

Nai Sarak

Dariba Kalan

Meena Bazar · Neta Subhas Park

Chauk Hauz Qazi

Chawri Bazar

Chawri Bazar

Jama Masjid

Kasturb

MULTANI DHANDA

RAMNAGAR

Ajmeri Gate Rd

Sita Ram Bazar

Churi Walan Chowk

Desh Bandhu Gupta Rd

Ajmeri Gate

Kamla

PAHARGANJ

New Delhi Station

New Delhi Station

Bhavbhuti Marg

Vivekanand Marg (Minto) Rd

J Nehru Marg

Asaf Ali Rd

Ramila Grounds

Turkman Gate

Main Bazar

N

200 metres
200 yards

① ② ③ ④

A

B

C

D

E

motifs in many colours, especially gilt. Silk carpets and heavy curtains hung from the canopy rings outside the building, such interiors reminders of the Mughals' nomadic origins in Central Asia, where royal durbars were held in tents.

At the back of the hall is a platform for the emperor's throne. Around this was a gold railing, within which stood the princes and great nobles separated from the lesser nobles inside the hall. Behind the throne canopy are 12 marble panels inlaid with motifs of fruiting trees, parrots and cuckoos. Figurative workmanship is very unusual in Islamic buildings, and these panels are the only example in the Red Fort.

As well as matters of official administration, Shah Jahan would listen to accounts of illness, dream interpretations and anecdotes from his ministers and nobles. Wednesday was the day of judgement. Sentences were often swift and brutal and sometimes the punishment of dismemberment, beating or death was carried out on the spot. The executioners were close at hand with axes and whips. On Friday, the Muslim holy day, there would be no business.

Inner palace buildings Behind the Diwan-i-Am is the private enclosure of the fort. Along the east wall, overlooking the River Yamuna, Shah Jahan set six small palaces (five survive). Also within this compound are the Harem, the Life-Bestowing Garden and the Nahr-i-Bihisht (Stream of Paradise).

Life-Bestowing Gardens (Hayat Baksh Bagh) The original gardens were landscaped according to the Islamic principles of the Persian *char bagh*, with pavilions, fountains and water courses dividing the garden into various but regular beds. The two pavilions **Sawan** and **Bhadon**, named after the first two months of the rainy season (July-August), reveal something of the character of the garden. The garden used to create the effect of the monsoon and contemporary accounts tell us that in the pavilions, some of which were especially erected for the **Teej** festival, which marks the arrival of the monsoon, the royal ladies would sit in silver swings and watch the rains. Water flowed from the back wall of the pavilion through a slit above the marble shelf and over the niches in the wall. Gold and silver pots of flowers were placed in these alcoves during the day whilst at night candles were lit to create a glistening and colourful effect.

Shahi Burj From the pavilion next to the Shahi Burj (**Royal Tower**) the canal known as the **Nahr-i-Bihisht** (Stream of Paradise) began its journey along the Royal Terrace. The three-storey octagonal tower was seriously damaged in 1857 and is still unsafe. In Shah Jahan's time the Yamuna lapped the walls. Shah Jahan used the tower as his most private office and only his sons and a few senior ministers were allowed with him.

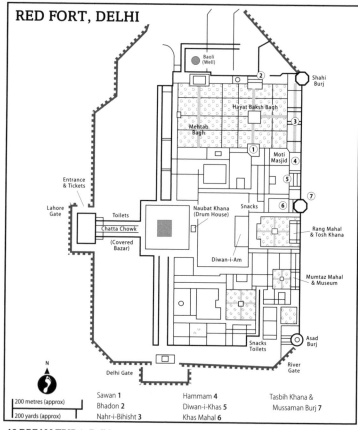

RED FORT, DELHI

Baoli (Well)

Shahi Burj

Hayat Baksh Bagh

Mehtab Bagh

Moti Masjid

Entrance & Tickets

Lahore Gate

Toilets

Naubat Khana (Drum House)

Snacks

Chatta Chowk

(Covered Bazar)

Rang Mahal & Tosh Khana

Diwan-i-Am

Mumtaz Mahal & Museum

Snacks Toilets

Asad Burj

N

Delhi Gate

River Gate

200 metres (approx)
200 yards (approx)

Sawan 1
Bhadon 2
Nahr-i-Bihisht 3

Hammam 4
Diwan-i-Khas 5
Khas Mahal 6

Tasbih Khana & Mussaman Burj 7

Moti Masjid To the right are the three marble domes of Aurangzeb's 'Pearl Mosque' (shoes must be removed). Bar the cupolas, it is completely hidden behind a wall of red sandstone, now painted white. Built in 1662 of polished white marble, it has some exquisite decoration. All the surfaces are highly decorated in a fashion similar to rococo, which developed at the same time as in Europe. Unusually the prayer hall is on a raised platform with inlaid outlines of individual *musallas* ('prayer mats') in black marble. While the outer walls were aligned to the cardinal points like all the other fort buildings, the inner walls were positioned so that the mosque would correctly face Mecca.

Hammam The **Royal Baths** have three apartments separated by corridors with canals to carry water to each room. The two flanking the entrance, for the royal children, had hot and cold baths. The room furthest away from the door has three basins for rose water fountains.

Diwan-i-Khas Beyond is the single-storeyed **Hall of Private Audience**, topped by four Hindu-style *chhattris* and built completely of white marble. The *dado* (lower part of the wall) on the interior was richly decorated with inlaid precious and semi-precious stones. The ceiling was silver but was removed by the Marathas in 1760. Outside, the hall used to have a marble pavement and an arcaded court. Both have gone.

This was the Mughal office of state. Shah Jahan spent two hours here before retiring for a meal, siesta and prayers. In the evening he would return to the hall for more work before going to the harem. The hall's splendour moved the 14th-century poet Amir Khusrau to write the lines inscribed above the corner arches of the north and south walls: "*Agar Firdaus bar rue Zamin-ast/Hamin ast o Hamin ast o Hamin ast*" (If there be a paradise on earth, it is here, it is here, it is here).

Royal palaces Next to the Diwan-i-Khas is the three-roomed **Khas Mahal** (Private Palace). Nearest the Diwan-i-Khas is the **Tasbih Khana** (Chamber for the Telling of Rosaries) where the emperor would worship privately with his rosary of 99 beads, one for each of the mystical names of Allah. In the centre is the Khwabgah (Palace of Dreams) which gives on to the octagonal **Mussaman Burj** tower. Here Shah Jahan would be seen each morning. A balcony was added to the tower in 1809 and here George V and Queen Mary appeared in their Coronation Durbar of 1911. The **Tosh Khana** (Robe Room), to the south, has a beautiful marble screen at its north end, carved with the scales of justice above the filigree grille. If you are standing with your back to the Diwan-i-Khas you will see a host of circulating suns (a symbol of royalty), but if your back is to the next building (the Rang Mahal), you will see moons surrounding the scales. All these rooms were sumptuously decorated with fine silk carpets, rich silk brocade curtains and lavishly decorated walls. After 1857 the British used the Khas Mahal as an officer's mess and sadly it was defaced.

The **Rang Mahal** (Palace of Colours), the residence of the chief *sultana*, was also the place where the emperor ate most of his meals. It was divided into six apartments. Privacy and coolness were ensured by the use of marble *jali* screens. Like the other palaces it was beautifully decorated with a silver ceiling ornamented with golden flowers to reflect the water in the channel running through the building. The north and south apartments were both known as **Sheesh Mahal** (Palace of Mirrors) since into the ceiling were set hundreds of small mirrors. In the evening when candles were lit a starlit effect would be produced.

Through the palace ran the **Life-bestowing Stream** and at its centre is a lotus-shaped marble basin which had an ivory fountain. As might be expected in such a cloistered and cosseted environment, the ladies sometimes got bored. In the 18th century the **Empress of Jahandar Shah** sat gazing out at the river and remarked that she had never seen a boat sink. Shortly afterwards a boat was deliberately capsized so that she could be entertained by the sight of people bobbing up and down in the water crying for help.

The southernmost of the palaces, the **Mumtaz Mahal** (Palace of Jewels) ① *Tue-Sun 1000-1700*, was also used by the harem. The lower half of its walls are of marble and it contains six apartments. After the Mutiny of 1857 it was used as a guardroom and since 1912 it has been a museum with exhibits of textiles, weapons, carpets, jade and metalwork as well as works depicting life in the court. It should not be missed.

SPICE MARKET

Outside the Red Fort, cycle-rickshaws offer a trip to the spice market, Jama Masjid and back through the bazar. You travel slowly westwards down Chandni Chowk passing the town hall. Dismount at Church Road and follow your guide into the heart of the market on Khari Baoli where wholesalers sell every conceivable spice. Ask to go to the roof for an excellent view over the market and back towards the Red Fort. The ride back through the bazar is equally fascinating – look up at the amazing electricity system. The final excitement is getting back across Netaji Subhash Marg. Panic not, the rickshaw wallahs know what they are doing. Negotiate for one hour and expect to pay about Rs 100. The spice-laden air may irritate your throat. Also ask a cycle-rickshaw to take you to Naughara Street, just off Kinari Bazar, a very pretty street amidst the chaos of Old Delhi.

JAMA MASJID (FRIDAY MOSQUE)
① *Visitors welcome from 30 mins after sunrise until 1215; and from 1345 until 30 mins before sunset, free, still or video cameras Rs 150, tower entry Rs 20.*

The magnificent Jama Masjid is the largest mosque in India and the last great architectural work of Shah Jahan, intended to dwarf all mosques that had gone before it. With the fort, it dominates Old Delhi. The mosque is much simpler in its ornamentation than Shah Jahan's secular buildings – a judicious blend of red sandstone and white marble, which are interspersed in the domes, minarets and cusped arches.

The gateways Symbolizing the separation of the sacred and the secular, the threshold is a place of great importance where the worshipper steps to a higher plane. There are three huge gateways, the largest being to the east. This was reserved for the royal family who gathered in a private gallery in its upper storey. Today, the faithful enter through the east gate on Fridays and for **Id-ul-Fitr** and **Id-ul-Adha**. The latter commemorates Abraham's (Ibrahim's) sacrificial offering of his son Ishmael (Ismail). Islam (unlike the Jewish and Christian tradition) believes that Abraham offered to sacrifice Ishmael, Isaac's brother.

The courtyard The façade has the main *iwan* (arch), five smaller arches on each side with two flanking minarets and three bulbous domes behind, all perfectly proportioned. The *iwan* draws the worshippers' attention into the building. The minarets have great views from the top; well worth the climb for Rs 10 (women may not be allowed to climb alone). The **hauz**, in the centre of the courtyard, is an ablution tank placed as usual between the inner and outer parts of the building to remind the worshipper that it is through the ritual of baptism that one first enters the community of believers. The **Dikka**, in front of the ablution tank, is a raised platform. Muslim communities grew so rapidly that by the eighth century it sometimes became necessary to introduce a second *muballigh* (prayer leader) who stood on this platform and copied the postures and chants of the *imam* inside to relay them to a much larger congregation. With the introduction of the loudspeaker and amplification, the *dikka* and the *muballigh* became redundant. In the northwest corner of the masjid there is a small shed. For a small fee, the faithful are shown a hair from the beard of the prophet, as well as his sandal and his footprint in rock.

The Kawthar Inscription Set up in 1766, the inscription commemorates the place where a worshipper had a vision of the Prophet standing by the celestial tank in paradise. It is here that the Prophet will stand on Judgment Day. In most Islamic buildings, the inscriptions are passages from the Koran or Sayings of the Prophet. Shah Jahan, however, preferred to have sayings extolling the virtues of the builder and architect as well. The 10 detailed panels on the façade indicate the date of construction (1650-1656), the cost (10 lakhs – one million rupees), the history of the building, the architect (Ustad Khalil) and the builder (Nur Allah Ahmed, probably the son of the man who did most of the work on the Taj Mahal).

→NEW DELHI

Delhi's present position as capital was only confirmed on 12 December 1911, when George V announced at the Delhi Durbar that the capital of India was to move from Calcutta to Delhi. The new city, New Delhi, planned under the leadership of British architect Edwin Lutyens with the assistance of his friend Herbert Baker, was inaugurated on 9 February 1931.

The city was to accommodate 70,000 people and have boundless possibilities for future expansion. The king favoured something in form and flavour similar to the Mughal masterpieces but fretted over the horrendous expense that this would incur. A petition signed by eminent public figures such as Bernard Shaw and Thomas Hardy advocated an Indian style and an Indian master builder. Herbert Baker had made known his own views even before his appointment when he wrote "first and foremost it is the spirit of British sovereignty which must be imprisoned in its stone and bronze". Lutyens himself despised Indian architecture. "Even before he had seen any examples of it", writes architectural historian Giles Tillotson, "he pronounced Mughal architecture to be 'piffle', and seeing it did not disturb that conviction". Yet in the end, Lutyens was forced to settle for the compromise.

INDIA GATE AND AROUND

A tour of New Delhi will usually start with a visit to India Gate. This war memorial is situated at the eastern end of **Rajpath**. Designed by Lutyens, it commemorates more than 70,000 Indian soldiers who died in the First World War. Some 13,516 names of British and Indian soldiers killed on the Northwest Frontier and in the Afghan War of 1919 are engraved on the arch and foundations. Under the arch is the Amar Jawan Jyoti, commemorating Indian armed forces' losses in the Indo-Pakistan War of 1971. The arch (43 m high) stands on a base of Bharatpur stone and rises in stages. Similar to the Hindu *chhattri* signifying regality, it is decorated with nautilus shells symbolizing British maritime power. Come at dusk to join the picnicking crowds enjoying the evening. You may even be able to have a pedalo ride if there's water in the canal.

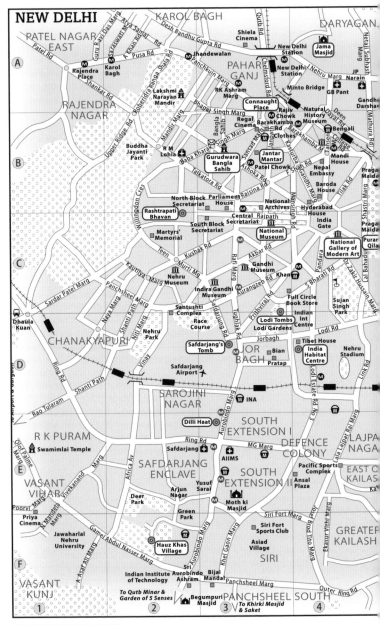

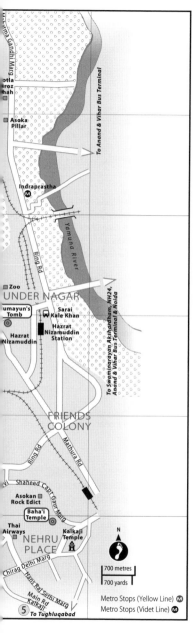

To the northwest of India Gate are two impressive buildings, **Hyderabad House** and **Baroda House**, built as residences for the Nizam of Hyderabad and the Gaekwar of Baroda. Now used as offices, both were carefully placed to indicate the paramountcy of the British Raj over the Princely States. The Nizam, reputed to be the richest man in the world, ruled over an area equal to that of France. The Gaekwar belonged to the top level of Indian princes and both, along with the maharajas of Mysore, Jammu and Kashmir and Gwalior were entitled to receive 21-gun salutes.

Rajpath leads west from India Gate towards **Janpath**. To the north are the Lutyens-designed **National Archives**, formerly the Imperial Record Office. To the south is the National Museum (see below).

NATIONAL GALLERY OF MODERN ART

ⓘ *Jaipur House, near India Gate, T011-2338 4640, www.ngmaindia.gov.in, Tue-Sun 1000-1700, Rs 150 foreigners, Rs 10 Indians.*

There is now a new air-conditioned wing of this excellent gallery and select exhibits from the old building are housed in a former residence of the Maharaja of Jaipur. In the Seeds of Time traces the trajectory of modern Indian art. Artists include **Amrita Shergil**, with over 100 exhibits, synthesizing the flat treatment of Indian painting with a realistic tone, and **Rabindranath Tagore** (ground floor), with examples from a brief but intense spell in the 1930s. The Bombay School or Company School (first floor) includes Western painters who documented their visits to India. Realism is reflected in Indian painting of the early 19th century represented by the schools of Avadh, Patna, Sikkim and Thanjavur. The Bengal School (the late 19th-century Revivalist Movement) is represented by artists such as Abanindranath Tagore and Nandalal Bose. Western influence was discarded in response to the nationalist movement. Inspiration derived from Indian folk art is evident in the works of Jamini Roy and YD Shukla. Prints from the gallery shop are incredibly good value – up to Rs 80 for poster-size prints of famous works.

NATIONAL MUSEUM

ⓘ *Janpath, T011-2301 9272, www.nationalmuseumindia.gov.in, daily 1000-1700, foreigners Rs 300 (including audio tour), Indians Rs 10, camera Rs 300; free guided tours 1030, 1130, 1200, 1400, films are screened every day (1430), marble squat toilets, but dirty.*

The collection was formed from the nucleus of the Exhibition of Indian Art, London (1947). Now merged with the Asian Antiquities Museum it displays a rich collection of the artistic treasure of Central Asia and India including ethnological objects from prehistoric archaeological finds to the late Medieval period. Replicas of exhibits and books on Indian culture and art are on sale. There is a research library.

Ground floor Prehistoric: seals, figurines, toy animals and jewellery from the Harappan civilization (2400-1500 BC). **Maurya Period**: terracottas and stone heads from around the third century BC include the *chaturmukha* (four-faced) *lingam*. **Gandhara School**: stucco heads showing the Graeco Roman influence. **Gupta terracottas** (circa AD 400): include two life-size images of the river goddesses Ganga and Yamuna and the four-armed bust of Vishnu from a temple near Lal Kot. **South Indian sculpture**: from Pallava and early Chola temples and relief panels from Mysore. Bronzes from the Buddhist monastery at Nalanda. Some of Buddha's relics were placed in the Thai pavilion in 1997.

First floor Illustrated manuscripts: include the *Babur-i-nama* in the emperor's own handwriting and an autographed copy of Jahangir's memoirs. **Miniature paintings**: include the 16th-century Jain School, the 18th-century Rajasthani School and the Pahari Schools of Garhwal, Basoli and Kangra. **Aurel Stein Collection** consists of antiquities recovered by him during his explorations of Central Asia and the western borders of China at the turn of the 20th century.

Second floor Pre-Columbian and Mayan artefacts: anthropological section devoted to tribal artefacts and folk arts. **Sharad Rani Bakkiwal Gallery of Musical Instruments**: displays over 300 instruments collected by the famous *sarod* player.

THE SECRETARIATS

At the Secretariat and Rashtrapati Bhavan gates, the mounted and unmounted troops parade in full uniform on Saturdays at 1030 are worth attending. Standing on either side of Raisina Hill, **North Block** houses the Home and Finance Ministries, **South Block** the Ministry of Foreign Affairs. These long classical buildings topped by Baroque domes, designed by Baker, were derived from Wren's Royal Naval College at Greenwich. The towers were originally designed to be twice the height of the buildings and to act as beacons guarding the way to the inner sanctum. The domes are decorated with lotus motifs and elephants, while the north and south gateways are Mughal in design. On the northern Secretariat building is the imperialistic inscription "Liberty will not descend to a people: a people must raise themselves to liberty. It is a blessing that must be earned before it can be enjoyed".

In the **Great Court** between the Secretariats are the four **Dominion Columns**, donated by the governments of Australia, Canada, New Zealand and South Africa – ironically, as it turned out. Each is crowned by a bronze ship sailing east, symbolizing the maritime and mercantile supremacy of the British Empire. In the centre of the court is the Jaipur column of red sandstone topped with a white egg, bronze lotus and six-pointed glass star of India (which has evolved into today's five-pointed star).

RASHTRAPATI BHAVAN AND NEHRU MEMORIAL MUSEUM

Once the Viceroy's House, Rashtrapati Bhavan is the official residence of the President of India. The Viceroy's House, New Delhi's centrepiece of imperial proportions, was 1 km around the foundations, bigger than Louis XIV's palace at Versailles. It had a colossal dome surmounting a long colonnade and 340 rooms in all. It took nearly 20 years to complete, similar to the time it took to build the Taj Mahal. In the busiest year, 29,000 people were working on the site and buildings began to take shape. The project was surrounded by controversy from beginning to end. Opting for a fundamentally classical structure, both Baker and Lutyens sought to incorporate Indian motifs, many entirely superficial. While some claim that Lutyens achieved a unique synthesis of the two traditions, Tillotson asks whether "the sprinkling of a few simplified and classicized Indian details (especially *chhattris*) over a classical palace" could be called a synthesis. The Durbar Hall, 23 m in diameter, has coloured marble from all parts of India.

To the south is Flagstaff House, formerly the residence of the commander-in-chief. Renamed Teen Murti Bhawan it now houses the **Nehru Memorial Museum** ① *T011-2301 4504, Tue-Sun 1000-1500, planetarium Mon-Sat 1130-1500, library Mon-Sat 0900-1900, free.* Designed by Robert Tor Russell, in 1948 it became the official residence of India's first prime minister, Jawaharlal Nehru. Converted after his death (1964) into a national memorial, the reception, study and bedroom are intact. A *Jyoti Jawahar* (torch) symbolizes the eternal values he inspired and a granite rock is carved with extracts from his historic speech at midnight on 14 August 1947; an informative and vivid history of the Independence Movement.

The **Martyr's Memorial**, at the junction of Sardar Patel Marg and Willingdon Crescent, is a magnificent 26-m-long, 3-m-high bronze sculpture by DP Roy Chowdhury. The 11 statues of national heroes are headed by Mahatma Gandhi.

ETERNAL GANDHI MULTIMEDIA MUSEUM

① *Birla House, 5 Tees Jan Marg (near Claridges Hotel), T011-3095 7269, www.eternal gandhi.org, closed Mon and 2nd Sat, 1000-1700, free, film at 1500.*
Gandhi's last place of residence and the site of his assassination, Birla House has been converted into a whizz-bang display of 'interactive' modern technology. Over-attended by young guides eager to demonstrate the next gadget, the museum seems aimed mainly at those with a critically short attention span, and is too rushed to properly convey the story of Gandhi's life. However, a monument in the garden marking where he fell is definitely worth a visit. Other museums in the city related to Gandhi include **National Gandhi Museum** ① *opposite Raj Ghat, T011-2331 1793, www.gandhimuseum.org, Tue-Sat 0930-1730*, with five pavilions – sculpture, photographs and paintings of Gandhi and the history of the *Satyagraha* movement, the philosophy of non-violence; **Gandhi Smarak Sangrahalaya** ① *Raj Ghat, T011-2301 1480, Fri-Wed 0930-1730*, displays some of Gandhi's personal belongings and a small library includes recordings of speeches; **Indira Gandhi Museum** ① *1 Safdarjang Rd, T011-2301 0094, Tue-Sun 0930-1700, free*, charts the phases of her life from childhood to the moment of her death. Fascinating if rather gory exhibits – you can see the blood-stained, bullet-ridden sari she was wearing when assassinated.

PARLIAMENT HOUSE AND AROUND

Northeast of the Viceroy's House is the **Council House**, now **Sansad Bhavan**. Baker designed this based on Lutyens' suggestion that it be circular (173 m diameter). Inside are the library and chambers for the Council of State, Chamber of Princes and Legislative Assembly – the **Lok Sabha**. Just opposite the Council House is the **Rakabganj Gurudwara** in Pandit Pant Marg. This 20th-century white marble shrine, which integrates the late Mughal and Rajasthani styles, marks the spot where the headless body of Guru Tegh Bahadur, the ninth Sikh Guru, was cremated in 1657. West of the Council House is the Cathedral **Church of the Redemption** (1927-1935) and to its north the Italianate Roman Catholic **Church of the Sacred Heart** (1930-1934), both conceived by Henry Medd.

CONNAUGHT PLACE AND CONNAUGHT CIRCUS

Connaught Place and its outer ring, Connaught Circus (now officially named **Rajiv Chowk** and **Indira Chowk**, but still commonly referred to by their old names), comprise two-storey arcaded buildings, arranged radially around a circular garden that was completed after the Metro line was installed. Designed by Robert Tor Russell, they have become the main commercial and tourist centre of New Delhi. Sadly, the area also attracts bands of insistent touts ready to take advantage of the unwary traveller by getting them into spurious 'official' or 'government' shops and travel agencies. The area (and Palika Bazar, a humid and dingy underground market hidden beneath it) has long been renowned for its shoe-shine tricksters. Large wadges of slime appear mysteriously on shoes and are then pointed out eagerly by attendant boys or men who offer to clean them off at a price. This can just be the start of 'necessary repairs' to the shoes for which bills of over Rs 300 are not unknown. If caught – increasingly unlikely as the scammers seem to be on the way out – insist politely but firmly that the dirt is cleaned off free of charge.

PAHARGANJ

Delhi's backpacker ghetto occupies a warren of lanes and dingy alleys immediately to the west of New Delhi railway station, a few hundred metres north of Connaught Circus. The crowded Main Bazar offers an instant immersion into the chaos of which India is capable, as stray cows and cycle-rickshaws tangle with a throng of pedestrians, hotel touts, and salesmen hawking knock-off handbags, books and cheap clothing. Though there's little other than shopping to hold your interest, the hundreds of guesthouses here offer the greatest concentration of genuinely cheap accommodation in the city, and the area contains a number of appealing rooftop cafés that provide a respite from the madness below. In 2010, the Main Bazar had an overhaul. Ignoring the strikes of the shopkeepers, bulldozers moved in and widened the road by essentially cutting off the front of the buildings that were encroaching onto it. Now the streets are wider and the businesses are giving themselves a facelift.

Northwest of Paharganj, the grid of streets comprising **Karol Bagh** contains what is, by some definitions, the biggest market in Asia. Conveniently linked to the city by Metro, the area is full of mid-range hotels, but mainly populated by Indians.

LAKSHMI NARAYAN MANDIR

To the west of Connaught Circus is the Lakshmi Narayan **Birla Temple** in Mandir Marg. Financed by the prominent industrialist Raja Baldeo Birla in 1938, this is one of the most popular Hindu shrines in the city and one of Delhi's few striking examples of Hindu architecture. Dedicated to Lakshmi, the goddess of well-being, it is commonly referred to as **Birla Mandir**. The design is in the Orissan style with tall curved *sikharas* (towers) capped by large *amalakas*. The exterior is faced with red and ochre stone and white marble. Built around a central courtyard, the main shrine has images of Narayan and his consort Lakshmi while two separate cells have icons of Siva (the Destroyer) and Durga (the 10-armed destroyer of demons). The temple is flanked by a *dharamshala* (rest house) and a Buddhist *vihara* (monastery).

GURUDWARA BANGLA SAHIB

ⓘ *Baba Kharak Singh Rd, free.*

This is a fine example of Sikh temple architecture, featuring a large pool reminiscent of Amritsar's Golden Temple. The 24-hour reciting of the faith's holy book adds to the atmosphere, and there's free food on offer, although don't be surprised if you're asked to help out with the washing up! You must remove your shoes and cover your head to enter – suitable scarves are provided if you arrive without.

Further northeast on Baba Kharak Singh Marg is **Hanuman Mandir**. This small temple was built by Maharaja Jai Singh II of Jaipur. **Mangal haat** (Tuesday Fair) is a popular market.

JANTAR MANTAR

Just to the east of the Hanuman Mandir in Sansad Marg (Parliament Street) is Jai Singh's **observatory** (Jantar Mantar) ⓘ *sunrise to sunset, Rs 100 foreigners, Rs 5 Indians*. The Mughal Emperor Mohammad Shah (ruled 1719-1748) entrusted the renowned astronomer Maharaja Jai Singh II with the task of revising the calendar and correcting the astronomical tables used by contemporary priests. Daily astral observations were made for years before construction began and plastered brick structures were favoured for the site instead of brass instruments. Built in 1725 it is slightly smaller than the later observatory at Jaipur.

MEMORIAL GHATS

Beyond Delhi Gate lies the **Yamuna River**, marked by a series of memorials to India's leaders. The river itself, a kilometre away, is invisible from the road, protected by a low rise and banks of trees. The most prominent memorial, immediately opposite the end of Jawaharlal Nehru Road, is that of Mahatma Gandhi at **Raj Ghat**. To its north is **Shanti Vana** (Forest of Peace), landscaped gardens where Prime Minister Jawaharlal Nehru was cremated in 1964, as were his grandson Sanjay Gandhi in 1980, daughter Indira Gandhi in 1984 and elder grandson, Rajiv, in 1991. To the north again is **Vijay Ghat** (Victory Bank) where Prime Minister Lal Bahadur Shastri was cremated.

→ SOUTH DELHI

South Delhi is often overlooked by travellers. This is a real pity as it houses some of the city's most stunning sites, best accommodation, bars, clubs and restaurants, as well as some of its most tranquil parks. However be warned, South Delhi can be hell during rushhour when the traffic on the endless flyovers comes to a virtual standstill. But with the metro, you can explore all the way down to Gurgaon with relative ease.

LODI GARDENS

These beautiful gardens, with mellow stone tombs of the 15th- and 16th-century Lodi rulers, are popular for gentle strolls and jogging. In the middle of the garden facing the east entrance from Max Mueller Road is **Bara Gumbad** (Big Dome), a mosque built in 1494. The raised courtyard is provided with an imposing gateway and *mehman khana* (guest rooms). The platform in the centre appears to have had a tank for ritual ablutions.

The **Sheesh Bumbad** (Glass Dome, late 15th century) is built on a raised incline north of the Bara Gumbad and was once decorated with glazed blue tiles, painted floral designs and Koranic inscriptions. The façade gives the impression of a two-storeyed building, typical of Lodi architecture. **Mohammad Shah's Tomb** (1450) is that of the third Sayyid ruler. It has sloping buttresses, an octagonal plan, projecting eaves and lotus patterns on the ceiling. **Sikander Lodi's Tomb**, built by his son in 1517, is also an octagonal structure decorated with Hindu motifs. A structural innovation is the double dome which was later refined under the Mughals. The 16th-century **Athpula** (Bridge of Eight Piers), near the northeastern entrance, is attributed to Nawab Bahadur, a nobleman at Akbar's court.

SAFDARJANG'S TOMB
ⓘ *Sunrise to sunset, Rs 100 foreigners, Rs 5 Indians.*

Safdarjang's Tomb, seldom visited, was built by Nawab Shuja-ud-Daulah for his father Mirza Mukhim Abdul Khan, entitled Safdarjang, who was Governor of Oudh (1719-1748), and Wazir of his successor (1748-1754). Safdarjang died in 1754. With its high enclosure walls, *char bagh* layout of gardens, fountain and central domed mausoleum, it follows the tradition of Humayun's tomb. Typically, the real tomb is just below ground level. Flanking the mausoleum are pavilions used by Shuja-ud-Daulah as his family residence. Immediately to its south is the battlefield where Timur and his Mongol horde crushed Mahmud Shah Tughluq on 12 December 1398.

HAZRAT NIZAMUDDIN
ⓘ *Dress ultra-modestly if you don't want to feel uncomfortable or cause offence.*

At the east end of the Lodi Road, Hazrat Nizamuddin Dargah (Nizamuddin 'village') now tucked away behind the residential suburb of Nizamuddin West, off Mathura Road, grew up around the shrine of Sheikh Nizamuddin Aulia (1236-1325), a Chishti saint. This is a wonderfully atmospheric place. *Qawwalis* are sung at sunset after *namaaz* (prayers), and are particularly impressive on Thursdays – be prepared for crowds. Highly recommended.

West of the central shrine is the **Jama-at-khana Mosque** (1325). Its decorated arches are typical of the Khalji design also seen at the Ala'i Darwaza at the Qutb Minar. South of the main tomb and behind finely crafted screens is the grave of princess Jahanara, Shah Jahan's eldest and favourite daughter. She shared the emperor's last years when he was imprisoned at Agra Fort. The grave, open to the sky, is in accordance with the epitaph written by her: "Let naught cover my grave save the green grass, for grass suffices as the covering of the lowly". Pilgrims congregate at the shrine twice a year for the Urs (fair) held to mark the anniversaries of Hazrat Nizamuddin Aulia and his disciple Amir Khusrau, whose tomb is nearby.

HUMAYUN'S TOMB
ⓘ *Sunrise to sunset, Rs 250 foreigners, Rs 10 Indians, video cameras Rs 25, located in Nizamuddin, 15-20 mins by taxi from Connaught Circus, allow 45 mins.*

Eclipsed later by the Taj Mahal and the Jama Masjid, this tomb is the best example in Delhi of the early Mughal style of tomb. Superbly maintained, it is well worth a visit, preferably before visiting the Taj Mahal. Humayun, the second Mughal emperor, was forced into exile in Persia after being heavily defeated by the Afghan Sher Shah in 1540. He returned to

India in 1545, finally recapturing Delhi in 1555. The tomb was designed and built by his senior widow and mother of his son Akbar, Hamida Begum. A Persian from Khurasan, after her pilgrimage to Mecca she was known as Haji Begum. She supervised the entire construction of the tomb (1564-1573), camping on the site.

The plan The tomb has an octagonal plan, lofty arches, pillared kiosks and the double dome of Central Asian origin, which appears here for the first time in India. Outside Gujarat, Hindu temples make no use of the dome, but the Indian Muslim dome had until now, been of a flatter shape as opposed to the tall Persian dome rising on a more slender neck. Here also is the first standard example of the garden tomb concept: the **char bagh** (garden divided into quadrants), water channels and fountains. This form culminated in the gardens of the Taj Mahal. However, the tomb also shows a number of distinctively Hindu motifs. Tillotson has pointed out that in Humayun's tomb, Hindu *chhattris* (small domed kiosks), complete with temple columns and *chajjas* (broad eaves), surround the central dome. The bulbous finial on top of the dome and the star motif in the spandrels of the main arches are also Hindu, the latter being a solar symbol.

The approach The tomb enclosure has two high double-storeyed gateways: the entrance to the west and the other to the south. A *baradari* occupies the centre of the east wall, and a bath chamber that of the north wall. Several Moghul princes, princesses and Haji Begum herself lie buried here. During the 1857 Mutiny Bahadur Shah II, the last Moghul emperor of Delhi, took shelter here with his three sons. Over 80, he was seen as a figurehead by Muslims opposing the British. When captured he was transported to Yangon (Rangoon) for the remaining four years of his life. The tomb to the right of the approach is that of Isa Khan, Humayun's barber.

The dome Some 38 m high, the dome does not have the swell of the Taj Mahal and the decoration of the whole edifice is much simpler. It is of red sandstone with some white marble to highlight the lines of the building. There is some attractive inlay work, and some *jalis* in the balcony fence and on some of the recessed keel arch windows. The interior is austere and consists of three storeys of arches rising up to the dome. The emperor's tomb is of white marble and quite plain without any inscription. The overall impression is that of a much bulkier, more squat building than the Taj Mahal. The cavernous space under the main tombs is home to great colonies of bats.

HAUZ KHAS
① *1-hr cultural show, 1845, Rs 100 (check with Delhi Tourism, see page 40).*
South of Safdarjang's Tomb, and entered off either Aurobindo Marg on the east side or Africa Avenue on the west side, is Hauz Khas. Ala-ud-din Khalji (ruled 1296-1313) created a large tank here for the use of the inhabitants of Siri, the second capital city of Delhi founded by him. Fifty years later Firoz Shah Tughluq cleaned up the silted tank and raised several buildings on its east and south banks which are known as Hauz Khas or Royal Tank.

Firoz Shah's austere tomb is found here. The multi-storeyed wings, on the north and west of the tomb, were built by him in 1354 as a *madrasa* (college). The octagonal and square *chhattris* were built as tombs, possibly to the teachers at the college. Hauz Khas is now widely used as a park for early-morning recreation – walking, running and yoga *asanas.* Classical music concerts, dance performances and a *son et lumière* show are held in the evenings when monuments are illuminated by thousands of earthen lamps and torches. Wandering the streets of Haus Khaz village, you can almost forget that you are in India. Labyrinthine alleys lead to numerous galleries, boutiques and restaurants. There are a lot of little design studios here and a more boho vibe.

QUTB MINAR COMPLEX

① *Sunrise to sunset, Rs 250 foreigners, Rs 10 Indians. The metro goes to Qutb Minar. Bus 505 from New Delhi Railway Station (Ajmeri Gate), Super Bazar (east of Connaught Circus) and Cottage Industries Emporium, Janpath. Auto Rs 110, though drivers may be reluctant to take you. This area is also opening up as a hub for new chic restaurants and bars.*

Muhammad Ghuri conquered northwest India at the very end of the 12th century. The conquest of the Gangetic plain down to Benares (Varanasi) was undertaken by Muhammad's Turkish slave and chief general, Qutb-ud-din-Aibak, whilst another general took Bihar and Bengal. In the process, temples were reduced to rubble, the remaining Buddhist centres were dealt their death blow and their monks slaughtered. When Muhammad was assassinated in 1206, his gains passed to the loyal Qutb-ud-din-Aibak. Thus the first sultans or Muslim kings

QUTB MINAR COMPLEX

To Mehrauli
To Delhi
Aurobindo Marg
Graves
Mosque
Entrance
6
4
2
Gupta Pillar
Court of Ala-ud-din
PWD Rest House
To Badarpur
3
Court of Iltutmish
1
8
Qutb Canopy
Qutb Restaurant
To Gurgaon
5
7
9

N
200 metres
200 yards

1192-1199
Qutb Minar **1**
Quwwat-ul-Islam Mosque **2**

1210-1236
Screens **3**
Iltutmish's Tomb **6**

1300-1312
Ala'i Minar **4**
Ala'i Darwaza **5**
Ala-ud-din Khalji's Tomb **7**
Madrasa **8**

Early 16th century
Tomb of Imam Zamin **9**

of Delhi became known as the **Slave Dynasty** (1026-1290). For the next three centuries the Slave Dynasty and the succeeding Khalji (1290-1320), Tughluq (1320-1414), Sayyid (1414-1445) and Lodi (1451-1526) dynasties provided Delhi with fluctuating authority. The legacy of their ambitions survives in the tombs, forts and palaces that litter Delhi Ridge and the surrounding plain. Qutb-ud-din-Aibak died after only four years in power, but he left his mark with the **Qutb Minar** and his **citadel**. Qutb Minar, built to proclaim the victory of Islam over the infidel, dominates the countryside for miles around. Visit the *minar* first.

Qutb Minar (1) In 1199 work began on what was intended to be the most glorious tower of victory in the world and was to be the prototype of all *minars* (towers) in India. Qutb-ud-din-Aibak had probably seen and been influenced by the brick victory pillars in Ghazni in Afghanistan, but this one was also intended to serve as the minaret attached to the Might of Islam Mosque. From here the muezzin could call the faithful to prayer. Later every mosque would incorporate its minaret.

As a mighty reminder of the importance of the ruler as Allah's representative on earth, the Qutb Minar (literally 'axis minaret') stood at the centre of the community. A pivot of Faith, Justice and Righteousness, its name also carried the message of Qutb-ud-din's (Axis of the Faith) own achievements. The inscriptions carved in Kufi script tell that "the tower was erected to cast the shadow of God over both east and west". For Qutb-ud-din-Aibak it marked the eastern limit of the empire of the One God. Its western counterpart is the Giralda Tower built by Yusuf in Seville.

The Qutb Minar is 73 m high and consists of five storeys. The diameter of the base is 14.4 m and 2.7 m at the top. Qutb-ud-din built the first three and his son-in-law Iltutmish embellished these and added a fourth. This is indicated in some of the Persian and Nagari (North Indian) inscriptions which also record that it was twice damaged by lightning in 1326 and 1368. While repairing the damage caused by the second, Firoz Shah Tughluq added a fifth storey and used marble to face the red and buff sandstone. This was the first time contrasting colours were used decoratively, later to become such a feature of Mughal buildings. Firoz's fifth storey was topped by a graceful cupola but this fell down during an earthquake in 1803. A new one was added by a Major Robert Smith in 1829 but was so out of keeping that it was removed in 1848 and now stands in the gardens.

The original storeys are heavily indented with different styles of fluting, alternately round and angular on the bottom, round on the second and angular on the third. The beautifully carved honeycomb detail beneath the balconies is reminiscent of the Alhambra Palace in Spain. The calligraphy bands are verses from the Koran and praises to its patron builder.

Quwwat-ul-Islam Mosque (2) The Quwwat-ul-Islam Mosque (The Might of Islam Mosque), the earliest surviving mosque in India, is to the northwest of the Qutb Minar. It was begun in 1192, immediately after Qutb-ud-din's conquest of Delhi and completed in 1198, using the remains of no fewer than 27 local Hindu and Jain temples.

The architectural style contained elements that Muslims brought from Arabia, including buildings made of mud and brick and decorated with glazed tiles, *squinches* (arches set diagonally across the corners of a square chamber to facilitate the raising of a dome and to effect a transition from a square to a round structure), the pointed arch and the true dome. Finally, Muslim buildings came alive through ornamental calligraphy and geometric patterning. This was in marked contrast to indigenous Indian styles of architecture. Hindu,

Buddhist and Jain buildings relied on the post-and-beam system in which spaces were traversed by corbelling, ie shaping flat-laid stones to create an arch. The arched screen that runs along the western end of the courtyard beautifully illustrates the fact that it was Hindu methods that still prevailed at this stage, for the 16-m-high arch uses Indian corbelling, the corners being smoothed off to form the curved line.

Screens (3) Qutb-ud-din's screen formed the façade of the mosque and, facing in the direction of Mecca, became the focal point. The sandstone screen is carved in the Indo-Islamic style, lotuses mingling with Koranic calligraphy. The later screenwork and other extensions (1230) are fundamentally Islamic in style, the flowers and leaves having been replaced by more arabesque patterns. Indian builders mainly used stone, which from the fourth century AD had been intricately carved with representations of the gods. In their first buildings in India the Muslim architects designed the buildings and local Indian craftsmen built them and decorated them with typical motifs such as the vase and foliage, tasselled ropes, bells and cows.

Iltutmish's extension The mosque was enlarged twice. In 1230 Qutb-ud-din's son-in-law and successor, Shamsuddin Iltutmish, doubled its size by extending the colonnades and prayer hall – 'Iltutmish's extension'. This accommodated a larger congregation, and in the more stable conditions of Iltutmish's reign, Islam was obviously gaining ground. The arches of the extension are nearer to the true arch and are similar to the Gothic arch that appeared in Europe at this time. The decoration is Islamic. Almost 100 years after Iltutmish's death, the mosque was enlarged again, by Ala-ud-din Khalji. The conductor of tireless and bloody military campaigns, Ala-ud-din proclaimed himself 'God's representative on earth'. His architectural ambitions, however, were not fully realized, because on his death in 1316 only part of the north and east extensions were completed.

Ala'i Minar (4) and the Ala'i Darwaza (5) To the north of the Qutb complex is the 26-m **Ala'i Minar**, intended to surpass the tower of the Qutb, but not completed beyond the first storey. Ala-ud-din did complete the south gateway to the building, the **Ala'i Darwaza**; inscriptions testify that it was built in 1311 (Muslim 710 AH). He benefited from events in Central Asia: since the early 13th century, Mongol hordes from Central Asia fanned out east and west, destroying the civilization of the Seljuk Turks in West Asia, and refugee artists, architects, craftsmen and poets fled east. They brought to India features and techniques that had developed in Byzantine Turkey, some of which can be seen in the Ala'i Darwaza.

The gatehouse is a large sandstone cuboid, into which are set small cusped arches with carved *jali* screens. The lavish ornamentation of geometric and floral designs in red sandstone and white marble produced a dramatic effect when viewed against the surrounding buildings.

The inner chamber, 11 sq m has doorways and, for the first time in India, true arches. Above each doorway is an Arabic inscription with its creator's name and one of his self-assumed titles – 'The Second Alexander'. The north doorway, which is the main entrance, is the most elaborately carved. The dome, raised on squinched arches, is flat and shallow. Of the effects employed, the arches with their 'lotus-bud' fringes are Seljuk, as is the dome with the rounded finial and the façade. These now became trademarks of the **Khalji style**, remaining virtually unchanged until their further development in Humayun's Tomb.

Iltutmish's Tomb (6) Built in 1235, Iltutmish's Tomb lies in the northwest of the compound, midway along the west wall of the mosque. It is the first surviving tomb of a Muslim ruler in India. Two other tombs also stand within the extended Might of Islam Mosque. The idea of a tomb was quite alien to Hindus, who had been practising cremation since around 400 BC. Blending Hindu and Muslim styles, the outside is relatively plain with three arched and decorated doorways. The interior carries reminders of the nomadic origins of the first Muslim rulers. Like a Central Asian *yurt* (tent) in its decoration, it combines the familiar Indian motifs of the wheel, bell, chain and lotus with the equally familiar geometric arabesque patterning. The west wall is inset with three *mihrabs* that indicate the direction of Mecca.

The tomb originally supported a dome resting on *squinches* which you can still see. The dome collapsed (witness the slabs of stone lying around) suggesting that the technique was as yet unrefined. From the corbelled squinches it may be assumed that the dome was corbelled too, as found in contemporary Gujarat and Rajput temples. The blocks of masonry were fixed together using the Indian technology of iron dowels. In later Indo-Islamic buildings lime plaster was used for bonding.

Other tombs To the southwest of the uncompleted Quwwat-ul-Islam mosque, an L-shaped ruin marks the site of **Ala-ud-din Khalji's Tomb (7)** within the confines of a **madrasa (college) (8)**. This is the first time in India that a tomb and *madrasa* are found together, another custom inherited from the Seljuks. Immediately to the east of the Ala'i Darwaza stands the **Tomb of Imam Zamin (9)**, an early 16th-century *sufi* 'saint' from Turkestan. It is an octagonal structure with a plastered sandstone dome and has *jali* screens, a characteristic of the Lodi style of decoration.

TUGHLUQABAD

ⓘ *Sunrise to sunset, foreigners Rs 100, Indians Rs 5, video camera Rs 25, allow 1 hr for return rickshaws, turn right at entrance and walk 200 m. The site is often deserted so don't go alone. Take plenty of water.*

Tughluqabad's ruins, 7.5 km east from Qutb Minar, still convey a sense of the power and energy of the newly arrived Muslims in India. From the walls you get a magnificent impression of the strategic advantages of the site. **Ghiyas'ud-Din Tughluq** (ruled 1321-1325), after ascending the throne of Delhi, selected this site for his capital. He built a massive fort around his capital city which stands high on a rocky outcrop of the Delhi Ridge. The fort is roughly octagonal in plan with a circumference of 6.5 km. The vast size, strength and obvious solidity of the whole give it an air of massive grandeur. It was not until Babur (ruled 1526-1530) that dynamite was used in warfare, so this is a very defensible site.

East of the main entrance is the rectangular **citadel**. A wider area immediately to the west and bounded by walls contained the **palaces**. Beyond this to the north lay the **city**. Now marked by the ruins of houses, the streets were laid out in a grid fashion. Inside the citadel enclosure is the **Vijay Mandal tower** and the remains of several halls including a long underground passage. The fort also contained seven tanks.

A causeway connects the fort with the tomb of Ghiyas'ud-Din Tughluq, while a wide embankment near its southeast corner gave access to the fortresses of **Adilabad** about 1 km away, built a little later by Ghiyas'ud-Din's son Muhammad. The tomb is very well preserved and has red sandstone walls with a pronounced slope (the first Muslim building in India to have sloping walls), crowned with a white marble dome. This dome, like that of the Ala'i Darwaza at the Qutb, is crowned by an *amalaka*, a feature of Hindu architecture. Also Hindu is the trabeate arch at the tomb's fortress wall entrance. Inside are three cenotaphs belonging to Ghiyas'ud-Din, his wife and son Muhammad.

Ghiyas'ud-Din Tughluq quickly found that military victories were no guarantee of lengthy rule. When he returned home after a victorious campaign the welcoming pavilion erected by his son and successor, Muhammad-bin Tughluq, was deliberately collapsed over him. Tughluqabad was abandoned shortly afterwards and was thus only inhabited for five years. The Tughluq dynasty continued to hold Delhi until Timur sacked it and slaughtered its inhabitants. For a brief period Tughluq power shifted to Jaunpur near Varanasi, where the Tughluq architectural traditions were carried forward in some superb mosques.

BAHA'I TEMPLE (LOTUS TEMPLE)

ⓘ *1 Apr-30 Sep 0900-1900, 1 Oct-31 Mar Tue-Sun 0930-1730, free entry and parking, visitors welcome to attend services, at other times the temple is open for silent meditation and prayer. Audio-visual presentations in English are at 1100, 1200, 1400 and 1530, remove shoes before entering. Bus 433 from the centre (Jantar Mantar) goes to Nehru Place, within walking distance (1.5 km) of the temple at Kalkaji, or take a taxi or auto-rickshaw.*

Architecturally the Baha'i Temple is a remarkably striking building. Constructed in 1980-1981, it is built out of white marble and in the characteristic Baha'i temple shape of a lotus flower – 45 lotus petals form the walls – which internally creates a feeling of light and space (34 m high, 70 m in diameter). It is a simple design, brilliantly executed and very elegant in form. All Baha'i temples are nine-sided, symbolizing 'comprehensiveness, oneness and unity'. The Delhi Temple, which seats 1300, is surrounded by nine pools, an attractive feature also helping to keep the building cool. It is particularly attractive when flood-lit. Baha'i temples are "dedicated to the worship of God, for peoples of all races, religions or castes. Only the Holy Scriptures of the Baha'i Faith and earlier revelations are read or recited".

→ EAST OF THE YAMUNA

Designated as the site of the athletes' village for the 2010 Commonwealth Games, East Delhi has just one attraction to draw visitors across the Yamuna.

SWAMINARAYAN AKSHARDHAM

ⓘ *www.akshardham.com, Apr-Sep Tue-Sun 1000-1900, Oct-Mar Tue-Sun 0900-1800, temple free, Rs 170 for 'attractions', musical fountain Rs 20, no backpacks, cameras or other electronic items (bag and body searches at entry gate). Packed on Sun; visit early to avoid crowds.*

Opened in November 2005 on the east bank of the Yamuna, the gleaming Akshardham complex represents perhaps the most ambitious construction project in India since the foundation of New Delhi itself. At the centre of a surreal 40-ha 'cultural complex' complete with landscaped gardens, cafés and theme park rides, the temple-monument is dedicated to the 18th-century saint Bhagwan Swaminarayan, who abandoned his home at the age of 11 to embark on a lifelong quest for the spiritual and cultural uplift of Western India. It took 11,000 craftsmen, all volunteers, no less than 300 million hours to complete the temple using traditional building and carving techniques.

If this is the first religious site you visit in India, the security guards and swarms of mooching Indian tourists will hardly prepare you for the typical temple experience. Yet despite this, and the boat rides and animatronic shows which have prompted inevitable comparisons to a 'spiritual Disneyland', most visitors find the Akshardham an inspiring, indeed uplifting, experience, if for no other reason than that the will and ability to build something of its scale and complexity still exist.

The temple You enter the temple complex through a series of intricately carved gates. The Bhakti Dwar (Gate of Devotion), adorned with 208 pairs of gods and their consorts, leads into a hall introducing the life of Swaminarayan and the activities of BAPS (Bochasanwasi Shri Akshar Purushottam Swaminarayan Sanstha), the global Hindu sect-cum-charity which runs Akshardham. The main courtyard is reached through the Mayur Dwar (Peacock Gate), a conglomeration of 869 carved peacocks echoed by an equally florid replica directly facing it.

From here you get your first look at the central monument. Perfectly symmetrical in pink sandstone and white marble, it rests on a plinth encircled by 148 elephants, each sculpted from a 20-tonne stone block, in situations ranging from the literal to the mythological: mortal versions grapple with lions or lug tree trunks, while Airavatha, the eight-trunked mount of Lord Indra, surfs majestically to shore after the churning of the oceans at the dawn of Hindu creation. Above them, carvings of deities, saints and *sadhus* cover every inch of the walls and columns framing the inner sanctum, where a gold-plated *murti* (idol) of Bhagwan Swaminarayan sits attended by avatars of his spiritual successors, beneath a staggeringly intricate marble dome. Around the main dome are eight smaller domes, each carved in hypnotic fractal patterns, while paintings depicting Swaminarayan's life of austerity and service line the walls (explanations in English and Hindi).

Surrounding the temple is a moat of holy water supposedly taken from 151 sacred lakes and rivers visited by Swaminarayan on his seven-year barefoot pilgrimage. 108 bronze *gaumukhs* (cow heads) representing the 108 names of God spout water into the tank, which is itself hemmed in by a 1-km-long *parikrama* (colonnade) of red Rajasthani sandstone.

The exhibition halls and grounds Much of the attention paid to Akshardham revolves around the Disneyesque nature of some of its attractions. Deliberately populist, they aim to instil a sense of pride in the best of Indian values and cultural traditions, and may come across to some as overly flag-waving and patriotic. **Sahajanand Darshan** is an animatronic rendition of Swaminarayan's life, told over a series of rooms through which you are shepherded by an attendant. A beautifully shot Imax movie, *Neelkanth Darshan*, tells the story of the young yogi's seven-year pilgrimage, with dance routines and scenic set pieces worthy of a Bollywood ad campaign. **Sanskruti Vihar** is a 14-minute boat ride along the mythical Saraswati River where visitors are introduced to Indian pioneers in the fields of science, technology, medicine and philosophy.

A similar message imbues the **Cultural Garden**, an avenue of bronze statues extolling the cardinal virtues of prominent figures from Hindu mythology and Indian history. Between the exhibition halls and the main Akshardham is the **Yagnapurush Kund**, an enormous step well (claimed to be the biggest in the world) overlooked by a 9-m bronze statue of Neelkanth. This is the scene for a dramatic and popular musical fountain show each evening.

DELHI LISTINGS

WHERE TO STAY

$$$$ Claridges, 12 Aurangzeb Rd,
T011-3955 5000, www.claridges.com.
138 refurbished, classy rooms, art deco-
style interiors, colonial atmosphere,
attractive restaurants – **Jade Garden**
is good as is the newer tapas inspired
Sevilla, slick **Aura** bar, impeccable
service, more atmosphere than most.
$$$$ Imperial, Janpath, T011-2334 1234,
www.theimperialindia.com. Quintessential
Delhi. 230 rooms and beautiful 'deco suites'
in supremely elegant Lutyens-designed
1933 hotel. Unparalleled location, great
bar, antiques and art everywhere, beautiful
gardens with spa and secluded pool,
amazing **Spice Route** restaurant, classy and
knows it but still quite an experience.
$$$$ Manor, 77 Friends Colony, T011-
2692 5151, www.themanordelhi.com.
Contemporary boutique hotel with 10
stylish rooms, heavenly beds, polished
stone surfaces and chrome, relaxing garden,
a haven. This is where Sir Terence Conran
stays so quality can be guaranteed. Beautiful
artwork and relaxed vibe. Acclaimed
restaurant **Indian Accent**. Charming service.
$$$$-$$$ Amarya Haveli, P5 Hauz Khas
Enclave, T011-4175 9268, www.amarya
group.com. Luxury, boutique, hip French-
run guesthouse. Bright en suite rooms,
with TV, Wi-Fi. Fantastic roof garden.
Great home-cooked food. Book ahead.
They have a sister property, **Amarya Villa**,
in Safdarjung Enclave – the decor there
is inspired by *Navratna* (nine gems).
Both properties are effortlessly chic.
$$$$-$$$ The Rose, T-40 Hauz Khas
Village, T011-6450 0001, www.therosenew
delhi.com. Stylish accommodation in funky
neighbourhood. Beautifully decorated
spacious rooms – with one budget
contender 'The Cabin'. All walls adorned
with artwork – they have an artist in
residence. Rave reviews in their restaurant.

$$$ Broadway, 4/15A Asaf Ali Rd, T011-
4366 3600, www.hotelbroadwaydelhi.com.
Interior designer Catherine Levy has
designed some of the 36 rooms in a
quirky kitsch style, brightly coloured with
psychedelic bathroom tiles. The other rooms
have a more classic design. **Chor Bizarre**
restaurant and bar is highly regarded, as
is the unfortunately named 'Thugs' pub.
Morning and afternoon walking tours of
Old Delhi. Book in advance.
$$$ Hotel Corus, B-49 Connaught Pl,
T011-4365 2222, www.hotelcorus.com.
Comfortable hotel right at the heart of
things. Great location and simple, good
value rooms. You get 15% discount in
their onsite **Life Caffe**.
$$$-$$ Master Guest House, R-500
New Rajendra Nagar (Shankar Rd and
GR Hospital Rd crossing), T011-2874
1089, www.masterbedandbreakfast.com.
3 beautiful rooms, a/c, Wi-Fi, rooftop for
breakfast, *thalis*, warm welcome, personal
attention, secure, recommended. Each
room has the theme of a different god,
complete with appropriate colour schemes.
Very knowledgeable, caring owners run
excellent tours of 'hidden Delhi'. They make
Delhi feel like home.
$$$-$$ Tree of Life B&B, D-193, Saket,
T(0)9810-277699, www.tree-of-life.in.
Stylish B&B with beautifully decorated
rooms, simple but chic. Kitchen access,
excellent onsite reflexology and yoga –
really good atmosphere. The owner also
runs **Metropole Tourist Service**, www.
metrovista.co.in, so is a font of all travelling
knowledge. Close to Saket metro station
and to **PVR** cinema and malls.
$$-$ Wongdhen House, 15A New Tibetan
Colony, Manju-ka-Tilla, T011-2381 6689,
wongdhenhouse@hotmail.com. Very clean
rooms, some with a/c and TV, safe, cosy,
convivial, good breakfast and great Tibetan

meals, an insight into Tibetan culture, peacefully located by Yamuna River yet 15 mins by auto-rickshaw north of Old Delhi Station. For more information on the Tibetan colony of Manju-ka-Tilla, check out www.manjukatilla.com.

RESTAURANTS

$$$ Bukhara, ITC Maurya Sheraton Sardar Patel Marg, T011-2611 2233. Stylish Northwest Frontier cuisine amidst rugged walls draped with rich rugs (but uncomfortable seating). Outstanding meat dishes and dhal. Also tasty vegetable and paneer dishes, but vegetarians will miss out on the best dishes.

$$$ Indian Accent, at The Manor, 77 Friends Colony West, T011-4323 5151. With a menu designed by Manish Mehotra, who runs restaurants in Delhi and London, this acclaimed restaurant offers up Indian food with a modern twist. Your *dosas* will reveal masala morel mushrooms; rather than the traditional Goan prawns *balchao* here you will find it with roasted scallops. Or raw mango masala candy floss for desert? The menu reflects the changing of the seasons and there is live fusion music on Sat.

$$$ Latitude, 9 Khan Market, above Good Earth, T011-2462 1013. This is like sitting in someone's very chic living room and getting served delicious Italian numbers such as bruschetta, salads and pastas, topped off with top-notch coffees. It's run by the Queen of Italian food, Ritu Dalmia, whose restaurant Diva in Greater Kailash is an institution. This is a great pit-stop when shopping in Khan Market.

$$$ Olive at the Qutb, T011-2957 4444, www.olivebarand kitchen.com. Branch of the ever-popular Mumbai restaurant; some people say the Delhi version wins hands down. They serve up delicious platters of Mediterranean food and good strong cocktails. Or head to their sister restaurant Olive Beach, in the Diplomat Hotel, especially for their legendary blow-out Sun brunches: for Rs 2195 you get open access to a mind-boggling buffet and as many martini's as you can drink.

$$$ Spice Route, Imperial Hotel (see Where to stay). Award-winning restaurant charting the journey of spices around the world. Extraordinary temple-like surroundings (it took 7 years to build) and magical atmosphere for enjoying Kerala, Thai, Vietnamese cuisine.

$$ Gunpowder, 22 Hauz Khaz Village, 3rd floor, T011-2653 5700. Wander around the labyrinthine streets of Hauz Khaz and hopefully stumble upon this great restaurant. Specializing in spicy flavours from South India, these are tastes you don't often find north of Mumbai. Try the *Toddy Shop Meen Curry*, *Malabar parotta* and spicy dry pickle *Vepilakkati*. Great views from the terrace and deservedly popular, so book ahead.

$$ Naivedyam, 1 Hauz Khas Village, T011-2696 0426. Exceptionally good South Indian food, great service and very good value. Try the Malabar parantha with kurma or a feast of a *thali*, as well as all the usual *dosas* and *idlis*. It's a beautifully decorated restaurant with murals and columns – a bit like stepping back in time.

$ Karim's, Gali Kababiyan (south of Jama Masjid), Mughlai. Authentic, busy, plenty of local colour. The experience, as much as the food, makes this a must. Not a lot to tempt vegetarians though. In the malls in Saket, you will also find branches of Karim's.

$ Saravana Bhavan, P-15/90, near McDonalds, T011-2334 7755; also at 46 Janpath. Chennai-based chain, light and wonderful South Indian, superb chutneys, unmissable *kaju anjeer* ice cream with figs and nuts. It can take hours to get a table at night or at weekends. If your name's not on the list, you're not getting a *dosa*.

AGRA AND AROUND

The romance of what is arguably the world's most famous building still astonishes in its power. In addition to the Taj Mahal, Agra also houses the great monuments of the Red Fort and the I'timad-ud-Daulah, but to experience their beauty you have to endure the less attractive sides of one of India's least prepossessing towns. A big industrial city, the monuments are often covered in a haze of polluted air, while visitors may be subjected to a barrage of high-power selling. Despite it all, the experience is unmissable. The city is also the convenient gateway to the wonderful, abandoned capital of Fatehpur Sikri, the beautifully serene Akbar's Mauseuleum and some of Hinduism's most holy sites.

→ ARRIVING IN AGRA

GETTING THERE
By far the best way to arrive is by the *Shatabdi Express* train from Delhi, which is much faster than travelling by car and infinitely more comfortable than the frequent 'express' buses, which can take five tiring hours. The best time to visit is between November and March.

MOVING ON
There are regular trains from Agra for **Ranthambhore National Park** (see page 84; the train station is Sawai Madhopur). One of the best – the *Ibadat Express (12395)* – leaves Agra Fort at 0730 and takes 3½ hours, getting you in on time potentially for an afternoon safari. Another option – the *Azimabad Expres (12948)* – leaves at 1230 and arrives in Sawai Madhopur at 1620. The trains are definitely better than road options, which take longer and often route you through Jaipur.

GETTING AROUND
Buses run a regular service between the station, bus stands and the main sites. Cycle-rickshaws, autos and taxis can be hired to venture further afield, or hire a bike if it's not too hot.

TOURIST INFORMATION
Government of India tourist office ① *191 The Mall, T0562-222 6378*. Guides available (Rs 100), helpful and friendly. **UPTDC** ① *64 Taj Rd, T0562-236 3377, also at Agra Cantt, T0562-242 1204*, and **Tourist Bungalow** ① *Raja-ki-Mandi, T0562-285 0120*. **UP Tours** ① *Taj Khema, Taj East Gate, T0562-233 0140*.

Note that there is an **Agra Development Authority Tax** of Rs 500 levied on each day you visit the Taj Mahal and includes Red Fort, Fatehpur Sikri and other attractions. This is in addition to the individual entry fees to the monuments.

→ BACKGROUND

With minor interruptions Agra alternated with Delhi as the capital of the Mughal Empire. **Sikander Lodi** seized it from a rebellious governor and made it his capital in 1501. He died in Agra but is buried in Delhi (see page 56). Agra was Babur's capital. He is believed to have laid out a pleasure garden on the east bank of the River Yamuna and his son Humayun built a mosque here in 1530. **Akbar** lived in Agra in the early years of his reign. Ralph Fitch, the English Elizabethan traveller, described a "magnificent city, with broad streets and tall buildings". He also saw Akbar's new capital at Fatehpur Sikri, 40 km west, describing a route lined all the way with stalls and markets. Akbar moved his capital again to Lahore, before returning to Agra in 1599, where he spent the last six years of his life. **Jahangir** left

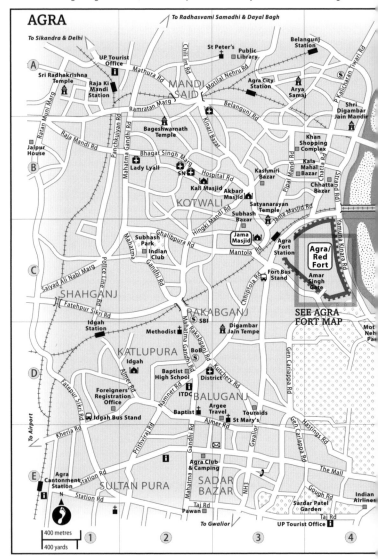

Agra for Kashmir in 1618 and never returned. Despite modifying the Red Fort and building the Taj Mahal, **Shah Jahan** also moved away in 1638 to his new city Shah Jahanabad in Delhi, though he returned in 1650, taken prisoner by his son Aurangzeb and left to spend his last days in the Red Fort. It was **Aurangzeb**, the last of the Great Mughals, who moved the seat of government permanently to Delhi. In the 18th century Agra suffered at the hands of the Jats, was taken, lost and retaken by the Marathas who, in turn, were ousted by the British in 1803. It was the centre of much fighting in the 'Uprising' and was the administrative centre of the Northwest Provinces and Oudh until that too was transferred to Allahabad in 1877.

→ TAJ MAHAL

ⓘ *Sat-Thu sunrise to sunset (last entry 1700), foreigners Rs 750 (including Development Tax), Indians Rs 20, cash only, includes still camera, video cameras, tripods, other electronic items eg mobile phones not allowed, lockers at East and West Gates Rs 1. No photos inside the tomb (instant fines). Allow at least 1 hr. Full moon viewing 2 nights either side of full moon (see www.stardate.org/nightsky/moon for full moon dates), 2030-0030, separate entry fee of foreigners Rs 750, Indians Rs 510, book tickets day before at Architectural Survey of India, 22 The Mall, T0562-222 7261.*

Of all the world's great monuments, the Taj Mahal is one of the most written about, photographed, televized and talked about. To India's Nobel Laureate poet, Tagore, the Taj was a "tear drop on the face of humanity", a building to echo the cry "I have not forgotten, I have not forgotten, O beloved" and its mesmerizing power is such that despite the hype, no one comes away disappointed.

Shah Jahan, the fifth of the Great Mughals, was so devoted to his favourite wife, Mumtaz Mahal (Jewel of the Palace) that he could not bear to be parted from her and insisted that she always travel with him, in all states of health. While accompanying him on a military campaign, she died at the age of 39 giving birth to their 14th child. On her deathbed, it is said, she asked the emperor to show the world how much they loved one another.

The grief-stricken emperor went into mourning for two years. He turned away from the business of running the empire and dedicated himself to architecture, resolving to build his wife the most magnificent memorial on earth. On the right bank of the River Yamuna in full view of his fortress palace, it was to be known as the Taj-i-Mahal (Crown of the Palace).

According to the French traveller Tavnier, work on the Taj commenced in 1632 and took 22 years to complete, employing a workforce of 20,000. The red sandstone was available locally but the white marble was quarried at Makrana in Rajasthan and transported 300 km by a fleet of 1000 elephants. Semi-precious stones for the inlay came from far and wide: red carnelian from Baghdad; red, yellow and brown jasper from the Punjab; green jade and crystal from China; blue lapis lazuli from Ceylon and Afghanistan; turquoise from Tibet; chrysolite from Egypt; amethyst from Persia; agates from the Yemen; dark green malachite from Russia; diamonds from Central India and mother-of-pearl from the Indian Ocean. A 3-km ramp was used to lift material up to the dome and, because of the sheer weight of the building; boreholes were filled with metal coins and fragments to provide suitable foundations. The resemblance of the exquisite double dome to a huge pearl is not coincidental; a saying of the Prophet describes the throne of God as a dome of white pearl supported by white pillars.

Myths and controversy surround the Taj Mahal. On its completion it is said the emperor ordered the chief mason's right hand to be cut off to prevent him from repeating his masterpiece. Another legend suggests that Shah Jahan intended to build a replica for himself in black marble on the other side of the river, connected to the Taj Mahal by a bridge built with alternate blocks of black and white marble. Some have asserted that architects responsible for designing this mausoleum must have come from Turkey, Persia or even Europe (because of the pietra dura work on the tomb). In fact, no one knows who drew the plans. What is certain is that in the Taj Mahal, the traditions of Indian Hindu and Persian Muslim architecture were fused together into a completely distinct and perfect art form.

VIEWING

The white marble of the Taj is extraordinarily luminescent and even on dull days seems bright. The whole building appears to change its hue according to the light in the sky. In winter (December to February), it is worth being there at sunrise. Then the mists that often lie over the River Yamuna lift as the sun rises and casts its golden rays over the pearl-white tomb. Beautifully lit in the soft light, the Taj appears to float on air. At sunset, the view from across the river is equally wonderful. The **Archaeological Survey of India** explicitly asks visitors not to make donations to anyone including custodians in the tomb.

ENTRANCES

To reduce damage to the marble by the polluted atmosphere, local industries are having to comply with strict rules now and vehicles emitting noxious fumes are not allowed within 2 km of the monument. People are increasingly using horse-drawn carriages or walking. You can approach the Taj from three directions. The western entrance is usually used by those arriving from the fort and is an easy 10-minute walk along a pleasant garden road. At the eastern entrance, rickshaws and camel drivers offer to take visitors to the gate for up to Rs 100 each; however, an official battery bus ferries visitors from the car park to the gate for a small fee.

THE APPROACH

In the unique beauty of the Taj, subtlety is blended with grandeur and a massive overall design is matched with immaculately intricate execution. You will already have seen the dome of the tomb in the distance, looking almost like a miniature, but as you go into the open square, the Taj itself is so well hidden that you almost wonder where it can be. The glorious surprise is kept until the last moment, for wholly concealing it is the massive red sandstone gateway of the entrance, symbolizing the divide between the secular world and paradise.

The gateway was completed in 1648, though the huge brass door is recent. The original doors (plundered by the Jats) were solid silver and decorated with 1100 nails whose heads were contemporary silver coins. Although the gateway is remarkable in itself, one of its functions is to prevent you getting any glimpse of the tomb inside until you are right in the doorway itself. From here only the tomb is visible, stunning in its nearness, but as you move forward the minarets come into view.

THE GARDEN

The Taj garden, well kept though it is nowadays, is nothing compared with its former glory. The guiding principle is one of symmetry. The *char bagh*, separated by the watercourses (rivers of heaven) originating from the central, raised pool, were divided into 16 flower beds, making a total of 64. The trees, all carefully planted to maintain the symmetry, were either cypress (signifying death) or fruit trees (life). The channels were stocked with colourful fish and the gardens with beautiful birds. It is well worth wandering along the side avenues for not only is it much more peaceful but also good for framing photos of the tomb with foliage. You may see bullocks pulling the lawnmowers around.

THE MOSQUE AND ITS JAWAB

On the east and west sides of the tomb are identical red sandstone buildings. On the west (left-hand side) is a mosque. It is common in Islam to build one next to a tomb. It sanctifies the area and provides a place for worship. The replica on the other side is known as the **Jawab** (answer). This can't be used for prayer as it faces away from Mecca.

THE TOMB

There is only one point of access to the **plinth** and tomb, where shoes must be removed (socks can be kept on; remember the white marble gets very hot) or cloth overshoes worn (Rs 2, though strictly free).

The **tomb** is square with bevelled corners. At each corner smaller domes rise while in the centre is the main dome topped by a brass finial. The dome is actually a double dome and this device, Central Asian in origin, was used to gain height. The resemblance of the dome to a huge pearl is not coincidental. The exterior ornamentation is calligraphy (verses of the Koran), beautifully carved panels in bas relief and superb inlay work.

The **interior** of the mausoleum comprises a lofty central chamber, a *maqbara* (crypt) immediately below this, and four octagonal corner rooms. The central chamber contains replica tombs, the real ones being in the crypt. The public tomb was originally surrounded by a jewel-encrusted silver screen. Aurangzeb removed this, fearing it might be stolen, and replaced it with an octagonal screen of marble carved from one block of marble and inlaid with precious stones. It is an incredible piece of workmanship. This chamber is open at sunrise, but may close during the day.

Above the tombs is a **Cairene lamp** whose flame is supposed never to go out. This one was given by Lord Curzon, Governor General of India (1899-1905), to replace the original which was stolen by Jats. The tomb of Mumtaz with the 'female' slate, rests immediately beneath the dome. If you look from behind it, you can see how it lines up centrally with the main entrance. Shah Jahan's tomb is larger and to the side, marked by a 'male' pen-box, the sign of a cultured or noble person. Not originally intended to be placed there but squeezed in by Aurangzeb, this flaws the otherwise perfect symmetry of the whole complex. Finally, the acoustics of the building are superb, the domed ceiling being designed to echo chants from the Koran and musicians' melodies.

The **museum** ⓘ *above the entrance, Sat-Thu 1000-1700*, has a small collection of Mughal memorabilia, photographs and miniatures of the Taj through the ages but has no textual information. Sadly, the lights do not always work.

→ AGRA FORT (RED FORT)

ⓘ *0600-1800, foreigners Rs 300 (Rs 250 if you've been to the Taj on the same day), Indians Rs 15, video Rs 25; allow a minimum of 1½ hrs for a visit. The best route round is to start with the building on your right before going through the gate at the top of the broad 100 m ramp; the gentle incline made it suitable for elephants.*

On the west bank of the River Yamuna, Akbar's magnificent fort dominates the centre of the city. Akbar erected the walls and gates and the first buildings inside. **Shah Jahan** built the impressive imperial quarters and mosque, while Aurangzeb added the outer ramparts. The outer walls, just over 20 m high and faced with red sandstone, tower above the outer moat. The fort is crescent-shaped with a long, nearly straight wall facing the river, punctuated at regular intervals by bastions. The main entrance used to be in the centre of the west wall, the **Delhi Gate**, facing the bazar. It led to the Jami Masjid in the city but is now permanently closed. You can only enter now from the **Amar Singh Gate** in the south. Although only the southern third of the fort is open to the public, this includes nearly all the buildings of interest. At the gate you will have to contend with vendors of cheap soapstone boxes and knick-knacks. If you want to buy something, bargain hard. Guides will offer their services – most are not particularly good.

FORTIFICATIONS

The fortifications tower above the 9-m-wide, 10-m-deep moat (still evident but containing stagnant water) formerly filled with water from the Yamuna River. There is an outer wall on the riverside and an imposing 22-m-high inner, main wall, giving a feeling of great defensive power. Although it served as a model for Shah Jahan's Red Fort in Delhi, its own model was the Rajput fort built by Raja Man Singh Tomar of Gwalior in 1500, see page 190. If an aggressor managed to get through the outer gate they would have to make a right-hand turn and thereby expose their flank to the defenders on the inner wall. The inner gate is solidly powerful but has been attractively decorated with tiles. The similarities with Islamic patterns of the tilework are obvious, though the Persian blue was also used in the Gwalior Fort and may well have been imitated from that example. The incline up to this point and beyond was suitable for elephants and as you walk past the last gate and up the broad brick-lined ramp with ridged slabs, it is easy to imagine arriving on elephant back. At the top of this 100-m ramp is a gate with a map and description board on your left.

Jahangiri Mahal (1) Despite its name, this was built by Akbar (circa 1570) as women's quarters. It is all that survives of his original palace buildings. In front is a large **stone bowl**, with steps both inside and outside, which was probably filled with fragrant rose water for bathing. Almost 75 m sq, the palace has a simple stone exterior. Tillotson has pointed out that the blind arcade of pointed arches inlaid with white marble which decorate the façade

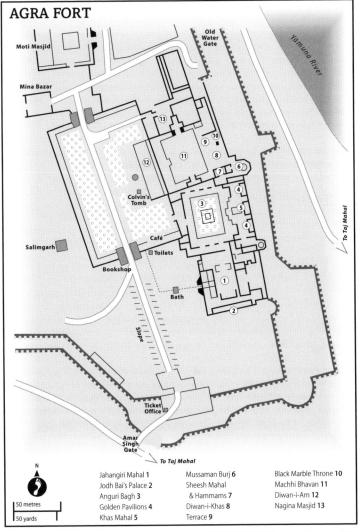

AGRA FORT

Old Water Gate

Yamuna River

Moti Masjid

Mina Bazar

13

10
9
11   8

12

7   6

Colvin's Tomb

3   4

Café

5

Salimgarh

4

Toilets

Bookshop

1

To Taj Mahal

Bath

2

Slope

Ticket Office

Amar Singh Gate

→ To Taj Mahal

N

50 metres
50 yards

Jahangiri Mahal **1**	Mussaman Burj **6**	Black Marble Throne **10**
Jodh Bai's Palace **2**	Sheesh Mahal	Machhi Bhavan **11**
Anguri Bagh **3**	& Hammams **7**	Diwan-i-Am **12**
Golden Pavilions **4**	Diwan-i-Khas **8**	Nagina Masjid **13**
Khas Mahal **5**	Terrace **9**	

is copied from 14th-century monuments of the Khaljis and Tughluqs in Delhi. He notes that they are complemented by some features derived from Hindu architecture, including the *jarokhas* (balconies) protruding from the central section, the sloping dripstone in place of *chajja* (eaves) along the top of the façade, and the domed *chhattris* at its ends. The presence of distinctively Hindu features does not indicate a synthesis of architectural styles at this early stage of Mughal architecture, as can be seen much more clearly from inside the Jahangiri Mahal. Here most of the features are straightforwardly Hindu; square-headed arches and extraordinarily carved capitals and brackets illustrate the vivid work of local Hindu craftsmen employed by Akbar without any attempt either to curb their enthusiasm for florid decoration and mythical animals nor to produce a fusion of Hindu and Islamic ideas. Tillotson argues that the central courtyard is essentially Hindu, in significant contrast with most earlier Indo-Islamic buildings. In these, an Islamic scheme was modified by Hindu touches. He suggests, therefore, that the Jahangiri Mahal marks the start of a more fundamental kind of Hinduization, typical of several projects during Akbar's middle period of rule, including the palace complex in Fatehpur Sikri. However, it did not represent a real fusion of ideas – something that only came under Shah Jahan – simply a juxtaposition of sharply contrasting styles.

Jodh Bai's Palace (2) On the south side, this is named after one of Jahangir's wives. On the east the hall court leads onto a more open yard by the inner wall of the fort. In contrast to other palaces in the fort, this is quite simple. Through the slits in the wall you can see the Taj.

SHAH JAHAN'S PALACE BUILDINGS
Turn left through to Shah Jahan's Khas Mahal (1636). The open tower allows you to view the walls and see to your left the decorated Mussaman Burj tower. The use of white marble transforms the atmosphere, contributing to the new sense of grace and light.

Anguri Bagh (3) (Vine Garden) The formal, 85-m-sq, geometric gardens are on the left. In Shah Jahan's time the geometric patterns were enhanced by decorative flower beds. In the middle of the white marble platform wall in front is a decorative water slide. From the pool with its bays for seating and its fountains, water would drain off along channels decorated to mimic a stream. The surface was scalloped to produce a rippling waterfall, or inlaid to create a shimmering stream bed. Behind vertical water drops, there are little cusped arch niches into which flowers would be placed during the day and lamps at night. The effect was magical.

Golden Pavilions (4) The curved *chala* roofs of the small pavilions by the Khas Mahal are based on the roof shape of Bengali village huts constructed out of curved bamboo, designed to keep off heavy rain. The shape was first expressed in stone by the Sultans of Bengal. Originally gilded, these were probably ladies' bedrooms, with hiding places for jewellery in the walls. These pavilions are traditionally associated with Shah Jahan's daughters, Roshanara and Jahanara.

Khas Mahal (5) This was the model for the Diwan-i-Khas at the Red Fort in Delhi. Some of the original interior decoration has been restored (1895) and gives an impression of how splendid the painted ceiling must have been. The metal rings were probably used for *punkhas*. Underneath are cool rooms used to escape the summer heat. The Khas Mahal illustrates Shahs' original architectural contribution.

The buildings retain distinctively Islamic Persian features – the geometrical planning of the pavilions and the formal layout of the gardens, for example. Tillotson points out that here "Hindu motifs are treated in a new manner, which is less directly imitative of the Hindu antecedents. The temple columns and corbel capitals have been stripped of their rich carving and turned into simpler, smoother forms ... the *chhattris* have Islamic domes. Through these subtle changes the indigenous motifs have lost their specifically Hindu identity; they therefore contrast less strongly with the Islamic components, and are bound with them into a new style. The unity is assisted by the use of the cusped arch and the *Bangladar* roof". Seen in this light, the Khas Mahal achieves a true synthesis which eluded Akbar's designs.

Mussaman Burj (6) On the left of the Khas Mahal is the Mussaman Burj (Octagonal Tower, though sometimes corrupted into Saman Burj, then translated as Jasmine Tower). It is a beautiful octagonal tower with an open pavilion. With its openness, elevation and the benefit of cooling evening breezes blowing in off the Yamuna River, this could well have been used as the emperor's bedroom. It has been suggested that this is where Shah Jahan lay on his deathbed, gazing at the Taj. Access to this tower is through a magnificently decorated and intimate apartment with a scalloped fountain in the centre. The inlay work here is exquisite, especially above the pillars. In front of the fountain is a sunken courtyard which could be filled by water carriers, to work the fountains in the pool.

Sheesh Mahal (7) (Mirror Palace) Here are further examples of decorative water engineering in the *hammams*; the water here may have been warmed by lamps. The mirrors, which were more precious than marble, were set into the walls, often specially chiselled to accommodate their crooked shape. The defensive qualities of the site and the fortifications are obvious. In the area between the outer rampart and the inner wall gladiatorial battles were staged pitting man against tiger, or elephant against elephant. The tower was the emperor's grandstand seat.

Diwan-i-Khas (8) (Hall of Private Audience, 1637) This is next to the Mussaman Burj, approached on this route by a staircase which brings you out at the side. The interior of the Diwan-i-Khas, a three-sided pavilion with a terrace of fine proportions, would have been richly decorated with tapestries and carpets. The double columns in marble inlaid with semi-precious stones in delightful floral patterns in pietra dura have finely carved capitals.

TERRACE AND MACHHI BHAVAN

In front of the Diwan-i-Khas are two throne 'platforms' on a **terrace (9)**. Gascoigne recounts how Shah Jahan tried to trick a haughty Persian ambassador into bowing low as he approached the throne by erecting a fence with a small wicket gate so that his visitor would have to enter on hands and knees. The ambassador did so, but entered backwards, thus presenting his bottom first to the Emperor. The **black marble throne (10)** at the rear of the terrace was used by Jahangir when claiming to be Emperor at Allahabad. The emperor sat on the white marble platform facing the **Machhi Bhavan (11)** (Fish Enclosure), which once contained pools and fountains, waiting to meet visiting dignitaries.

Diwan-i-Am (12) Go down an internal staircase and you enter the Diwan-i-Am from the side. The clever positioning of the pillars gives the visitor arriving through the gates in the right- and left-hand walls of the courtyard an uninterrupted view of the throne. On the back wall of the pavilion are *jali* screens to enable the women of the court to watch without being seen. The open-sided, cusped arched hall built of plaster on red stone, is very impressive. The throne alcove of richly decorated white marble completed in 1634 after seven years' work used to house the Peacock Throne. Its decoration made it extraordinary: "the canopy was carved in enamel work and studded with individual gems, its interior was thickly encrusted with rubies, garnets and diamonds, and it was supported on 12 emerald covered columns" writes Tillotson. When Shah Jahan moved his capital to Delhi he took the throne with him to the Red Fort, only for it to be taken back to Persia as loot by Nadir Shah in 1739.

Nagina Masjid (13) From the corner opposite the Diwan-i-Khas two doorways lead to a view over the small courtyards of the *zenana* (harem). Further round in the next corner is the Nagina Masjid. Shoes must be removed at the doorway. Built by Shah Jahan, this was the private mosque of the ladies of the court. Beneath it was a *mina* bazar for the ladies to make purchases from the marble balcony above. Looking out of the Diwan-i-Am you can see the domes of the **Moti Masjid** (Pearl Mosque, 1646-1653), an extremely fine building closed to visitors because of structural problems. Opposite the Diwan-i-Am are the barracks and **Mina Bazar**, also closed to the public. In the paved area in front of the Diwan-i-Am is a large well and the **tomb of Mr John Russell Colvin**, the Lieutenant Governor of the Northwest Provinces who died here during the 1857 'Uprising'. Stylistically it is sadly out of place. The yellow buildings date from the British period.

JAMA MASJID

The mosque built in 1648, near the fort railway, no longer connected to the fort, is attributed to Shah Jahan's dutiful elder daughter Jahanara. In need of repair and not comparable to buildings within the fort, its symmetry has suffered since a small minaret fell in the 1980s. The fine marble steps and bold geometric patterns on the domes are quite striking.

→ AROUND AGRA

I'TIMAD-UD-DAULAH

ⓘ *Old City, State Highway 39, Moti Bagh, Etmadpur. Sunrise-sunset, foreigners Rs 100 plus Rs 10 tax, Indians Rs 10, video Rs 25.*

The tomb of I'timad-ud-Daulah (or 'Baby Taj') sets a startling precedent as the first Mughal building to be faced with white marble inlaid with contrasting stones. Unlike the Taj it is small, intimate and has a gentle serenity, but is just as ornate. The tomb was built for **Ghiyas Beg**, a Persian who had obtained service in Akbar's court, and his wife. On Jahangir's succession in 1605 he became *Wazir* (chief minister). Jahangir fell in love with his daughter, **Mehrunissa**, who at the time was married to a Persian. When her husband died in 1607, she entered Jahangir's court as a lady-in-waiting. Four years later Jahangir married her. Thereafter she was known first as **Nur Mahal** (Light of the Palace), later being promoted to **Nur Jahan** (Light of the World). Her niece Mumtaz married Shah Jahan.

Nur Jahan built the tomb for her father in the *char bagh* that he himself had laid out. It is beautifully conceived in white marble, mosaic and lattice. There is a good view from the roof of the entrance. Marble screens of geometric lattice work permit soft lighting of the inner chamber. The yellow marble caskets appear to have been carved out of wood. On the engraved walls of the chamber is the recurring theme of a wine flask with snakes as handles – perhaps a reference by Nur Jahan, the tomb's creator, to her husband Jahangir's excessive drinking. Stylistically, the tomb marks a change from the sturdy and manly buildings of Akbar's reign to softer, more feminine lines. The main chamber, richly decorated in pietra dura with mosaics and semi-precious stones inlaid in the white marble, contains the tomb of I'timad-ud-Daulah (Pillar of the Goverment) and his wife. Some have argued that the concept and skill must have travelled from its European home of 16th-century Florence to India. However, Florentine pietra dura is figurative whereas the Indian version is essentially decorative and can be seen as a refinement of its Indian predecessor, the patterned mosaic.

SIKANDRA

ⓘ *12 km northwest of Agra. Sunrise-sunset, foreigners Rs 100, Indians Rs 10, includes camera, video Rs 25. Better known as Akbar's Mausoleum. Morning is the quietest time to visit.*

Following the Timurid tradition, Akbar (ruled 1556-1605) had started to build his own tomb at Sikandra. He died during its construction and his son **Jahangir** completed it in 1613. The result is an impressive, large but architecturally confused tomb. A huge gateway, the **Buland Darwaza**, leads to the great garden enclosure, where spotted deer run free on the immaculate lawns. The decoration on the gateway is strikingly bold, with its large mosaic patterns, a forerunner of the pietra dura technique. The white minarets atop the entrance were an innovation which reappear, almost unchanged, at the Taj Mahal. The walled garden enclosure is laid out in the *char bagh* style, with the mausoleum at the centre.

A broad paved path leads to the 22.5-m-high tomb with four storeys. The lowest storey, nearly 100 m sq and 9 m high, contains massive cloisters. The entrance on the south side leads to the tomb chamber. Shoes must be removed or cloth overshoes worn (hire Rs 2). In a niche opposite the entrance is an alabaster tablet inscribed with the 99 divine names of Allah. The sepulchre is in the centre of the room, whose velvety darkness is pierced by a single slanting shaft of light from a high window. The custodian, in expectation of a donation, makes "Akbaaarrrr" echo around the chamber.

Some 4 km south of Sikandra, near the high gateway of the ancient **Kach ki Sarai** building, is a sculptured horse, believed to mark the spot where Akbar's favourite horse died. There are also *kos minars* (marking a *kos*, about 4 km) and several other tombs on the way.

→ FATEHPUR SIKRI

The red sandstone capital of Emperor Akbar, one of his architectural achievements, spreads along a ridge. The great mosque and palace buildings, deserted after only 14 years are still a vivid reminder of his power and vision. Perfectly preserved, it conjures up the lifestyle of the Mughals at the height of their glory.

BACKGROUND

The first two Great Mughals, Babur (ruled 1526-1530) and his son Humayun (ruled 1530-1540, 1555-1556) both won (in Humayun's case, won back) Hindustan at the end of their lives, and they left an essentially alien rule. Akbar, the third and greatest of the Mughals changed that. By marrying a Hindu princess, forging alliances with the Rajput leaders and making the administration of India a partnership with Hindu nobles and princes rather than armed foreign minority rule, Akbar consolidated his ancestors' gains, and won widespread loyalty and respect. Akbar had enormous magnetism. Though illiterate, he had great wisdom and learning as well as undoubted administrative and military skills. Fatehpur Sikri is testimony to this remarkable character.

Although he had many wives, the 26-year-old Akbar had no living heir; the children born to him had all died in infancy. He visited holy men to enlist their prayers for a son and heir. **Sheikh Salim Chishti**, living at Sikri, a village 37 km southwest of Agra, told the emperor that he would have three sons. Soon after, one of his wives, the daughter of the Raja of Amber, became pregnant, so Akbar sent her to live near the sage. A son Salim was born, later to be known as **Jahangir**. The prophecy was fulfilled when in 1570 another wife gave birth to Murad and in 1572, to Daniyal. Salim Chishti's tomb is here.

Akbar, so impressed by this sequence of events, resolved to build an entirely new capital at Sikri in honour of the saint. The holy man had set up his hermitage on a low hill of hard reddish sandstone, an ideal building material, easy to work and yet very durable. The building techniques used imitated carvings in wood, as well as canvas from the Mughal camp (eg awnings). During the next 14 years a new city appeared on this hill – 'Fatehpur' (town of victory) added to the name of the old village, 'Sikri'. Later additions and alterations were made and debate continues over the function and dates of the various buildings. It is over 400 years old and yet perfectly preserved, thanks to careful conservation work carried out by the Archaeological Survey of India at the turn of the century. There are three sections to the city: the 'Royal Palace', 'Outside the Royal Palace' and the 'Jami Masjid'.

FATEHPUR SIKRI

Sights ○
Pachisi Board **1**
Turkish Sultana's House **2**
Dawlatkhana-i-Khas **3**

Sunahra Makan **4**
Panch Mahal **5**
Jodh Bai's Palace **6**
Hawa Mahal **7**

Nagina Masjid **8**
Raja Birbal's Palace **9**
Tomb of Sheikh
    Salim Chishti **10**

When Akbar left, it was slowly abandoned to become ruined and deserted by the early 1600s. Some believe the emperor's decision was precipitated by the failure of the water supply, whilst local folklore claims the decision was due to the loss of the court singer Tansen, one of the 'nine gems' of Akbar's court. However, there may well have been political and strategic motives. Akbar's change in attitude towards orthodox Islam and his earlier veneration of the Chishti saints supplanted by a new imperial ideology, may have influenced his decision. In 1585 he moved his court to Lahore and when he returned south again, it was to Agra. But it was at Fatehpur Sikri that Akbar spent the richest and most productive years of his 49-year reign.

THE ENTRANCE

ⓘ *Sunrise to sunset, foreigners Rs 250, Indians Rs 5. It is best to visit early, before the crowds. Official guides are good (about Rs 100; Rs 30 off season) but avoid others. Avoid the main entrance (lots of hawkers); instead, take the right-hand fork after passing through Agra gate to the hassle-free 2nd entrance. Allow 3 hrs and carry plenty of drinking water.*

Entry to Fatehpur Sikri is through the **Agra Gate**. The straight road from Agra was laid out in Akbar's time. If approaching from Bharatpur you will pass the site of a large lake, which provided one defensive barrier. On the other sides was a massive defensive wall with nine gates (clockwise): Delhi, Lal, Agra, Bir or Suraj (Sun), Chandar (Moon), Gwaliori, Tehra (Crooked), Chor (Thief's) and Ajmeri. Sadly there are men with 'performing' bears along the road from Agra – they should be discouraged – avoid stopping to photograph or tip.

From the Agra Gate you pass the sandstone **Tansen's Baradari** on your right and go through the triple-arched **Chahar Suq** with a gallery with two *chhattris* above which may have been a **Nakkar khana** (Drum House). The road inside the main city wall leading to the entrance would have been lined with bazars. Next on your right is the square, shallow-domed **Mint** with artisans' workshops or animal shelters, around a courtyard. Workmen still chip away at blocks of stone in the dimly lit interior.

ROYAL PALACE

The **Diwan-i-Am** (Hall of Public Audience) was also used for celebrations and public prayers. It has cloisters on three sides of a rectangular courtyard and to the west, a pavilion with the emperor's throne, with *jali* screens on either side separating the court ladies. Some scholars suggest that the west orientation may have had the added significance of Akbar's vision of himself playing a semi-divine role.

This backed onto the private palace. In the centre of the courtyard behind the throne is the **Pachisi Board (1)** or Chaupar. It is said that Akbar had slave girls dressed in yellow, blue and red, moved around as 'pieces'!

The **Diwan-i-Khas** (Hall of Private Audience) to your right, is a two-storey building with corner kiosks. It is a single room with a unique circular throne platform. Here Akbar would spend long hours in discussion with Christians, Jains, Buddhists, Hindus and Parsis. They would sit along the walls of the balcony connected to the **Throne Pillar** by screened 'bridges', while courtiers could listen to the discussions from the ground floor. Decorative techniques and metaphysical labels are incorporated here – the pillar is lotus shaped (a Hindu and Buddhist motif), the Royal Umbrella (*chhattri*) is Hindu, and the Tree of Life, Islamic. The bottom of the pillar is carved in four tiers; Muslim, Hindu, Christian and Buddhist designs. The Throne Pillar can be approached by steps from the outside although there is no access to the upper floor. The design of the Hall deliberately followed the archaic universal pattern of establishing a hallowed spot from which spiritual influence could radiate. In his later years, Akbar developed a mystical cult around himself that saw him as being semi-divine.

An Archaeological Survey of India team recently discovered an 'air-conditioned palace' built for Akbar, while digging up steps leading down to a water tank set in the middle of the main palace complex. The subterranean chambers were found under the small quadrangle in sandstone, set in the middle of a water tank and connected on all four sides by narrow corridors. It's not yet open to the public.

In the **Treasury** in the northwest corner of the courtyard is the **Ankh Michauli** (Blind Man's Buff), possibly used for playing the game, comprising three rooms each protected by a narrow corridor with guards. The *makaras* on brackets are mythical sea creatures who guard the treasures under the sea. Just in front of the Treasury is the **Astrologer's Seat**, a small kiosk with elaborate carvings on the Gujarati 'caterpillar' struts which may have been used by the court astrologer or treasurer.

The **Turkish Sultana's House (2)** or Anup Talao Pavilion is directly opposite, beyond the Pachisi Board. Sultana Ruqayya Begum was Akbar's favourite and her 'house', with a balcony on each side, is exquisitely carved with Islamic decorations. Scholars suggest this may have been a pleasure pavilion. The geometrical pattern on the ceiling is reminiscent of Central Asian carvings in wood while the walls may have been set originally with reflecting glass to create a Sheesh Mahal (Mirror Palace). In the centre of this smaller south courtyard is the **Anup Talao** where the Emperor may have sat on the platform, surrounded by perfumed water. The *Akbarnama* mentions the emperor's show of charity when he filled the Talao with copper, silver and gold coins and distributed them over three years.

Dawlatkhana-i-Khas (3), the emperor's private chambers, are next to the rose-water fountain in the corner. There are two main rooms on the ground floor. One housed his library – the recesses in the walls were for manuscripts. Although unable to read or write himself, Akbar enjoyed having books read to him. Wherever he went, his library of 50,000 manuscripts accompanied him. The larger room behind was his resting area. On the first floor is the **Khwabgah** (Palace of Dreams) which would have had rich carpets, hangings and cushions. This too was decorated with gold and ultramarine paintings. The southern window (Jharokha Darshan) was where the emperor showed himself to his people every morning.

Leaving the Dawlatkhana-i-Khas you enter another courtyard which contained the **Ladies' garden** for the *zenana*, and the **Sunahra Makan (4)** or the Christian wife **Maryam's** House, a two-storeyed affair for the emperor's mother, which was embellished with golden murals in the Persian style. The inscriptions on the beams are verses by **Fazl**, Akbar's poet laureate, one of the '*Navaratna*' (Nine Jewels) of the Court. Toilets in the corner of the garden are quite clean.

The **Panch Mahal (5)** is an elegant, airy five-storeyed pavilion just north of this, each floor smaller than the one below, rising to a single domed kiosk on top. The horizontal line of this terraced building is emphasized by wide overhanging eaves (for providing shade), parapets broken by the supporting pillars of which there are 84 on the ground floor (the magic number of seven planets multiplied by 12 signs of the zodiac). The 56 carved columns on the second floor are all different and show Hindu influence. Originally dampened scented *khuss* (grass screens) which were hung in the open spaces, provided protection from the heat and sun, as well as privacy for the women who used the pavilion.

Jodh Bai, the daughter of the Maharaja of Amber, lived in Raniwas. The spacious **palace (6)** in the centre, assured of privacy and security by high walls and a 9-m-high guarded gate to the east. Outside the north wall is the 'hanging' **Hawa Mahal (7)** (Palace of Winds) with beautiful *jali* screens facing the *zenana* garden which was once enclosed, and the bridge (a later addition) led to the Hathipol. Through the arch is the small **Nagina Masjid (8)**, the mosque for the ladies of the court. The *hammams* (baths) are to the south of the palace. The centre of the building is a quadrangle around which were the harem quarters, each section self-contained with roof terraces. The style, a blend of Hindu and Muslim (the lotus, chain and bell designs being Hindu, the black domes Muslim), is strongly reminiscent of Gujarati temples, possibly owing to the craftsmen brought in (see *jarokha* windows, niches, pillars and brackets). The upper pavilions north and south have interesting ceiling structure (imitating the bamboo and thatch roof of huts), here covered with blue glazed tiles, adding colour to the buildings of red sandstone favoured by Akbar. Jodh Bai's vegetarian kitchen opposite the palace has attractive chevron patterns.

Raja Birbal's Palace (9) is a highly ornamented house to the northwest of Jodh Bai's Palace. It has two storeys – four rooms and two porches with pyramidal roofs below, and two rooms with cupolas and screened terraces above. Birbal, Akbar's Hindu prime minister, was the brightest of Akbar's 'Nine Jewels'. Again the building combines Hindu and Islamic elements (note the brackets, eaves, *jarokhas*). Of particular interest is the insulating effect of the double-domed structure of the roofs and cupolas which kept the rooms cool, and the diagonal positioning of the upper rooms which ensured a shady terrace. Some scholars believe that this building, *Mahal-i-Ilahi*, was not for Birbal, but for Akbar's senior queens.

South of the Raja's house are the **stables**, a long courtyard surrounded by cells which probably housed zenana servants rather than the emperor's camels and horses, though the rings suggest animals may have been tied there.

JAMI MASJID

Leaving the Royal Palace you proceed across a car park to the Jami Masjid and the sacred section of Fatehpur Sikri. The oldest place of worship here was the **Stone Cutters' Mosque** (circa 1565) to the west of the Jami Masjid. It was built near Sheikh Salim Chishti's cell which was later incorporated into it by stonecutters who settled on the ridge when quarrying for the Agra Fort began. It has carved monolithic 'S' brackets to support the wide sloping eaves.

The **Badshahi Darwaza** (King's Gate) is the entrance Akbar used. Shoes must be left at the gate but there are strips of carpet cross the courtyard to save burning your feet. The porch is packed with aggressive salesmen. The two other gates on the south and north walls were altered by subsequent additions. Built in 1571-1572, this is one of the largest mosques in India. Inside is the congregational courtyard (132 m by 111 m). To your right in the corner is the **Jamaat Khana Hall** and next to this the **Tomb of the Royal Ladies** on the north wall. The square nave carries the principal dome painted in the Persian style, with pillared aisles leading to side chapels carrying subsidiary domes. The **mihrab** in the centre of the west wall orientates worshippers towards Mecca. The sanctuary is adorned with carving, inlay work and painting.

The **Tomb of Sheikh Salim Chishti (10)**, a masterpiece in brilliant white marble, dominates the northern half of the courtyard. The Gujarati-style serpentine 'S' struts, infilled with *jali*, are highly decorative while the carved pillar bases and lattice screens are stunning pieces of craftsmanship. The canopy over the tomb is inlaid with mother of pearl. On the cenotaph is the date of the saint's death (1571) and the date of the building's completion (1580); the superb marble screens enclosing the veranda were added by Jahangir's foster brother in 1606. Around the entrance are inscribed the names of God, the Prophet and the four Caliphs of Islam. The shrine inside, on the spot of the saint's hermitage, originally had a red sandstone dome, which was marble veneered around 1806. Both Hindu and Muslim women pray at the shrine, tying cotton threads, hoping for the miracle of parenthood that Akbar was blessed with.

Next to it, in the courtyard, is the larger, red, sandstone tomb of **Nawab Islam Khan**, Sheikh Salim's grandson, and other members of the family.

Buland Darwaza (Triumphal Gate) dominates the south wall but it is a bit out of place. Built to celebrate Akbar's brilliant conquest of Gujarat (circa 1576), it sets the style for later gateways. The high gate is approached from the outside by a flight of steps which adds to its grandeur. The decoration shows Hindu influence, but is severe and restrained, emphasizing the lines of its arches with plain surfaces. You see an inscription on the right of a verse from the Qur'an:

Said Jesus Son of Mary (on whom be peace):
The world is but a bridge; pass over it but build no houses on it.
He who hopes for an hour, hopes for Eternity.
The world is an hour.
Spend it in prayer, for the rest is unseen.

OUTSIDE THE ROYAL PALACE

Between the Royal Palace and the Jami Masjid, a paved pathway to the northwest leads to the **Hathipol** (Elephant Gate). This was the ceremonial entrance to the palace quarters, guarded by stone elephants, with its *nakkar khana* and bazar alongside. Nearby are the **waterworks**, with a deep well which had an ingenious mechanism for raising water to the aqueducts above ridge height. The **caravanserai** around a large courtyard fits on the ridge side, and was probably one of a series built to accommodate travellers, tradesmen and guards. Down a ramp immediately beyond is the **Hiran Minar**, an unusual tower studded with stone tusks, thought to commemorate Akbar's favourite elephant, Hiran. However, it was probably an *Akash Diya* (lamp to light the sky) or the 'zero point' for marking road distances in *kos*. You can climb up the spiral staircase inside it but take care as the top has no rail. This part of Fatehpur Sikri is off the main tourist track, and though less well preserved it is worth the detour to get the 'lost city' feeling, away from the crowds.

AGRA AND AROUND LISTINGS

WHERE TO STAY

$$$$ Amar Vilas, near Taj East Gate, T0562-223 1515, www.amarvilas.com. 102 rooms, all Taj-facing – the only place in Agra with such superlative views. You can feel like a Maharajah here – designed in strict adherence to the Mughal style. Beautiful rooms, with the best feature being the view. Stunning swimming pool, lovely gardens, extraordinary ambience. Guests are entertained at sunset with traditional dancing and musicians. If you can splash out on your trip, this is the place to do it. A magical experience.

$$$$ The Mughal, Fatehabad Rd, T0562-233 1701, www.itcwelcomgroup.in. Stunning suites, beautiful gardens, delightful pool. The new wing is particularly lovely. They have the award-winning **Kaya** Kalp spa. Low-rise construction means only the rooftop observatory offers good views of the Taj. Excellent restaurant.

$$$ Hotel Taj Plaza, close to **Amar Vilas Oberoi**, Shilp Gram "VIP" Rd, T0562-223 2515, www.hoteltajplaza.in. Good rooms in simple hotel. Views of the Taj Mahal from the rooftop. Great location within walking distance of the main event.

$$-$ Hotel Kamal, South Gate, near Taj Ganj police station, T0562-233 0126, www.hotelkamal.com. Good option in this area with variety of rooms; some with mod cons and a/c. Great view from the rooftop restaurant although the food is fairly mediocre. Website makes the place looks swankier than it is.

RESTAURANTS

$$$ Esphahan, Amar Vilas (see Where to stay). Outstanding, rich Avadhi food in high-class setting, but non-residents will find it hard to get a table.

$$ Dasaprakash, Meher Theatre Complex, 1 Gwalior Rd, T0562-246 3535. Comprehensive range of South Indian offerings, *thalis* and *dosas* a speciality.

$$ Only, 45 Taj Rd, T0562-236 4333. Interesting menu, attractive outside seating, popular with tour groups, live entertainment.

RANTHAMBHORE

Ranthambhore National Park is one of the finest tiger reserves in the country, although even here their numbers have dwindled due to poachers. Most visitors spending a couple of nights here are likely to spot one of these wonderful animals, although many leave disappointed. Set in dry deciduous forest, some trees trailing matted vines, the park's rocky hills and open valleys are dotted with small pools and fruit trees. The reserve covers 410 sq km between the Aravalli and Vindhya hills. Scrubby hillsides surrounding Ranthambhore village are pleasantly peaceful, their miniature temples and shrines glowing pink in the evening sun before they become silhouetted nodules against the night sky. Once the private tiger reserve of the Maharajah of Jaipur, in 1972 the sanctuary came under the Project Tiger scheme following the government Wildlife Protection Act. By 1979, 12 villages inside the park had been 'resettled' into the surrounding area, leaving only a scattering of people still living within the park's boundaries. Should the tigers evade you, as you pass along misty dust tracks as the crisp morning air disperses with the sunrise, you may well spot leopard, hyena, jackal, marsh crocodile, wild boar, langur monkey, bear and many species of deer and birdlife. The park's 10th-century fort, proudly flanked by two impressive gateways, makes a good afternoon excursion after a morning drive.

→ ARRIVING IN RANTHAMBHORE NATIONAL PARK

GETTING THERE
The closest station for Ranthambhore is Sawai Madhopur; alas most of the trains leaving Agra for Sawai Madhopur are at anti-social hours, but there is one option leaving Agra at 0600 and arriving Sawai Madhopur at 2100 (Pnbe Kota Express 13239) travelling on Monday, Wednesday, Thursday and Friday. If you were to drive, it wopuld take about six hours and you could have lunch in Bharatpur and visit the Keoladeo Ghana National Park.

MOVING ON
Sawai Madhopur is a train hub so it is easy to get connections onto **Jaipur** (see page 89). The most convenient is the *Ranthambore Express (12465)* taking just over two hours and arriving in Jaipur at 1645; best to opt for the chair car carriage. Buses will take a lot longer.

GETTING AROUND
The national park is 10 km east of Sawai Madhopur, with the approach along a narrow valley; the main gate is 4 km from the boundary. The park has good roads and tracks. Entry is by park jeep (gypsy) or open bus (canter) on four-hour tours; 16 jeeps and 20 canters are allowed in at any one time to minimize disturbance. You can book online. Some lodges can organize trips for you or there are a couple of jeeps and canters reserved for same-day bookings, which involves a queue and elbows and you may get gazumped by hotels paying over the odds for a private jeep. Jeeps are better but must be booked in advance so request one at the time of booking your lodge (passport number and personal details required) or try online. Visitors are picked up from their hotels.

TOURIST INFORMATION
The park is open 1 October-30 June for two sessions a day: winter 0630-1030, 1400-1800; summer 0600-1000, 1430-1830, but check as times change. Jeep hire: Rs 800-1200 per person for up to five passengers; jeep entry Rs 125; guide Rs 150. A seat in a canter,

Rs 500-550, can often be arranged on arrival, bookings start at 0600 and 1330 for same-day tours; advance bookings from 1000-1330. Individual entry fees are extra: foreigners Rs 200, Indians Rs 25, camera free, video Rs 200. The powers-that-be do keep changing regulations on all park entry in India, so double check with your hotel beforehand.

Rajasthan Tourism ⓘ *Hotel Vinayak, T07462-220808. Conservator of Forests/Field Director, T07462-220223.* **Forest Officer** ⓘ *T07462-221142.* A very informative background with photography tips is available on www.ranthambhore.com.

BEST TIME TO VISIT

The climate is best from November to April, though vegetation dies down in April exposing tigers. Maximum temperatures from 28-49°C. It can be very cold at dawn in winter.

→ BACKGROUND

Much of the credit for Ranthambhore's present position as one of the world's leading wildlife resorts goes to India's most famous 'tiger man', Mr Fateh Singh Rathore. His enthusiasm for all things wild has been passed on to his son, Dr Goverdhan Singh Rathore, who set up the Prakratik Society in 1994. This charitable foundation was formed in response to the increasing human encroachment on the tiger's natural forest habitat; in 1973 there were 70,000 people living around Ranthambhore Park, a figure which has now increased to 200,000.

The human population's rapidly increasing firewood requirements were leading to ever-more damaging deforestation, and the founders of the Prakratik Society soon realized that

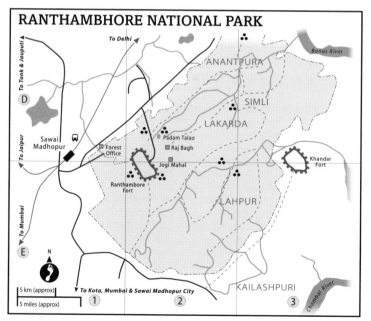

RANTHAMBHORE NATIONAL PARK

something needed to be done. Their solution was as brilliant as it was simple; enter the 'biogas digester'. This intriguingly named device, of which 225 have so far been installed, uses cow dung as a raw material, and produces both gas for cooking, negating the need for firewood, and organic fertilizer, which has seen crop yields increase by 25%. The overwhelming success of this venture was recognized in June 2004, when the Prakratik Society was presented with the prestigious Ashden Award for Sustainable Energy in London.

→ WILDLIFE

Tiger sightings are recorded almost daily, usually in the early morning, especially from November to April. Travellers report the tigers seem "totally unconcerned, ambling past only 10 m away". Sadly, poaching is prevalent: between 2003 and 2005, 22 tigers were taken out of the park by poachers operating from surrounding villages, a wildlife scandal that spotlighted official negligence in Ranthambhore. Since then the population has recovered somewhat, with about six cubs being born each year. Across the country the Tiger Census of 2010 has revealed that tiger numbers are up by 295 making a total of 1706 tigers. Current estimate is 31 adult tigers in the park. As well as Save the Tiger campaigns from Aircel, there is a Travel Operators for Tigers group who many of the hotels in Ranthambhore are a part of. The lakeside woods and grassland provide an ideal habitat for herds of chital and sambar deer and sounders of wild boar. Nilgai antelope and chinkara gazelles prefer the drier areas of the park. Langur monkeys, mongoose and hare are prolific. There are also sloth bear, a few leopards, and the occasional rare caracal. Crocodiles bask by the lakes, and some rocky ponds have freshwater turtles. Extensive birdlife includes spurfowl, jungle fowl, partridges, quails, crested serpent eagle, woodpeckers, flycatchers, etc. There are also water birds such as storks, ducks and geese at the lakes and waterholes. Padam Talao by the Jogi Mahal is a favourite water source; there are also water holes at Raj Bagh and Milak.

→ RANTHAMBHORE FORT

ⓘ *The entrance to the fort is before the gate to the park. Open from dawn to dusk, though the Park Interpretation Centre near the small car park may not be open. Free entry.*

There is believed to have been a settlement here in the eighth century. The earliest historic record is of it being wrested by the Chauhans in the 10th century. In the 11th century, after Ajmer was lost to Ghori, the Chauhans made it their capital. Hamir Chauhan, the ruler of Ranthambhore in the 14th century, gave shelter to enemies of the Delhi sultanate, resulting in a massive siege and the Afghan conquest of the fort. The fort was later surrendered to Emperor Akbar in the 16th century when Ranthambhore's commander saw resistance was useless, finally passing to the rulers of Jaipur. The forests of Ranthambhore historically guarded the fort from invasions but with peace under the Raj they became a hunting preserve of the Jaipur royal family. The fort wall runs round the summit and has a number of semi-circular bastions, some with sheer drops of over 65 m and stunning views. Inside the fort you can see a Siva temple – where Rana Hamir beheaded himself rather than face being humiliated by the conquering Delhi army – ruined palaces, pavilions and tanks. Mineral water, tea and soft drinks are sold at the foot of the climb to the fort and next to the Ganesh temple near the tanks.

GOING FURTHER
Bundi

Bundi lies in a beautiful narrow valley with Taragarh Fort towering above. Much less developed than the other fort towns, Bundi is starting to blossom, with classic *havelis* being turned into boutique guesthouses and more family guesthouses are springing up too. Yet it is still a long way off the bazar bustle of Pushkar and the speed and hustle of Jodhpur and Jaisalmer. Bundi is especially colourful and interesting during the many festivals.

Getting there and moving on There are several convenient morning trains that take you from Sawai Madhopur to Kota Junction, the best takes just 1½ hours leaving at 0810 from Sawai Madhopur (Hmh Kota Specia 09733). From Kota Junction, there are hourly buses to Bundi, although a taxi will only take 30 minutes and cost around Rs 300. Avoid the bus as roads are under development. **Tourist office** ① *Circuit House, near Raniji ki Baori, T0747-244 3697*. From Kota Junction there are several convenient trains to **Jaipur** (see page 89) which take around four hours. For a morning departure, opt for the *Bct Jp Express (12955)* leaving Kota Junction at 0855. For a late afternoon departure try the *Kota Hmh Specia (99734)* leaving at 1655 and arriving in Jaipur at 2105.

Places in Bundi Taragarh Fort ① *0600-1800, foreigners Rs 100, Indians Rs 20, camera Rs 50, video Rs 100* (1342), stands in sombre contrast to the beauty of the town and the lakes below. There are excellent views but it is a difficult 20-minute climb beset in places by aggressive monkeys; wear good shoes and wield a big stick. The eastern wall is crenellated with high ramparts while the main gate to the west is flanked by octagonal towers. The **Bhim Burj** tower dominates the fort and provided the platform for the Garbh Ganjam ('Thunder from the Womb'), a huge cannon. A pit to the side once provided shelter for the artillery men. Cars can go as far as the TV tower then it is 600 m along a rough track.

The **Palace Complex** ① *below Taragarh, 0900-1700, foreigners Rs 100, Indians Rs 20*, which was begun around 1600, is at the northern end of the bazar, and was described by Kipling as "such a palace as men build for themselves in uneasy dreams – the work of goblins rather than of men". A steep, rough stone ramp leads up through the **Hazari Darwaza** (Gate of the Thousand) where the garrison lived. The palace entrance is through the **Hathi Pol** (Elephant Gate, 1607-1631), which has two carved elephants with a water clock. Steps lead up to **Ratan Daulat** above the stables, the unusually small Diwan-i-Am which was intended to accommodate a select few at public audience. A delicate marble balcony overhangs the courtyard. The **Chattar Mahal** (1660), the newer palace of green serpentine rock, is pure Rajput in style and contains private apartments decorated with wall paintings, glass and mirrors. The **Chitrashala** ① *0900-1700, Rs 20*, a cloistered courtyard with a gallery running around a garden of fountains, has a splendid collection of miniatures showing scenes from the Radha Krishna story. The murals (circa 1800) are some of the finest examples of Rajput art but are not properly maintained. At night, the palace is lit up and thousands of bats pour out of its innards. There are several 16th- to 17th-century step wells and 'tanks' (*kunds*) in town. The 46-m-deep **Raniji-ki-baori** ① *Mon-Sat 1000-1700, closed 2nd Sat each month, free, caretaker unlocks the gate*, with beautiful pillars and bas relief sculpture panels of Vishnu's 10 *avatars*, is the most impressive. **Sukh Mahal**, a summer pleasure palace, faces the **Jait Sagar** lake; Kipling spent a night in the original pavilion.

RANTHAMBHORE LISTINGS

WHERE TO STAY

$$$$ Sherbagh Tented Camp,
Sherpur-Khiljipur, T07462-252120,
www.sujanluxury.com. Open 1 Oct-30 Mar.
Award-winning eco-camp with luxury
tents and hot showers, bar, dinner around
fire, lake trips for birders, stunning grounds
and seated areas for quiet contemplation,
jungle ambience, well organized. All meals
included. Beautiful shop on site. Owner
Jaisal Singh has put together a new book
Ranthambhore – The Tiger's Realm.

$$$$ Vanyavilas (Oberoi), T07462-223999,
www.oberoihotels.com. Very upmarket
garden resort set around a recreated *haveli*
with fantastic frescoes. 25 unbelievably
luxurious a/c tents (wooden floors,
marble baths), billiards, elephant rides,
wildlife lectures, dance shows in open-air
auditorium, "fabulous spa", friendly and
professional. Elephants greet you at the door.

$$$-$$ Ranthambore Bagh,
Ranthambhore Rd, T(0)8239 166777,
www.ranthambhore.com. 12 luxury tents
and 12 simple but attractive rooms in
this pleasantly laid-back property owned
by a professional photographer and his
lovely family. Pride has been taken in
every detail; the public areas and dining
hall are particularly well done. Fantastic
food, including traditional Rajasthani, and
atmospheric suppers around the campfire.

$$ Tiger Vilas, Ranthambore Rd,
T07462-221121, www.tigervilla.in.
10 clean, modern rooms in convenient
location for park, beautiful decor,
reasonably priced veggie food.

$$ Tiger Safari, T07462-221137, www.tiger
safariresort.com. 14 cosy rooms, 4 attractive
a/c cottages, very clean, hot shower, quiet,
jeep/bus to park, very helpful, good value,
ordinary food but few other options.

WHAT TO DO

Tour operators
Bagh Safari, www.baghsafari.com.
Offer exceptional wildlife tours. They
are passionate about wildlife and
photography, running trips and events
in Ranthambhore, but also to Africa
and Sri Lanka. In Ranthambhore, you
can stay at their beautiful guesthouse
Ranthambhore Bagh (see above) and,
as well a tiger safaris, you can opt for village
treks and birdwatching. The founder of
Ranthambhore Bagh and **Bagh Safari**,
Dicky Singh, is an incredible photographer
and has many a fascinating story to share.

Indiabeat, www.indiabeat.co.uk.
Jaipur-based **Indiabeat** have fantastic
guides Chandrakant and Nafis (based
in Ranthambhore) with expert wildlife
knowledge. They can also arrange
interesting and thought-provoking talks
with Divya from charity **Tiger Watch**, who
offers a real insight into the protection of
tigers and the role of the national parks.
**Ranthambhore Nature Guide
Association** (**RNGA**), www.ranthambhore
guides.com. Another good group to check
out. They are committed to the preservation
of tigers and their natural habitat and are
keen to introduce tourists to the wonders
of Indian wildlife.

JAIPUR AND AROUND

The sandstone 'pink city' of Jaipur, Rajasthan's capital, is the heady gateway to the state. It is on the popular 'Golden Triangle' route (Delhi–Agra–Jaipur–Delhi), which, for many short-haul visitors, is their only experience of Rajasthan. The steady stream of tourists means the city has to make little effort to attract visitors; as a result its pastel-hued buildings are not what they used to be and many of the sights are poorly maintained. Nonetheless it's a worthwhile stopover in itself, as well as a staging post for the surrounding area. The old city, with its bazars, palaces and havelis, *along with a couple of forts and the ancient city of Amber nearby, are well worth a wander. Knotted, narrow streets hold cupboard-sized workshops where elderly women dash out clothes on rusty Singers; men energetically stuff mattresses with piles of rags; boys mend bicycles next to old men rolling pellets of paste into sweets; whole families carve table legs or hammer bed headboards out of sheet metal; and 'gold men' leave the old city's textile houses sprinkled with metallic pigment from a day's work rubbing the powder into fabric patterned with resin glue. Escape the bustle and head up to the Tiger Fort (Nahargarh) for sunset, where proud peacocks pick among the ruins and monkeys scamper about in the twilight against the backdrop of Man Sagar Lake and its Jal Mahal (Water Palace).*

→ JAIPUR

ARRIVING IN JAIPUR

Getting there Sanganer Airport is 15 km south of town. Airport buses, taxis and auto-rickshaws take 30 minutes to the centre. The railway station has links with most major cities. The Ranthambore Express (12465) takes just over two hours from Sawai Madhopur (near Ranthambhore) and arrives in Jaipur at 1645. Buses will take a lot longer. The Main Bus Terminal at Sindhi Camp is used by state and private buses. Buses from Delhi use the dramatically improved NH8; the journey now takes under four hours by car. Most hotels are a short auto-rickshaw ride away from the station and bus terminal.

Moving on It is a relatively short trip by Indian standards from Jaipur to **Pushkar** (see page 105), the next stop on Dream Trip 1, and easy on public transport. Your best option is by train: there are numerous services from Jaipur to Ajmer Junction taking around two hours. From Ajmer, it is a 30-minute taxi ride (Rs 300) to Pushkar. You can opt for a direct bus from Jaipur to Pushkar, but the train/taxi combo is preferable.

Getting around The walled Old City, to the northeast of town, holds most of the sights and the bazar. Take a rickshaw to the area, then explore on foot. What few attractions the new town holds are spread out so it's best explored by rickshaw, bus or taxi. There is also a new metro system under construction which should ease the traffic above ground.

Tourist information Government of India Tourism ① *Hotel Khasa Kothi, T0141-511 0598*, also has counters at the **Railway Station** ① *T0141-231 5714*, and **Central Bus Stand** ① *T0141-506 4102*. Guides for four to eight hours cost Rs 250-400 (Rs 100 extra for French, German, Japanese, Spanish). *Jaipur for Aliens*, a free miniature guidebook created by the owner of the **Hotel Pearl Palace**, has regularly updated information on transport and attractions; available at the hotel (see Where to stay, page 103).

BACKGROUND

Jaipur ('City of Victory') was founded in 1727 by **Maharaja Jai Singh II**, a Kachhawaha Rajput, who ruled from 1699 to 1744. He had inherited a kingdom under threat not only from the last great Mughal Emperor Aurangzeb, but also from the Maratha armies of Gujarat and Maharashtra. Victories over the Marathas and diplomacy with Aurangzeb

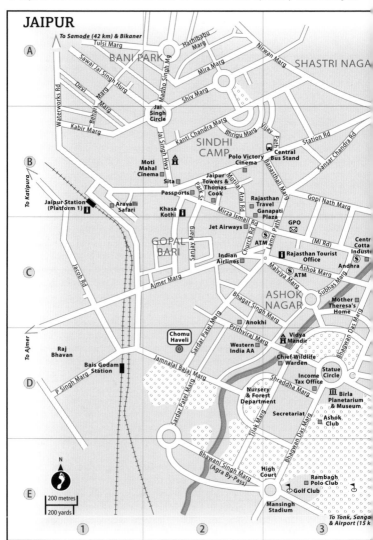

won back the favour of the ageing Mughal, so that the political stability that Maharaja Jai Singh was instrumental in creating was protected, allowing him to pursue his scientific and cultural interests. Jaipur is very much a product of his intellect and talent. A story relates an encounter between the **Emperor Aurangzeb** and the 10-year-old Rajput prince. When asked what punishment he deserved for his family's hostility and resistance to the

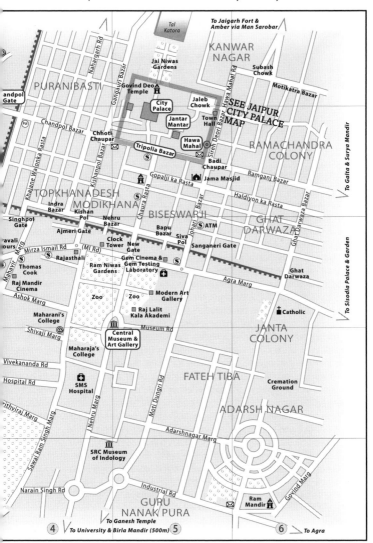

Mughals, the boy answered "Your Majesty, when the groom takes the bride's hand, he confers lifelong protection. Now that the Emperor has taken my hand, what have I to fear?" Impressed by his tact and intelligence, Aurangzeb bestowed the title of *Sawai* (one and a quarter) on him, signifying that he would be a leader.

Jai Singh loved mathematics and science, and was a keen student of astronomy, via Sanskrit translations of Ptolemy and Euclid. A brilliant Brahmin scholar from Bengal, Vidyadhar Bhaṭṭacharya, helped him to design the city. Work began in 1727 and it took four years to build the main palaces, central square and principal roads. The layout of streets was based on a mathematical grid of nine squares representing the ancient Hindu map of the universe, with the sacred Mount Meru, home of Siva, occupying the central square. In Jaipur the royal palace is at the centre. The three-by-three square grid was modified by relocating the northwest square in the southeast, allowing the hill fort of Nahargarh (Tiger Fort) to overlook and protect the capital. At the southeast and southwest corners of the city were squares with pavilions and ornamental fountains. Water for these was provided by an underground aqueduct with outlets for public use along the streets. The main streets are 33 yds wide (33 is auspicious in Hinduism). The pavements were deliberately wide to promote the free flow of pedestrian traffic and the shops were also a standard size. Built with ancient Hindu rules of town planning in mind, Jaipur was advanced for its time. Yet many of its buildings suggest a decline in architectural power and originality. The architectural historian Giles Tillotson argues that the "traditional architectural details lack vigour and depth and are also flattened so that they become relief sculpture on the building's surface, and sometimes they are simply drawn on in white outline".

In addition to its original buildings, Jaipur has a number of examples of late 19th-century buildings which marked an attempt to revive Indian architectural skills. A key figure in this movement was Sir Samuel Swinton Jacob. A school of art was founded in 1866 by a group of English officers employed by Maharaja Sawai Madho Singh II to encourage an interest in Indian tradition and its development. In February 1876 the Prince of Wales visited Jaipur, and work on the Albert Hall, now the Central Museum, was begun to a design of Jacob. It was the first of a number of construction projects in which Indian craftsmen and designers were employed in both building and design. This ensured that the Albert Hall was an extremely striking building in its own right. The opportunities for training provided under Jacob's auspices encouraged a new school of Indian architects and builders. One of the best examples of their work is the Mubarak Mahal (1900), now Palace Museum, designed by Lala Chiman Lal.

HAWA MAHAL

ⓘ *Enter from Tripolia Bazar, Sat-Thu 0900-1630, foreigners Rs 50, Indians Rs 10 – audio tours possible; for the best views accept invitations from shop owners on upper floors across the street.*

The 'Palace of the Winds' (circa 1799) forms part of the east wall of the City Palace complex and is best seen from the street outside. Possibly Jaipur's most famous building, this pink sandstone façade of the palace was built for the ladies of the harem by Sawai Pratap Singh. The five storeys stand on a high podium with an entrance from the west. The elaborate façade contains 953 small casements in a huge curve, each with a balcony and crowning arch. The windows enabled *hawa* (cool air) to circulate and allowed the women who were secluded in the *zenana* to watch processions below without being seen. The museum has second-century BC utensils and old sculpture. It's a magical place.

CITY PALACE (1728-1732)

ⓘ *0930-1700 (last entry 1630), foreigners Rs 300 (includes still camera and a good audio guide), Indians Rs 75 (camera Rs 50 extra); includes Sawai Man Singh II Museum and Jaigarh Fort, valid for 1 week. Video (unnecessary) Rs 200; doorkeepers expect tips when photographed. Photography in galleries prohibited.*

The City Palace occupies the centre of Jaipur, covers one seventh of its area and is surrounded by a high wall – the Sarahad. Its style differs from conventional Rajput fort palaces in its separation of the palace from its fortifications, which in other Rajput buildings are integrated in one massive interconnected structure. In contrast, the Jaipur Palace has much more in common with Mughal models, with its main buildings scattered

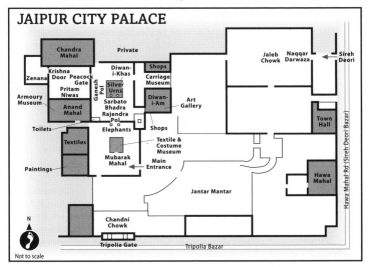

in a fortified campus. To find the main entrance, from the Hawa Mahal go north about 250 m along the Sireh Deori Bazar past the Town Hall (Vidhan Sabha) and turn left through an arch – the Sireh Deori (boundary gate). Pass under a second arch – the Naqqar Darwaza (drum gate) – into Jaleb Chowk, the courtyard which formerly housed the palace guard. Today it is where coaches park. This is surrounded by residential quarters which were modified in the 19th century under Sawai Ram Singh II. A gateway to the south leads to the Jantar Mantar, the main palace buildings and museum and the Hawa Mahal.

Mubarak Mahal The main entrance leads into a large courtyard at the centre of which is the Mubarak Mahal, faced in white marble. Built in 1890, originally as a guesthouse for the Maharaja, the Mubarak Mahal is a small but immaculately conceived two-storeyed building, designed on the same cosmological plan in miniature as the city itself – a square divided into a three by three-square grid.

The **Textile and Costume Museum** on the first floor has fine examples of fabrics and costumes from all over India, including some spectacular wedding outfits, as well as musical instruments and toys from the royal nursery. In the northwest corner of the courtyard is the **Armoury Museum** containing an impressive array of weaponry – pistols, blunderbusses, flintlocks, swords, rifles and daggers, as well as some fascinating paintings on the way in. This was originally the common room of the harem. From the north-facing first-floor windows you can get a view of the Chandra Mahal (see below). Just outside the Armoury Museum is **Rajendra Pol**, a gate flanked by two elephants, each carved from a single block of marble, which leads to the inner courtyard. There are beautifully carved alcoves with delicate arches and *jali* screens and a fine pair of patterned brass doors.

Diwan-i-Khas (Sarbato Bhadra) The gateway leads to the courtyard known variously as the Diwan-i-Am, the Sarbato Bhadra or the Diwan-i-Khas Chowk. Today, the building in its centre is known as the Diwan-i-Khas (circa 1730). Originally the Diwan-i-Am, it was reduced to the hall of private audience (Diwan-i-Khas) when the new Diwan-i-Am was built to its southeast at the end of the 18th century. The courtyard itself reflects the overwhelming influence of Mughal style, despite the presence of some Hindu designs, a result of the movement of Mughal-trained craftsmen from further north in search of opportunities to practise their skills. In the Diwan-i-Khas (now known by the Sanskrit name Sarbato Bhadra) are two huge silver urns – ratified by Guinness as being the largest pieces of silver in the world – used by Sawai Madho Singh for carrying Ganga water to England.

Diwan-i-Am (Diwan Khana) Art Gallery With its entrance in the southeast corner of the Diwan-i-Am courtyard, the 'new' Hall of Public Audience built by Maharaja Sawai Pratap Singh (1778-1803) today houses a fine collection of Persian and Indian miniatures, some of the carpets the maharajas had made for them and an equally fine collection of manuscripts. To its north is the **Carriage Museum**, housed in a modern building. In the middle of the west wall of the Diwan-i-Am courtyard, opposite the art gallery, is the **Ganesh Pol**, which leads via a narrow passage and the Peacock Gate into **Pritam Niwas Chowk**. This courtyard has the original palace building 'Chandra Mahal' to its north, the *zenana* on its northwest, and the Anand Mahal to its south. Several extremely attractive doors, rich and vivid in their peacock blue, aquamarine and amber colours, have small marble Hindu gods watching over them.

Chandra Mahal Built between 1727 and 1734 the Moon Palace is the earliest building of the palace complex. Externally it appears to have seven storeys, though inside the first and second floors are actually one high-ceilinged hall. The top two floors give superb views of the city and Tiger Fort. On the ground floor (north) a wide veranda – the **Pritam Niwas** (House of the Beloved) – with Italian wall paintings, faces the formal Jai Niwas garden. The main section of the ground floor is an Audience Hall. The palace is not always open to visitors.

The hall on the first and second floors, the **Sukh Niwas** (House of Pleasure), underwent a Victorian reconstruction. Above it are the **Rang Mandir** and the **Sobha Niwas**, built to the same plan. The two top storeys are much smaller, with the mirror palace of the **Chavi Niwas** succeeded by the small open marble pavilion which crowns the structure, the **Mukat Niwas**.

In the northeast corner of the Pritam Niwas Chowk, leading into the *zenana*, is the **Krishna door**, its surface embossed with scenes of the deity's life. The door is sealed in the traditional way with a rope sealed with wax over the lock.

Govind Deo Temple and beyond North of the Chandra Mahal, the early 18th-century Govind Deo Temple, which was probably built as a residence, has been restored by an ancient technique using molasses, curd, coconut water, fenugreek, rope fibres and lime, but is again not always open to visitors. The furniture is European – Bohemian glass chandeliers – the decoration Indian. Following the steps around you will see a *mandala* (circular diagram of the cosmos), made from rifles around the royal crest of Jaipur. The ceiling of this hall is in finely worked gold. Further on are the beautiful Mughal-style fountains and the **Jai Niwas gardens** (1727), laid out as a *char bagh*, the **Badal Mahal** (circa 1750) and the **Tal Katora** tank. The view extends across to the maharaja's private Krishna temple and beyond the compound walls to the Nahargarh (Tiger Fort) on the hills beyond.

JANTAR MANTAR (OBSERVATORY)

① *0900-1630, foreigners Rs 200, Indians Rs 40.*
Literally 'Instruments for measuring the harmony of the heavens', the Jantar Mantar was built between 1728 and 1734. Jai Singh wanted things on a grand scale and chose stone with a marble facing on the important planes. Each instrument serves a particular function and each gives an accurate reading. Hindus believe that their fated souls move to the rhythms of the universe, and the matching of horoscopes is still an essential part in the selection of partners for marriage. Astrologers occupy an important place in daily life and are consulted for all important occasions and decision-making. The observatory is fascinating. We recommend you hire a guide to explain the functions of the instruments. There is little shade so avoid the middle of the day. Moving clockwise the *yantras* (instruments) are as follows:
Small 'Samrat' is a large sundial (the triangular structure) with flanking quadrants marked off in hours and minutes. The arc on your left shows the time from sunrise to midday, the one on the right midday to sundown. Read the time where the shadow is sharpest. The dial gives solar time, so to adjust it to Indian Standard Time (measured from Allahabad) between one minute 15 seconds and 32 minutes must be added according to the time of year and solar position as shown on the board.
'Dhruva' locates the position of the Pole Star at night and those of the 12 zodiac signs. The graduation and lettering in Hindi follows the traditional unit of measurement based on the human breath, calculated to last six seconds. Thus: four breaths = one *pala* (24 seconds), 60 *palas* = one *gati* (24 minutes), 60 *gatis* = one day (24 hours).

'**Narivalya**' has two dials: south facing for when the sun is in the southern hemisphere (21 September-21 March) and north facing for the rest of the year. At noon the sun falls on the north-south line.

The Observer's Seat was intended for Jai Singh.

Small 'Kranti' is used to measure the longitude and latitude of celestial bodies.

'**Raj**' (King of Instruments) is used once a year to calculate the Hindu calendar, which is based on the Jaipur Standard as it has been for 270 years. A telescope is attached over the central hole. The bar at the back is used for sighting, while the plain disk is used as a blackboard to record observations.

'**Unnathamsa**' is used for finding the altitudes of the celestial bodies. Round-the-clock observations can be made and the sunken steps allow any part of the dial to be read.

'**Disha**' points to the north.

'**Dakshina**', a wall aligned north-south, is used for observing the position and movement of heavenly bodies when passing over the meridian.

Large 'Samrat' is similar to the small one (see above) but 10 times larger and thus accurate to two seconds instead of 20 seconds. The sundial is 27.4 m high. It is used on a particularly holy full moon in July/August, to predict the length and heaviness of the monsoon for the local area.

'**Rashivalayas**' has 12 sundials for the signs of the zodiac and is similar to the Samrat yantras. The five at the back (north to south), are Gemini, Taurus, Cancer, Virgo and Leo. In front of them are Aries and Libra, and then in the front, again (north-south), Aquarius, Pisces, Capricorn, Scorpio and Sagittarius. The instruments enable readings to be made at the instant each zodiacal sign crosses the meridian.

'**Jai Prakash**' acts as a double check on all the other instruments. It measures the rotation of the sun, and the two hemispheres together form a map of the heavens. The small iron plate strung between crosswires shows the sun's longitude and latitude and which zodiacal sign it is passing through.

Small 'Ram' is a smaller version of the Jai Prakash Yantra (see above).

Large 'Ram Yantra' Similarly, this finds the altitude and the azimuth (arc of the celestial circle from Zenith to horizon).

'**Diganta**' also measures the azimuth of any celestial body.

Large 'Kranti' is similar to the smaller Kranti (see above).

GATORE KI CHHATRIYAN (ROYAL GAITOR)

ⓘ *Foreigners Rs 30, Indians Rs 20, camera Rs 20.*

The gaitor is a complex of temples and tombs in the foothills of the the Nahargarh (Tiger Fort), see below. It has a dramatic rocky setting and good views of the crenellated city wall snaking up and over the dusty hills behind. Creamy marble domes with interiors of beautiful stonework encrusted with carvings of elephants, battle scenes and wild flowers. The site is barely maintained and the lawns are parched lawns, but endearingly so. It's a very peaceful, restful spot.

NAHARGARH (TIGER FORT)

ⓘ *1000-1630, foreigners Rs 30, Indians Rs 5, camera Rs 30, video Rs 70. Rickshaw for sunset Rs 400-500 return. Snacks and drinks are available at the Durg Café.*

The small fort with its immense walls and bastions stands on a sheer rock face. The city at its foot was designed to give access to the fort in case of attack. To get there on foot you have to first walk through some quiet and attractive streets at the base of the hill, then 2 km up a steep, rough winding path to reach the top. Alternatively, it can also be reached by road via Jaigarh Fort. Beautifully floodlit and incredibly atmospheric after dark, it dominates the skyline by day. Much of the original fort (1734) is in ruins but the walls and 19th-century additions survive, including rooms furnished for maharajas. This is a 'real fort', quiet and unrushed, and well worth visiting for the breathtaking views, to look inside the buildings and to walk around the battlements. However, it is an active fort used as a training ground for soldiers; women alone may feel quite vulnerable here. You can combine this visit with Jaigarh Fort (see page 99), 7 km away along the flat-topped hill, which is part of the same defensive network.

CENTRAL MUSEUM AND MODERN ART GALLERY
① *Museum Sat-Thu 1000-1630, foreigners Rs 150, Indians Rs 20; gallery 1000-1700, free, closed 2nd Sat of month and Sun; garden 0900-1700, foreigners Rs 100, Indians Rs 10.*
Within the Ram Niwas Gardens you can visit the museum, gallery and a zoological garden. Housed in the beautiful Albert Hall is the **Central Museum**, displaying mainly excellent decorative metalware, miniature portraits and other art pieces. It also features Rajasthani village life – including some gruesome torture techniques – displayed through costumes, pottery, woodwork, brassware, etc. The first-floor displays are covered in dust and poorly labelled. **Modern Art Gallery**, Ravindra Rang Manch, has an interesting collection of contemporary Rajasthani art. Finally, in the gardens is the **Zoological Garden** containing lions, tigers, panthers, bears, crocodiles and deer, plus a bird park opposite.

→ AROUND JAIPUR

Amber Fort is one of Jaipur's biggest draws, with an elephant ride to the top a priority on many people's 'to do' list. It's still an impressive building but has been poorly maintained in recent years. Sanganer and Bagru offer good opportunities to see handicrafts in production, while Samode is perhaps the last word in elegant living.

AMBER (AMER)
Today there is no town to speak of in Amber, just the palace clinging to the side of the rocky hill, overlooked by the small fort above, with a small village at its base. In the high season this is one of India's most popular tourist sites, with a continuous train of colourfully decorated elephants walking up and down the ramp to the palace. One penalty of its popularity is the persistence of the vendors.

Background Amber, which takes its name from Ambarisha, a king of the once-famous royal city of Ayodhya, was the site of a Hindu temple built by the Mina tribes as early as the 10th century. Two centuries later the Kachhawaha Rajputs made it their capital, which it remained until Sawai Jai Singh II moved to his newly planned city of Jaipur in 1727. Its location made Amber strategically crucial for the Mughal emperors as they moved south, and the Maharajahs of Amber took care to establish close relations with successive Mughal rulers. The building of the fort palace was begun in 1600 by Raja Man Singh, a noted Rajput general in Akbar's army, and Mughal influence was strong in much of the subsequent building.

The approach ① *Around Rs 550 per elephant carrying 4, no need to tip, though the driver will probably ask, takes 10 mins. Jeeps Rs 100 each way, or Rs 10 per seat. It can be quite a long wait in a small garden with little shade and you will be at the mercy of the hawkers. If you do want to buy, wait until you reach the steps when the price will drop dramatically.* From the start of the ramp you can either walk or ride by elephant; the walk is quite easy and mainly on a separate path. Elephants carry up to four people on a padded seat. The ride can be somewhat unnerving when the elephant comes close to the edge of the road, but it is generally perfectly safe. You have to buy a 'return ticket' even if you wish to walk down later. The elephants get bad tempered as the day wears on. If you are interested in finding out more about the welfare of Amber's elephants, or indeed any of Jaipur's street animals, you should contact an organization called **Help in Suffering** ① *T0141-276 0803, www.his-india.org.au.*

The Palace ① *0900-1630 (it's worth arriving at 0900), foreigners Rs 150, Indians Rs 10, camera Rs 75, video Rs 150 (tickets in the Chowk, below the steps up to Shila Mata). Take the green bus from the Hawa Mahal, Rs 5. Auto-rickshaw Rs 80 (Rs 200 for return, including the wait). Guides are worth hiring, Rs 400 for a half day (group of 4), find one with a government guide licence.* After passing through a series of five defensive gates, you reach the first courtyard of the **Raj Mahal** built by Man Singh I in 1600, entered through the **Suraj Pol** (Sun Gate). Here you can get a short ride around the courtyard on an elephant, but bargain very hard. There are some toilets near the dismounting platform. On the south side of this Jaleb Chowk with the flower beds, is a flight of steps leading up to the **Singh Pol** (Lion Gate) entrance to the upper courtyard of the palace.

A separate staircase to the right leads to the green marble-pillared **Shila Mata Temple** (to Kali as Goddess of War), which opens at certain times of the day and then only allows a limited number of visitors at a time (so ask before joining the queue). The temple contains a black marble image of the goddess that Man Singh I brought back from Jessore (now in Bangladesh; the chief priest has always been Bengali). The silver doors with images of Durga and Saraswati were added by his successor.

In the left-hand corner of the courtyard, the **Diwan-i-Am** (Hall of Public Audience) was built by Raja Jai Singh I in 1639. Originally, it was an open pavilion with cream marble pillars supporting an unusual striped canopy-shaped ceiling, with a portico with double red sandstone columns. The room on the east was added by Sawai Ram Singh II. **Ganesh Pol** (circa 1700-1725), south of the *chowk*, colourfully painted and with mosaic decoration, takes its name from the prominent figure of Ganesh above the door. It separates the private from the public areas.

This leads onto the **Jai Singh I** court with a formal garden. To the east is the two-storeyed cream-coloured marble pavilion – **Jai Mandir** (Diwan-i-Khas or Hall of Private Audience) below and **Jas Mandir** (1635-1640) with a curved Bengali roof, on the terrace above. The former, with its marble columns and painted ceiling, has lovely views across the lake. The latter has colourful mosaics, mirrors and marble *jali* screens which let in cooling breezes. Both have **Shish Mahals** (Mirror Palaces) faced with mirrors, seen to full effect when lit by a match. To the west of the chowk is the **Sukh Niwas**, a pleasure palace with a marble water course to cool the air, and doors inlaid with ivory and sandalwood. The Mughal influence is quite apparent in this chowk.

Above the Ganesh Pol is the **Sohag Mandir**, a rectangular chamber with beautiful latticed windows and octagonal rooms to each side. From the rooftop there are stunning views over the palace across the town of Amber, the long curtain wall surrounding the town and further north, through the 'V' shaped entrance in the hills, to the plains beyond. Beyond this courtyard is the **Palace of Man Singh I**. A high wall separates it from the Jai Singh Palace. In the centre of the chowk which was once open is a *baradari* (12-arched pavilion), combining Mughal and Hindu influences. The surrounding palace, a complex warren of passages and staircases, was turned into *zenana* quarters when the newer palaces were built by Jai Singh. Children find it great fun to explore this part.

Old Palace and Anokhi Museum Old Palace of Amber (1216) lies at the base of Jaigarh Fort. A stone path (currently being restored) from the Chand Pol in the first courtyard of Amber Palace leads to the ruins. Though there is little interest today, nearby are several worthwhile temples. These include the **Jagatsiromani Temple** dedicated to Krishna, with carvings and paintings; it is associated with Mira Bai. Take time to visit the fantastic Anokhi Museum of hand-printing. There's a great textile collection and you can even try your hand at handblock printing.

NORTH OF JAIPUR

Jaigarh Fort ⓘ *0900-1630, foreigners Rs 35, Indians Rs 20, free with City Palace entry ticket (use within 48 hrs), still camera Rs 40, video Rs150, vehicle entry Rs 50. To reach the fort, from Amber Palace turn right out of the Suraj Pol and follow a stone road past the old elephant quarters. This is the start of the ascent – a steady climb of about 25 mins, or take a taxi. What appears at first to be 2 adjoining forts is in fact all part of the same structure. There is also a good road from the Jaipur–Amber road which goes straight to Jaigarh Fort and on to Nahargarh.* Above the palace on the hill top stands the gigantic bulk of Jaigarh, impressively lit at night; its *parkotas* (walls), bastions, gateways and watchtowers a testimony of the power of the Jaipur rulers. It is well worth a visit. The forbidding medieval fort was never captured and so has survived virtually intact which makes it particularly interesting. In the 16th-century cannon foundry you can see the pit where the barrels were cast, the capstan-powered lathe which bored out the cannon and the iron-workers' drills, taps and dies. The armoury has a large collection of swords and small arms, their use in the many successful campaigns having been carefully logged. There is an interesting photograph collection and a small café outside the armoury. There are gardens, a granary, open and closed reservoirs; the ancient temples of Ram Harihar (10th century) and Kal Bhairava (12th century) are within the fort. You can explore a warren of complicated dark passageways among the palaces. Many of the apartments are open and you can see the collections of coins and puppets (shows on demand). The other part of the fort, at a slightly higher elevation, has a tall watch tower. From here there are tremendous views of the surrounding hills. The massive 50-tonne **Jai Ban cannon** stands on top of one tower. Allegedly the largest cannon on wheels in the world, with an 8-m barrel, it had a range of around 20 km, but it was never used. Some 7 km further along the top of the hill is the smaller Nahargarh Fort overlooking Jaipur itself (see page 96).

Ramgarh Lake and Jamwa Sanctuary The 15-sq-km lake of Jamwa Ramgarh attracts large flocks of waterfowl in winter, and lies within a game sanctuary with good boating and birdwatching. Built to supply Jaipur with water, it now provides less than 1% of the city's needs and in years of severe drought may dry up completely. The 300-sq-km Jamwa Sanctuary, which once provided the Jaipur royal family with game, still has some panthers, nilgai and small game. Contact the tourist office in Jaipur (see page 89) for details of public buses. It is about a 45-minute drive.

Samode At the head of the enclosed valley in the dry rugged hills of the northern Aravallis, Samode stands on a former caravan route. The sleepy village, with its local artisans producing printed cloth and glass bangles, nestles within a ring of old walls. The painted *havelis* are still full of character. Samode is well worth the visit from Jaipur, and makes a good stop en route to the painted towns of Shekhawati (see opposite). Both the palace and the *bagh* are wonderful, peaceful places to spend a night.

The **palace** ⓘ *now a heritage hotel, entry Rs 500 for non-residents includes tea/coffee*, which dominates the village, is fabulously decorated with 300-year-old wall paintings (hunting scenes, floral motifs, etc) which still look almost new. Around the first floor of the Darbar Hall are magnificent alcoves, decorated with mirrors like *shish mahal* and *jali* screens through which the royal ladies would have looked down into the grand jewel-like Darbar Hall.

Towering immediately above the palace is **Samode Fort**, the maharajah's former residence, reached in times of trouble by an underground passage. The old stone zigzag path has been replaced by 300 steps. Though dilapidated, there are excellent views from the ramparts; a caretaker has the keys. The main fort gate is the starting point of some enticing walks into the Aravallis. A paved path leads to a shrine about 3 km away. There are two other powerful forts you can walk to, forming a circular walk ending back in Samode. Allow three hours, wear good shoes, a hat and carry water.

Samode Bagh, a large 400-year-old Mughal-style formal garden with fountains and pavilions, has been beautifully restored. It is 3 km southeast of Samode, towards the main Jaipur-Agra road. Within the grounds are modest-sized but elaborately decorated tents.

GOING FURTHER
Shekhawati

Shekhawati is famous for its beautiful painted *havelis*; its like an 'open-air art gallery' of paintings dating from the mid-19th century. Although a day trip gives you an idea of its treasures, it is better to spend two or three nights in Shekhawati to see the temples, frescoed forts, chhatris and step wells at leisure. There are other diversions laid on such as horse or camel safaris and treks into the hills. Shekhawati sees far fewer visitors than the better-known areas of Rajasthan.

Ramgarh has the highest concentration of painted *havelis*, though they are not as well maintained as those of Nawalgarh, which has the second largest selection. It is easier to visit *havelis* in towns that have hotels, especially Nawalgarh and Mandawa. There are a choice of interesting properties to stay in; we recommend **Mandawa Haveli** (near Sonthaliya Gate, Mandawa, T01592-233088) and **Apani Dhani** (Jhunjhunu Road, Nawalgarh, www.apanidhani.com).

ARRIVING IN SHEKHAWATI

Getting there You can get to the principal Shekhawati towns by train but road access is easier. A car comes in handy, though there are crowded buses from Delhi, Jaipur and Bikaner to some towns. Buses leave every 30 minutes (0500-2000) from Jaipur's Main Bus Station and take three hours.

Moving on Unless you have a driver, it is best to go to **Pushkar** (see page 105) via Jaipur from the Shekhawati region. It is possible to take a local bus from Mandawa to Kuchaman and then onto Pushkar, but much faster to go via Jaipur (see page 89).

BACKGROUND

The 'Garden of Shekha' was named after Rao Shekhaji of Amarsar (1433-1488) who challenged the Kachhawahas, refusing to pay tribute to the rulers at Amber. These Rajput barons made inroads into Muslim territory even during Mughal rule, and declared Shekhawati independent from the Jaipur suzerainty until 1738. During this period the merchants lavishly decorated their houses with paintings on religious, folk and historical themes. As Mughal power collapsed Shekhawati became a region of lawless banditry. In the early 19th century the British East India Company brought it under their control, bringing peace but also imposing taxes and tolls on trade which the Marwaris resented. Many of the merchants migrated to other parts of the country to seek their fortune and those who flourished returned their wealth to their homeland and took over as patrons of the arts.

PLACES IN SHEKHAWATI

There are two districts Sikar and Jhunjhunun. The key places to visit are Mandawa and Nawalgarh. Nawalgarh was founded in 1737 by Thakur Nawal Singh. There are numerous *havelis* worth visiting here and **Nawalgarh Fort** has fine examples of maps and plans of Shekhawati and Jaipur. The **Bala Kila**, which has a kiosk with beautiful ceiling paintings, is approached via the fruit market in the town centre and entered through the **Hotel Radha**. There are some beautiful 18th-century temples and it's worth visiting the Ganga Mai temple near Nansa Gate.

The **Anandilal Poddar Haveli**, now converted to the **Poddar Haveli Museum** ⓘ *foreigners Rs 100, includes camera and guide*, is perhaps the best restored *haveli* of Shekhawati. The 1920s *haveli* has around 700 frescoes including a Gangaur procession, scenes from the Mahabharata, trains, cars, the avatars of Vishnu, bathing scenes and British characters.

Other remarkable Murarka *havelis* include the 19th-century **Kesardev Murarka**, which has a finely painted façade and the early 20th-century **Radheshyam Murarka**. The latter portrays processions, scenes from folk tales and various Hindu and Christian religious themes, sometimes interspersed with mirror-work.

Similar to Nawalgarh, Mandawa has a high density of *havelis* in its pleasant streets and is one of the preferred places to stay in the area with plenty of characterful accommodation. Even the State Bank of Bikaner and Jaipur is an old *haveli*.

Baggar is10 km north east of Jhunjhunun and is worth seeing if only for the wall paintings of gods and angels being transported in motor cars. While Mahansar, 30 km northeast of Jhunjhunun, has a distinctly medieval feel. It has the Poddar *haveli* of **Son Chand**, the **Rama Temple** (ask for the key to the Golden Room; expensive at Rs 100 but very well preserved) and the large **Raghunath Temple** with some of the finest paintings of the region.

Churu, northwest of Baggar, was believed to have been a Jat stronghold in the 16th century. The town, which thrived during the days of overland desert trade, has some interesting 1870s Oswal Jain *havelis*. The main attraction, however, is the extraordinary '**Malji-ka-Kamra**', a crumbling, colonnaded *haveli* which houses some amazing interior scenes.

Ramgarh and Fatehpur are in the Sikar district. Ramgarh was settled by the Poddars in the late 18th century. In addition to their many *havelis*, visit the *chhatris* with painted entrances near the bus stand, as well as the temples to Shani (with mirror decoration) and to Ganga.

Fatehpur is worth a visit simply for the **Nadine Le Prince Haveli Cultural Centre**, near Chauhan Well (www.cultural-centre.com, T0157-123 1479). Following a visit to the area, Nadine Le Prince took it upon herself to safeguard the cultural heritage of Fatehpur and the restoration of this *haveli* is exceptional. The frescoes are exquisite and have served as an inspiration to Nadine's own artwork. As well as the restored *haveli*, there is a fine art gallery, sculpture garden and tribal art gallery and she hopes to create an artistic exchange between local and international artists.

JAIPUR AND AROUND LISTINGS

WHERE TO STAY

Jaipur

$$$$ Rambagh Palace (Taj), Bhawani Singh Rd, T0141-221 1919, www.tajhotels.com. 90 luxuriously appointed rooms and extraordinary suites arranged around a courtyard in the former maharaja's palace; it still feels like the real thing. Set in 19 ha of beautifully maintained garden, larger groups are invited to participate in elephant polo on the back lawn! Stunning indoor pool and a tented spa, but the real pièce de résistance is the spectacular dining hall, reminiscent of Buckingham Palace. Pleasant, relaxed atmosphere, good food and friendly staff.

$$$$-$$$ Diggi Palace, SMS Hospital Rd, T0141-237 3091, www.hoteldiggi palace.com. 43 attractive rooms in charming 125-year-old building. Not as glitzy as some but effortlessly chic with large range of rooms. Lovely open restaurant, great home-grown food, peaceful garden, enthusiastic, helpful owners who co-host the **Jaipur Literature and Heritage Festival** with William Dalrymple (see box, page 92). Calming atmosphere; you can really feel at home here – you will often bump into one of the family members who still live here. They also host lots of craft and cookery workshops here and trips to their organic farm.

$$$-$$ Pratap Bhawan Bed & Breakfast, A-4 Jamnalal Bajaj Marg, C-Scheme, T(0)98290 74354, www.pratapbhawan.com. Run by a delightful couple, this is a lovely homestay with delicious food. Nicely decorated rooms full of excellent wildlife photography which is one of owner Himanshu's passions – food is the other. Their cookery lessons will let you into the secrets of traditional Rajput cooking.

$$ Arya Niwas, Sansar Chandra Rd (behind Amber Tower), T0141-407 3546, www.aryaniwas.com. 95 very clean, simple but not always quiet rooms are modernized and smart. They serve good very cheap vegetarian food, there's a pleasant lounge, travel desk, tranquil lawn, friendly, helpful, impressive management. Book ahead (arrive by 1800). Great value.

$$ Umaid Bhawan, D1-2A Bani Park, T0141-231 6184, www.umaidbhawan.com. 28 beautifully decorated and ornately furnished rooms, many with balconies, one of the most charming *haveli*-style guesthouses with a lovely pool and friendly, knowledgeable owners.

$ Hotel Pearl Palace, Hari Kishan Somani Marg, Hathroi Fort, Ajmer Rd, T0141-237 3700, www.hotelpearlpalace.com. A real gem. Rooms are quirky and all slightly

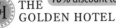

different with art pieces gathered or designed by the charming owner, modern, comfortable, some with a/c, Wi-Fi, lots of character. The pinnacle is the **Peacock** restaurant on the roof serving excellent food with great views of Jaipur, surrounded by plants and artworks. Booking ahead is essential. The owner Mr Singh has also created a beautiful heritage-style property nearby, the **Pearl Palace Heritage**.

Around Jaipur
$$$$ Samode Haveli Gangapole, T0141-263 2407, www.samode.com. 150-year-old, beautifully restored *haveli* with a leafy courtyard and gardens. 30 rooms and 2 suites (the spectacular Maharaja and Maharani suites have original mirrored mosaics, faded wall paintings, pillars, lamp-lit alcoves, cushions and carved wooden beds). Evening meals are served in the peaceful, atmospheric courtyard or in the magnificent, somewhat over-the-top dining room. Large pool with bar. Excellent food, including a good Western selection, huge wine list. You can also stay at the stunning **Samode Palace** 1 hr outside Jaipur.

$$$$ The Treehouse Resort, Km 35 – NH-8, T(0)90017 97422, www.treehouseresort.in. Inspired by naturalist Jim Corbett's tree-houses, Sunil Mehta has built what they call 'deluxe nests' in the trees. These treehouses have great eco-credentials and a back-to-nature vibe. There is a good restaurant and stunning **Peacock Bar** reconstructed from a 400-year-old heritage building.

RESTAURANTS

Jaipur
$$ Four Seasons, D-43A2 Subhash Mg, C-Scheme, T0141-227 5450. High-quality vegetarian Indian and Chinese food, with an extensive menu, pleasantly smart ambience and good staff. A cut above.

$$ Niros, Mirza Ismail Rd, T0141-237 4493. International. This is a characterful restaurant serving up good Indian and the obligatory Chinese and continental dishes.

$$-$ Anokhi Café, KK Square Shopping Complex, Prithviraj Rd, C-Scheme, T0141-400 7244. Great café serving international tastes such as Thai green bean salad, quiches and sandwiches. Try the pomegranate and pineapple juice, great filter coffee and an array of cakes and biscuits. A little oasis and right next door to the beautiful **Anokhi** shop with handblock prints galore.

$$-$ Chokhi Dhani, 19 km south on Tonk Rd, T0141-277 0555, www.chokhidhani. com. Enjoyable 'village' theme park with camel and elephant rides, traditional dancing and puppet shows popular with families from Delhi. If you are only coming to Jaipur, this gives you a Disney view of the rest of Rajasthan, but it is done very well. Food-wise there are 2 options, the 1st for Rs 350 gets you a traditional Rajasthani *thali* and you sit on the floor in an outdoor space. The Royal Rajasthani Dinner is Rs 650 and offers up a huge menu; not for the faint-hearted.

$$-$ Peacock, on roof of **Hotel Pearl Palace** (see above). Probably the most charming restaurant in town, very atmospheric with excellent Indian and continental dishes (vegetarian and non-vegetarian food prepared in separate kitchens). There are even fresh croissants in the morning from a French baker. Superb views by day and night from this 2-tiered restaurant, eclectic collection of quirky furniture designed by the owner and watched over by a giant peacock. Worth seeking out if you're not staying here.

$ Lassiwala, Mirza Ismail Rd, opposite Niro's. The unrivalled best *lassis* in the city, served in rough clay cups and topped off with a crispy portion of milk skin. Of the 3 'original' **Lassiwalas** parked next to each other, the genuine one is on the left, next to the alley. Come early; they run out by afternoon.

JAIPUR TO UDAIPUR

Pushkar lies in a narrow valley overshadowed by rocky hills, which offer spectacular views of the desert at sunset. The lake at its heart, almost magically beautiful at dawn and dusk, is one of India's most sacred. The village is transformed during the celebrated camel fair into a colourful week of heightened activity, but a visit outside this annual extravaganza is also worthwhile.

The village has been markedly changed in recent years by the year-round presence of large numbers of foreigners originally drawn by the Pushkar Fair, but there are still plenty of chances for an unhurried stroll around the lake that uncovers a very holy site: ghats dotted with shrines to the elephant-god Ganesh; little alcoves filled with candles, flowers and burning incense; here and there a wild-haired, spindly sadhu sits in repose by a tiny charcoal fire, knees brought up to his chin ...

Dozens of hotels, restaurants, cafés and shops cater to Western tastes and many travellers find it hard to drag themselves away from such creature comforts. The village's main bazar, though busy, has banned rickshaws so is relieved of revving engines and touting drivers. Take the short trek up to the Savitri Temple (3 km along a sandy track and jagged stone steps cut into the mountain), and you can swap village activity for open swathes of valley and fringes of desert beyond. From on high, the houses crowd the lake's edges as if it's a plug-hole down which all of Pushkar is slowly being drawn. Come the evening, groups of women promenade the bazars, the clashing colours of their saris all flowing together. Men dry their turbans in the evening sun after washing them in the lake, wafting the metres of filmy fabric in the breeze or draping it on nearby trees. Note that Pushkar is not to everybody's taste as there is a high hassle factor from cash-seeking ubiquitous Brahmin 'priests' requesting a donation receipt for the 'Pushkar Passport' (a red string tied around the wrist as part of a puja/blessing). After a two-year lake cleaning project, hopefully now the lake is healthy and thriving.

→ PUSHKAR

ARRIVING IN PUSHKAR

Getting there Pushkar is accessible via Ajmer Junction. Many trains serve Ajmer from Jaipur and then it is a 30-minute pretty taxi drive through the hills to Pushkar.

Moving on Venturing to the small towns of **rural Rajasthan** (see page 107) is naturally easiest by car; however, there are some local bus services from Pushkar but the going is slow. **Ekta Travels** ① *T0941-430 0313*, in Pushkar can offer onward journey advice.

Getting around The main sights and congested bazars of Ajmer, which can be seen in a day at a pinch, are within 15 to 20 minutes' walk of the railway station but you'll need a rickshaw to get to Ana Sagar. Pushkar is small enough to explore on foot. Hire a bike to venture further.

PLACES IN PUSHKAR

① *There are dozens of temples here, most of which are open 0500-1200, 1600-2200.*
Pushkar Lake is one of India's most sacred lakes. It is believed to mark the spot where a lotus thrown by Brahma landed. Fa Hien, the Chinese traveller who visited Pushkar in the fifth century AD, commented on the number of pilgrims, and although several of the older temples were subsequently destroyed by Aurangzeb, many remain. Ghats lead down to

the water to enable pilgrims to bathe, cows to drink, and the town's young folk to wash off after the riotous Holi celebrations. They also provide a hunting ground for Brahmin 'priests', who press a flower into the hand of any passing foreigner and offer – even demand – to perform *puja* (worship) in return for a sum of money. If this hard-sell version of spirituality appeals, agree your price in advance – Rs 50 should be quite sufficient – and be aware that a proportion of so-called priests are no such thing.

The **Brahma temple** ① *0600-1330, 1500-2100 (changes seasonally)*, beyond the western end of the lake, is a particularly holy shrine and draws pilgrims throughout the year. Although it isn't the only Brahma temple in India, as people claim, it is the only major pilgrim place for followers of the Hindu God of Creation. It is said that when Brahma needed a marital partner for a ritual, and his consort Saraswati (Savitri) took a long time to come, he married a cow-girl, Gayatri, after giving her the powers of a goddess (Gayatri because she was purified by the mouth of a cow or *gau*). His wife learnt of this and put a curse on him – that he would only be worshipped in Pushkar.

There are 52 ghats around the lake, of which the Brahma Ghat, Gan Ghat and Varah Ghat are the most sacred. The medieval **Varah Temple** is dedicated to the boar incarnation of Vishnu. It is said the idol was broken by Emperor Jahangir as it resembled a pig. The **Mahadev Temple** is said to date from 12th century while the **Julelal Temple** is modern and jazzy. Interestingly enough the two wives of Brahma have hilltop temples on either side of the lake, with the Brahma temple in the valley. A steep 3-km climb up the hill which leads to the **Savitri Temple** (dedicated to Brahma's first wife), offers excellent views of the town and surrounding desert.

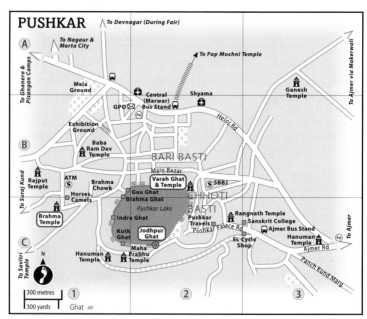

ON THE ROAD
The pull of the cattle and camels

The huge Mela is Pushkar's biggest draw. Over 200,000 visitors and pilgrims and hordes of cattle and camels with their semi-nomadic tribal drivers, crowd into the town. Farmers, breeders and camel traders buy and sell. Sales in leather whips, shoes, embroidered animal covers soar while women bargain over clay pots, bangles, necklaces and printed cloth.

Events begin four to five days before the full moon in November. There are horse and camel races and betting is heavy. In the Ladhu Umt race teams of up to 10 men cling to camels, and one another, in a hilarious and often chaotic spectacle. The Tug-of-War between Rajasthanis and foreigners is usually won by the local favourites. There are also sideshows with jugglers, acrobats, magicians and folk dancers. At nightfall there is music and dancing outside the tents, around friendly fires – an unforgettable experience despite its increasingly touristy nature, even including a laser show. The cattle trading itself actually takes place during the week before the fair; some travellers have reported arriving during the fair and there being no animals left.

The **Main (Sadar) Bazar** is full of shops selling typical tourist, as well as pilgrim knick-knacks and is usually very busy. At full moon, noisy religious celebrations last all night so you may need your ear plugs here.

→ RURAL RAJASTHAN

The magic of Rajasthan is often found off the trodden path and this state is renowned for its nature and birdlife and for some stunning fort palaces seemingly in the middle of nowhere. Places not to miss if you have time to detour are **Chhatra Sagar** close to Pushkar – a stunning camp set on the banks of a reservoir with amazing birdlife and village walks. Alternatively, Deogarh Mahal, on the way to Udaipur, is a stunning fort palace lovingly restored; they also have an amazing camp where you might just hear the rumble of a leopard's roar at night.

DEOGARH

Deogarh (Devgarh) 2 km off the NH8, is an excellent place to break journey between Pushkar and Udaipur. It is a very pleasant, little frequented town with a dusty but interesting bazar (if you are interested in textiles, visit **Vastra Bhandar** ① *T02904-252187*, for reasonably priced and good-quality textiles). Its elevation makes it relatively cool and the countryside and surrounding hills are good for gentle treks. There is an old fort on a hill as well as a magnificent palace on a hillock in the centre with murals illustrating the fine local school of miniature painting. **Raghosagar Lake**, which is very pleasant to walk around, has an island with a romantic ruined temple and centotaphs (poor monsoons leave the lake dry). It attracts numerous migratory birds and is an attractive setting for the charming 200-year-old palace, **Gokal Vilas**, the home of the present Rawat Saheb Nahar Singhji and the Ranisahiba. Their two sons have opened the renovated 17th-century **Deogarh Mahal Palace** to guests, see Where to stay, page 108. The Rawat, a knowledgeable historian and art connoisseur, has a private collection of over 50 paintings which guests may view, advance notice required. The shop at the hotel has good modern examples to buy. There is plenty to do here including an excellent 45-minute train journey from Deogarh to Phulud which winds down through the Aravalli hills to the plain below through tunnels and bridges.

WHERE TO STAY

Pushkar

$$$$-$$$ Greenhouse Resort, Tilora village, 8 km from Pushkar, T0145-230 0079, www.thegreenhouseresort.com. This is a truly unique place with luxurious tents mixed with giant greenhouses growing roses and strawberries and lots of organic vegetables for the kitchen. With a nod to the environment, they are experimenting with water conservation, innovative irrigation and solar panels and the resort is staffed mainly by local people. The beds are stunning and there are all mod cons in the tents. This is a serene place, relaxing and inspiring.

$$-$ Inn Seventh Heaven, next to Mali ka Mandir, T0145-510 5455, www. inn-seventh-heaven.com. Beautiful rooms spiral out from the inner courtyard in this fantastically well-restored 100-year-old *haveli*, plus a handful of ascetic but much cheaper rooms in the neighbouring building. Lots of seating areas are dotted throughout the 3-storey building, even some lovely swinging *diwans*. Very friendly, informal, excellent rooftop restaurant (baked potatoes from open coal fire in winter), the restaurant goes from strength to strength, charming owner and a sociable atmosphere. Exceptionally good value.

$$-$ U-Turn, Lake Vahara Ghat Choti Basti, T(0)992-873 7798, www.hotelurn.com. A new chic little number right on the lake. The rooms are small due to the age of the building, but with bags of charm. Formerly the **Bhola Guest House**, the 2nd oldest guesthouse in Pushkar. Of the 6 beautifully decorated rooms, you can choose from the 'Princess Villa' or the 'Kama Sutra Villa'. The rooftop café is also a cut above, with nice fabrics and comfy chairs and serving up the usual global fare.

$ Sunset, on the lake, T0145-277 2382, hotelsunset@hotmail.com. 20 plain, clean rooms, 3 a/c, around a lovely garden, lots of flowers and papaya trees. Well located close to the lake and with the popular **Sunset Café**.

Rural Rajasthan

$$$$ Chhatra Sagar, 4 km from Nimaj, Pali, T02939-230118, www.chhatrasagar. com. Open 1 Oct-31 Mar. 11 beautiful colonial-style tents on the banks of a very picturesque reservoir, south of Pushkar, just west of the main Jaipur–Udaipur highway. The ex-rulers of Nimaj have recreated the hunting lodge of their forefathers to great effect with amazing views over the water. The family still live on the lake themselves, so there's a very convivial family atmosphere. You might see a peacock fly across the lake. Safaris and bird walks can be arranged, all meals included in the tariff (and the food is delicious).

$$$$ Lakshman Sagar, near Raipur village, Pali, T011-2649 4531, www.sewara. com. Lakeside cottages in stunning desert landscape. Although super stylish, the decor borrows from classic Rajasthan village life so it has a rustic chic vibe. There are plenty of outdoor spaces to sit and gaze out into the desert and a beautiful swimming pool. to lounge by.They are working on other old properties across Rajasthan so check their website for new places to lay your hat.

$$$$-$$$ Deogarh Mahal, T(0)992-883 4777, www.deogarhmahal.com. This labyrinthine fort dates back to 1617 and boasts 50 beautifully restored rooms, including atmospheric suites furnished in traditional style with good views; the best have balconies with private jacuzzis, but not all are up to the same standard. Fabulous lotus flower-shaped pool, Keralan massage, Mewari meals, home-grown produce, bar, great gift shop, log fires, folk entertainment, boating, birdwatching, jeep safaris, audio tour by William Dalrymple, talks on art history, hospitable and delightful hosts. They can organize romantic dinners in private courtyards around the mahal or out in abandoned forts in the surrounding countryside, or gala dinners with camel cart rides and fireworks. Outstanding hotel and highly recommended. Reserve well ahead. The family have also renovated the **Fort Singh Sagar**, 5 km from Deogarh. This is where the man of the house at Deogarh Mahal used to bring his shooting parties. With more contemporary decor, there are 4 stylish suites and amazing sunken bathrooms. It is in the middle of a small lake, very serene and is an ideal hideaway. Prices start at US$350 per night. Stunning.

$$$ Deogarh Khayyam, 4 km from Deogarh, T(0)992-883 4777, www.deogarh mahal.com. These stunning tents are perched on a jungle plateau – you are utterly surrounded by nature. The 16 luxurious tents are fairly spread out so you feel the birds and wildlife are your neighbours not your fellow guests. Log fires and starry skies in the evening and the same amazing food as Deogarh Mahal served up. Camping was never so exciting.

RESTAURANTS

Pushkar

$$-$ Little Italy Pizzeria, Panch Kund Rd. High-quality Italian dishes plus Israeli and Indian specialities, pleasant garden setting. They have opened another restaurant **La Pizzeria**, near Varah Temple, Chhoti Basti.

$$-$ Sixth Sense, perched at the top of **Inn at Seventh Heaven** (see Where to stay) this is by far the most stylish dining experience in Pushkar. Serving up the usual Indian and international fare, with baked potatoes, pastas and fantastic home-baked desserts.

$ Neem Tree Farm, outside Pushkar, T(0)7737-777903, www.neemtreefarm. weebly.com. This place specializes in permaculture, natural farming and solar architecture. You can head out during the day for a 'permaculture' picnic or have dinner in the desert. A unique experience.

$ Halwai ki gali (alley off Main Bazar). Sweet shops sell *malpura* (syrupy pancake), as well as other Rajasthani/ Bengali sweets.

UDAIPUR AND AROUND

Enchanting Udaipur, set in the Girwa Valley in the Aravalli Hills of south Rajasthan, must be one of the most romantic cities in India, with white marble palaces, placid blue lakes, attractive gardens and green hills that are a world away from the surrounding desert. High above the lake towers the massive palace of the Maharanas. From its rooftop gardens and balconies, you can look over Lake Pichola, the Lake Palace "adrift like a snowflake" in its centre. The monsoons that deserted the city earlier in the decade have returned – though water shortage remains a threat – to replenish the lakes and ghats, where women thrash wet heaps of washing with wooden clubs, helped by splashing children. The houses and temples of the old city stretch out in a pale honeycomb, making Udaipur an oasis of colour in a stark and arid region. Sunset only intensifies the city's beauty, turning the city palace's pale walls to gold, setting the lake to shimmer in silvery swathes against it, while mynah birds break out into a noisy twilight chorus. Ochre and orange skies line the rim of the westernmost hills while countless roof terraces light up and the lake's islands appear to float on waters dancing in the evening breeze and turning purple in the fading light.

→UDAIPUR

ARRIVING IN UDAIPUR

Getting there The airport, about 30-45 minutes by taxi or city bus, is well connected. The main bus stand is east of Udai Pol, 2-3 km from most hotels, while Udaipur City Railway Station is another 1 km south. Both have auto-rickshaw stands outside as well as pushy hotel touts.

Travelling around Rural Rajasthan you are limited to local buses or you can opt for your own driver. There is a convenient train which leaves Jaipur at 0645, calling at Ajmer Junction at 0850 and Bhilwara at 1038 (where it's possible to get a taxi to Deogarh) and finishing in Udaipur at 1345 (*Jp Udz Sf Spl 09721*).

Moving on There is a regular bus service from Udaipur to **Kumbhalgarh** (see page 121) and **Ranakpur** (see page 123). Kumbhalgarh is 80 km from Udaipur and many tour operators have taxi services (although most of them offer one-day excursions from Udaipur); try the friendly **Shree Ji Travels** ① *www.shreejitoursudaipur.com*.

Getting around The touristy area around the Jagdish temple and the City Palace, the main focus of interest, is best explored on foot but there are several sights further afield. Buses, shared tempos, auto-rickshaws and taxis cover the city and surrounding area; some travellers prefer to hire a scooter or bike.

Tourist information Be prepared for crowds, dirt and pollution and persistent hotel touts who descend on new arrivals. It is best to reserve a hotel ahead or ask for a particular street or area of town. Travellers risk being befriended by someone claiming to show you the city for free. If you accept, you run the risk of visiting one shop after another with your 'friend'. **Rajasthan Tourism Development Corporation (RTDC)** ① *Tourist Reception Centre, Fateh Memorial, Suraj Pol, T0294-241 1535, open 1000-1700, guides 4-8 hrs, Rs 250-400.*

BACKGROUND

The legendary **Ranas of Mewar** who traced their ancestry back to the Sun, first ruled the region from their seventh-century stronghold Chittaurgarh. The title 'Rana', peculiar to the rulers of **Mewar**, was supposedly first used by Hammir who reoccupied Mewar in 1326. In 1568, **Maharana Udai Singh** founded a new capital on the shores of Lake Pichola and named it Udaipur (the city of sunrise) having selected the spot in 1559. On the advice of an

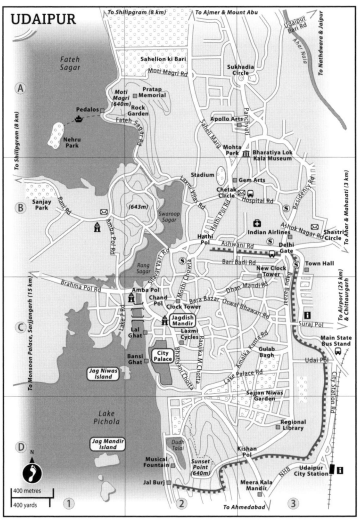

ascetic who interrupted his rabbit hunt, Udai Singh had a temple built above the lake and then constructed his palace around it.

In contrast to the house of Jaipur, the rulers of Udaipur prided themselves on being independent from other more powerful regional neighbours, particularly the Mughals. In a piece of local princely one-upmanship, **Maharana Pratap Singh**, heir apparent to the throne of Udaipur, invited Raja Man Singh of Jaipur to a lakeside picnic. Afterwards he had the ground on which his guest had trodden washed with sacred Ganga water and insisted that his generals take purificatory baths. Man Singh reaped appropriate revenge by preventing Pratap Singh from acceding to his throne. Udaipur, for all its individuality, remained one of the poorer princely states in Rajasthan, a consequence of being almost constantly at war. In 1818, Mewar, the Kingdom of the Udaipur Maharanas, came under British political control but still managed to avoid almost all British cultural influence.

OLD CITY

Udaipur is a traditionally planned fortified city. Its bastioned rampart walls are pierced by massive gates, each studded with iron spikes as protection against enemy war elephants. The five remaining gates are: **Hathi Pol** (Elephant Gate – north), **Chand Pol** (Moon Gate – west), **Kishan Pol** (south), the main entrance **Suraj Pol** (Sun Gate – east) and **Delhi Gate** (northeast). On the west side, the city is bounded by the beautiful Pichola Lake and to the east and north, by moats. To the south is the fortified hill of Eklingigarh. The main street leads from the Hathi Pol to the massive City Palace on the lake side.

The walled city is a maze of narrow winding lanes flanked by tall whitewashed houses with doorways decorated with Mewar folk art, windows with stained glass or *jali* screens, majestic *havelis* with spacious inner courtyards and shops. Many of the houses here were given by the Maharana to retainers – barbers, priests, traders and artisans while many rural landholders (titled jagirdars), had a *haveli* conveniently located near the palace.

The **Jagdish Mandir** ① *150 m north of the palace, 0500-1400, 1600-2200*, was built by Maharana Jagat Singh in 1651. The temple is a fine example of the Nagari style, and contrasts with the serenity of Udaipur's predominantly whitewashed buildings, surrounded as it often is by chanting Sadhus, gambolling monkeys and the smell of incense. A shrine with a brass Garuda stands outside and stone elephants flank the entrance steps; within is a black stone image of Vishnu as Jagannath, the Lord of the Universe.

A quiet, slightly eccentric museum, including what they claim is the world's largest turban, now lies in the lovely 18th-century **Bagore ki Haveli** ① *1000-1900, Rs 25, camera Rs 10*, has 130 rooms and was built as a miniature of the City Palace. There are cool shady courtyards containing some peacock mosaics and fretwork, and carved pillars made from granite, marble and the local blueish-grey stone. A slightly forlorn but funny puppet show plays several times a day on the ground floor.

CITY PALACE

① *0930-1730, last entry 1630. From Ganesh Deori Gate: Rs 50 (more from near Lake Palace Ghat). Camera Rs 100, video Rs 300. From 'Maharajah's gallery', you can get a pass for Fateh Prakash Palace, Shiv Niwas and Shambu Niwas, Rs 75. Guided tour, 1 hr, Rs 100 each. Guides hang around the entrance; standards vary wildly and they can cause a scene if you already have hired a guide. Ask at the ticket office. Rs 25 gets you access to the complex and a nice walk down to the jetty.*

This impressive complex of several palaces is a blend of Rajput and Mughal influences. Half of it, with a great plaster façade, is still occupied by the royal family. Between the **Bari Pol**

(Great Gate, 1608, men traditionally had to cover their heads with a turban from this point on) to the north, and the **Tripolia Gate** (1713), are eight *toranas* (arches), under which the rulers were weighed against gold and silver on their birthdays, which was then distributed to the poor. One of the two domes on top of the Tripolia originally housed a water clock; a glass sphere with a small hole at the base was filled with water and would take exactly one hour to empty, at which point a gong would be struck and the process repeated. The gate has three arches to allow the royal family their private entrance, through the middle, and then a public entry and exit gate to either side. Note the elephant to the far left (eastern) end of the gate structure; they were seen as bringers of good fortune and appear all over the palace complex. The Tripolia leads in to the **Manak Chowk**, originally a large courtyard which was converted in to a garden only in 1992. The row of lumps in the surface to the left are original, and demarcate elephant parking bays! Claiming descent from Rama, and therefore the sun, the Mewars always insured that there was an image of the sun available for worship even on a cloudy day, thus the beautiful example set in to the exterior wall of the palace. The large step in front of the main entrance was for mounting horses, while those to the left were for elephants. The family crest above the door depicts a Rajput warrior and one of the Bhil tribesmen from the local area whose renowned archery skills were much used in the defence of the Mewar household. The motto translates as 'God protects those who stand firm in upholding righteousness'.

As you enter the main door, a set of stairs to the right leads down to an armoury which includes an impressive selection of swords, some of which incorporate pistols in to their handles. Most people then enter the main museum to the right, although it is possible to access the government museum from here (see below). The entrance is known as **Ganesh Dori**, meaning 'Ganesh's turn'; the image of the elephant God in the wall as the steps start to turn has been there since 1620. Note the tiles underneath which were imported from Japan in the 1930s and give even the Hindu deities an Oriental look to their eyes. The second image is of Laxmi, bringer of good fortune and wealth.

The stairs lead in to **Rai Angan**, 'Royal Court' (1559). The temple to the left is to the sage who first advised that the royal palace be built on this side. Opposite is a display of some of Maharana Pratap Singh's weapons, used in some of his many battles with the Mughals, as well as his legendary horse, Chetak. The Mughals fought on elephants, the Mewars on horses; the elephant trunk fitted to Chetak's nose was to fool the Mughal elephants in to thinking that the Mewar horses were baby elephants, and so not to be attacked. A fuller version of this nosepiece can be seen in one of the paintings on the walls, as indeed can an elephant wielding a sword in its trunk during battle.

The stairs to the left of the temple lead up to **Chandra Mahal**, featuring a large bowl where gold and silver coins were kept for distribution to the needy. Note that the intricately carved walls are made not from marble but a combination of limestone powder, gum Arabic, sugar cane juice and white lentils. From here steps lead up in to **Bari Mahal** (1699-1711), situated on top the hill chosen as the palace site; the design has incorporated the original trees. The cloisters' cusped arches have wide eaves and are raised above the ground to protect the covered spaces from heavy monsoon rain. This was an intimate 'playground' where the royal family amused themselves and were entertained. The painting opposite the entrance is an aerial view of the palace; the effect from the wall facing it is impressive. The chair on display was meant for Maharana Fateh Singh's use at the Delhi Darbar, an event which he famously refused to attend. The chair was sent on and has still never been used.

The picture on the wall of two elephants fighting shows the area that can be seen through the window to the left; there is a low wall running from the Tripolia Gate to the main palace building. An elephant was placed either side of the wall, and then each had to try to pull the other until their opponent's legs touched the wall, making them the victor.

The next room is known as **Dil Kushal Mahal** ('love entertainment room'), a kind of mirrored love nest. This leads on to a series of incredibly intricate paintings depicting the story of life in the palace, painted 1782-1828. The **Shiv Vilas Chini ki Chatar Sali** incorporates a large number of Chinese and Dutch tiles in to its decoration, as well as an early petrol-powered fan. Next is the Moti Mahal, the ladies' portion of the men's palace, featuring a changing room lined with mirrors and two game boards incorporated into the design of the floor.

Pritam Niwas was last lived in by Maharana Gopal Singh, who died in 1955 having been disabled by polio at a young age. His wheel armchair and even his commode are on display here. This leads on to **Surya Chopar**, which features a beautiful gold-leaf image of the sun; note the 3D relief painting below. The attractive **Mor Chowk** court, intended for ceremonial darbars, was added in the mid-17th century, and features beautiful late 19th-century peacock mosaics. The throne room is to its south, the **Surya Chopar**, from which the Rana (who claimed descent from the Sun) paid homage to his divine ancestor. The **Manak Mahal** (Ruby Palace) was filled with figures of porcelain and glass in the mid-19th century. To the north, the **Bari Mahal** or Amar Vilas (1699-1711) was added on top of a low hill. It has a pleasant garden with full grown trees around a square water tank in the central court.

A plain, narrow corridor leads in to the **Queen's Palace**, featuring a series of paintings, lithographs and photographs, and leading out in to **Laxmi Chowk**, featuring two cages meant for trapping tigers and leopards. The entrance to the **government museum** ① *Sat-Thu 1000-1600, Rs 3,* is from this courtyard. The rather uncared for display includes second century BC inscriptions, fifth- to eighth-century sculptures and 9000 miniature paintings of 17th- and 19th-century Mewar schools of art but also a stuffed kangaroo and Siamese twin deer.

On the west side of the Tripolia are the **Karan Vilas** (1620-1628) and **Khush Mahal**, a rather grotesque pleasure palace for European guests, whilst to the south lies the **Shambhu Niwas Palace** the present residence of the Maharana.

Maharana Fateh Singh added to this the opulent **Shiv Niwas** with a beautiful courtyard and public rooms, and the **Fateh Prakash Palace**. Here the Darbar Hall's royal portrait gallery displays swords still oiled and sharp. The Bohemian chandeliers (1880s) are reflected by Venetian mirrors, the larger ones made in India of lead crystal. Both, now exclusive hotels (see Where to stay, below), are worth visiting.

On the first floor is the **Crystal Gallery** ① *0900-2000, Rs 500 for a guided tour with a talk on the history of Mewar, followed by a cup of tea (overpriced with a cold reception according to some; avoid the cream tea as the scones are so hard they will crack your teeth).* The gallery has an extensive collection of cut-crystal furniture, vases, etc, made in Birmingham, England in the 1870s, supplemented by velvet, rich 'zardozi' brocade, objects in gold and silver and a precious stone-studded throne.

'The Legacy of honour', outlining the history of the Mewar dynasty, is a good **Son et Lumière**, the first privately funded one in India. There are two shows daily at 1930 and 2030, Rs 100 for ground seating, Rs 300 on terrace; book at the City Palace ticket office.

LAKE PICHOLA

Fringed with hills, gardens, *havelis*, ghats and temples, Lake Pichola is the scenic focus of Udaipur though parts get covered periodically with vegetation, and the water level drops considerably during the summer. Set in it are the Jag Niwas (Lake Palace) and the Jag Mandir Palaces.

Jag Mandir, built on an island in the south of the lake, is notable for the Gul Mahal, a domed pavilion started by Karan Singh (1620-1628) and completed by Jagat Singh (1628-1652). It is built of yellow sandstone inlaid with marble around an attractive courtyard. Maharajah Karan Singh gave the young Prince Khurram (later Shah Jahan), refuge here when he was in revolt against his father Jahangir in 1623, cementing a friendly relationship between the Mewar Maharaja and the future Mughal Emperor. Refugee European ladies and children were also given sanctuary here by Maharana Sarap Singh during the Mutiny. There is a lovely pavilion with four stone elephants on each side (some of the broken trunks have been replaced with polystyrene!). You get superb views from the balconies. It's possible to take an enjoyable **boat trip** ① *Apr-Sep 0800-1100, 1500-1800, Oct-Mar 1000-1700, on the hour, Rs 300 for 1-hr landing on Jag Mandir, Rs 200 for boat ride without stop*, from Rameshwar Ghat, south of City Palace complex. It's especially attractive in the late afternoon light. Rates from the boat stand at Lal Ghat may be slightly cheaper. There is a pricey bar/restaurant on the island but it's worth stopping for the stunning views.

Jag Niwas Island (Lake Palace) ① *it is no longer possible to go to the Lake Palace for lunch or dinner unless you are a resident at Lake Palace, Leela or Oberoi*. The Dilaram and Bari Mahal Palaces were built by **Maharana Jagat Singh II** in 1746 and cover the whole island. Once the royal summer residences and now converted into a hotel, they seem to float like a dream ship on the blue waters of the lake. The courtly atmosphere, elegance and opulence of princely times, the painted ceilings, antique furniture combined with the truly magical setting make it one of the most romantic buildings in India. There are, of course, superb views.

Jal Burj is on the water's edge, south of the town. From the small **Dudh Talai** nearby, there is an attractive walk alongside the main lake (especially pleasant in the evening; large fruit bats can also often be seen). A left turn up a new road leads to **Manikya Lal Verma Park** ① *Rs 5 during the day, Rs 10 evening*, which has great lake views and a delightfully kitsch 'musical fountain', switched on in the evening – a favourite with Indian families.

On the hill immediately to the east of Dudh Talai, a pleasant two-hour walk to the south of the city, is **Sunset Point** which has excellent free views over the city. The path past the café (good for breakfast) leads to the gardens on the wall; a pleasant place to relax. Although it looks steep it is only a 30-minute climb from the café.

FATEH SAGAR AND AROUND

This lake, north of Lake Pichola, was constructed in 1678 during the reign of Maharana Jai Singh and modified by Maharana Fateh Singh. There is a pleasant lakeside drive along the east bank but, overall, it lacks the charm of the Pichola. **Nehru Park** on an island (accessible by ferry) has a restaurant.

Overlooking the Fateh Sagar is the **Moti Magri (Pearl Hill)** ① *0900-1800, Rs 20, camera free*. There are several statues of local heroes in the attractive rock gardens including one of Maharana Pratap on his horse Chetak, to which he owed his life. Local guides claim that Chetak jumped an abyss of extraordinary width in the heat of the battle of Haldighati (1576) even after losing one leg. To find out more look at *Hero of Haldighati*.

Sahelion ki Bari (Garden of the Maids of Honour) ⓘ *0900-1800, Rs 10, plus Rs 2 for 'fountain show'*, a little north from Moti Magri, is an ornamental pleasure garden; a great spot, both attractive and restful. There are many fountains including trick ones along the edge of the path which are operated by the guide clapping his hands! In a pavilion in the first courtyard, opposite the entrance, a children's museum has curious exhibits including a pickled scorpion, a human skeleton and busts of Einstein and Archimedes. Beautiful black marble kiosks decorate the corners of a square pool. An elegant round lotus pond has four marble elephants spouting water. To the north is a rose garden with over 100 varieties.

At **Ahar** (3 km east) are the remains of the ancient city which has some Jain *chhatris* set on high plinths in the Mahasati (royal cremation ground). A small **museum** ⓘ *1000-1700, closed Fri and holidays, Rs 3*, contains pottery shards and terracotta toys from the first century BC and 10th-century sculptures. Nearby are the temples of Mira Bai (10th century), Adinatha (11th century) and Mahavira (15th century).

→ AROUND UDAIPUR

The area around Udaipur is dotted with a wide range of attractions, from some of the grandest of Rajasthan's heritage hotels to some of its cosiest castles, from secluded forest lakes, surrounded by wildlife, to one of the largest reservoirs in Asia. It's also home to some ancient temples and perhaps the most evocative of Rajasthan's plentiful palaces, the Juna Mahal near Dungarpur.

Most of the sights in this area are a little isolated and so not well connected by train. However, the quality of the region's roads has greatly improved recently, making travel either by bus or taxi both quick and convenient.

MONSOON PALACE
ⓘ *15 km west. In order to reach the Monsoon Palace, you enter into Sajjangarh: foreigners Rs 160, Indians RS 20, Car RS 130. Allow about 3 hrs for the round trip. rickshaws cannot make it up the steep hill to the palace, so expect a good hike up or get a taxi.*
There are good views from this deserted palace on a hilltop. The unfinished building on **Sajjangarh**, at an altitude of 335 m, which looks picturesque from the west-facing battlements, was named after Sajjan Singh (1874-1884) and was planned to be high enough to see his ancestral home, Chittaurgarh. Normally, you need a permit from the police in town to enter, though many find a tip to the gateman suffices. It offers panoramic views of Udaipur (though the highest roof is spoilt by radio antennas); the windows of the Lake Palace can be seen reflecting the setting sun. The palace itself is very run down but the views from the hill top are just as good. The views to the other sides of the rolling hills is equally as sublime. A visit in the late afternoon is recommended – sunset is spectacular, take binoculars.

JAISAMAND LAKE
Before the building of huge modern dams in India, Jaisamand was the second largest artificial lake in Asia, 15 km by 10 km. Dating from the late 17th century, it is surrounded by the summer palaces of the Ranis of Udaipur. The two highest surrounding hills are topped by the **Hawa Mahal** and **Ruti Rani palaces**, now empty but worth visiting for the architecture and views. A small sanctuary nearby has deer, antelope and panther. Tribals still inhabit some islands on the lake while crocodiles, keelback water snakes and turtles bask on others.

BAMBORA

The imposing 18th-century hilltop fortress of Bambora has been converted to a heritage hotel by the royal family of Sodawas at an enormous restoration cost yet retaining its ancient character. The impressive fort is in Mewari style with domes, turrets and arches. To get here from Udaipur, go 12 km east along the airport road and take the right turn towards Jaisamand Lake passing the 11th-century Jagat Temple (38 km) before reaching Bambora.

SITAMATA WILDLIFE SANCTUARY

The reserve of dense deciduous forests covers over 400 sq km and has extensive birdlife (woodpeckers, tree pies, blue jays, jungle fowl). It is one of the few sanctuaries between the Himalaya and the Nilgiris where giant brown flying squirrels have been reported. Visitors have seen hordes of langur monkey, nilgai in groups of six or seven, four-horned antelope, jackal and even panther and hyena, but the thick forests make sighting difficult. There are crocodiles in the reservoirs.

RISHABDEO

Rishabdeo, off the highway, has a remarkable 14th-century Jain temple with intricate white marble carving and black marble statuary, though these are not as fine as at Dilwara or Ranakpur. Dedicated to the first Jain Tirthankar, Adinath or Rishabdev, Hindus, Bhils as well as Jains worship there. An attractive bazar street leads to the temple, which is rarely visited by tourists. Special worship is conducted several times daily when Adinath, regarded as the principal focus of worship, is bathed with saffron water or milk. The priests are friendly; a small donation (Rs 10-20) is appreciated.

DUNGARPUR

Dungarpur (City of Hills) dates from the 13th century. The district is the main home of the Bhil tribal people. It is also renowned for its stone masons, who in recent years have been employed to build Hindu temples as far afield as London. The attractive and friendly village has one of the most richly decorated and best-preserved palaces in Rajasthan, the Juna Mahal. Surrounded on three sides by Lake Gaibsagar and backed by picturesque hills, the more recent **Udai Bilas Palace** (now a heritage hotel, see page 119) was built by Maharawal Udai Singhji in the 19th century and extended in 1943. The huge courtyard surrounds a 'pleasure pool' from the centre of which rises a four-storeyed pavilion with a beautifully carved wooden chamber.

The **Juna Mahal**, above the village, dates from the 13th century when members of the Mewar clan at Chittaur moved south to found a new kingdom after a family split. It is open to guests staying at Udai Bilas and by ticket (Rs 150) for non-residents, obtainable at the hotel. The seven-storeyed fortress-like structure with turrets, narrow entrances and tiny windows has colourful and vibrant rooms profusely decorated over several centuries with miniature wall paintings (among the best in Rajasthan), and glass and mirror inlay work. There are some fine *jarokha* balconies and sculpted panels illustrating musicians and dancers in the local green-grey parava stone which are strikingly set against the plain white walls of the palace to great effect. The steep narrow staircases lead to a series of seven floors giving access to public halls, supported on decorated columns, and to intimate private chambers. There is a jewel of a Sheesh Mahal and a cupboard in the Maharawal's bedroom on the top floor covered in miniatures illustrating some 50 scenes from the Kama Sutra. Windows and balconies open to the breeze command lovely views over the town below. Perhaps nowhere else in Rajasthan gives as good an impression of how these palaces must have been hundreds of years ago; it is completely unspoilt and hugely impressive. It is amazing, but not very accessible to elderly people. There is no actual path.

Some interesting temples nearby include the 12th-century Siva temple at **Deo Somnath**, 12 km away, and the splendid complex of temple ruins profusely decorated with stone sculptures.

UDAIPUR AND AROUND LISTINGS

WHERE TO STAY

$$$$ Devi Garh, Delwara, 5 km from Eklingji, T02953-289211, www.lebua.com/devigarh. For the ultimate in luxury. **Devi Garh** is spectacular – this is not a typical palace renovation, it is chic and super stylish with amazing attention to detail. The rooms are themed, so you might find yourself in the Lapis Lazuli room or the Marigold room. The original paintings in the restaurant are exquisite. Recently taken over by the **Lebua** group so there might be changes afoot. It's stunning but bear in mind it is about 22 km outside Udaipur.

$$$$ Shiv Niwas (HRH), City Palace (turn right after entrance), T0294-252 8016, www.hrhindia. com. 19 tasteful rooms, 17 luxurious suites including those stayed in by Queen Elizabeth II and Roger Moore, some with superb lake views, very comfortable, good restaurant, very pleasant outdoor seating for all meals around a lovely marble pool (non-residents pay Rs 300 to swim), tennis, squash, excellent service, beautiful surroundings, reserve ahead in season. This place will have you feeling like a Maharani.

$$$$ Udaivilas (Oberoi), Lake Pichola, T0294-243 3300, www.oberoihotels.com. The elegant but monochrome exterior of this latter-day palace does nothing to prepare you for the opulence within; the spectacular entry courtyard sets the scene for staggeringly beautiful interiors. The 87 rooms are the last word in indulgence; some have one of the hotel's 9 swimming pools running alongside their private balcony. The setting, overlooking both the lake and city palaces, is superb, as are the food and service. This is probably one of the most perfect hotels in India. Outstanding.

$$$ Amet Haveli, Outside Chandpole, T0294-243 1085, amethaveli@sify.com. Enviable location on the lakefront. Beautiful rooms – some with unparalleled views across the lake. The highly recommended **Ambrai** restaurant is on site.

$$$-$$ Kankarwa Haveli, 26 Lal Ghat, T0294-241 1457, www.kankarwahaveli.com. Wide range of rooms in renovated 250-year-old *haveli* on lake shore, some with views and some with beautiful original artwork and features – each room is different. 2 modern, glass-fronted suites have been built but they fit in seamlessly with this classic building; one suite has possibly the best view of the lake in this area. The roof terrace has also had a revamp and you can sample some great home cooking. Lots of cosy nooks to sit in. You will be welcomed warmly by Janardan Singh and his family. Very atmospheric.

$$$-$$ Udai Garh, 21 Lal Ghat, behind Jagdish Temple, T0294-242 1239, www.udaigarhudaipur.in. Beautiful rooms with classic furniture, but the crowning glory is the roof-top swimming pool with great views across the lake. Seductive rooftop restaurant too.

$$ Hibiscus Guest House, 190 Naga Nagri, Chandpol, follow signs to **Leela Palace Hotel**, T0294-280 3490, www.hibiscusinudaipur.com. Tucked away on the Chandpol side of the lake, this lovely guesthouse run by Carol and Babu has a relaxed vibe. Beautifully decorated rooms, lovely dining room, pretty garden, massive dog (Great Dane!)

$$-$ Jheel Guest House, 56 Gangaur Ghat (behind temple), T0294-242 1352, www.jheelguesthouse.com. Friendly owner and fantastic views. Don't be deceived by the unremarkable entrance, one room in particular practically hangs over the ghats with a spectacular view all the way towards the **Lake Palace** hotel. New extension has 6 pleasant rooms with bath and hot water; 8 rooms in older part, good rooftop restaurant. There is the **Ginger** café downstairs too.

RESTAURANTS

\$\$\$ Ambrai, Lake Pichola Rd. Magical garden restaurant with tables under trees by lake shore, superb views of City Palace, fantastic at sunset. **Ambrai** serve all of the usual classic Indian dishes and good fish. If you want a lakeside table, be sure to book ahead. Recommended by everyone you speak to in Udaipur.

\$\$\$ Upre by 1559AD, Lake Pichola Hotel, Hanuman Ghat, T0294-243 1197, www.1559AD.com. Run by Arwan Shaktawat, this is a chic rooftop restaurant and lounge with great Udaipur views – best at night. Interesting menu of Indian classics and European treats.

\$\$\$-\$\$ Savage Garden, up alley near east end of Chandpol bridge. Particularly lovely in the evenings with its striking blue interior and superior food. You can sit in the courtyard or up in the beautifully decorated elevated restaurant. Under the watchful eye of French owner and chef, they prepare a small menu done well. Highlights are delicious pasta dishes, risottos and great mezze. The fish is good too. There is a lovely atmosphere here – very romantic.

\$\$ Sankalp, outside Suraj Pol, City Station Rd, T0294-510 2686. This is a fantastic branch of the Ahmedabad-based Sankalp chain – if you tire of the richer North Indian fare, this place serves deliciously light South Indian food. All the usual favourites are on the menu, including *masala dosa* and *idlis*, with an amazing range of chutneys.

\$\$ Whistling Teal, Jhadol Haveli, 103 Bhattiyana Chohatta, T0294-242 2067. Delicious traditional Rajasthani food, such as *kadai pakoda* and *gatta curry*, as well as a bit of everything from around the globe. It's in a lovely open courtyard with gardens and relaxed seating.

\$ Garden Hotel, opposite Gulab Bagh, Excellent Gujarati/Rajasthani vegetarian *thalis*, Rs 50, served in the former royal garage of the Maharanas of Mewar, an interesting circular building. The original fuel pumps can still be seen in the forecourt where 19 cars from the ancestral fleet have been displayed. Packed at lunch, less so for dinner, elderly Laurel-and-Hardyesque waiters shout at each other and forget things, food may arrive cold, but worth it for the experience.

UDAIPUR TO JODHPUR

Little-known Kumbhalgarh is one of the finest examples of defensive fortification in Rajasthan. You can wander around the palace, the many temples and along the walls – 36 km long in all – to savour the great panoramic views. It is two hours (63 km) north of Udaipur through the attractive Rajasthani countryside. The small fields are well kept and Persian wheels and 'tanks' are dotted across the landscape. In winter, wheat and mustard grow in the fields, and the journey there and back is as magical as the fort.

The temples of Ranakpur are incredibly ornate and amazingly unspoilt by tourism, having preserved a dignified air which is enhanced by the thick green forests that surround them. There are a number of interesting villages and palaces in the nearby area; if time allows this is a great region to explore at leisure, soaking in the unrushed, rural way of life.

Journeying between Udaipur and Jodhpur, there are many smaller oases to decamp to, including the beautiful Rawla Narlai which is dominated by a huge boulder and if you have the inclination you can climb to the beautiful Shiva temple at the very top of it. This area is rich in natural beauty and it's a great place to step back in time and take in what Rajasthan was like centuries ago.

→ NORTH OF UDAIPUR

EKLINGJI

ⓘ *0400-0700, 1000-1300 and 1700-1900. No photography. Occasional buses go from Udaipur to Eklingji and Nagda which are set in a deep ravine containing the Eklingji Lake. The RTDC (see page 110) run tours from Udaipur, 1400-1900.*

The white marble **Eklingji Temple** has a two-storey mandapa to Siva, the family deity of the Mewars. It dates from AD 734 but was rebuilt in the 15th century. There is a silver door and screen and a silver Nandi facing the black marble Siva. The evenings draw crowds of worshippers and few tourists. Many smaller temples surround the main one and are also worth seeing. Nearby is the large but simple **Lakulisa Temple** (AD 972), and other ruined semi-submerged temples. The back-street shops sell miniature paintings. It is a peaceful spot attracting many waterbirds.

→ KUMBHALGARH AND AROUND

KUMBHALGARH FORT

ⓘ *Foreigners Rs 100, Indians Rs 5.*

Kumbhalgarh Fort, off the beaten tourist track, was the second most important fort of the Mewar Kingdom after Chittaurgarh. Built mostly by Maharana Kumbha (circa 1485), it is situated on a west-facing ridge of the Aravalli hills, commanding a great strategic position on the border between the Rajput kingdoms of Udaipur (Mewar) and Jodhpur (Marwar). It is accessible enough to make a visit practicable and getting there is half the fun. There are superb views over the lower land to the northwest, standing over 200 m above the pass leading via Ghanerao towards Udaipur.

The approach Passing though charming villages and hilly terrain, the route to the fort is very picturesque. The final dramatic approach is across deep ravines and through thick scrub jungle. Seven gates guarded the approaches while seven ramparts were reinforced by semicircular bastions and towers. The 36-km-long black walls with curious bulbous towers exude a feeling of power as they snake their way up and down impossibly steep terrain. They were built to defy scaling and their width enabled rapid deployment of forces – six horses could walk along them side by side. The walls enclose a large plateau containing the smaller Katargarh Fort with the decaying palace of Fateh Singh, a garrison, 365 temples and shrines, and a village. The occupants (reputedly 30,000) could be self-sufficient in food and water, with enough storage to last a year. The fort's dominant location enabled defenders to see aggressors approaching from a great distance. Kumbhalgarh is believed to have been taken only once and that was because the water in the ponds was poisoned by enemy Mughals during the reign of Rana Pratap.

The gates The first gate **Arait Pol** is some distance from the main fort; the area was once thick jungle harbouring tigers and wild boar. Signals would be flashed by mirror in times of emergency. **Hulla Pol** (Gate of Disturbance) is named after the point reached by invading Mughal armies in 1567. **Hanuman Pol** contains a shrine and temple. The **Bhairava Pol** records the 19th-century chief minister who was exiled. The fifth gate, the **Paghra (Stirrup) Pol** is where the cavalry assembled; the Star tower nearby has walls 8 m thick. The Top-Khana (Cannon Gate) is alleged to have a secret escape tunnel. The last, **Nimbu (Lemon) Pol** has the Chamundi temple beside it.

The palace It is a 30-minute walk (fairly steep in parts) from the car park to the roof of the Maharana's darbar hall. Tiers of inner ramparts rise to the summit like a fairytale castle, up to the appropriately named Badal Mahal (19th century) or 'palace in the clouds', with the interior painted in pastel colours. Most of the empty palace is usually unlocked (a *chaukidar* holds the keys). The views over the walls to the jungle-covered hillsides (now a wildlife reserve) and across the deserts of Marwar towards Jodhpur, are stunning. The palace rooms are decorated in a 19th-century style and some have attractive coloured friezes, but are unfurnished. After the maze-like palace at Udaipur, this is very compact. The Maharana's palace has a remarkable blue darbar hall with floral motifs on the ceiling. Polished *chunar* (lime) is used on walls and window sills, but the steel ceiling girders give away its late 19th-century age. A gap separated the *mardana* (men's) palace from the *zenana* (women's) palace. Some of the rooms in the *zenana* have an attractive painted frieze with elephants, crocodiles and camels. A circular Ganesh temple is in the corner of the *zenana* courtyard. A striking feature of the toilets was the ventilation system which allowed fresh air into the room while the toilet was in use.

KUMBHALGARH WILDLIFE SANCTUARY
ⓘ *Foreigners Rs 100, Indians Rs 10, car Rs 65, open sunrise to sunset.*
The sanctuary to the west of the fort covering about 600 sq km has a sizeable wildlife population but you have to be extremely lucky to spot any big game in the thick undergrowth. Some visitors have seen bear, panther, wolf and hyena but most have to be contented with seeing nilgai, sambhar deer, wild boar, jackal, jungle cat and birds. Crocodiles and water fowl can be seen at **Thandi Beri Lake**. Jeep and horse safaris can be organized from hotels in the vicinity including **Aodhi**, **Ranakpur**, **Ghanerao** and **Narlai**. The rides can be quite demanding as the tracks are very rough. There is a 4WD jeep track and a trekking trail through the safari area can be arranged through **Shivika Lake Hotel**, Ranakpur (http://shivikalakehotel.com).

The tribal Bhils and Garasias – the latter found only in this belt – can be seen here, living in their traditional huts. The Forest Department may permit an overnight stay in their **Rest House** in **Kelwara**, the closest town, 6 km from sanctuary. With steep, narrow streets devoid of cars it is an attractive little place.

GHANERAO

Ghanerao was founded in 1606 by Gopal Das Rathore of the Mertia clan, and has a number of red sandstone *havelis* as well as several old temples, *baolis* and marble *chhatris*, 5 km beyond the reserve. The village lay at the entrance to one of the few passes through the Aravallis between the territories held by the Rajput princes of Jodhpur and Udaipur. The beautiful 1606 **royal castle** has marble pavilions, courtyards, paintings, wells, elephant stables and walls marked with canon balls. The present Thakur Sajjan Singh has opened his castle to guests and organizes two- to three-day treks to Kumbhalgarh Fort, 50 km by road accessible to jeep, and Ranakpur.

The **Mahavir Jain Temple**, 5 km away, is a beautiful little 10th-century temple. It is a delightful place to experience an unspoiled rural environment.

RAWLA NARLAI

Some 25 km from Kumbhalgarh Fort, and an hour's drive from Ranakpur, is a Hindu and Jain religious centre. It has a 17th-century fort with interesting architecture, right in the heart of the village, which is ideal for a stopover.

RANAKPUR

ⓘ *Daily; non-Jains are only allowed to visit the Adinatha 1200-1700, free. Photos with permission from Kalyanji Anandji Trust office next to the temple, camera Rs 50, video Rs 150, photography of the principal Adinatha image is prohibited. Shoes and socks must be removed at the entrance. Black clothing and shorts are not permitted. No tips, though unofficial 'guides' may ask for baksheesh.*

One of five holy Jain sites and a popular pilgrimage centre, it has one of the best-known Jain temple complexes in the country. Though not comparable in grandeur to the Dilwara temples in Mount Abu, it has very fine ornamentation and is in a wonderful setting with peacocks, langurs and numerous birds. The semi-enclosed deer park with spotted deer, nilgai and good birdlife next to the temple, attracts the occasional panther! You can approach Ranakpur from Kumbhalgarh through the wildlife reserve in 1½ hours although you will need to arrange transport from the Sanctuary entrance. A visit is highly recommended.

The **Adinatha** (1439), the most noteworthy of the three main temples here, is dedicated to the first Tirthankar. Of the 1444 engraved pillars, in Jain tradition, no two are the same, each individually carved. The sanctuary is symmetrically planned around the central shrine and is within a 100-sq-m raised terrace enclosed in a high wall with 66 subsidiary shrines lining it, each with a spire; the gateways consist of triple-storey porches. The sanctuary with a clustered centre tower contains a *chaumukha* (four-fold) marble image of Adinatha. The whole complex, including the extraordinary array of engraved pillars, carved ceilings and arches are intricately decorated, often with images of Jain saints, friezes of scenes from their lives and holy sites. The lace-like interiors of the corbelled domes are a superb example of western Indian temple style. The **Parsvanatha** and **Neminath** are two smaller Jain temples facing this, the former with a black image of Parsvanatha in the sanctuary and erotic carvings outside. The star-shaped **Surya Narayana Temple** (mid-15th century) is nearby.

There is a beautiful 3.7-km trek around the wildlife sanctuary, best attempted from November to March, contact sanctuary office next to temples for information.

→ SOUTH OF JODHPUR

The area south of Jodhpur is refreshingly green and fertile compared to the desert landscapes of most of Western Rajasthan (although it can be very dry from March until the monsoon). The landscape is mostly agricultural, punctuated by small, friendly villages, some housing stunning heritage hotels.

ROHET

Rohet, 50 km south of Jodhpur, was once a picturesque hamlet settled by the Bishnoi community. It is now a busy highway village although it has a busy bazar and is pleasant to wander around. At the end of the village a lake attracts numerous winter migrants in addition to resident birds. Here also are the family cenotaphs. Rohetgarh, a small 'castle' beside the lake, which has been converted in to a hotel, has a collection of antique hunting weapons. The hotel will organize trips to the local Bishnoi villages. It is quite usual to see blue bull, black buck and other antelopes in the fields. Village life can be very hard in this arid environment but the Bishnoi are a dignified people who delight in explaining their customs. You can take part in the opium tea ceremony which is quite fun and somewhat akin to having a pint with the locals down at the pub.

LUNI

The tiny bustling village of Luni, 40 km from Jodhpur, sits in the shadow of the 19th-century red sandstone Fort Chanwa which has been converted to a hotel. With its complex of courtyards, water wheels, and intricately carved façades, the fort and its village offer an attractive and peaceful alternative to the crowds of Jodhpur. The village of **Sanchean**, which you will pass through on the way, is worth exploring.

UDAIPUR TO JODHPUR LISTINGS

WHERE TO STAY

Kumbhalgarh and around

$$$$ Aodhi (HRH), 2 km from Kumbhalgarh Fort gate, T02954-242341, www.eternal mewar.in. Closest place to the fort, great location set in to the rock face. 27 rooms in modern stone 'cottages' decorated in colonial style to good effect with attached modern bathrooms. Beautiful restaurant and coffee shop, pool, relaxing atmosphere, very helpful staff, fabulous views, very quiet, superb horse safaris (US$200 per night), trekking, tribal village tours.

$$$$ Fort Rawla Narlai, Rawla Narlai, T(0)992-875 4913, www.rawlanarlai.com. Overlooked by a huge granite boulder, this place is rather special. The energy of the boulder and the temples and caves that are dotted around it, plus the beautifully renovated fort create a very serene place to hide away. 20 rooms (11 a/c) individually decorated with antiques, new showers, plus 5 luxurious, well-appointed 'tents', good simple meals under the stars, helpful, friendly staff, attractive garden setting, good riding. You can wander up to the Shiva temple on top of the boulder by scaling 700 steps. Check out the special dinner they host at a candlelit step well – so romantic.

$$$$-$$$ The Mana Hotel, Ranakpur–Sadri Rd, T011-4808 0000 (Delhi), www.manahotels.in. Innovative contemporary design in rural Rajasthan – quite unexpected and pulled off successfully. Lovely common areas, large glass and steel villas and a variety of rooms.

$$$ Maharani Bagh (WelcomHeritage), Ranakpur Rd, T02934-285105, www.welcomheritagehotels.in. 18 well-furnished modern bungalows with baths in lovely 19th-century walled orchard of Jodhpur royal family, full of bougainvillea and mangos, outdoor Rajasthani restaurant (traditional Marwari meals Rs 400), pool, jeep safaris, horse riding. Wake up call is care of the peacocks or langur monkeys tap dancing on the roof.

$$ Dera, Kelwara, T02954-242400, www.derakumbhalgarh.com. Great array of tents in 3 categories – some with a/c. Some of the tents are semi-permanent so are beautifully furnished, others are a fabulous purple inside rather than the standard white. Great views. Recommended.

Rural retreats south of Jodhpur

$$$$ Mihirgarh, an hour from Rohet, T982-902 3453, www.mihirgarh.com. The 'sun fortress' is a new venture from the team at **Rohetgarh** (see below) offering stunning suites with private courtyards and plunge pools. There is also an infinity pool, spa, beautiful restaurant and barbecue area and 360° views of the desert landscape. Breathtaking.

$$$ Rohetgarh, Rohet, T02936-268 231, www.rohetgarh.com. Come here to write a book. Both William Dalrymple and Bruce Chatwin have used the inspiring Rohetgarh to put pen to paper. Dating from 1622, there are a range of rooms (avoid rooms near outdoor restaurant). Fine Rajasthani food, ordinary architecture but in a beautiful environment, pleasant lake-view terraces, lovely pool, health club, riding and safaris to Bishnoi, Raika and artisans' villages, boating on the lake, a relaxing getaway. They have also set up a **Wilderness Camp** 17 km away in the desert.

$ Chhotaram Prajapat's Home Stay, Village Salawas, 20 km from Jodhpur on the way to Luni, T0291 2696744, www.salawashomestay.com. Atmospheric taste of village life, in fact they call themselves "an initiative in reality" rather than a hotel! Simple mud hut rooms, local food, village walks and friendly atmosphere.

JODHPUR AND AROUND

Rajasthan's second largest city, Jodhpur is entirely dominated by its spectacular Mehrangarh Fort, towering over proceedings below with absolute authority. You could spend most of a day wandering this grand stone edifice on its plinth of red rock, pausing in the warm shafts of sunlight in its honey-coloured courtyards and strolling its chunky, cannon-lined ramparts high above the moat of blue buildings which make up the old city. Up there, birds of prey circle on the thermals, close to eye level, while the city hums below, its rickshaw horns and occasional calls to prayer still audible. Jodhpur's fascinating old city is a hive of activity, the colourful bazars, narrow lanes and bustling Sardar Market frequented by equally colourful tribal people from the surrounding areas. South of the railway line things are altogether more serene, and nowhere more so than the impressive Umaid Bhawan Palace, its classic exterior belying the art deco extravaganza within. There are also some remarkable sights around Jodhpur: the temples of Osian and Nagaur are well worth a visit and there are some great heritage hotels set in quiet nearby villages.

→ JODHPUR

ARRIVING IN JODHPUR

Getting there Jodhpur has good air, rail and road links with the other major cities of Rajasthan as well as Delhi and Mumbai. From Udaipur it is a stunning drive through the hills to Kumbhalgarh and Ranakpur, but alas after Ranakpur the road deteriorates and it's a bumpy old journey onto Jodhpur, so it's good to stop along the way at Kumbhalgarh or Rawla Narlai. There is no train line, but regular buses ply this route, or you can opt for a driver if you prefer.

Moving on Nagaur (see page 131) is just 137 km from Jodhpur and there are regular bus services from the RST bus stand. Alternatively, you can opt for a driver to make the going easier.

Getting around The train and bus stations are conveniently located close to the old city, with most hotels a Rs 20-30 rickshaw ride away, while the airport is 5 km south of town. The old city is small enough to walk around, although many people find a rented bicycle the best way to get about.

Tourist information The government tourist office is on the grounds of the RTDC ① *Hotel Ghoomar*, High Court Rd, T0291-254 4010. As well as the usual supply of maps and pamphlets, it also organize half-day city tours and village safaris. Also, **Tourist Assistance Force** has a presence at the railway station bus stand and clock tower.

BACKGROUND

The **Rathore** Rajputs had moved to **Marwar** – the 'region of death' – in 1211, after their defeat at Kanauj by Muhammad Ghori. In 1459 Rao Jodha, forced to leave the Rathore capital at Mandore, 8 km to the north, chose this place as his capital because of its strategic location on the edge of the Thar Desert. The Rathores subsequently controlled wide areas of Rajasthan. Rao Udai Singh of Jodhpur (died 1581) received the title of Raja from Akbar, and his son, Sawai Raja Sur Singh (died 1595), conquered Gujarat and part of the Deccan for the emperor. Maharaja Jaswant Singh (died 1678), having supported Shah Jahan in the Mughal struggle for succession in 1658, had a problematic relationship with the subsequent Mughal rule of Aurangzeb, and his son Ajit Singh was only able to succeed him after Aurangzeb's own death in 1707. In addition to driving the Mughals out of Ajmer he added substantially to the Mehrangarh Fort in Jodhpur. His successor, Maharaja Abhai Singh (died 1749) captured Ahmedabad, and the state came into treaty relations with the British in 1818.

Jodhpur lies on the once-strategic Delhi–Gujarat trading route and the Marwaris managed and benefited from the traffic of opium, copper, silk, sandalwood, dates, coffee and much more besides.

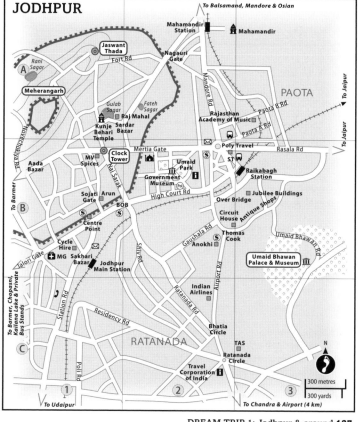

The Old City is surrounded by a huge 9.5-km-long wall which has 101 bastions and seven gates, above which are inscribed the names of the places to which the roads underneath them lead. It comprises a labyrinthine maze of narrow streets and lively markets, a great place to wander round and get lost. Some of the houses and temples are of richly carved stone, in particular the red sandstone buildings of the Siré (Sardar) Bazar. Here the **Taleti Mahal** (early 17th century), one of three concubines' palaces in Jodhpur, has the unique feature of *jarokhas* decorated with temple columns.

MEHRANGARH

ⓘ *T0291-254 8790, 0900-1700, foreigners Rs 400 (including audio), students Rs 300, Indians Rs 60, includes excellent MP3 audio guide and camera fee, video Rs 200, allow at least 2 hrs, there is a pleasant restaurant on the terrace near the ticket office. For a novel way of viewing the fort, try ziplining with Flying Fox, www.flyingfox.asia (there are 6 ziplines).*

The 'Majestic Fort' sprawls along the top of a steep escarpment with a sheer drop to the south. Originally started by Rao Jodha in 1459, it has walls up to 36 m high and 21 m wide, towering above the plains. Most of what stands today is from the period of Maharajah Jaswant Singh (1638-1678). On his death in 1678, Aurangzeb occupied the fort. However, after Aurangzeb's death Mehrangarh returned to Jaswant Singh's son Ajit Singh and remained the royal residence until the Umaid Bhavan was completed in 1943. It is now perhaps the best preserved and presented palace in Rajasthan, an excellent example which the others will hopefully follow.

The summit has three areas: the palace (northwest), a wide terrace to the east of the palace, and the strongly fortified area to the south. There are extensive views from the top. One approach is by a winding path up the west side, possible by rickshaw, but the main approach and car park is from the east. The climb is quite stiff; those with walking difficulties may use the elevator (Rs 15 each way).

The gateways There were originally seven gateways. The first, the **Fateh Gate**, is heavily fortified with spikes and a barbican that forces a 45° turn. The smaller **Gopal Gate** is followed by the **Bhairon Gate**, with large guardrooms. The fourth, **Toati Gate**, is now missing but the fifth, **Dodhkangra Gate**, marked with cannon shots, stands over a turn in the path and has loopholed battlements for easy defence. Next is the **Marti Gate**, a long passage flanked by guardrooms. The last, **Loha (Iron) Gate**, controls the final turn into the fort and has handprints (31 on one side and five on the other) of royal *satis*, the wives of maharajas. It is said that six queens and 58 concubines became *satis* on Ajit Singh's funeral pyre in 1724. *Satis* carried the Bhagavad Gita with them into the flames and legend has it that the holy book would never perish. The main entrance is through the **Jay (Victory) Pol.**

The palaces From the Loha Gate the ramp leads up to the Suraj (Sun) Pol, which opens onto the Singar Choki Chowk, the main entrance to the museum, see below. Used for royal ceremonies such as the anointing of rajas, the north, west and southwest sides of the Singar Choki Chowk date from the period immediately before the Mughal occupation in 1678. The upper storeys of the chowk were part of the *zenana*, and from the **Jhanki Mahal** (glimpse palace) on the upper floor of the north wing the women could look down on the activities of the courtyard. Thus the chowk below has the features characteristic of much of the rest of the *zenana*, *jarokhas* surmounted by the distinctive Bengali-style eaves and beautifully ornate *jali* screens. These allowed cooling breezes to ventilate rooms and corridors in the often stiflingly hot desert summers.

Also typical of Mughal buildings was the use of material hung from rings below the eaves to provide roof covering, as in the columned halls of the **Daulat Khana** and the **Sileh Khana** (armoury), which date from Ajit Singh's reign. The collection of Indian weapons in the armoury is unequalled, with remarkable swords and daggers, often beautifully decorated with calligraphy. Shah Jahan's red silk and velvet tent, lavishly embroidered with gold thread and used in the Imperial Mughal campaign, is in the **Tent Room**. The **Jewel House** has a wonderful collection of jewellery, including diamond eyebrows held by hooks over the ears. There are also palanquins, howdahs and ornate royal cradles, all marvellously well preserved.

The **Phool Mahal** (Flower Palace), above the Sileh Khana, was built by Abhai Singh (1724-1749) as a hall of private audience. The stone *jali* screens are original and there are striking portraits of former rulers, a lavishly gilded ceiling and the Jodhpur coat of arms displayed above the royal couch; the murals of the 36 musical modes are a late 19th-century addition.

The **Umaid Vilas**, which houses Rajput miniatures, is linked to the **Sheesh Mahal** (Mirror Palace), built by Ajit Singh between 1707 and 1724. The room has characteristic large and regularly sized mirror work, unlike Mughal 'mirror palaces'. Immediately to its south, and above the Sardar Vilas, is the **Takhat Vilas**. Added by Maharajah Takhat Singh (1843-1873), it has wall murals of dancing girls, love legends and Krishna Lila, while its ceiling has two unusual features: massive wooden beams to provide support and the curious use of colourful Belgian Christmas tree balls.

The **Ajit Vilas** has a fascinating collection of musical instruments and costumes. On the ground floor of the Takhat Vilas is **Sardar Vilas**, and to its south the **Khabka** and **Chandan Mahals** (sleeping quarters). The **Moti Vilas** wings to the north, east and south of the Moti Mahal Chowk, date from Jaswant Singh's reign. The women could watch proceedings in the courtyard below through the *jali* screens of the surrounding wings. Tillotson suggests that the **Moti Mahal** (**Pearl Palace**) ① *Rs 150 for 15 mins*, to the west, although placed in the *zenana* of the fort, was such a magnificent building that it could only have served the purpose of a Diwan-i-Am (Hall of Public Audience). The Moti Mahal is fronted by excellently carved 19th-century woodwork, while inside waist-level niches housed oil lamps whose light would have shimmered from the mirrored ceiling. A palmist reads your fortune at Moti Mahal Chowk (museum area).

Mehrangarh Fort Palace Museum is in a series of palaces with beautifully designed and decorated windows and walls. It has a magnificent collection of the maharajas' memorabilia – superbly maintained and presented.

Jaswant Thada ① *off the road leading up to the fort, 0900-1700, Rs 30*, is the cremation ground of the former rulers with distinctive memorials in white marble which commemorate Jaswant Singh II (1899) and successive rulers of Marwar. It is situated in pleasant and well-maintained gardens and is definitely worth visiting on the way back from the fort.

→ THE NEW CITY

The new city beyond the walls is also of interest. Overlooking the Umaid Sagar is the **Umaid Bhawan Palace** on Chittar Hill. Building started in 1929 as a famine relief exercise when the monsoon failed for the third year running. Over 3000 people worked for 14 years, building this vast 347-room palace of sandstone and marble. The hand-hewn blocks are interlocked into position, and use no mortar. It was designed by HV Lanchester, with the most modern furnishing and facilities in mind, and completed in 1943. The interior decoration was left to the artist JS Norblin, a refugee from Poland; he painted the frescoes in the Throne Room (East Wing). For the architectural historian, Tillotson, it is "the finest example of Indo-Deco. The forms are crisp and precise, and the bland monochrome of the stone makes the eye concentrate on their carved shapes". The royal family still occupy part of the palace.

The **Umaid Bhawan Palace Museum** ① *T0291-251 0101, 0900-1700, Rs 50*, includes the Darbar Hall with its elegantly flaking murals plus a good collection of miniatures, armour and quirky old clocks as well as a bizarre range of household paraphernalia; if it was fashionable in the 1930s, expensive and not available in India, it's in here. Many visitors find the tour and the museum in general disappointing with not much to see (most of the china and glassware you could see in your grandma's cabinets). The palace hotel which occupies the majority of the building has been beautifully restored, but is officially inaccessible to non-residents; try sneaking in for a cold drink and a look at the magnificent domed interior, a remarkable separation from the Indian environment in which it is set.

Government Museum ① *Umaid Park, Sat-Thu 1000-1630, Rs 3*, is a time-capsule from the British Raj, little added since Independence, with some moth-eaten stuffed animals and featherless birds, images of Jain Tirthankars, miniature portraits and antiquities. A small zoo in the gardens has a few rare exotic species.

Just southeast of Raikabagh Station are the **Raikabagh Palace** and the **Jubilee Buildings**, public offices designed by Sir Samuel Swinton Jacob in the Indo-Saracenic style. On the Mandore Road, 2 km to the north, is the large **Mahamandir Temple**.

→ EXCURSIONS FROM JODHPUR

A village safari visiting a **Bishnoi village** is recommended, although they have naturally become more touristy over the years. Most tours include the hamlets of **Guda**, famous for wildlife, **Khejarali**, a well-known Bishnoi village, **Raika** cameleers' settlement and **Salawas**, see page 125.

Majestic Marwar – Rural Villages Tours, created by the excellent **Virasat Experiences** (www.virasatexperiences.com, based in Jaipur), run a very intesting non-touristy trip into the villages around Jodhpur with an interesting twist. The tour costs Rs 2500 per person, but Rs 500 of that goes to the villages to create rainwater harvesting projects and improve hygiene. You are really giving something back here, in contrast to some of the other 'tribal' tours touted locally which are exploitative.

The small, semi-rural village of **Jhalamand**, 12 km south of Jodhpur, is a good alternative to staying in the city, particularly if you have your own transport. It works especially well as a base from which to explore the Bishnoi and Raika communities.

Marwar, 8 km north of Jodhpur, is the old 14th-century capital of Mandore, situated on a plateau. Set around the old cremation ground with the red sandstone *chhatris* of the Rathore rulers, the gardens are usually crowded with Indian tourists at weekends. The **Shrine of the 33 Crore Gods** is a hall containing huge painted rock-cut figures of heroes and gods, although some of the workmanship is a little crude. The largest deval, a combination of temple and cenotaph, is Ajit Singh's (died 1724); it is worth a closer look but is unkempt. The remains of an eighth-century Hindu temple is on a hilltop nearby.

Bal Samand Lake is the oldest artificial lake in Rajasthan, 5 km north. Dating from 1159, it is surrounded by parkland laid out in 1936 where the 19th-century **Hawa Mahal** was turned into a royal summer palace. Although the interior is European in style, it has entirely traditional red sandstone filigree windows and beautifully carved balconies. The peaceful and well-maintained grounds exude calm and tranquillity, while the views over the lake are simply majestic.

→ AROUND JODHPUR

The temples of Osian are remarkable as much for their location in the middle of the desert as their architecture, while Nagaur is one of Rajasthan's busiest but most unaffected cities. Leaving the city, the landscape soon becomes agricultural, punctuated by small, friendly villages, some housing stunning heritage hotels.

OSIAN

Surrounded by sand dunes, this ancient town north of Jodhpur in the Thar Desert contains the largest group of eighth- to 10th-century Hindu and Jain temples in Rajasthan. The typical Pratihara Dynasty **temple complex** is set on a terrace whose walls are finely decorated with mouldings and miniatures. The sanctuary walls have central projections with carved panels' and above these rise curved towers. The doorways are usually decorated with river goddesses, serpents and scrollwork. The 23 temples are grouped in several sites north, west and south of the town. The western group contains a mixture of Hindu temples, including the **Surya Temple** (early eighth century) with beautifully carved pillars. The Jain **Mahavira Temple** (eighth- to 10th-century), the best preserved, 200 m further on a hillock, rises above the town and boasts a fantastically gaudy interior. The 11th- to 12th-century **Sachiya Mata Temple** is a living temple of the Golden Durga. Osian is well worth visiting.

KHIMSAR

On the edge of the desert, 80 km northeast of Jodhpur, Khimsar was founded by the Jain saint Mahavir 2500 years ago. The isolated, battle scarred, 16th-century moated castle of which a section remains, had a *zenana* added in the mid-18th century and a regal wing added in the 1940s.

NAGAUR

ⓘ *Foreigners Rs 50, Indians Rs 10, camera Rs 25, video Rs 50.*

Nagaur, 137 km north of Jodhpur, was a centre of Chishti Sufis. It attracts interest as it preserves some fine examples of pre-Mughal and Mughal architecture. The dull stretch of desert is enlivened by Nagaur's fort palace, temples and *havelis*. The city walls are said to date from the 11th- to 12th-century Chauhan period. Akbar built the mosque here and there is a shrine of the disciple of Mu'inuddin Chishti of Ajmer. **Ahhichatragarh Fort**, which dominates the city, is absolutely vast, contains palaces of the Mughal emperors and of the Marwars, and was restored with help from the Paul Getty Foundation and under the watchful eye of Maharah Gaj Singh of Jodhpur. It is quite an exceptional renovation The Akbar Mahal is stunningly elegant and perfectly proportioned. The fort also has excellent wall paintings and interesting ancient systems of rainwater conservation and storage, ably explained by a very knowledgeable curator. It was awarded a UNESCO Heritage Award in 2000. One of the most spectacular forts in Rajasthan with its conscientious renovation and going back to it's ancient Sufi history, it now hosts the **World Sufi Spirit Festival** every February.

KHICHAN

Four kilometres from Phalodi, southwest of Bikaner just off the NH15, is a lovely, picturesque village with superb red sandstone *havelis* of the Oswal Jains. Beyond the village are sand dunes and mustard fields, and a lake which attracts ducks and other waterfowl. The once-small, quiet village has grown into a bustling agricultural centre and a prominent bird-feeding station. Jain villagers put out grain behind the village for winter visitors; up to 8000 demoiselle cranes and occasionally common eastern cranes can be seen in December and January on the feeding grounds. At present you can go along and watch without charge.

POKARAN

Pokaran, between Jaisalmer and Jodhpur, stands on the edge of the great desert with dunes stretching 100 km west to the Pakistan border. It provides tourists with a mid-way stopover between Bikaner/Jodhpur and Jaisalmer as it did for royal and merchant caravans in the past. The impressive 16th-century yellow sandstone **Pokaran fort** ① *foreigners Rs 50, Indians Rs 10, camera Rs 50*, overlooking a confusion of streets in the town below, has a small museum with an interesting collection of medieval weapons, costumes and paintings. There are good views from the ramparts. Pokaran is also well known for its potters who make red-and-white pottery and terracotta horses/elephants. **Ramdeora**, the Hindu and Jain pilgrim centre nearby, has Bishnoi hamlets and a preserve for blackbuck antelope, Indian gazelle, bustards and sand grouse. **Ramdeora Fair** (September) is an important religious event with cattle trading.

JODHPUR AND AROUND LISTINGS

WHERE TO STAY

Jodhpur

$$$$ Raas, Tunvarji Ka Jhalra, Makrana Mohalla, www.raasjodhpur.com, T0291-263 6455. **Raas** is a gem at the heart of the city, built from the same warm rose-red sandstone as the fort that towers above it. Stunning balconies with carved stone shutters discreetly open up to reveal exceptional fort views. There is a contemporary vibe inspired by the essence of Rajasthan, rather than the traditional 'heritage-style' and yet it blends into the old city – it looks chic and stylish without looking out of place. As well as all the mod cons, you will find sumptuous fabrics and evocative photographs in every room. There are 2 restaurants, one open for non-residents as well as a very inviting pool.

$$$$-$$$ Ajit Bhawan, Circuit House Rd, T0291-251 3333, www.ajitbhawan.com. With a rather imposing palace façade, it is hard to imagine the variety of rooms, cottages and tents at this fantastic property. All luxuriously kitted out, the cottages are particularly beautiful. There is a very ornate swimming pool, several restaurants on site, an opulent bar and heaps of character. This, India's first heritage hotel, started in 1927 and still leads the way.

$$$ Bal Samand Palace (WelcomHeritage), T0291-257 2321, www.welcomheritagehotels.com. Just north of Jodhpur city, this is essentially 2 properties together, the Palace and the Garden Retreat. In extensive grounds on the lake, there are 10 attractively furnished suites in an atmospheric palace and 26 'garden retreat' rooms in the imaginatively renovated stables. There's a restaurant (mainly buffet), lovely pool, boating, pleasant orchards which attract nilgai, jackals and peacocks, and a calming, tranquil atmosphere.

$$ Devi Bhavan, 1 Ratanada Circle, T0291-251 1067, www.devibhawan.com. Beautiful rooms with bath and most with a/c, delightful shady garden with lovely new pool, excellent Indian dinner (set timings), Rajput family home. This is a very special place.

$$ Haveli Inn Pal, T0291-261 2519, www.haveliinnpal.com. Quirkily designed rooms, some have huge windows overlooking the fort, others have lake views and unusual marble shower troughs, while others still have beds you need a ladder to get into. Fantastic furniture, great rooftop restaurant with commanding views and a rare patch of lawn, pleasant.

$$ Juna Mahal, Ada Bazar, Daga St, T0291-244 5511, www.junamahal.com. A special little place, this recently renovated 472-year-old *haveli* has bags of charm and stylish decor. Lord Krishna room is particularly lovely.

$$-$ Singhvi's Haveli, Navchokiya, Ramdevjika Chowk, T0291-262 4293, singhvi15adhaveli@ hotmail.com. 11 rooms in charming, 500-year-old *haveli* (one of the oldest), tastefully decorated, friendly family. New extra-special suite with mirror-work ceiling reminiscent of the fort that towers above. Nice chill-out area.

$ Yogi's Guest House, Raj Purohit Ji Ki Haveli, Manak Chowk, old town, T0291-264 3436, yogiguesthouse@hotmail.com. 12 rooms, most in 500-year-old *haveli*, clean, modern bathrooms, camel/jeep safaris, experienced management. Very popular – book ahead. Lovely atmosphere.

Nagaur

$$$$ Ranvas, T0291-257 2321 (Jodhana Heritage), www.ranvasnagaur.com. Stunningly restored *havelis* within the magical fort of Nagaur. This new venture is extremely stylish and yet comfortable.

Beautiful furnishings, sumptuous fabrics, rare artefacts, charming courtyards and secluded spots, **Ranvas** is effortlessly chic. The rooms are converted from the *havelis* of the 16 wives of the Royal Court. There is an amazing pool and delicious restaurant. You also get a spectacular private tour of the fort.

$$$$ Royal Camp, T0291-257 2321, www.jodhanaheritagehotels.com. Operates Oct-Mar and during the camel fair (when the price rises.) 20 delightful deluxe 2-bed furnished tents (hot water bottles, heaters, etc), flush toilets, hot water in buckets, stunning dining area, all inside fort walls. Although you seem very secluded, Nagaur Fort is right in the middle of the city and not elevated, so you do get traffic and mosque noise. An experience.

$ Mahaveer International, Vijay Vallabh Chowk, near bus stand, T01582-243158, www.minagaur.com. 15 reasonable rooms, 7 a/c, huge dining hall, friendly knowledgeable manager.

RESTAURANTS

Jodhpur

$$$ Bijolai, Water Habitat Retreat, Air Force Radar Rd, Kailana Lake, T(0)810-400 0909, www.1559AD.com. This is another serving by the team behind **1559AD** Udaipur (see page 120). There are mixed reports on the food and service, although the location and ambience is unbeatable. There is indoor dining as well as lakeside gazebos. It's 8 km from city.

$$$ Chokelao Terrace, T0291-255 5389, www.mehrangarh.org. What a backdrop! Great Rajasthani food as you sit perched over the city of Jodhpur at the majestic Mehrengarh Fort. Breathtaking.

$$ Indique, Pal Haveli behind clock tower and next to **Haveli Inn Pal**. Beautiful rooftop restaurant by the clock tower. They describe their food as "good, wholesome, spicy and traditional" with recipes passed down through the generations. Great views.

$$ On the Rocks, near **Ajit Bhawan**, T0291-510 2701. Good mix of Indian and continental, plus a relaxing bar, patisserie, ice cream parlour and lovely gardens.

$$ Sankalp, 12th Rd (west of city centre). 1030-2300. Upmarket a/c South Indian, *dosas* come with a fantastic range of chutneys, good service.

$ Jhankar, follow signs to next to **Ganesh Guest House**. This little courtyard café has great character – very pretty and a menu of all the usual traveller favourites to boot.

JAISALMER AND AROUND

The approach to Jaisalmer is magical as the city rises out of the vast barren desert like an approaching ship. With its crenellated sandstone walls and narrow streets lined with exquisitely carved buildings, through which camel carts trundle leisurely, it has an extraordinarily medieval feel and an incredible atmosphere. The fort inside, perched on its hilltop, contains some gems of Jain temple building, while beautifully decorated merchants' havelis are scattered through the town. Once inside the fort walls looking out to the desert, it's easy to imagine caravans and camels sweeping across towards you in a dream of Arabian nights, but what you actually see are growing legions of windmills flanking the dunes in the distance. Unlike the other forts you visit in Rajasthan, Jaisalmer's is fully alive with shops, restaurants and guesthouses inside its walls and labyrinthine alleyways. It's beautiful to wander the tiny streets always finding a new nook or a great view.

All this has not failed to attract the attention of mass tourism, and at times Jaisalmer can feel overrun with package tourists, being swept from one shop to the next in a whirlwind of rapid consumption by insistent guides. Over the years, increased development of guesthouses and businesses within the walls has put pressure on the sewage, drainage and foundations of the fort. Three of the 99 bastions crumbled a couple of years ago and several people were killed. These bastions have now been replaced, but if you look at the fort bastions from the outside you can see signs of water discolouration.

If you find Jaisalmer's magic diminished there's always the romantic desolation of the Thar Desert, easily accessible beyond the edge of the city. Many of the settlements close to the city have become well used to tourists, so it's worth venturing a little further out to get an idea of life in the desert. Highlights include the remarkable ghost city of Khuldera and, of course, the chance to take it all in from on top of a camel.

ARRIVING IN JAISALMER

Getting there The nearest airport is at Jodhpur, 275 km away, which is connected to Jaisalmer by buses and several daily trains.

There are regular buses from Bikaner, Nagaur and Jodhpur to Jaisalmer and the train from Jodhpur is slightly faster than it used to be – it can be quicker to take the bus. The *Dli Jsm Express (14659)* leaves at the rather unsocial hour of 0530 but arrives in Jaisalmer at 1115. Most long-distance buses arrive at the bus stand, a 15-minute walk from the fort. Your hotel may offer a pick-up. If not, have a place in mind and prepare for a barrage of competing touts.

Moving on The new civil airport in Jaisalmer is due to open in 2013. Spicejet will be operating flights back to Delhi for the final stage of this trip.

If you have more time on your hands, you could take the train or bus, breaking your journey in the fort town of Bikaner before making your way back to Delhi. The other cross-country train route would be onward to Jodhpur–Ajmer–Jaipur and finally into Delhi.

Getting around Unmetered jeeps and auto-rickshaws can be hired at the station but they are no help inside the fort so you may have to carry your luggage some distance uphill if you choose a fort hotel. Rickshaws are allowed into the fort at certain times.

You can hire a bike from **Gopa Chowk** (Rs 30), though the town is best explored on foot. Most hotels and restaurants are clustered around the two chowks and inside the fort.

Tourist information RTDC ⓘ *near TRC, Station Rd, Gadi Sagar Pol, T02992-252406, 0800-1200, 1500-1800.* Counter at railway station.

BACKGROUND

Founded by Prince Jaisal in 1156, Jaisalmer grew to be a major staging post on the trade route across the forbidding Thar Desert from India to the West. The merchants prospered and invested part of their wealth in building beautiful houses and temples with the local sandstone. The growth of maritime trade between India and the West caused a decline in trade across the desert which ceased altogether in 1947. However, the wars with Pakistan (1965 and 1971) resulted in the Indian government developing the transport facilities to the border to improve troop movement. This has also helped visitors gain access. Today, the army and tourism are mainstays of the local economy; hotel touts and pushy shopkeepers have become a problem in recent years.

→ PLACES IN JAISALMER

THE FORT

ⓘ *Best light for photography is late afternoon.*

On the roughly triangular-shaped Trikuta Hill, the fort stands 76 m above the town, enclosed by a 9-km wall with 99 bastions (mostly 1633-1647). Often called the Golden

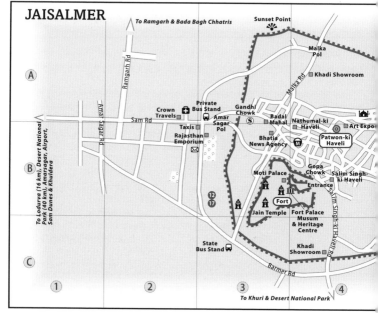

JAISALMER

Fort because of the colour of its sandstone walls, it dominates the town. You enter the fort from the east from Gopa Chowk. The Suraj Pol (1594), once an outer gate, is flanked by heavy bastions and has bands of decoration which imitate local textile designs. Take a walk through the narrow streets within the fort, often blocked by the odd goat or cow, and see how even today about 1000 of the town's people live in tiny houses inside the fort often with beautiful carvings on doors and balconies. It is not difficult to get lost.

As with many other Rajput forts, within the massive defences are a series of palaces, the product of successive generations of rulers' flights of fancy. The local stone is relatively easy to carve and the dry climate has meant that the fineness of detail has been preserved through the centuries. The *jali* work and delicately ornamented balconies and windows with wide eaves break the solidity of the thick walls, giving protection from the heat, while the high plinths of the buildings keep out the sand.

The entire **Fort Palace Museum and Heritage Centre** ① *0800-1800 summer, 0900-1800 winter, foreigners Rs 250 includes an excellent audio guide and camera, Indians Rs 10, video Rs 150*, has been renovated and an interesting series of displays established, including sculpture, weapons, paintings and well-presented cultural information. The view from the roof, the highest point inside the fort, is second to none. The **Juna Mahal** (circa 1500) of the seven-storey palace with its *jali* screens is one of the oldest Rajasthani palaces. The rather plain *zenana* block to its west, facing the *chauhata* (square) is decorated with false *jalis*. Next to it is the *mardana* (men's quarters) including the Rang Mahal above the Hawa Pol, built during the reign of Mulraj II (1762-1820), which has highly detailed murals and mirror decoration. **Sarvotam Vilas** built by Akhai Singh (1722-1762) is ornamented with blue tiles and glass mosaics. The adjacent **Gaj Vilas** (1884) stands on a high plinth. Mulraj II's **Moti Mahal** has floral decoration and carved doors.

To Mohangarh (NH15)

Kishanghat Pol

Jethwai Rd

To Jodhpur (30 km)

To Wood Fossil Park (17 km)

Auto Stand

Gadi Sagar Pol

Barmer Rd

Desert Cultural Centre

Desert National Park Office

Tilon-ki Pol

N

Gadi Sagar

200 metres

200 yards

5   6

The open square beyond the gates has a platform reached by climbing some steps; this is where court was held or royal visitors entertained. There are also fascinating **Jain temples** (12th-16th centuries) ① *0700-1200, Rs 10, camera Rs 50, video Rs 100, leather shoes not permitted*, within the fort. Whilst the Rajputs were devout Hindus they permitted the practice of Jainism. The **Parsvanatha** (1417) has a fine gateway, an ornate porch and 52 subsidiary shrines surrounding the main structure. The brackets are elaborately carved as maidens and dancers. The exterior of the **Rishbhanatha** (1479) has more than 600 images as decoration whilst clusters of towers form the roof of the **Shantinatha** built at the same time. **Ashtapadi** (16th century) incorporates the Hindu deities of Vishnu, Kali and Lakshmi

ON THE ROAD

On a camel's back

Camel safaris draw many visitors to Jaisalmer. They allow an insight into otherwise inaccessible desert interiors and a chance to see rural life, desert flora and wildlife. The 'safari' is not a major expedition into the middle of nowhere. Instead, it is often along tracks, stopping off for sightseeing at temples and villages along the way. The camel driver/owner usually drives the camel or rides alongside (avoid one sharing your camel), usually for two hours in the morning and three hours in the afternoon, with a long lunch stop in between. There is usually jeep or camel cart backup with tents and 'kitchen' close by, though thankfully out of sight. It can be fun, especially if you are with companions and have a knowledgeable camel driver.

Camel safaris vary greatly in quality with prices ranging from around Rs 500 per night for the simplest (sleeping in the open, vegetarian meals) to those costing Rs 4500 (deluxe double-bedded tents with attached Western baths). Bear in mind that it is practically impossible for any safari organizer to cover his costs at anything less than Rs 500 – if you're offered cheaper tours, assume they'll be planning to get their money back by other means, ie shopping/drug selling along the way. Safaris charging Rs 500-1000 can be adequate (tents, mattresses, linen, cook, jeep support, but no toilets). It's important to ascertain what is included in the price and what are extras.

The popular 'Around Jaisalmer' route includes **Bada Bagh**, **Ramkunda**, **Moolsagar**, **Sam dunes**, **Lodurva** and **Amar Sagar** with three nights in the desert. Some routes now include **Kuldhara**'s medieval ruins and the colourful **Kahla** village, as well as **Deda**, **Jaseri lake** (good birdlife) and **Khaba** ruins (with a permit). Most visitors prefer to take a two-day/one-night or three-day/two-night camel safari, with jeep transfer back to Jaisalmer. A more comfortable alternative is to be jeeped to a tented/hut camp in the desert as a base for a night and enjoy a camel trek during the day without losing out on the evening's entertainment under the stars. A short camel ride in town up to Sunset Point (or at Sam/ Khuri) is one alternative to a safari before deciding on a long haul, and also offers great views of upper levels of *havelis* – but watch out for low-slung electric wires! Prepaid camel rides have now been introduced – Rs 80 for a 30-minute ride. For some, "half an hour is enough to ride a tick-ridden animal". Make sure you cover up all exposed skin and use sunscreen to avoid getting burnt.

Sunny Tours, Shahi Palace, T(0)94143-65495, www.sunnytourntravels.com, is one of the oldest tour operators in Jaisalmer. They offer fantastic camel and jeep safaris. You are in good hands with this professional team, they have separate bed rolls for sleeping (not just what you have been sitting on for sunset and dinner), they provide tents in the winter as well as delicious food, fruit and cookies and your very own camel. You can go on camel safari for half a day up to as many days as you like (or can stand). Their route takes in the usual peaceful dunes and tribal villages. If you fancy a more regal and upmarket affair try **Rajasthan Desert Safaris**, T(0)9414-140109, www.desertsafarijaisalmer.com, who have Swiss-cottage tents with attached toilets near the dunes at Rs 4500 per night. It is quite magical to be in the lap of luxury under the desert sky.

into its decoration. The **Mahavir Temple** ⓘ *view 1000-1100*, has an emerald statue. The **Sambhavanatha** ⓘ *1000-1100*, (1431) has vaults beneath it that were used for document storage. The **Gyan Bhandar** here is famous for its ancient manuscripts.

HAVELIS

There are many exceptional *havelis* in the fort and in the walled town. Many have beautifully carved façades, *jali* screens and oriel windows overhanging the streets below. The ground floor is raised above the dusty streets and each has an inner courtyard surrounded by richly decorated apartments. Further east, **Patwon-ki Haveli** (1805) ① *1030-1700, foreigners Rs 150, Indians Rs 50 (audio tour Rs 250/ camera Rs 50) is the best of the restored havelis* and you get a beautiful view from the rooftop. It's a cluster of five *havelis* built for five brothers. They have beautiful murals and carved pillars. A profusion of balconies cover the front wall and the inner courtyard is surrounded by richly decorated apartments; parts have been well restored. The main courtyard and some roofs are now used as shops. The views from the decorative windows are stunning.

Inside Amar Sagar Pol, the former ruler's 20th-century palace **Badal Mahal** with a five-storeyed tower, has fine carvings. **Nathumal-ki Haveli** (1885), nearer Gandhi Chowk, was built for the prime minister. Partly carved out of rock by two craftsmen, each undertaking one half of the house, it has a highly decorative façade with an attractive front door guarded by two elephants. Inside is a wealth of decoration; notice the tiny horse-drawn carriage and a locomotive showing European influence.

DESERT CULTURAL CENTRE

① *Gadisar Circle, T02992-252 188, 1000-1700, Rs 10.*

The Desert Cultural Centre was established in 1997 with the aim of preserving the culture of the desert. The museum contains a varied display of fossils, paintings, instruments, costumes and textiles which give an interesting glimpse in to life in the desert. The charismatic founder, Mr Sharma, has written several books on Jaisalmer.

GADI SAGAR TANK

The Gadi Sagar (Gadisar or Gharisar) tank, southeast of the city walls, was the oasis which led Prince Jaisal to settle here. Now connected by a pipe to the Indira Gandhi Canal, it has water all year. It attracts migratory birds and has many small shrines around it and is well worth visiting, especially in the late afternoon. The delightful archway is said to have been constructed by a distinguished courtesan who built a temple on top to prevent the king destroying the gate.

→ AROUND JAISALMER

AMAR SAGAR AND LODURVA

The pleasant **Amar Sagar** ① *5 km northwest of Jaisalmer, foreigners Rs 30, Indians free, camera Rs 50, video Rs 100*, was once a formal garden with a pleasure palace of Amar Singh (1661-1703) on the bank of a lake which dries up during the hot season. The Jain temple there has been restored.

A further 10 km away is **Lodurva** ① *0630-1930, foreigners Rs 20, Indians free, camera Rs 50, video Rs 100*, which contains a number of Jain temples that are the only remains of a once-flourishing Marwar capital. Rising honey-coloured out of the desert, they are beautifully carved with *jali* outside and are well maintained and worth visiting.

KHULDERA

This is a fascinating ghost town, and well worth stopping at on the way to Sam. The story goes that 400 or so years ago, Salim Singh, the then prime minister of Jaisalmer, took a distinct shine to a Paliwal girl from this village. The rest of the Paliwal people did not want this beautiful girl taken away from them, and so after intense pressure from the prime minister decided to abandon the village one night, with everyone dispersing in different directions, never to return. It is remarkably well preserved, and best visited with a guide who can point out the most interesting buildings from the many still standing. **Khabha**, just south of here, is also recommended.

SAM DUNES (SAIN)
ⓘ *Rs 10, car Rs 20 (camera fees may be introduced), camel rates start at Rs 100 per hr.*
Sam dunes, 40 km west of Jaisalmer, is popular for sunset camel rides. It's not a remote spot in the middle of the desert but the only real large stretch of sand near town; the dunes only cover a small area, yet they are quite impressive. Right in the middle of the dunes, **Sunset View** is like a fairground, slightly tacky with lots of day-trippers – as many as 500 in the high season; the only escape from this and the camel men is to walk quite a way away.

KHURI
ⓘ *Rs 10, buses from Jaisalmer take 1½ hrs, jeep for 4 people Rs 450 for a sunset tour.*
Khuri, 40 km southwest of Jaisalmer, is a small picturesque desert village of decorated mud-thatched buildings which was ruled by the Sodha clan for four centuries. Visitors are attracted by shifting sand dunes, some 80 m high, but the peace of the village has been spoilt by the growing number of huts, tents and guesthouses. Persistent hotel and camel agents board all buses bound for Khuri. The best months to visit are from November to February.

THAR DESERT NATIONAL PARK
ⓘ *Rs 150 per person; car permits Rs 500; permits are required, apply 2 days in advance to Forest Department, T02992-252489, or through travel agents.*
The Thar Desert National Park is near Khuri, the core being about 60 km from Jaisalmer (the road between Sam and Khuri is passable with a high-clearance vehicle). The park was created to protect 3000 sq km of the Thar Desert, the habitat for drought resistant, endangered and rare species which have adjusted to the unique and inhospitable conditions of extreme temperatures. The desert has undulating dunes and vast expanses of flat land where the trees are leafless, thorny and have long roots. Fascinating for birdwatching, it is one of the few places in India where the **great Indian bustard** is proliferating (it can weigh up to 14 kg and reach a height of 40 cm). In winter it also attracts the migratory **houbara bustard**. You can see imperial black-bellied and common Indian sand grouse, five species of vulture, six of eagle, falcons, and flocks of larks at Sudasari, in the core of the park, 60 km from Jaisalmer. Chinkaras are a common sight, as are desert and Indian foxes. Blackbuck and desert cat can be seen at times. Close to sunset, you can spot desert hare in the bushes.

MOVING ON
To Delhi
At the end of Dream Trip 1, you will return to Delhi (see Moving on, page 135), to connect with your international flight home.

JAISALMER AND AROUND LISTINGS

WHERE TO STAY

\$\$\$\$ The Serai, near Chandan village, 30 km outside Jaisalmer, T02997-200014, www.sujanluxury.com. Already starring on the front cover of *Condé Nast Traveller* magazine, this luxurious resort is inspired by the colours of the desert, with warm sandstone and beautiful natural textiles. The swimming pool is based on an Indian step well and 6 of the luxury tents have their own plunge pools. Sit by the swimming pool and get treated to sorbet and ice cold *nimbu pani*, while the restaurant serves up global fusion food. This is the most stylish way to experience desert life. It's a place for landmark moments – honeymoons, engagements or 'big' birthdays.

\$\$\$\$ Suryagarh, Kahala Phata, Sam Rd, T02992-269269, www.suryagarh.com. Stunning heritage-style project and the outer façade of the hotel mirrors the famous Jaisalmer Fort. Beautiful suites, vibey bar area and lovely indoor pool. The spa is exceptional. Attention to detail everywhere you turn.

\$\$\$ The Mama's Resort and Camp, T03014-274042, www.themamasjaisalmer. com. Stay in the desert in style with luxury tents and 4-poster beds. There are also nice rooms, but the tents win. You can book packages which, naturally, always include a camel.

\$\$ Nachana Haveli, Gandhi Chowk, T02992-252 110, www.nachanahaveli. com. Converted 18th-century Rajput *haveli* with carved balconies and period artefacts. Rooms are stylishly done with great bathrooms, particularly upstairs suites. Rooftop restaurant in the season, has very authentic feel overall. Friendly family.

\$\$-\$ Shahi Palace, Shiv St, near SBBJ bank, outside fort, T02992-255920, www.shahipalacehotel.com. 16 super-stylish rooms in a beautiful sandstone building with fabulous bathrooms. The team of 4 brothers here work hard to make everyone feel at home. Beautiful chic rooftop restaurant with lots or archways and even a wooden boat from Karnataka masquerading as a flowerpot. The view of the fort is outstanding as is their food. They provide free station pickup and all manner of travel support. Excellent reports on their camel safaris.

\$ The Desert Haveli, near Jain Temple, T(0)756-845 5656, www.deserthaveli-hostel.com. 7 characterful rooms in charming, 400-year-old *haveli*, honest, friendly owner. Very atmospheric.

RESTAURANTS

\$\$-\$ Desert Boy's Dhani, near Nagar Palika, Dhibba. Lovely garden restaurant with good range of Indian classics and traditional Rajasthani food. Folk dance and music.

\$\$-\$ 1st Gate Fusion, Dhibba (see Where to stay). Stylish place with great views and lovely decor. And on the menu all things Italian as well as a fair amount of good Indian food.

\$ Jaisal Italy, in the main fort gate. Charming, cool interiors with windows looking up the pathway to the fort. Excellent bruschetta and a great meeting point before or after fort walks.

ON THE ROAD

For some of us the ultimate Dream Trip will be our honeymoon. And increasingly, it might be the wedding party as more people are choosing to marry abroad.

A wedding in India is only limited by your imagination. The magic is that anything is possible. Weddings are a big deal in India and the celebrations usually last three days. And the investment is huge. However, coming to India for a wedding can work out a lot cheaper than doing it at home. Bridalwear, custom-made rings, decor and food can all come in at a fraction of the price. Or not, depending on how you want to play it. You can do ultimate luxury wedding or 'budget' luxury!

"The best thing about India for weddings," says Victoria Dyer who runs **IndiaBeat**, www.indiabeat.co.uk, and had her own wedding in Jaipur, "is that there is no limit to what you can do. We started our wedding with a Holi (throwing of colour) party, then had drinks and fireworks up at the Moti Dongri Fort in Jaipur. We were married the next day in an English church built in the 1850s and then arrived with the rest of the wedding party at the reception by elephant!"

There are many great locations across India. **Samode Palace**, close to Jaipur is very special, as is **Diggi Palace** in Jaipur itself. Udaipur is dubbed the Venice of the East and has many magical properties. Or how about a wedding party in the desert? **Indiabeat** (www.indiabeat.co.uk) recently organized a wedding party in Udaipur that included a market complete with circus performers, fire breathers and elephants, overlooking Lake Pichola.

Naturally there is a fair amount of paperwork if you decide to have a legal wedding in India, rather than a blessing, but it is possible. Even if you're a non-resident, it is possible to be legally married with a local civil registrar, although you should factor in spending 60 days in India. There's a 30-day residency requirement, so either the bride or the groom has to be living in India for at least 30 days before applying to the local registry office to get married. For foreigners, this means getting a certificate from the local police station. Hiring a wedding planner in India is going to make the process smoother, whether you decide to have a legal ceremony or just a blessing.

If you are just planning your honeymoon India has many magical and unforgettable places. The beautiful **Amarvilas** in Agra will hire a Hindu priest to perform a wedding *puja* for you at the hotel with a view of the Taj Mahal – even if it's just the two of you on your honeymoon. You get to dress up in traditional clothes and make your intentions again.

Deogarh Mahal and **Devi Garh**, both in Rajasthan, can create stunning private dinners in their grounds – maybe in the turret of the palace, or in the beautiful **Sheesh Mahal** (crystal palace), or under a starry sky in the jungle close by. Or how about hiding away in the desert at **The Serai** near Jaisalmer? The stunning **Mihir Garh** between Jodhpur and Udaipur has been voted one of the best honeymoon resorts in India. While **Rawla Narlai** close by hosts a candlelit step-well dinner – the ultimate in romance.

You might want a more exhilarating honeymoon trekking in the Himalaya. Many Indian newlyweds head to Manali on honeymoon, so you could take a leaf out of their book. The most romantic honeymoon hideaway in Manali is **Baikunth Magnolia**, or you could escape to the peace and luxury of **Samode Safari Lodge** in Bandhavgarh National Park.

Keep dreaming, *sab kuch milega* – anything is possible.

142 DREAM TRIP 1: Jaisalmer & around

DREAM TRIP 2
Delhi→Amritsar→Srinagar→Leh→Delhi 21 days

Delhi 2 nights, page 35

Amritsar 2 nights, page 145
Train/overnight bus/flight (6 hrs/9 hrs/
1 hr 20 mins) from Delhi

Srinagar 1 night, page 154
Flight from Amritsar (1 hr 20 mins)

Houseboat in Srinagar 3 nights,
page 161
Dal Lake and Nagin Lake are accessed
by boat (or road) from Srinagar city

Pahalgam or Gulmarg 1 night, page 160
Jeep from Srinagar to Pahalgam (2½ hrs);
to Gulmarg (1-1½ hrs)

Kargil 1 night, page 163
Jeep/bus from Srinagar to Kargil
(205 km, 9 hrs/11-12 hrs)

Lamayuru en route or overnight stay,
page 163
Jeep from Srinagar/Kargil
(11-12 hrs/4-5 hrs)

Alchi 1 night, page 164
Jeep from Kargil with lunch stop
at Lamayuru (5-6 hrs)

Lekir en route or overnight stay,
page 166
Jeep from Alchi (2-2½ hrs)

Phyang en route or overnight stay,
page 167
Jeep from Alchi via Lekir,
45 mins before Leh

Leh 3 nights, page 171
From Alchi, via Lekir and Phyang
(2½ hrs plus stopping time)

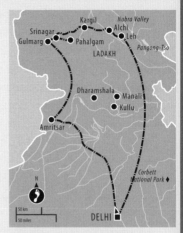

Trekking or trip to Nubra Valley
3 nights, page 178
Short trekking trips or jeep excursions
to Nubra leave from Leh

Leh 2 nights, page 171
Return to Leh by private jeep, at the
end of a trek or Nubra Valley trip

Delhi 2 nights, page 35
Flight from Leh (1 hr 20 mins)
for international flight home

GOING FURTHER

Dharamsala page 152
Train to Pathankot or Kangra plus taxi
(15 hrs); flight to Kangra from Delhi
(1 hr 20 mins)

Manali and Kullu Valley page 183
Bus from Leh (2 days)

Corbett National Park page 185
Flight/car from Delhi (1 hr/5 hrs)

DREAM TRIP 2
Delhi → Amritsar → Srinagar → Leh → Delhi

This itinerary begins in Delhi where the remnants of the Mughal Empire mix into a modern and sprawling metropolis. The Red Fort and the Jama Masjid form the heart of the Old City, while majestic tombs of the emperors intersperse the broad avenues of Lutyens' Delhi. Next destination is Amritsar and the magical Golden Temple where you can easily spend a whole day soaking up the atmosphere.

From Amritsar, it's a short flight to Srinagar and the Kashmir Valley. Spend some time on one of hundreds of houseboats moored on the lakes, and being paddled around in a *shikara* or simply watching the birdlife from the veranda as the sun goes down. From Srinagar you can easily make a day or overnight trip to the hill station of Pahalgam or the snow resort of Gulmarg. It's a long road on to Leh – but one of the most spectacular and unforgettable – winding over mountain passes and criss-crossing the Indus River. After Kargil, the culture abruptly changes from Muslim to Buddhist, and the wild mountain valleys are home to tiny villages and active monasteries poised on peaks. There is accommodation dotted throughout the villages, so if you want to slow things down, Lamayuru, Alchi, Likir and Phyang are all possible night-stops.

Leh is the perfect antidote to a gruelling journey. The new museum, the old bazaar, relaxing garden restaurants and the impressive palace keep you busy in the city, while day trips can be made to the famous monasteries nearby, such as Hemis and Thikse. A three-day trek can be arranged when you've acclimatized, as can an excursion to the remote Nubra Valley. Those who have plenty of time might choose to take the road back to Delhi, stopping in laid-back Manali, or to fly on to Corbett National Park to spot a tiger or two.

AMRITSAR AND AROUND

After two nights in Delhi (see page 35), Dream Trip 2 moves north to Amritsar ('Pool of the Nectar of Immortality'), named after the sacred pool in the Golden Temple, the holiest of Sikh sites. The temple itself, the city's singular attraction, is a haven of peace amidst an essentially congested city. The atmosphere is particularly powerful during amritvela *(dawn to early light), when the surrounding glistening white-marble pavement is still cold under foot and the gold begins to shimmer on the lightening water. Sunset and evening prayers are also a special time to visit. You cannot help but be touched by the sanctity and radiance of the place, the friendly welcome of the people and the community spirit. Music constantly plays from within the inner sanctum of the Hari Mandir.*

→ AMRITSAR

ARRIVING IN AMRITSAR
Getting there Rajasansi Airport is 11 km away with taxi or auto-rickshaw transfers. The railway is central, the bus station 2 km east; *Shatabdi Express* trains run between Delhi and Amritsar. It's a 15-minute auto-rickshaw ride from the Golden Temple to the south.

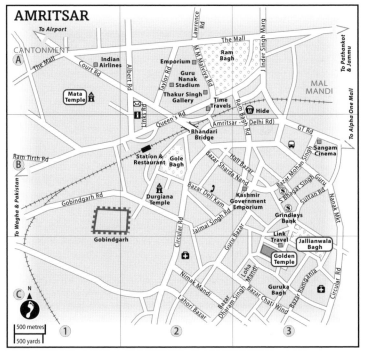

Before entering a temple, gurudwara or mosque, check when you are required to remove your shoes. Most places have a cloakroom, where you can leave them for a few rupees until you have finished looking around. In a Sikh temple, both men and women should cover their heads and wear long sleeves. You can make a contribution to the shrine's upkeep by putting a donation in the green *tameer* (building) fund box.

Moving on From Amritsar the flight to **Srinagar** (see page 154) takes one hour 20 minutes. Those with plenty of time could travel overland to Srinagar, spending a night in **Pahalgam** (see page 160) en route.

Getting around The city is quite spread out. Cycle-rickshaws squeeze through the crowded lanes. Auto-rickshaws are handy for longer journeys unless you get a bike. **Tourist office** ⓘ *opposite the railway station, T0183-240 2452*.

BACKGROUND

The original site for the city was granted by the Mughal Emperor Akbar (ruled 1556-1605) who visited the temple, and it has been sacred to the Sikhs since the time of the fourth guru, Guru Ram Das (1574-1581). He insisted on paying its value to the local Jats who owned it, thereby eliminating the possibility of future disputes on ownership. Guru Ram Das then invited local merchants to live and trade in the immediate vicinity. In 1577 he heard that a cripple had been miraculously cured while bathing in the pool here. The pool was enlarged and named Amrit Sarovar (Immortality). Guru Arjan Dev (1581-1601), Guru Ram Das' son and successor, enlarged the tank further and built the original temple at its centre from 1589-1601. The Afghan Ahmad Shah Durrani desecrated the Golden Temple in 1757. The Sikhs united and drove him out, but four years later he defeated the Sikh armies, sacking the town and blowing up the temple. Later, the Sikhs re-conquered the Punjab and restored the temple and tank. Under their greatest secular leader, Maharaja Ranjit Singh, the temple was rebuilt in 1764. In 1830 he donated 100 kg (220 lbs) of gold which was applied to the copper sheets on the roof and much of the exterior of the building, giving rise to the name the 'Golden Temple'. Now Punjab's second largest town, Amritsar was a traditional junction of trade routes. The different peoples, Yarkandis, Turkomans, Kashmiris, Tibetans and Iranians indicate its connections with the Old Silk Road.

GOLDEN TEMPLE

The spiritual nerve centre of the Sikh faith, every Sikh tries to make a visit and bathe in the holy water. It is immensely powerful, spiritual and welcoming to all, with an all-pervasive air of strength and self-sufficiency.

Visiting the temple Shoes, socks, sticks and umbrellas can be left outside the cloakroom free of charge. Visitors should wash their feet outside the entrance. It is best to go early as for much of the year the marble gets too hot by noon. Dress appropriately and cover your head in the temple precincts. Head scarves are available during the day but not at night; a handkerchief suffices. Avoid sitting with your back towards the temple or with your legs stretched out. Tobacco, narcotics and intoxicants are not permitted. The community kitchen provides food all day, for a donation. The **information office** ⓘ *near the main entrance, T0183-255 3954,* is very helpful.

Worship Singing is central to Sikh worship, and the 24-hour chanting at the Golden Temple adds greatly to the reverential atmosphere. After building the temple, Guru Arjan Dev compiled a collection of hymns of the great medieval saints and this became the *Adi Granth* (Original Holy book). It was installed in the temple as the focus of devotion and teaching. Guru Gobind Singh, the 10th and last guru (1675-1708) revised the book and also refused to name a successor saying that the book itself would be the Sikh Guru. It thus became known as the *Guru Granth Sahib* (*The Holy Book as Guru*).

The temple compound Entering the temple compound through the main entrance or clock tower you see the **Harmandir** (the Golden Temple itself) beautifully reflected in the stunning expanse of water that surrounds it. Each morning (0400 summer, 0500 winter) the *Guru Granth Sahib* is brought in a vivid procession from the **Akal Takht** at the west end to the Harmandir, to be returned at night (2200 summer, 2100 winter). The former represents temporal power, the latter spiritual – and so they do not quite face each other.

All pilgrims walk clockwise round the tank, stopping at shrines and bathing in the tank on the way round to the Harmandir itself. The tank is surrounded by an 8-m-wide white marble pavement, banded with black and brown Jaipur marble.

East End To the left of the entrance steps are the bathing ghats and an area screened off from public view for women to dip. Also on this side are the **68 Holy Places** representing 68 Hindu pilgrimage sites as referenced in Guru Nanak's Japji Sahib. When the tank was built, Guru Arjan Dev told his followers that, rather than visit all the orthodox Hindu places of pilgrimage, they should just bathe here, thus acquiring equivalent merit.

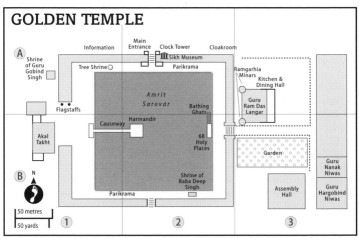

GOLDEN TEMPLE

A shrine contains a copy of the *Guru Granth Sahib*. Here and at other booths round the tank the Holy Book is read for devotees. The *granthi* (reader) is a temple employee and a standard reading lasts for three hours, while a complete reading takes 48 hours.

Dining hall, kitchen, assembly hall and guesthouses The surrounding *bunghas* (white arcade of buildings) are hostels for visitors. Through the archway a path leads to the **Guru Ram Das Langar** (kitchen and dining hall) immediately on the left, while two tall octagonal minarets, the 18th-century **Ramgarhia Minars**, provide a vantage point over the temple and inner city. At the far end of the path are a series of guesthouses including **Guru Ram Das Sarai**, where pilgrims can stay free for up to three nights. Sikhs have a community kitchen where all temple visitors, regardless of their religious belief, can eat together. The third Guru, Guru Amar Das (1552-1574), abolished the custom of eating only with others of the same caste. He even refused to bless the Mughal Emperor Akbar unless he was prepared to eat with everyone else who was present. *Seva* (voluntary service), which continues to be a feature of modern Sikhism, extends to the kitchen staff and workers; visitors are also welcome to lend a hand. The Amritsar kitchen may feed up to 10,000 people a day, with 3000 at a sitting and up to 1 Lakh (100,000) visitors at the weekends. Lunch is 1100-1500 and dinner 1900 onwards.

Returning to the temple tank, the **shrine** on the south side is to Baba Deep Singh. When Ahmad Shah Durrani attacked Amritsar in 1758, Baba Deep Singh was copying out the *Guru Granth Sahib*. He went out to fight with his followers, vowing to defend the temple with his life. He was mortally wounded, 6 km from town; some say that his head was hacked from his body. Grimly determined and holding his head on with one hand he fought on. On his way back to the temple he died on this spot. The story is recounted in the picture behind glass.

West end The complex to the west has the Akal Takht, the flagstaffs, and the Shrine of Guru Gobind Singh. The **flagstaffs** symbolize religion and politics, in the Sikh case intertwined. They are joined in the middle by the emblem of the Sikh nation, the two swords of Hargobind, representing spiritual and temporal authority. The circle is inscribed with the Sikh rallying call *Ek Onkar* (God is One).

Started when Arjan Dev was Guru (1581-1605), and completed by Guru Hargobind in 1609, the **Akal Takht** is the seat of the Sikhs' religious committee. It is largely a mixture of 18th- and early 19th-century building, the upper storeys being the work of Ranjit Singh. It has a first-floor room with a low balcony which houses a gilt-covered ark, central to the initiation of new members of the Khalsa brotherhood.

To the side of the flagstaffs is a **shrine** dedicated to the 10th and last guru, Gobind Singh (Guru 1675-1708). In front of the entrance to the temple causeway is a square, a gathering place for visitors.

Sometimes you may see Nihang (meaning 'crocodile') Sikhs, followers of the militant Guru Gobind Singh, dressed in blue and armed with swords, lances and curved daggers.

At the centre of the tank stands the most holy of all Sikh shrines, the **Harmandir** (Golden Temple). Worshippers obtain the sweet *prasad* before crossing the causeway to the temple where they make their offering. The 60-m-long bridge, usually crowded with jostling worshippers, is built out of white marble like the lower floor of the temple. The rest of the temple is covered in copper gilt. On the doorways verses from the *Guru Granth Sahib* are inscribed in Gurumukhi script while rich floral paintings decorate the walls and excellent silver work marks the doors. The roof has the modified onion-shaped dome, characteristic of Sikh temples, but in this case it is covered in the gold that Ranjit Singh added for embellishment.

The ground floor of the three-storey temple contains the Holy Book placed on a platform under a jewel-encrusted canopy. *Guru Granth Sahib* contains approximately 3500 hymns. Professional singers and musicians sing verses from the book continuously from 0400-2200 in the summer and 0500-2130 in winter. An excited crowd of worshippers attempts to touch the serpent horn. Each evening the holy book is taken ceremoniously to the Akal Takht and brought back the next morning; it's a great time to visit. The palanquin used for this, set with emeralds, rubies and diamonds with silver poles and a golden canopy, can be seen in the treasury on the first floor of the entrance to the temple. Throughout the day, pilgrims place offerings of flowers or money around the book. There is no ritual in the worship or pressure from temple officials to donate money. The marble walls are decorated with mirror-work, gold leaf and designs of birds, animals and flowers in semi-precious stones in the Mughal style.

On the first floor is a balcony on which three respected Sikhs always perform the **Akhand Path** (Unbroken Reading). In order to preserve unity and maintain continuity, there must always be someone practising devotions. The top floor is where the gurus used to sit and here again someone performs the *Akhand Path*; this is the quietest part of the building and affords a good view over the rest of the complex.

On the edge of the tank just west of the entrance is the **Tree Shrine**, a gnarled, 450-year-old *jubi* tree, reputed to have been the favourite resting place of the first chief priest of the temple. Women tie strings to the branches, hoping to be blessed with a son by the primaeval fertility spirits that choose such places as their home. The **Sikh Museum** ① *at the main entrance to the temple (just before steps leading down to the parikrama), 0700-1830, free*, is somewhat martial, reflecting the struggles against the Mughals, the British and the Indian Army. The **Sikh Library** ① *in the Guru Nanak Building, Mon-Sat 0930-1630*, has a good selection of books in English as well as current national newspapers.

THE TOWN

The old city is south of the railway station encircled by a ring road, which traces the line of the city walls built during the reign of Ranjit Singh. **Jallianwala Bagh**, noted for the most notorious massacre under British rule (see below), is 400 m north of the Golden Temple.

Relations with the British had soured in 1919. *Hartals* (general strikes) became a common form of demonstration. The Punjab, which had supplied 60% of Indian troops committed to the First World War, was one of the hardest hit economically in 1918 and tension was high. The lieutenant governor of the province decided on a 'fist force' to repulse the essentially non-violent but vigorous demonstrations. Some looting occurred in Amritsar and the British called in reinforcements. These arrived under the command of General Dyer.

Dyer banned all meetings but people were reported to be gathering on Sunday 13 April 1919 as pilgrims poured into Amritsar to celebrate **Baisakhi**, the Sikh New Year and the anniversary of the founding of the *khalsa* in 1699. That afternoon thousands were crammed into Jallianwala Bagh, a piece of waste ground popular with travellers, surrounded on all sides by high walls with only a narrow alley for access. Dyer personally led some troops to the place, gave the crowd no warning and ordered his men to open fire leaving 379 dead and 1200 wounded. Other brutal acts followed.

The **Jallianwala Bagh massacre** was hushed up and the British government in London was only aware of it six months later at which time the Hunter Committee was set up to investigate the incident. It did not accept Dyer's excuse that he acted as he did in order to prevent another insurrection on the scale of the Mutiny of 1857. He was asked to resign and returned to England where he died in 1927. However, he was not universally condemned. A debate in the House of Lords produced a majority of 126 to 86 in his favour and the *Morning Post* newspaper launched a fund for "The Man who Saved India".

India was outraged by Dyer's massacre. **Gandhi**, who had called the nationwide *hartal* in March, started the Non Co-operation Movement, which was to be a vital feature of the struggle for Independence. This was not the end of the affair. O'Dwyer, the governor of the province, was shot dead at a meeting in Caxton Hall, London, by a survivor of Jallianwala Bagh who was hanged for the offence. For a modern take on the whole story, check out the Bollywood movie *Rang de Basanti.*

Today the gardens are a pleasant enclosed park. They are entered by a narrow path between the houses, opening out over lawns. A **memorial plaque** recounts the history at the entrance, and a large memorial dominates the east end of the garden. There is an interesting museum. On the north side is a well in which many who tried to escape the bullets were drowned, and remnants of walls have been preserved to show the bullet holes.

The old town has a number of mosques and Hindu temples – the **Durgiana Temple** (16th century), and the new **Mata Lal Devi Temple**, which imitates the difficult access to the famous Himalayan Mata Vaishno Devi Cave Temple of Katra by requiring the worshipper to wade awkwardly through water and crawl through womb-like tunnels is well worth a visit. The whole temple area is Disneyesque with plastic grottoes and statues. Women who wish to have children come here to pray, there is community food and a charity hospital run from the temple's trust. It's a very popular and lively temple, definitely worth a visit. Northeast of the railway station are the **Ram Bagh gardens**, the Mall and Lawrence Road shopping areas.

WAGAH

The Wagar Border, 35 km from Amritsar, is a fun excursion. It's best to go late afternoon for the changing of the guards and the ceremonial lowering of the flags ceremony at sundown, carried out with great pomp and rivalry, are quite a spectacle. There is much synchronized foot stamping, gate slamming and displays of scorn by colourful soldiers! It is the ministry of funny walks. New viewing galleries have been built but crowds still clamour to get the best view. Women are allowed to get to the front, and there is a VIP section (open to foreign visitors) next to the gate. It is best to get there near closing time though photography is difficult with the setting sun.

AMRITSAR AND AROUND LISTINGS

WHERE TO STAY

Amritsar

$$$$ Hyatt, next to Alpha One Mall, GT Rd, T0183-287 1234, www.hyatt.com. Formerly **Ista** hotel, this is a beautiful boutique hotel offering up the most stylish rooms in Amritsar. There is a stunning spa with all the usual ayurvedic fare, but also rose quartz and amethyst facials inspired by the award-winning **Ananda Spa** in the Himalayas. Food-wise, you can choose between the all-day **Collage** with food from around the globe and a *teppenyaki* station or **Thai-Chi**, evenings only.

$$$$-$$$ Ranjit's Svaasa, 47-A The Mall Rd, T0183-256 6618, www.welcomheritage hotels.in. Tastefully restored rooms with huge windows in a 250-year-old red-brick manor surrounded by palms and lawns, elegant service, great food, beautiful Spa Pavilion offering Ayurvedic and international treatments.

$$$ Hotel Le Golden, clock tower Extension, outside Golden Temple complex, T0183-255 8800, www.hotellegolden.com. Modern rooms close to the temple, with views of Akal Takht. Rooftop restaurant **The Glass** has view of Siri Harmandir Sahib.

$$-$ Grace, 35 Braham Buta Market, close to Golden Temple, T0183-255 9355. Good range of rooms, friendly management.

$ Rest houses, in/near the Golden Temple, eg **Guru Ram Das Niwas** and **Guru Arjan Dev Niwas**. For a very atmospheric stay, you can stay in the rest houses at **The Golden Temple**. Some are free, for others there is a charge; please leave a donation. **Guru Ram Das Niwas** has a small foreigner-only enclave with guard. Tobacco, alcohol and drugs are prohibited. It can be noisy as sometimes it's so busy people stay in the courtyard; but it's an eye-opening experience.

RESTAURANTS

Amritsar

$$$-$$ Crystal, Queens Rd, T0183-222 5555. Good international food, excellent service, pleasant ambience, huge portions. There is **Crystal** on the ground floor proclaiming that there is only 1 branch. And there is **Crystal** on the 2nd floor proclaiming the same thing – the 2 brothers have fallen out and both refuse to change the name.

$$ Punjabi Rasoi, near Jallianwala Bagh, T0183-254 0140. The best option near the Golden Temple. Very good *thalis*, south Indian food and traditional Punjabi fare. Internet café upstairs too.

Langar at the Golden Temple, a beautiful way to connect to the spirit of the Golden Temple and the people that make their pilgrimage here is to sit in the communal dining hall and take food. The Langar caters for between 10,000 and 100,000 people a day – everyone sits together on the floor and eats a simple meal of dhal, vegetable and roti. Every Sikh temple has a community kitchen run by volunteers, but this is the largest. Try and get backstage and check out the size of the pots! Another highlight is after morning prayer at around 0600 when in front of the main entrance, huge cauldrons of piping hot fennel-laced chai are served – it's definitely the best way to start the day.

GOING FURTHER
Dharamsala

Dharamshala has a spectacular setting along a spur of the Dhauladhar range, varying in height from 1250 m at the 'Lower Town' bazar to 1768 m at McLeodganj. It is this 'Upper' and more attractive part of town that attracts the vast majority of visitors. McLeodganj is the home of His Holiness the Dalai Lama and so attracts many tourists and diplomats and there is a very definite Tibetan feel as many refugees have made it their home. Although the centre of McLeodganj itself has now become somewhat overdeveloped, it is surrounded by forests, set against a backdrop of high peaks, with superb views over the Kangra Valley and Shiwaliks. There is a choice of interesting properties to stay in; we recommend **Chonor House** (Thekchen Choeling Road, Mcleodganj, www.norbulingka.org) and **Grace Hotel** (558 Old Chari Road, Kotwali Bazar Dharamshala, www.welcomheritagehotels.in).

BACKGROUND

The hill station was established by the British between 1815 and 1847, but remained a minor town until the **Dalai Lama** settled here after Chinese invasion of Tibet in October 1959. The Tibetan community has tended to take over the hospitality business and many Westerners come here because they are particularly interested in Buddhism, meditation or the Tibetan cause. A visitor's attempt to use a few phrases in Tibetan is always warmly responded to: *tashi delek* (hello, good luck), *thukje-chey* (thank you), *thukje-sik* (please), *gong-thag* (sorry), and *shoo-den-jaa-go* (goodbye).

ARRIVING IN DHARAMSALA

Getting there Flights arrive at **Gaggal Airport** (Kangra, 13 km). Lower Dharamshala is well connected by bus. The nearest station on the scenic mountain railway is at Kangra, while Pathankot has daily trains to and from Delhi and Amritsar.

Getting around From Dharamshala, it is 10 km by the bus route to McLeodganj but a shorter, steeper path (3 km) takes about 45 minutes on foot. Local jeeps and rickshaws use this bumpy, potholed shortcut. Compact McLeodganj itself, and its surroundings, are ideal for walking.

PLACES IN DHARAMSALA

Namgyal Monastery ⓘ *0500-2100*, at McLeodganj, with the Buddhist School of Dialectics, mostly attended by small groups of animated 'debating' monks, is known as 'Little Lhasa'. This *tsuglagkhang* (cathedral) opposite the Dalai Lama's residence resembles the centre of the one in Lhasa and is five minutes' walk from the main bazar. It contains large gilded bronzes of the Buddha, Avalokitesvara and Padmasambhava. To the left of the Tsuglagkhang is the **Kalachakra Temple** with very good modern murals of *mandalas*, protectors of the Dharma, and Buddhist masters of different lineages of Tibetan Buddhism, with the central image of Shakyamuni. Sand *mandalas* (which can be viewed on completion) are constructed throughout the year, accompanied by ceremonies. The temple is very important as the practice of Kalachakra Tantra is instrumental in bringing about world peace and harmony. Within the monastery complex is the **Tibetan Museum** ⓘ *Tue-Sun 0900-1700, Rs 5*, with an interesting collection of documents and photographs detailing Tibetan history, the Chinese occupation of Tibet and visions of the future for the country. It is an essential and very thought-provoking visit for those interested in the Tibetan cause.

His Holiness the **Dalai Lama** ① www.dalailama.com, usually leads the prayers on special occasions – 10 days for **Monlam Chenmo** following **Losar**, **Saga Dawa** (May) and his own birthday (6 July). If you wish to have an audience with him, you need to sign up in advance at the Security Office (go upstairs) by **Hotel Tibet**. On the day, arrive early with your passport. Cameras, bags and rucksacks are not permitted. His Holiness is a Head of State and the incarnation of Avalokitesvara, the Bodhisattva of Love and Great Compassion; show respect by dressing appropriately (no shorts or sleeveless tops).

The little golden-roofed **Tsechokling Monastery**, in a wooded valley 300 m below McLeodganj (down rather slippery steps), was built between 1984 and 1986; the monks are known for their skill in crafting *tormas* (butter sculptures) and sand *mandalas*, which decorate the prayer hall.

Norbulingka Institute ① T01892-246405, www.norbulingka.org, is becoming a major centre for Buddhist teaching and practical work. Named after the summer residence of the Seventh Dalai Lama, it was set up to ensure the survival of Tibetan Buddhism's cultural heritage. Up to 100 students and 300 Tibetan employees are engaged in a variety of crafts and Tibetan language classes. The temple has a 4.5-m-high gilded statue of the Buddha and over 1000 painted images. There is a **Tibetan Library** with a good range of books and magazines. You can attend lectures and classes on Tibetan culture and language and Buddhism or attend two **meditation** classes (free but a donation is appreciated). Those attending regularly pay Rs 100 per meditation session.

Church of St John-in-the-Wilderness (1860) ① open for Sun morning service, with attractive stained-glass windows, is a short distance below McLeodganj. Along with other buildings in the area, it was destroyed by the earthquake of 1905 but has been rebuilt. In April 1998 thieves tried to steal the old bell, which was cast in London and installed in 1915, but could only move it 300 m.

Museum of Kangra Art ① Main Rd, Tue-Sun 1000-1330, 1400-1700, free, allow 30 mins, near the bus stand in Lower Dharamshala, includes regional jewellery, paintings, carvings, a reminder of the rich local heritage contrasted with the celebrated Tibetan presence. Copies of Roerich paintings will be of interest to those not planning to visit Naggar.

AROUND MCLEODGANJ

Bhagsu, an easy 2-km stroll east, or Rs 40 auto-rickshaw ride, has a temple to Bhagsunath (Siva). The mountain stream here feeds a small pool for pilgrims, while there is an attractive waterfall 1 km beyond. Unfortunately this has resulted in it becoming very touristy, with increasing building activity. Upper Bhagsu is lined with little shops, restaurants and guesthouses and some bigger hotels, but has great views. The further you walk up the hill the quieter it becomes and Bhagsu attracts many backpackers for long stays here.

Dharamkot, 3 km away (from McLeodganj by auto Rs 80, or on foot from Bhagsu), has very fine views and you can continue on towards the snowline. Villagers' homes and guesthouses are dotted up the hillside.

Naddi Gaon, 1.5 km further uphill from the bridge by Dal Lake (buses from Dharamshala, 0800-1900), has really superb views of the Dhauladhar Range. **Kareri Lake** is further on. The TCV (Tibetan Childrens' Village) nearby educates and trains children in traditional handicrafts.

It is an 8-km trek to **Triund**, 2827 m, at the foot of the Dhauladhar where there is a **Forest Lodge** on a hill top. Some trekkers pitch tents, whilst others make use of caves or shepherds' huts. Take provisions and warm sleeping gear if planning to stay overnight.

KASHMIR VALLEY

The beauty of the Vale of Kashmir, with its snow-dusted mountains looming in shades of purple above serene lakes and wildflower meadows, still has the power to reduce grown poets to tears. Nonetheless, the reality of military occupation pervades many aspects of daily life, with army camps, bunkers and checkposts positioned every few hundred metres along the highways and throughout the countryside.

→ SRINAGAR

Founded by Raja Pravarasen in the sixth century, ringed by mountains and alluringly wrapped around the Dal and Nagin lakes, Srinagar ('beautiful city') is divided in two by the River Jhelum. Once known as the city of seven *kadals* (bridges), there are now 12 that connect the two sides, the older ones giving their names to their adjoining neighbourhoods. It is the largest city in the state and the summer seat of government. Sadly the troubles of the past 20 years have scarred the town, leading to the desertion and neglect of many of its fine houses, buildings and Hindu temples. The famous Dal Lake has shrunk to a sixth of its former size and has become badly polluted. Older Srinagaris lament the passing of the formerly spruce city, yet even so, Srinagar is a charming city with a strong character, unique in India for its Central Asian flavour.

ARRIVING IN SRINAGAR

Getting there The airport is 14 km south of town; a taxi to the main tourist areas takes 30-45 minutes and costs Rs 400. As well as daily flights from Amritsar, Srinagar has several daily direct flights from Delhi and weekly flights from Leh. If you wish to travel overland from Amritsar, regular buses go to Jammu (six hours), where you can stop for a night or two. From Jammu, travel to the Kashmir Valley by jeep (eight or nine hours, including stops for lunch and tea). It's a stunning journey through the mountains as the bus winds its way up to the Jawahar tunnel that burrows through the Pir Panjal, the jade-green Chenab river flowing hundreds of feet below. Emerging from the tunnel on the other side, high in the hills of south Kashmir, travellers are treated to a breathtaking view of the valley spread before out before them.

Moving on Srinagar will be the base for a stay on a nearby **houseboat** (see page 161). Also from Srinagar, it's a 2½-hour jeep ride to the hill station of **Pahalgam** (see page 160) or a one- to 1½-hour ride to the snow resort of **Gulmarg** (see page 160). Next you'll be ready to head east by jeep or bus on the long and unforgettable **road to Leh** (see page 163).

Getting around There are government taxi stands with fixed rates at the Tourist Reception Centre (Residency Road), Dal Gate and Nehru Park, and an abundance of auto-rickshaws. Local buses are cheap, but can be crowded and slow. The days of dusk-to-dawn curfews are over, but even so, the city shuts down relatively early; by 2100 the streets are deserted and it can be tricky to find transport.

Tourist information The Tourist Reception Centre ① *Residency Rd, close to the tourist area of Dalgate, T0194-245 2691, www.jktourism.org, open 24/7,* houses the state

ON THE ROAD
Warning

Visitors to India have been advised against travel to the Kashmir Valley, with the exception of: the cities of Jammu and Srinagar; travel between these two cities on the Jammu–Srinagar highway; and the region of Ladakh. In the past, several of the splinter groups opposed to the Indian government have taken hostages as a means of putting pressure on the government, so the risks of travel in Kashmir are real. However, in recent years there has been an overall decline in violence and an increasing number of Indian and Western tourists are visiting the valley. Nevertheless, take advice from your own consulate, and be aware that travelling against their advice can render your travel insurance void.

department of tourism, the **Jammu and Kashmir Tourism Development Corporation** (**JKTDC**) ① *T0194-2457927, www.jktdc.co.in*, and **Adventure Tourism** for booking accommodation and tours. You can pick up an excellent map showing both the city and the whole state at the tourist information centre. Also within the complex is the **J&K State Transport Corporation** ① *T0194-245 5107*, for bus tickets.

Safety At time of writing the British **Foreign and Commonwealth Office** ① *www.fco. gov.uk*, advises against all rural travel in Jammu and Kashmir, except in Ladakh, and excepting the cities of Jammu and Srinagar, and along the Jammu–Srinagar highway. For an on-the-ground perspective, check www.greaterkashmir.com, www.kashmirtimes.com and www.freepresskashmir.com. Most travellers report no problems, but it is essential to be careful and keep informed about the situation.

Grenade attacks on army bunkers in the city used to be common, but are currently rare. However, in 2006 six Indian tourists were killed during grenade attacks on two bus loads of tourists from West Bengal. Given the tensions between Kashmir and the Indian government, Indian tourists are more likely to be directly targeted than foreigners.

If you are in town and see the shop shutters coming down before closing time, this is generally a sign that a protest is approaching. Either beat a hasty retreat in an auto-rickshaw, or take shelter in a shop until the demonstrators and police have passed. Always ask how the situation is before heading to the old city ('Downtown') and don't go there on Fridays, when spontaneous demonstrations following afternoon prayers are common.

PLACES IN SRINAGAR

The city falls into three parts; the commercial area (**Uptown**), the old city (**Downtown**) and the area around the lakes (**Dalgate**, the **Boulevard**, **Nehru Park**). Downtown can be reached from Uptown either directly, by driving through Dalgate or by driving all the way around Dal Lake, which takes you past the gardens of Cheshma Shahi, Nishat and the turning for the road to Shalimar. This route also takes you past the Grand Palace Hotel, the village of Brein, the Char Minar Island restaurant and reaches Downtown via the Hazrat Bal mosque and Makhdoom Sahib. Uptown is the place for shopping, particularly Polo View and the Bund, which is a footpath that runs along the Jhelum. Residency Road and Lal Chowk are also in Uptown.

Hotels on the Boulevard are popular – particularly with Indian tourists – but tend to be huge, impersonal and overpriced. The city is famous for its houseboats and staying on one can be a very pleasant experience, but it is necessary to book carefully; if the deal sounds too good to be true, then it probably is and you will end up paying in other ways (ie by being coerced into shopping trips, from which your hosts will take a hefty commission). Don't be bullied into booking a trip by pushy, Kashmiri travel agents in New Delhi – much better to book through the **Houseboat Owners Association** (see page 161). Try and find a boat with good references from other travellers. Also be aware that many boats in the Dal and Nagin lakes can only be accessed by *shikara*. While boat owners will insist that a *shikara* will always be at your disposal, some tourists have found that this has not been the case and have been marooned on boats with hosts they don't particularly like.

The Uptown area is good to stay in if you are interested in exploring the city and prefer to be away from the tourist rush. There are also some houseboats on the Jhelum River, with walk-on/walk-off access. You can hear the noise of the traffic from these boats, but there are no hawkers in this area.

Hotels around Dalgate tend to offer more budget options and can be very enjoyable. Those actually inside the lake are a good choice (Heaven Canal, Akbar) as the area is interesting with good views, but less hassle than the Boulevard.

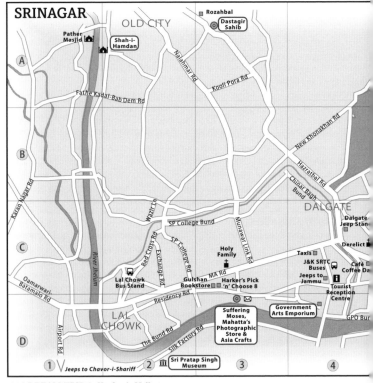

OLD CITY

Srinagar's old city (known locally as 'Downtown') is a fascinating area to wander around with a rather Central Asian feel. Once the manufacturing and trade hub of Kashmir, each *mohalla* (neighbourhood) had its own speciality, such as carpet weaving, goldsmithery and woodcarving. It was said that you could find even the milk of a pigeon in the thriving bazars and its traders grew rich, building themselves impressive brick and wood houses, in a style that is a charming fusion of Mughal and English Tudor.

In the north of the Old City is the distinctive mound of **Hari Parbat Hill**, on which stands a fort built by Shujah Shah Durrani in 1808 (closed to the public). On the southern side of Hari Parbat, the **Makhdoom Sahib shrine** is dedicated to Hazrat Sultan and affords wonderful views of the city. The actual shrine is off-limits to women and non-Muslims, but you can peek through the ornate, carved screen from outside and marvel at the fabulous array of chandeliers. In 2013, a **cable car** ① *tourists Rs 100*, up to the shrine was opened. Alternatively, you can access the steps up the hill from near the Sikh Gurdwara **Chhatti Padshahi**, by the imposing **Kathi Darwaza** (gate) in the Old City walls. This arched gateway (recently restored) was the principal entrance to the fort; a Persian inscription states that it was built by Akbar in 1597-1598. In the city wall on the opposite side of fort is the Sangeen Darwaza, which is more ornate (currently being restored).

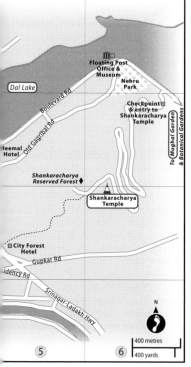

From Makhdoom Sahib take an auto-rickshaw (or walk 15 minutes) to the **Jama Masjid** (1674). The mosque is notable for the 370 wooden pillars supporting the roof, each is made from a single *deodar* tree. The building forms a square around an inner courtyard, with a beautiful fountain and pool at its centre. Its four entrance archways are topped by the striking, pagoda-like roofs that are an important architectural characteristic of the valley's mosques and shrines. The mosque was where the sacred hair of the Prophet Mohammed was kept before being moved to the Hazratbal Mosque.

About 10 minutes' walk to the southeast lies the 17th-century **tomb of Naqash Band Sahib**, a sufi saint. The interior of the shrine is covered with (modern) colourful papier-mâché flower designs; there is a women's section. The ornate mosque adjacent to the shrine is meticulously maintained, and is constructed of brick and wood alternate layers. Next to the shrine lie the graves of the 'martyrs' who died in the 1931 uprising against the Dogras. They are claimed as heroes by both the state government and the separatists – one of the few things both sides agree on.

Pampore, 11 km from Srinagar, is the centre of Kashmir's saffron industry. Saffron, a species of crocus (*Crocus sativus*), grows here in abundance, and in a few other places in the world, and is harvested by hand. Within each purple bloom, the three orange-red anthers yield pure saffron. Over 4500 blooms make one ounce (28 g) of the spice, so the price of this delicate flavouring and colouring in cooking is high (once far more valuable than gold). Its value has led the Indian government to set up a saffron research farm at Sangla in Himachal Pradesh.

The precious orange-coloured dye was used by royalty and the colour saffron was chosen by monks for their robes after the Buddha's death.

Enterprising traders have found a way to disguise dyed shreds of newspaper as saffron. You can test by rubbing a strand or two in a few drops of water on your palm: fake saffron will turn to red paste almost immediately, while the genuine article takes longer to stain and remains yellow.

Continue further in the same direction and you will reach the **Dastagir Sahib shrine**, which houses the tomb of Abdul Qazi Geelani. A fire in June 2012 almost entirely destroyed the main structure, including antique chandeliers, exquisite papier mâché and carved wood decoration. The 300-year-old, giant, handwritten *Qu'ran* and the holy relic of the saint were saved, as they were in a fireproof vault. The shrine is to be rebuilt according to its original structural character, and many devotees still come to pray here. A minute's walk away is little **Rozahbal shrine**, which claims to contain the 'tomb of Jesus' (Holger Kersten's *Jesus Lived in India* recounts the legend; also see www.tombofjesus.com). The community here are sensitive about inquiring visitors: do not produce a camera, and don't be surprised if locals warn you away. Head west, towards the river for the beautiful **Shah-i-Hamdan Masjid**, the site of Srinagar's first mosque, built in 1395 by Mir Sayed Ali Hamadni. The original building was destroyed by fire, the current wooden structure dating back to the 1730s. The entrance is worth seeing for its exquisite papier-mâché work and woodcarving, but non-Muslims are not allowed inside the actual shrine. However, there is a women's section at the rear which female non-Muslims can enter and you can linger by the doorway with devotees, peeping inside to see the richly painted walls and chandeliers. Facing Shah-i-Hamdan, across the river is the limestone **Pathar Masjid** (1623), built for the Empress Nur Jahan and renamed Shahi Mosque. Further up the river, on the same side as Shah-i-Hamdan lies the 15th-century bulbous brick **tomb of Zain-ul-Abidin's mother** ① *daily 0900-1700*, which is embellished with glazed turquoise tiles. The tomb adjoins a graveyard, containing the sultan Zain-ul-Abidin's grave and those of his wives and children, enclosed by an old stone wall that has been reused from an earlier Hindu temple. The area, Zaina Kadal, is interesting to walk around – carved copperwork is still produced here and you can see the craftsmen at work. It's the best place to buy your souvenir samovar.

South of the old city and the river is the remarkable **Sri Pratap Singh Museum** ① *Lal Mandi, Tue-Sun 1030-1630, foreigners Rs 50* (1898). Kashmir's Hindu and Buddhist past literally stares you in the face as 1000-year-old statues of Siva, Vishnu and the Buddha, excavated from all over the valley, casually line the walls. One room houses an eclectic mix of stuffed animals, bottled snakes and birds eggs, topped off by the dissembled skeleton of a woolly mammoth and looked down on by a collection of stags heads, mounted on the papier-mâché walls.

There are also miniature paintings, a selection of ancient manuscripts and coins, weapons, musical instruments and an anthropology section. Look out for the extraordinary 'Amli' shawl in the textiles room: an embroidered map of Srinagar, showing the Jamia mosque and the Jhelum dotted with houseboats (it took 37 years to complete). The collection will be displayed in full when the museum extends into the larger building being constructed next door.

DAL LAKE AND THE FLOATING GARDENS

Of all the city's sights, **Dal Lake** must be its trademark. Over 6.5 km long and 4 km wide, it is divided into three parts by manmade causeways. The small islands are willow covered, while round the lake are groves of *chinar*, poplar and willow. The Mihrbahri people have lived around the lakes for centuries and are market gardeners, tending the floating beds of vegetables and flowers that they have made and cleverly shielded with weeds to make them unobtrusive. *Shikaras*, the gondola-like pleasure boats that ply the lake, can be hired for trips around the Dal (official rate Rs 300 per hour, but it's possible to bargain for half that). The morning vegetable market is well worth seeing by boat, it starts around 0600 and a one-hour tour is adequate; it is in a Shi'ite area adorned with appropriate flags. If you're curious about the city, take a boat up the Jhelum as far as Shah-i-Hamdan, where you can get out for a walk. If you do this, it's worth taking a guide with you who can speak English.

Set up on a hill, behind the Boulevard (known as Takht-i-Sulaiman or 'Throne of Soloman'), is the **Shankaracharya Temple**, affording great views and a good place to orientate yourself. The temple was constructed during Jahangir's reign but is said to be on the same site as a second-century BC temple built by Asoka's son. The inelegant exterior houses a large lingum, while beneath is a cave where Shankaracharya is said to have performed a *puja*. The temple is 5.5 km up a steep road from the Boulevard; walking up the road is not permitted, although hitching a ride from the security check at the bottom is possible (open 0900-1700). There is an alternative rough path starting from next to the gate of the City Forest Hotel on Durganag Road (one hour up, 30 minutes down).

Set in front of a triangle of the lake created by intersecting causeways (now demolished) with a slender bridge at the centre lies the famous **Nishat Bagh** (Garden of Gladness) ① *Sat-Thu 0900-sunset, Rs 10*. Sandwiched between the hills and the lake, the steep terraces and central channel with fountains were laid out by Asaf Khan, Nur Jahan's brother, in 1632.

The **Shalimar Bagh** gardens ① *Apr-Oct 0900-sunset, Nov-Mar 1000-sunset, Rs 10*, are about 4 km away and set back from the lake. Built by Jahangir for his wife, Nur Jahan, the gardens are distinguished by a series of terraces linked by a water channel with central pavilions. These are surrounded by decorative pools, which can be crossed by stones. The uppermost pavilion has elegant black marble pillars and niches in the walls for flowers during the day and candles or lamps at night. The *chinar* (plane trees) have become so huge that some are falling down. **Chashma Shahi** (Royal Spring, 1632) ① *0900-sunset, Rs 10* is a much smaller garden built around the course of a renowned spring, issuing from a miniature stone dome at the garden's summit. It is attributed to Shah Jahan though it has been altered over the centuries. Nearby are the **Botanical Gardens** (Royal Spring, 1632) ① *Sat-Thu 0800-sunset, Rs 10*. Rather wilder than the other gardens, its tucked-away location makes it a good place for runners to stretch their legs.

West (2.5 km) of Chashmi Shahi, nestling in the hills, is the smallest and sweetest of the Mughal gardens, the charmingly named **Pari Mahal** (Fairy Palace) ① *sunrise-sunset, Rs 10*. Built in the 17th century by the ill-fated prince Dara Shikoh, who was later beheaded by his brother Aurangzeb, the garden has six terraces and the best sunset views of Srinagar. The terraced gardens, backed by arched ruins, are being restored and are illuminated at night.

Close to Nagin Lake, **Hazratbal Mosque** (Majestic Place) is on the western shore of Dal Lake and commands excellent lake views. The modern mosque stands out for its white, marble dome and has a special sanctity as a hair of the prophet Mohammad is preserved here. Just beyond is the **Nazim Bagh** (Garden of the Morning Breeze), one of the earliest Mughal gardens and attributed to Akbar.

At the end of the Boulevard in Nehru Park the tiny **Post Office Museum** ① *daily 1100-2000*, is unique in that it floats. You can send your mail from here.

DACHIGAM NATIONAL PARK
① *22 km east, past the Shalimar gardens. Passes available from the Tourist Reception Centre.* This park is home to the endangered Hangul deer as well as black and brown bears, leopards, musk deer and various migratory birds. Permits and further information about the best time to see the wildlife can be obtained from the Tourist Reception Centre in Srinagar (see page 154).

→ AROUND SRINAGAR

PAHALGAM
Pahalgam ('village of shepherds') sits at an altitude of 2133 m and is the main base for the yearly 'Amarnath Yatra' pilgrimage, which sees thousands of Hindu pilgrims climbing to a cave housing an 'ice lingam'. During the Yatra season, which runs from June to August, it gets very busy. Situated at the convergence of two dramatic river valleys, the town is surrounded by conifer forests and pastures. Central Pahalgam is packed with shawl shops, eateries and hotels; there's a striking mosque and pleasant parks (one of which surrounds the Pahalgam Club). The pointy-roofed Mamleshwar Temple, across Kolahoi stream, is devoted to Shiva, There are many short walks you can take from Pahalgam and it is also a good base for longer treks to the Suru Valley and Kishtwar. A good day walk is the 12 km up the beautiful Lidder Valley to Aru; from there you can continue on to to Lidderwat (22 km) and Kolahoi Glacier (35 km). A wide selection of accommodation caters for all budgets; some of the nicer options are a couple of kilometres up the valley from the town centre.

GULMARG
India's premier winter sports resort, Gulmarg attracts a colourful mix of characters, from the off-piste powder-addict adventurers who stay for months each year to the coach-loads of Indian tourists eager to see snow for the first time. Three times host of the country's annual Winter Games, it is one of the cheapest places in the world to learn to ski, although there are only a few beginners' runs. The resort is served by three ski lifts and boasts the world's second highest **gondola** ① *daily 1000-1800, Rs 800 return*, which stops at the Kangdori mid-station before rising up to Apharwat Top (4000 m), from where you can ski the 5.2 km back to Gulmarg. Or in summertime, take the cable car up and then halfway back, and walk down the remaining distance (take a picnic). Check with **Gulmarg J&K Tourism** ① *T01954-254 439*, about opportunities for heli-skiing. The season runs from December to April (best in January and February), and equipment is available for hire for around Rs 400-500 a day. Lift passes cost Rs 700-1250. Outside the winter season, Gulmarg is a popular day trip from Srinagar, with pony rides, walks and the world's highest green golf course being the main attractions.

KASHMIR VALLEY LISTINGS

WHERE TO STAY

Srinagar

$$$$ The Lalit Grand Palace, Gupkar Rd, a few km outside the city, T0194-250 1001, www.thelalit.com. This former palace was the residence of Kashmir's last maharajah, Hari Singh. Situated on a hillside overlooking Dal Lake, it has been tastefully kitted out with antiques befitting its history, including India's largest handmade carpet. One wing houses enormous, classically styled suites, while the other has 70 recently refurbished modern rooms. The restaurant, bar and health club are open to non-guests. It's a good place to go on a summer evening for the al fresco buffet.

$$$$ Vivanta by Taj – Dal View, Kralsangri Hill, Brein, T0194-246 1111, www.vivantabytaj.com. All-out luxury in this sprawling elegant resort with sublime Dal Lake views. Rooms are chic with Kashmiri details and warm colours. 24-hr fitness suite, fantastic restaurants, spa to open soon. Gorgeous place, worth going for a meal if you can't stay here.

$$$$-$$$ Hotel Broadway, Maulana Azad Rd, T0194-245 9001, www.hotel broadway.com. One of Srinagar's oldest and best-known hotels, the original 1970s interior has been well maintained. With lots of wood panelling, rooms can be a little dark. The staff are professional and polite, while the comfortable, centrally heated rooms, Wi-Fi service and city location make it popular with business travellers and journalists. It houses one of the city's few drinking spots, has an informal cinema and is attached to the city's 1st coffee shop, **Café Arabica**. Book online for discounts.

$$$ Dar-Es-Salam, Nandpora, Rainawari, T0194-242 7803, www.hoteldaressalam. com. This white Art Deco ex-stately home is the only hotel on Nagin Lake, with an established garden and a sweep of lawn onto the shore overlooking houseboats.

Mounted heads over the entrance set the colonial tone, while period furnishings in the 2 lounges include brass antique pots and a Raj-era tiger's head. An enclosed balcony surveys the lake. Modernized rooms (and **$$$$** suites), central heating, white duvets, meals available in the dining room.

$ Swiss Hotel, Old Gagribal Rd, T0194-2472766, www.swisshotelkashmir.com. The **Swiss** has 35 clean rooms with attached bath and hot water (morning and evening) that are offered at discounted rates to foreign tourists. The attractive red-painted old house has the best-value budget rooms in town. The new annex has large well-maintained rooms; prices increase as you go up to the 3rd floor where immaculate rooms have coffee-table, couch and numerous side lights. Look at a few rooms, as all washrooms are individually decorated, and some are simply enormous. There's a big front garden.

Houseboats

Houseboats are peculiar to Srinagar and can be seen moored along the shores of Dal Lake, the quieter Nagin Lake and along the Jhelum River. They were originally thought up by the British as a ruse to get around the law that foreigners could not buy land in the state

In the valley's heyday the boats were well kept and delightfully cosy; today some are still lavishly decorated with antiques and traditional Kashmiri handicrafts, but others have become distinctly shabby. Still mostly family-run, they usually include all meals and come in 5 categories: deluxe, A, B, C and D. The tariff for each category is given by the **Houseboat Owners Association**, T0194-245 0326, www.houseboatowners.org, through whom you can also make bookings.

Butt's Clermont Houseboats, west side of Dal Lake, T0194-242 0325, www.butts clermonthouseboat.com. Moored by Naseem Bagh, Garden of Breezes, shaded by *chinar* trees and a wall built by Emperor Akbar. Far from the densely packed south side of Dal Lake, 4 cream-painted boats are moored side-on to the shore. Crewelwork on fabrics, carved cedar panels, rosewood tables and a view of Hazratbal mosque. In operation since 1940, they are now on guestbook No 16. Former guests include Lord Mountbatten, George Harrison, PG Wodehouse, Ravi Shankar and Michael Palin.

Gurkha Houseboats, Nagin Lake, T0194-242 1001, www.nivalink.com/gurkha. The **Gurkha** group are renowned for their comfortable rooms and stylish boats on peaceful Nagin Lake. Good service and food.

Zaffer Houseboats, on Nagin Lake, T01954-250 0507, www.zafferhouse boats.com. Deluxe boats with a long history, walnut-panelled walls, single-piece walnut tables, old writing desks, backed onto the lake which means the front terrace is a delightful place to sit. Peaceful and quiet (despite the *sikhara* salesmen).

Pahalgam
$$$$ Pahalgam Hotel, T01936-243252, www.pahalgamhotel.com. Upper-end Raj-era hotel dating back to 1931, 4 buildings, with 36 of 40 rooms enjoying splendid views of forested peaks across the River Lidder. Rooms are tastefully decorated, centrally heated, very spacious, some have been recently renovated but all are pleasing (18 suites). Swimming pool in summer. Prices include all meals. Excellent shop.

$$-$ Himalaya House, 3 km from the bus stand, 1 km from Laripora village, T(0)9411-9045021, gulzarhakeem@hotmail.com. A cosy hotel on the river with an island garden and a restaurant of repute. 20 rooms, some with bathtub and balcony, nice crewelwork curtains and bedspreads. The comfortable lobby has a fireplace and is a good place to make friends. Free Wi-Fi.

Gulmarg
Prices can be negotiated in the winter months, particularly for longer stays.

$$$$ Khyber Himalayan Resort & Spa, T01954-254666, khyberhotels.com. Absolute luxury in a new resort with an Ayurvedic spa, gym, heated pool, and amazing restaurants. Rooms beautifully furnished with teak floors, silk carpets, walnut carving and rich Kashmiri fabrics. State-of-the-art bathrooms, huge windows make the most of views. Also 4 cottages, some with own pool.

$$$ Hotel Highlands Park, T01954-254430, www.hotelhighlandspark.com. Oozing old-world charm, rooms and suites are decorated with Kashmiri woodcraft and rugs. Renowned for its atmosphere – the best bar in Gulmarg is here, straight out of the 1930s – it's a wonderful place to unwind after a hard day on the slopes. Rooms have *bukharis* (wood stoves) to keep you warm and electric blankets are available on request. Recommended.

RESTAURANTS

Srinagar
For a special treat, dine at the **Vivanta by Taj** (with killer views), see above.

$$ Mughal Darbar, Residency Rd. Popular with middle-class locals, the cosy Mughal Darbar offers multi-cuisine fare, specializing in Kashmiri *wazwan*. It's located on the 1st floor, up the stairs.

$$ Tao Café, Residency Rd. A popular hangout with local journalists, politicians and artists, the **Tao** serves decent Kashmiri and Chinese food, as well as Tibetan *momos*, fish and various snacks. Its attractive gardens make it a good summer spot.

SRINAGAR TO LEH ROAD

The road from Srinagar to Leh must be one of the most fascinating journeys in the world as it negotiates high passes and fragile mountainsides. There are dramatic scenic and cultural changes as you go from verdant Muslim Kashmir to ascetic Buddhist Ladakh. When there is political unrest in Kashmir, the route, which runs very close to the Line of Control, may be closed to travellers. The alternative route to Manali from Leh is equally fascinating, see Going further, page 183.

→ SRINAGAR TO LAMAYURU

After passing through **Sonamarg**, you reach the pass of **Zoji La** (3528 m). The pass is slippery after rains and usually closed by snow during winter months (November to April). From Zoji La the road descends to **Minamarg meadow** and **Dras** (3230 m). The winter temperatures have been known to go down to -50°C, and heavy snow and strong winds cut off the town. Dras has a spectacular setting and a scruffy centre with restaurants and shops; there's a tourist information centre and decent enough J&K bungalows. The broad Kargil basin and its wide terraces are separated from the Mulbekh Valley by the 12-km-long **Wakha Gorge**.

KARGIL TO KHALTSE

On the bank of the River Suru, Kargil was an important trading post on two routes, from Srinagar to Leh, and to Gilgit and the lower Indus Valley. In 1999 the Pakistan army took control briefly of the heights surrounding the town before being forced to retreat. The town is considered grim by most visitors, however it is the main overnight stop on the Srinagar–Leh highway, and provides road access to the Zanskar Valley. With a largely Shi'ite population, Kargil has a very different atmosphere to both Srinagar and Leh. Centred around the busy main bazar are cheap internet cafés (unreliable), ATMs, a tourist office and plenty of hotels. Walking up the valley slope, perpendicular to the main bazar, takes you past old village houses to finish at Goma Kargil (4 km) for excellent views.

From Kargil the road continues 30 km to **Shargol** – the cultural boundary between Muslim and Buddhist areas, with a tiny, very ambient monastery located down a side-road – and then after another 10 km reaches **Mulbek**, a pretty village with a large (9 m) ancient Maitreya Buddha relief fronted by a *gompa* on the roadside. The ruins of Mulbek Khar (fort) sit atop a stalk of cliff next to two small *gompas*, a steep climb that affords fabulous views. Shortly after Mulbek is its larger sister village of Wahka, then the road crosses **Namika La**, at 3720 m (known as the 'Pillar in the Sky'). There is a tourist bungalow in tiny **Haniskut**, set in a pretty river valley marred by roads and pylons, where a very ruined fort lies on the northern side of the valley. The road then climbs to **Fotu La** at 4093 m, the highest pass on the route. From here you can catch sight of the monastery at Lamayuru (see below). The road does a series of loops to descend to the ramshackle village of **Khaltse** with a couple of garden-restaurants, shops and lodges, where it meets the milky green Indus River.

LAMAYURU

Lamayuru, 10 km before Khaltse, is worth a long lunch break or overnight stop. The famous monastery is perched on a crag overlooking the Indus in a striking lunar landscape

ON THE ROAD

Ecological implications aside, travel by road from Srinagar gives you an advantage over flying into Leh as it enables you to acclimatize to a high-altitude plateau. However, some people find the journey from Srinagar terrifying and very uncomfortable. If you are able to hire a jeep or car it will give you the flexibility of stopping to rest and to see the several sights on the way. Most healthy people find that if they relax completely for two days after flying in, they acclimatize without difficulty. If you have a heart condition, consult your doctor on the advisability of going to Leh.

between a drained lake and high mountains. Little medieval houses nestle on the steep slope beneath the monastery, and the effect is dramatically photogenic. The monastery complex, which includes a library thought to be the oldest in the region, was founded in the 11th century and belongs to the Tibetan Kagyupa sect. The present monastery dating from the 16th century was partly destroyed in the 19th. You can still see some of the murals, along with the redecorated *dukhang* (assembly hall). A small glass panel in the right hand wall of the *dukhang* protects a tiny holy cave, and there are many beautiful bronzes displayed. In a small temple, below the monastery, is an 11-headed and 1000-armed Avalokiteshvara image; the walls here are coated with murals – you will need to ask someone to get the key. Some of the upper rooms are richly furnished with carpets, Tibetan tables, statues, silver *stupas* and butter lamps. In June/July the monastery holds the famous **Yuru Kabgyat** festival, with colourful masked dancing, special prayers, and burning of sacrificial offerings. There are several guesthouses strung along the road and up the hillside; it's also possible to camp near the stream in a willow grove. Buses to Leh leave Lamayuru at around 0930.

There is a comfortable eco-camp in **Uletokpo**, just by the highway. From Uletokpo village a 6-km track leads to dramatic **Rizong**, with a monastery and nunnery, which may accommodate visitors. **Saspol** village marks the wide valley from which you can reach Alchi by taking a branch road across the Indus after passing some caves.

→ ALCHI TO LEH

ALCHI
ⓘ *0800-1300, 1400-1800, Rs 50, www.achiassociation.org.*
The road enters Saspol; about 2 km beyond the village, a link road with a suspension bridge over the river leads to Alchi, which is hidden from view as you approach. As the road enters the village, impressive old houses in various states of repair can be seen. It's possible to climb up the small rocky peak behind these, to a square white turret with graves around, for good views up the Indus valley and of the village. A patchwork of cultivated fields surrounds the monastery complex. A narrow path from the car park winds past village houses, donkeys and apricot trees to lead to the **Dharma Chakra** monastery. You will be expected to buy a ticket from one of the three *lamas* on duty. The whole complex, about 100 m long and 60 m wide, is enclosed by a whitewashed mud and straw wall. Alchi's large temple complex is regarded as one of the most important Buddhist centres in Ladakh and a jewel of monastic skill. A path on the right past two large prayer wheels and a row of smaller ones leads to the river which attracts deer down

to the opposite bank in the evenings. At the rear, small *chortens* with inscribed stones strewn around them, line the wall. It is worth walking around the exterior of the complex, and you'll get a beautiful view of the Indus River with mountains as a backdrop. For accommodation options, see page 169.

Founded in the 11th century by Rinchen Zangpo, the 'Great Translator', the monastery was richly decorated by artists from Kashmir and Tibet. Paintings of the mandalas, which have deep Tantric significance, are particularly fine; some decorations are reminiscent of Byzantine art. The monastery is maintained by monks from Lekir and is no longer a place for active worship.

The temple complex The entrance *chortens* are worth looking in to. Each has vividly coloured paintings within, both along the interior walls as well as in the small *chorten*-like openings on the ceilings. The first and largest of these has a portrait of the founder Rinchen Zangpo (closed at the time of research).

The first temple you come to is the **Sum-stek**, the three-tier temple with a carved wooden gallery on the façade, has triple arches. Inside are three giant four-armed, garlanded stucco figures of *Bodhisattvas*: the white *Avalokitesvara* on the left, the principal terracotta-red *Maitreya* in the centre at the back, and the ochre-yellow *Manjusri* on the right; their heads project to the upper storey which is reached by a rustic ladder (inaccessible). The remarkable features here are the brightly painted and gilded decorations on the clothing of the figures which include historical incidents, musicians, palaces and places of pilgrimage. Quite incongruous court scenes and Persian features appear on *Avalokitesvara* while the figures on *Maitreya* have Tantric connotations illustrating the very different styles of ornamentation on the three figures. The walls have numerous *mandalas* and inscriptions, as well as thousands of tiny Buddhas.

The oldest temple is the **dukhang**, which has a covered courtyard (originally open to the sky) with wooden pillars and painted walls; the left wall shows two rowing boats with fluttering flags, a reminder perhaps of the presence in ancient times of lakes in this desert. The brightly painted door to the *dukhang*, about 1.5 m high, and the entrance archway has some fine woodcarving. The subsidiary shrines on either side of the doorway contain *Avalokitesvaras* and *Bodhisattvas* including a giant four-armed Maitreya figure to the

ALCHI CHOSKOR

To Indus River ▲

Jampang
(Manjusri)
Temple

Lotsawa
(Translator's)
Temple

Avalokitesvara

Wall

Du-khang   Courtyard

Prayer
Wheels

Vairacona

Large
Prayer
Wheels

Manjusri

Sum-stek
(3-Tier)
Temple

Wooden
Porch

Entrance Chortens

Maitreya

Avalokitesvara

Lhakhang
Soma
(New Temple)

Kanjyur
Lhakhang

N

Sculptures

20 metres

20 yards

extreme right. This main assembly hall, which was the principal place of worship, suffers from having very little light so visitors need a good torch. The 'shrine' holds the principal gilded *Vairocana* (Resplendent) Buddha (traditionally white, accompanied by the lion) with ornate decorations behind, flanked by four important Buddha postures among others. The walls on either side of the main hall are devoted to fine but damaged *Mandala* paintings illustrating the four principal manifestations of the *Sarvavid* (Omniscient) Buddha – *Vairocana*, *Sakyamuni* (the Preacher), *Manjusri* (Lord of Wisdom) and as *Prajna Paramita* (Perfection of Wisdom). There are interesting subsidiary panels, friezes and inscriptions. On exiting, note the terrifying figure of *Mahakala* the guardian deity above the door with miniature panels of royal and military scenes. The one portraying a drinking scene shows the royal pair sanctified with haloes with wine-cups in hand, accompanied by the prince and attendants – the detail of the clothing clearly shows Persian influence.

The **Lotsawa** (Translator's) and **Jampang** (Manjusri) *Lhakhangs* were built later and probably neglected for some time. The former contains a statue of Rinchen Zangpo along with a seated Buddha while the latter has a finely carved doorway and exterior lintels. Ask for the lights to be switched on.

Lhakhang Soma (New Temple) is a square hall used as a meditation centre with a *chorten* within; its walls are totally covered with *mandalas* and paintings portraying incidents from the Buddha's life and historic figures; the main figure here is the preaching Buddha. There is an interesting panel of warriors on horseback near the door. Request the temple be opened if it is locked. **Kanjyur Lhakhang** in front of the Lhakhang Soma houses the scriptures.

LEKIR (LIKIR)

Some 8 km after Saspol, a road on the left leads up to Lekir Monastery via a scenic route. Lower Lekir, a scattering of houses where most accommodation is found, is about 1 km off NH1 accessed by confusing unpaved tracks. You can walk from Lower Likir up to the monastery, about 5 km on the road, or via shortcuts crossing the river. The picturesque whitewashed monastery buildings rise in different levels on the hillside across the Lekir River. A huge gold-coloured Maitreya Buddha flanks the complex. Lekir was built during the reign of Lachen Gyalpo who installed 600 monks here, headed by Lhawang Chosje (circa 1088). The *gompa* was invested with a collection of fine images, *thangkas* and murals to vie with those at Alchi. The present buildings date mainly from the 18th century since the original were destroyed by fire. A path up leads to the courtyard where a board explains the origin of the name: Klu-Khyil (snake coil) refers to the *nagas* here, reflected in the shape of the hill. Lekir was converted to the Gelugpa sect in the 15th century. The head *lama*, the younger brother of the Dalai Lama, has his apartments here, which were extended in the mid-1990s.

The **dukhang** (assembly hall) contains large clay images of the Buddhas (past, present and future), *thangkas*, and Kangyur and Tengyur manuscripts, the Kangyur having been first compiled in Ladakh during Lachen Gyalpo's reign. The **Nyenes-Khang** contains beautiful murals of the 35 confessional Buddhas and 16 arahats. Wooden steps lead up to the **Gon-Khang** housing a statue of the guardian deity here, as well as *thangkas* and murals. Further steps lead to a small but very interesting **museum** ① *Rs 20, opened on request (climb to a hall above, up steep wooden stairs)*, displays *thangkas*, old religious and domestic implements, costumes, etc, which are labelled in English.

ON THE ROAD
Gompas and festivals

Buddhist festivals usually take place in the bleak winter months when villagers gather together, stalls spring up around the *gompas* and colourful dance dramas and masked dances are performed in the courtyards. Musical instruments, weapons and religious objects are brought out during these dance performances. The *Kushak* (high priest) is accompanied by monks in monotonous recitation while others play large cymbals, trumpets and drums. The serious theme of victory of Good over Evil is lightened by comic interludes. A few monasteries celebrate their festivals in the summer months, for example Lamayuru, Hemis and Phyang.

Village craftsmen produce *thangkas*, carved wooden folding seats and clay pottery. If you wish to stay overnight, the monastery has guestrooms which share bathrooms (by donation); for further accommodation options in the villages, see page 169. A bus goes to Leh at 0730 from the monastery.

BASGO

Further along the road you catch sight of the ruins of Basgo before it crosses the Chargyal Thang plain with *chortens* and *mani* walls and enters Nimmu (see below). The road passes through Basgo village with the ruins of a Buddhist citadel impressively sited on a spur overlooking the Indus Valley. It served as a royal residence for several periods between the 15th and 17th centuries. The **fort palace** was once considered almost impregnable, having survived a three-year siege by Tibetan and Mongol armies in the 17th century.

Among the ruins two temples have survived. The higher **Maitreya Temple** (mid-16th century) built by Tashi Namgyal's son contains a very fine Maitreya statue at the rear of the hall, flanked by *bodhisattvas*. Some murals from the early period illustrating the Tibetan Buddhist style have also survived on the walls and ceiling; among the Buddhas and *bodhisattvas* filled with details of animals, birds and mermaids, appear images of Hindu divinities. The 17th-century **Serzang Temple** (gold and copper), with a carved doorway, contains another large Maitreya image whose head rises through the ceiling into a windowed box-like structure. The murals look faded and have been damaged by water. The fort is very photogenic, particularly so in the late afternoon light. The Chamba View guesthouse and restaurant is by the road, as you exit the village.

NIMMU

The road rejoins the Indus Valley and rises to a bare plateau to give you the first glimpse of Leh, 30 km away. Phyang is down a side valley to the north (left). The mud-brick houses of Nimmu have grass drying on the flat rooftops to provide fodder for the winter. A dry stone *mani* wall runs along the road; beyond Nimmu the walls become 2 m wide in places with innumerable *chortens* alongside. The rocky outcrops on the hills to the left appear like a natural fortress. Nimmu serves mainly as a bus rest-stop, but there are a couple of small hotels and a collection of *dhabas* and shops.

PHYANG

Phyang Gompa, 16 km from Leh, dominates a beautiful side valley dotted with poplars, homesteads and *chortens* with a village close by. It belongs to the Red-Hat Kagyupa sect, with its 16th-century Gouon monastery built by the founder of the Namgyal Dynasty which is marked by a flagstaff at the entrance. It houses 60 lamas and hundreds of statues including some Kashmiri bronzes (circa 14th century), *thangkas* and manuscript copies of the Kangyur and Tengyur. The temple walls have colourful paintings centring on the eight emblems of happiness. The walls in the main prayer hall are covered with ancient smoke-blackened murals, and a giant rolled-up *thangka* hangs from the ceiling. The faces of the statues in the Protector's Hall have been covered. A grand new wing is being constructed, with rather gawdy paintings by the artists (many of whom come from Bhutan). Morning prayers take place 0600-0730. Phyang is the setting for a spectacular July **Tseruk festival** with masked dancing. There are three buses daily from Leh; the morning bus allows you to explore the valley and walk back to Leh, but the afternoon bus only allows a short visit. However, it is worth overnighting in Phyang as there is a pleasing guesthouse (see, opposite), good walks around the traditional village and dramatic valley up to the fort, and stunning views to the pyramid-peak of Stok Kangri.

SPITUK

Finally, some 8 km from Leh, Spituk is reached. Standing on a conical hill, Spituk was founded in the 11th century. The buildings themselves, including three chapels, date from the 15th century and are set in a series of tiers with courtyards and steps. The Yellow-Hat Gelugpa monks created the precedent in Ladakh for building on mountain tops rather than valley floors. You can get good views of the countryside around.

The long 16th- to 17th-century *dukhang* (assembly hall) is the largest building and has two rows of seats along the length of the walls to a throne at the far end. Sculptures and miniature *chortens* are displayed on the altar. Spituk has a collection of ancient Jelbagh masks, icons and arms including some rescued from the Potala Palace in Lhasa.

Also 16th- to 17th-century, the **Mahakal Temple**, higher up the hill, contains a shrine of Vajrabhairava, often mistaken for the Goddess Kali. The terrifying face is only unveiled in January, during the **Gustor festival**. The bus from Srinagar can drop you on the highway (four daily, 20 minutes).

SRINAGAR TO LEH ROAD LISTINGS

WHERE TO STAY

Kargil

Hotels are quite expensive, but bargaining will secure a discount. On Hospital Rd, running uphill just off the Main Bazar, there's a cluster of budget hotels. Restaurants all serve meat; for vegetarian food look for signs advertising Punjabi meals.

$$$-$ Green Land, signed down an alley off Main Bazar, T01985-232324, www.hotelgreenlandkargil.com. A popular and well-kept place, it's not cheap but prices fairly reflect the standard of the rooms. Old block doubles Rs 1000, new block (much preferable) with a range of rooms including deluxe standard. Open all year round.

Lamayuru

$ Dragon, Lower Rd, T01982-224501, dragon_skyabu@yahoo.com. A range of spacious carpeted rooms, 4 with en suite by the garden restaurant, 8 with shared bath in the building to the rear, most are south-facing, and room 10 has attractively painted walls. Clean sheets and very reasonably priced. Restaurant serves up excellent Indian meals, and has a diverse menu. Internet available (during the 3 hrs of electricity in the evenings), as is hot water.

$ Niranjana Hotel, T01982-224555. Next to the monastery, this institutional-looking hotel has rooms on 3 levels with excellent valley views. Rooms are plain but comfortable. All share communal bathrooms which are modern and clean, hot shower in the evenings. Downstairs restaurant is good.

Alchi

$$ Alchi Resort, T(0)9419-218636, www.alchiresort.tripod.com. "The first never before hut type twin roomed resort in Ladakh"! A flowery fruit-filled garden edged by whitewashed cottages in adjoining pairs; cottages at the end enjoy more privacy. Well-appointed motel layout,

rooms, all have flatscreen TV, laminate or carpet floors, plain tiled bathrooms.

$ Heritage Home, right next to the monastery entrance. A very pleasant and convenient choice. Rooms are large, carpeted, freshly painted, en suite (hot water in the evening), soap and clean towel. Upstairs is more expensive, there's a decent restaurant out front with apricot trees above.

Lekir

$$ Lhukhil, T01982-253588, www.ladakhpackages.com. Grand gateway and luxuriant garden, although outdoor seating is on patchy grass next to scary statues and dragon-wrapped pillars. 24 rooms are well-fitted out and comfortable, with towels, toiletries and some views. Meals included.

$ Norboo Spon Guesthouse and Camping, Lower Lekir. Signed off the road to the monastery, or 300 m walk from Lower Likir on the way to the monastery. In a large Ladakhi house, roof decked with prayer flags, bright white paint and red trims, set among trees in a large garden with plenty of seating. Dining area of little tables, rugs and cushions with the odd decorative mask is cosy and homely; shared balcony. Rooms upstairs have good views and a very decent shared bathroom. Charming and kind family.

Phyang

$ Hidden North Guesthouse, T01982-226007, www.hiddennorth.com. This sweet guesthouse, set on a hillside, commands marvellous views. There are 7 clean unfussy rooms, most with views, one with private terrace, some with private bath; run by a nice Ladakhi-German couple. Huge shared terrace and garden. Meals available (Rs 70-150). It's perched at the top end of the village, a 5-min uphill walk from the last bus stop. Treks can also be arranged by their responsible outfit.

LADAKH

The mountains of Ladakh – literally 'many passes' – may not be as typically spectacular as some parts of the high Himalaya for, as even the valleys are at an altitude of 3500 m, the summits are only 3000 m higher. Because it is desert there is little snow on them and they look like big brown hills, dry and dusty, with clusters of willows and desert roses along the streams. Yet bright blue skies are an almost constant feature, as the monsoon rains do not reach here, and the contrast with the dramatic landscape creates a beautiful and heavenly effect. For thousands of visitors Ladakh is a completely magical place, remote and relatively unspoilt, with delightful, gentle, ungrasping people.

ARRIVING IN LADAKH

Getting around Inner Line Permits for the Nubra Valley, Tso-moriri and Pangong-Tso cost Rs 50 per person per day (for each area) for a maximum of seven days in each place, while trekkers in the Hemis High Altitude Park must pay Rs 25 per day. Permits are available from the District Commissioner's office in Leh, but all trekking/travel agents can arrange them for you – a much easier option. Allow at least half a day for an agent to obtain a permit, given only for groups of two or more. Permits are not extendable, but can be post-dated. Many people opt for permits covering all restricted areas. As a matter of course you should carry your passport with you since Ladakh is a sensitive border region. It's also worth carrying multiple photocopies of your passport and permits, as some checkpoints demand a copy.

Note Given the darkness of many buildings even at midday it is worth taking a torch wherever you go; it's a must at night.

Best time to visit The temperature can drop to -30°C in Leh and Kargil and -50°C in Dras, remaining sub-zero from December to February. Yet on clear sunny days in the summer, it can be scorching hot and you can easily get sunburnt; take plenty of sun cream. Ladakh lies beyond the monsoon line so rainfall is only 50 mm annually and there are even occasional dust storms. From October to May Leh is cut off by snow and you will have to fly in (see opposite).

BACKGROUND

Until recently Ladakhi society has generally been very introverted and the economy surprisingly self-sufficient. An almost total lack of precipitation has meant that cultivation must rely on irrigation. The rivers have been harnessed but with difficulty as the deep gorges presented a problem. Altitude and topography determine the choice of crop and farming is restricted to the areas immediately around streams and rivers. Barley forms the staple food while peas are the most common vegetable and apples and apricots the most popular fruits – the latter are dried for winter sustenance, while the kernel yields oil for burning in prayer-lamps. Because of the harshness of the climate and lack of rain, the cropping season usually lasts from April to October. At lower altitudes, grape, mulberry and walnut are grown.

Livestock is precious, especially the yak which provides meat, milk for butter, hair and hide for tents, boots, ropes and dung for fuel. Goats, especially in the eastern region, produce fine *pashm* for export. Animal transport is provided by yaks, ponies, Bactrian

ON THE ROAD
Traditional Ladakhi dress

Ladakhis dress in *gonchas*, loose woollen robes tied at the waist with a wide coloured band. Buddhists usually wear dark red while Muslims and nomadic tribes often use undyed material. The headdress varies from the simple Balti woollen cap with a rolled brim and the traditional *gonda* (a high embroidered hat) to the snake-shaped ornate black lambskin *perak* worn by some women. Studded with turquoise and lapis lazuli these are precious enough to be handed down as heirlooms.

camels and the broad-backed *hunia* sheep. The Zanskar pony is fast and strong and used for transport – and for the special game of Ladakhi polo. Travellers venturing out of Leh are likely to see villagers using traditional methods of cultivation with the help of *dzos* and donkeys and using implements that have not changed for centuries.

Cut off from the outside world for six months a year, Ladakh also developed a very distinct culture. Polyandry (where a woman has more than one husband) was common but many men became *lamas* (monks) and a few women *chomos* (nuns). Most people depended on subsistence agriculture but the harsh climate contributed to very high death rates and a stable population. That is rapidly changing. Imported goods are now widely available and more and more people are taking part in the monetary economy. Ladakh and its capital Leh have been open to tourists since 1974, and some feel there are now far too many; the pitfalls of modern society are all too evident in the mounds of plastic rubbish strewn along the roadsides. The population of Leh has increased by more than five times in the last decade, and during the summer months tourists descend in numbers that equal the local population. In winter, those who can, leave for the plains – so this is when a more traditional Leh experience can be had, if you can bear the cold and the inconvenience.

→ LEH

Mysterious dust-covered Leh sits in a fertile side valley of the Indus, about 10 km from the river. Encircled by stark awe-inspiring mountains with the cold desert beyond, it is the nearest experience to Tibet in India. The old Palace sits precariously on the hill to the north and looms over Leh. The wide Main Bazar Street (circa 1840s), which once accommodated caravans, has a colourful vegetable market where unpushy Ladakhi women sell local produce on the street side while they knit or chat. Makeshift craft and jewellery stalls line parts of Fort Road to the east to attract summer visitors along with Kashmiri shopkeepers who have come in search of greener pastures. The Old Town, mainly to the east of the Main Street, with its maze of narrow lanes, sits on the hillside below the palace and is worth exploring.

ARRIVING IN LEH
Getting there For seven to eight months in the year Leh is cut off by snow and the sole link with the outside world is by air. Tickets are in high demand so it is essential to book well ahead (on the internet). From mid-June to the end of September (weather permitting) the Manali–Leh highway opens to traffic, bringing travellers to the New Bus Stand south of town. Taxis wait at both the airport and bus stand to take you to town.

DREAM TRIP 2: Ladakh **171**

Moving on From Leh you can fly back to **Delhi** (see page 35) in one hour and 20 minutes, for your international flight home. If time is not an issue, you could travel overland to Delhi via **Manali** and the **Kullu Valley** (see page 183) or travel to **Corbett National Park** (see page 185) for a few days' wildlife spotting.

Getting around Many hotels are within a few minutes' walk of the Main Bazar Street around which Leh's activities are concentrated. All the places of interest in Leh itself can also be tackled on foot by most visitors though those arriving by air or from Manali are urged to acclimatize for 48 hours before exerting themselves. For visiting monasteries and spots out of town arrange a jeep or taxi, although there are some buses and hitchhiking is possible.

Tourist information J&K Tourism ① *2 km south on Airport Rd, T01982-252297, www.jktourism.org; or try the more convenient office on Fort Rd, T01982-253462, 1000-1600.*

BACKGROUND
The city developed as a trading post and market, attracting a wide variety of merchants from Yarkand, Kashgar, Kashmir, Tibet and North India. Tea, salt, household articles, wool and semi-precious stones were all traded in the market. Buddhism travelled along the Silk Road and the Kashmir and Ladakh feeder, which has also seen the passage of soldiers, explorers and pilgrims, forerunners of the tourists who today contribute most to the urban economy.

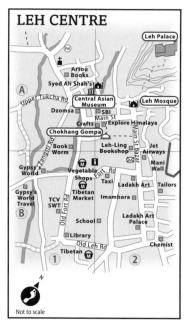

LEH CENTRE

Not to scale

PLACES IN LEH
Dun-coloured **Leh Palace** ① *sunrise to sunset, Rs 100*, has been described as a miniature version of Lhasa's Potala Palace. Built in the mid-16th century, the palace was partly in ruins by the 19th century. It has nine storeys, sloping buttresses and projecting wooden balconies. From the town below it is dazzling in the morning sun and ghostly at night. Built by King Singe Namgyal and still owned by the royal family, it is now unoccupied – they live in the palace at Stok. Visible damage was caused during Zorawar Singh's invasion from Kashmir in the 1830s. The palace is under restoration, with new window and door frames fitted, and structural improvements being made – but still be wary of hazardous holes in the floor. After a steep climb some find the palace disappointing, but the views from the roof are exceptional. Like the Lhasa Potala Palace it has numerous rooms, steps and narrow passages (take a torch). The central prayer room has religious texts

ON THE ROAD

Prepare for a different lifestyle in Leh

The whitewashed sun-dried brick walls of a typical two-storey, flat-roofed Ladakhi house, often with decorative woodwork around doors and windows and a carefully nurtured garden, look inviting to a traveller after a long hard journey. Many local families have opened up their homes to provide for the increasing demand for accommodation over a very short peak season and new hotels are springing up everywhere. However, prices do not reflect the type of furniture, furnishings and plumbing you might expect elsewhere in India although on the whole the rooms are kept clean. There is usually a space for sitting out – a 'garden' with a tree or two, some flower beds and some grass struggling to establish itself.

Electricity is limited, so expect power cuts, which are random and unpredictable. Some hotels have generators. Those without may run out of tap water but buckets are always at hand. Hot water is a luxury, available only during mornings and evenings. Plumbing allows for flush WCs in most hotels, although compost toilets are the more ecological method.

Guests are encouraged to economize on water and electricity – you will notice the low-power bulbs and scarcity of lights in rooms and public areas, so put away your reading material until sunrise.

lining the walls, and contains dusty deities and time-worn masks. The upper levels have some painted carved wooden lintels and old murals that give a hint of past splendours. The Archaeological Survey of India is responsible for restoration and you will be able to watch work in progress.

South of the palace, the architecturally striking **Leh Mosque** in the main bazar is worth visiting – the inner section is not open to women visitors. The Sunni Muslim mosque is believed to stand on land granted by King Deldan Namgyal in the 1660s; his grandmother was the Muslim Queen of Ladakh.

The new **Central Asian Museum** is housed in a beautifully constructed building in the Tsa Soma gardens, where camel caravans used to camp. The museum explores the history of the caravan trade that for centuries linked Ladakh, until its mid-20th-century isolation, with Tibet, Afghanistan, Samarkand, Kashmir and other city states. The museum is shaped like a Ladakhi fortress tower, with four floors inspired by the architecture of Ladakh, Kashmir, Tibet and Baltistan. Exhibits (metalware, coins, masks, etc) reveal the cultural exchange throughout the region; a garden café and museum shop are planned. A walking tour that includes the museum and visits restored buildings of the Old Town leaves daily (1000-1300, Rs 300) from **Lala's Art Café** (see Restaurants, page 182).

The **Chokhang Gompa** (New Monastery, 1957), off Main Bazar, was built to commemorate the 2500th anniversary of the birth of Buddha. The remains of the **Leh Gompa** houses a large golden Buddha.

The 15th-century **Tsemo Gompa** ('Red' Temple) is a strenuous walk north of the city and has a colossal two-storey-high image of Maitreya, flanked by figures of Avalokitesvara (right) and Manjusri (left). It was founded in 1430 by King Graspa Bum-Lde of the Namgyal rulers and a portrait of Tashi Namgyal hangs on the left at the entrance. Just bove the *gompa* is **Tsemo Fort** ① *dawn-dusk, Rs 20*, the classic landmark above Leh which can be seen from miles around.

ON THE ROAD
Volunteering

If you are interested in voluntary work, get in touch with the various organizations in Leh, such as **SECMOL**, www.secmol.org, or **LEDeG** (see below). There is a range of possibilities in and around Leh for potential volunteers, from teaching English to construction work. Alternatively, contact the **International Society for Ecology and Culture**, www.localfutures.org/ladakh-project. Farm volunteers with the **Learning from Ladakh** project are welcome (usually from July to September) for a minimum of a one-month to stay and work with a Ladakh farming family. A participation fee is expected (amount depends on where you are from) plus a nominal sum for daily lodging.

Sankar Gompa (17th-18th centuries) ① *3 km north of the centre, 0700-1000, 1700-1900, prayers at 1830 with chanting, drums and cymbals*, of the Yellow Hat Sect, is one of the few *gompas* built in the valley bottom; it's an enjoyable walk through fields from town. It houses the chief *lama* of Spituk and 20 others. The newer monks' quarters are on three sides of the courtyard with steps leading up to the *dukhang* (Assembly Hall). There are a number of gold statues, numerous wall paintings and sculptures including a large one of the 11-headed, 1000-armed *Avalokitesvara*. It's an atmospheric and beautiful enclave in the increasingly busy valley.

On Changspa Lane, across the stream from Sankar Gompa, you reach the start of the stiff climb up to the white Japanese **Shanti Stupa** (1989). This is one of a series of 'Peace Pagodas' built by the Japanese around the world. There are good views from the top where a café offers a welcome sight after the climb. There is also a road which is accessible by jeep. Below the *stupa*, the **New Ecology Centre**, has displays on 'appropriate technology', as well as a handicrafts centre, a technical workshop and an organic vegetable garden.

The **Ecological Centre of LEDeG** (Ladakh Ecological Development Group) and the **craft shop** ① *T01982-253221, www.ledeg.org, Mon-Fri 1000-1800*, opened in 1984 to spread awareness of Ladakhi environmental issues, encourage self-help and the use of alternative technology. It has a library of books on Ladakhi culture, Buddhism and the environment. Handicrafts are sold, and you can refill water for Rs 10.

The **Women's Alliance of Ladakh** (WAL) ① *Sankar Rd, Chubi, T01982-250293, www.womenallianceladakh.org, video shown Mon-Sat 1500 (minimum 10 people)*, is an alliance of 5000 Ladakhi women, concerned with raising the status of traditional agriculture, preserving the traditionally high status of women which is being eroded in the modern sector, and creating an alternative development model based on self-reliance for Ladakh. The centre has a café selling local and organic foods and a craft shop. They hold festivals, cultural shows, dances, etc which are advertised around Leh; it's mainly aimed at local people, but all visitors are welcome.

The **Donkey Sanctuary** ① *www.donkeysanctuary.in*, opened in 2008. This charity looks after 40 to 60 donkeys at any one time and is well worth a visit.

West of the centre, the non-profit making **Students' Educational and Cultural Movement of Ladakh** (SECMOL) ① *Karzoo, with an office on Old Leh Rd, T01982-252421, www.secmol.org*, encourages the teaching of Ladakhi history, culture and crafts.

From the radio station there are two long *mani* walls. **Rongo Tajng** is in the centre of the open plain and was built as a memorial to Queen Skalzang Dolma by her son Dalden

Namgyal. It is about 500 m long and was built in 1635. The stones have been meticulously carved. The other, a 350-m wall down the hill, is believed to have been built by Tsetan Namgyal in 1785 as a memorial to his father, the king.

→ SOUTHEAST OF LEH

South and east of Leh is an amazing stretch of road with some fascinating monasteries strung along it. Many of these make good day trips from Leh, and are possible excursions by bus and hitching. If you hire a car or jeep (which is good value when shared by four) you can visit many of the places below in a single day. Camera flash is not usually allowed in monasteries to reduce damage to wall paintings and *thangkas*. Carry a torch.

CHOGLAMSAR
Choglamsar, 7 km south of Leh on the east bank of the Indus, is a green oasis with poplars and willows where there are golf links and a polo ground as well as horticultural nurseries. The road between Leh and Choglamsar is now quite built up and at times clogged with traffic. The Central Institute of Buddhist Studies is here with a specialist library. Past the Tibetan refugee camps, children's village and the arts and crafts centre, the Choglamsar Bridge crosses the Indus. The **Chochot Yugma Imambara**, a few minutes' walk from the bridge, is worth a visit. Buses depart Leh hourly from 0800-1800.

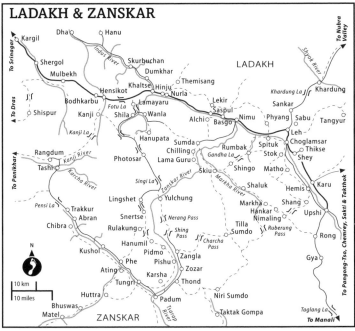

LADAKH & ZANSKAR

STOK

Across Choglamsar Bridge, 16 km south of Leh, is the royal palace dating from the 1840s when the King of Ladakh was deposed by the invading Dogra forces. The last king died in 1974 but his widow still lives here. His son continues the royal line and ascended to the throne in July 1993. The palace is a rambling building where only a dozen of the 80 rooms are used. The small **Palace Museum** ① *May-Oct 0900-1300 and 1400-1900, Rs 50*, with three rooms, is a showpiece for the royal *thangkas*, many 400 years old, crown jewels, dresses, coins, *peraks* (headdresses) encrusted with turquoise and lapis lazuli as well as religious objects. There's also a rather lovely café, which beckons with its views.

The **gompa**, a short distance away, has some ritual dance masks. Tsechu is in February. A three-hour walk up the valley behind Stok takes you to some extraordinary mountain scenery dominated by the 6121-m-high Stok Kangri.

There is an **archery contest** in July. There are at least three simple guesthouses in town, of which the Yarsta is most comfortable. Buses to Stok leave Leh at 0730 and 1700. Taxis from the Leh central taxi stand are available at fixed rates at any time.

SHEY

① *Palace open all day; try to be there 0700-0900, 1700-1800 when prayers are chanted, Rs 20.*
Until the 16th century, Shey was the royal residence, located at an important vantage point in the Indus Valley. Kings of Leh were supposed to be born in the monastery. The royal family moved to Stok in order to escape advancing Dogra forces from Kashmir who came to exploit the trade in pashmina wool. Shey, along with Thikse, is also regarded as an auspicious place for cremation.

Most of the fort walls have fallen into disrepair but the palace and its wall paintings have now been restored. The palace *gompa* with its 17.5-m-high blue-haired Maitreya Buddha, imitating the one at Tsemo Gompa, is attended by Drukpa monks from Hemis. It is made of copper and brass but splendidly gilded and studded with precious gem stones. Paintings in the main shrine have been chemically cleaned by the Archaeological Society of India. The large victory *stupa* is topped with gold. Extensive grounds covering the former lake bed to the east contain a large number of *chortens* in which cremated ashes of important monks, members of the royal family and the devout were buried. A newer temple houses another old giant Buddha statue. There are several rock carvings; particularly noteworthy is that of five *dhyani* Buddhas (circa eighth century) at the bottom of the hill. The small hotel below the *gompa* has spartan but clean rooms. It is 15 km southeast of Leh on the Indus River or can be reached along a stone path from Thikse. Hourly buses leave Leh 0800-1800.

THIKSE

① *Rs 30, hourly buses from Leh 0800-1800.*
Situated 25 km south of Leh on a crag overlooking the flood plain on the east bank of the Indus, this is one of the most imposing monasteries in Ladakh and was part of the original Gelugpa order in the 15th century. The 12-storey monastery, with typical tapering walls painted deep red, ochre and white, has 10 temples, a nunnery and 80 *lamas* in residence whose houses cling to the hillside below. The complex contains numerous *stupas*, statues, *thangkas*, wall paintings (note the fresco of the 84 Mahasiddhas, high above) swords and a large pillar engraved with the Buddha's teachings.

The new temple interior is dominated by a giant 13-m-high Buddha figure near the entrance. The principal *Dukhang* (assembly hall) at the top of the building has holes in the wall for storing religious texts and contains the guardian deities. At the very top, the Old Library has old wooden bookcases with ancient texts and statues; adjacent is the tiny *Chamsing Lhakhang*. Views from the roof are staggeringly good. The slightly creepy *Gonkhang* has Tibetan-style wall paintings. The **museum** ① *0600-1800, lunch break 1300-1330*, is near the entrance, and also sells souvenirs. There's a restaurant and guestrooms, below the museum. Thikse is a popular place to watch religious ceremonies, usually at 0630 or 1200. An early start by taxi makes even the first possible, or it's possible to stay overnight. They are preceded by the playing of large standing drums and long horns similar to *alpenstock*. Masked dances are performed during special festivals.

STAKNA

Across the valley on a hill, Stakna is the earliest Drukpa monastery, built before Hemis though its decorations are not as ancient. It is also called 'Tiger's nose' because of the shape of the hill site. This small but well-kept monastery has a beautiful silver-gilt *chorten* in the assembly hall, installed around 1955, and some interesting paintings in the dark temple at the back. No need for a local guide as the *lamas* are always willing to open the doors. There are excellent views of the Indus Valley and the Zanskar range.

HEMIS

① *0800-1300, 1400-1800.*

On the west bank of the Indus, 45 km southeast of Leh, the monastery, built on a green hillside surrounded by spectacular mountain scenery, is tucked into a gorge. The **Drukpa Monastery** was founded by Stagsang Raspa during the reign of Senge Namgyal (circa 1630). It is the biggest (350 *lamas*) and wealthiest in Ladakh and it's a 'must', thus is busy with tourists. Pass by *chortens* and sections of *mani* walls to enter the complex through the east gate which leads into a large 40 m by 20 m courtyard. Colourful flags flutter in the breeze from posts, and the balconied walls of the buildings have colourfully painted door and window frames. On the north side are two assembly halls approached by steps. The large three-tiered *Dukhang* to the right used for ceremonies is old and atmospheric; the smaller *Tshogskhang* (main temple) contains three silver gilt *chortens* and is covered in murals. The murals in the verandas depict guardian deities, the *kalachakra* (wheel of life) and 'Lords of the four quarters' are well preserved. A staircase alongside the *Tshogskhang* leads to a roof terrace where there are a number of shrines including a bust of the founder. The *Tsom Lakhang* (chapel) has ancient Kashmiri bronzes, a golden Buddha and a silver *chorten*. The largest of the monastery's prized possession is a heavy silk *thangka*, beautifully embroidered in bright coloured threads and pearls, which is displayed every 12 years (next 2016). The museum contains an important library of Tibetan-style books and an impressive collection of *thangkas*.

Not many people make the walk to the new golden Buddha on a nearby cliff, and there is also a pleasant 3-km walk uphill to another *gompa*. A stay in Hemis overnight enables you to attend early-morning prayers, a moving experience and recommended. Bus services make a day trip possible.

CHEMREY

Picture-perfect Chemrey is a short way off the main road, walkable from where the bus drops passengers. Perched on a little peak above encircling barley fields is **Thekchok Gompa**, home to 70 monks. A road winds to the top, but it's nicer to walk up the steep steps through traditional homesteads. The wonky prayer hall has countless murals of the Buddha, and there are three further *lhakhang* (image halls) to visit; a museum on the roof contains *thangkas* and statues. The beautiful setting and relative lack of visitors makes Chemrey a very worthwhile stop.

SAKTI AND TAKTHOK

The road continues through a sloping valley to Takthok, first passing Sakti village with the dramatic ruins of a fortress by the roadside. At ancient **Takthok Gompa** ① *Rs 30*, there is a holy cave-shrines in which the sage Padmasambhava meditated in the eighth century. The walls and ceiling are papered with rupee notes and coins, numerous statues are swathed in prayer scarves, and centuries of butter lamps have left their grime. A highly colourful *dukhang* hall contains three beautiful statues. It is the only monastery in Ladakh belonging to the Nyingma sect of Buddhism; about 60 *lamas* reside here, and at the new *gompa* constructed nearby in 1980. It's possible to take a morning bus from Leh to Takthok and walk the 5 km back down the valley to Chemrey. Should you get stranded in Takthok, a **Tourist Bungalow**, T(0)9622-959513, opposite the *gompa*, has four jaded but sunny rooms, some with squat toilets.

PANGONG-TSO

A popular excursion from Leh (permit required) is to the narrow 130-km-long Pangong-Tso, at 4250 m, the greater part of which lies in Tibet. The road, which is only suitable for 4WD in places, is via **Karu** on the Leh–Manali Highway, where the road east goes through **Zingral** and over the Chang La pass. Beyond are **Durbuk**, a small village with low-roofed houses, and **Tangste**, the 'abode of Chishul warriors' with a Lotswa Temple, which is also an army base with a small bank. The rough jeep track takes you through an impressive rocky gorge which opens out to a valley which has camping by a freshwater stream in the hamlet of **Mugleb** and then on to **Lukung** and finally **Spangmik**, 153 km from Leh. On the way you will be able to see some Himalayan birds including *chikhor* (quail) which may end up in the cooking pot.

An overnight stop on the lake shore allows you to see the blue-green lake in different lights. You can walk between Lukung and Spangmik, 7 km, on the second day, passing small settlements growing barley and peas along the lake shore. You return to Leh on the third day. There are tented camps at Durbuk, Tangtse and Lukung. At Spangmik there is a wider choice of accommodation, in the form of homestays (mats on floor) or in the rather pricey Pangong Tso Resort (rooms have attached bath). Buses go from Leh at 0630 on Saturdays and Sundays, but almost everyone makes the journey by private jeep.

→ NUBRA VALLEY

These once-restricted areas are now open to visitors with an Inner Line Permit. Permits are issued in Leh to groups of two or more travelling together by jeep, for a maximum of seven days. You can get a joint permit to cover all areas. Allow a day to get a permit. A lot of ground can be covered in the period but it is best to consult a Leh-based trekking and travel agent. Always carry multiple photocopies of your passport and ILP with you, to facilitate the crossing of checkpoints.

For an exhilarating high-altitude experience over possibly the highest motorable pass in the world, travel across the Ladakh range over the 5600-m **Khardung La**. This is along the old Silk Route to the lush green Nubra Valley up to **Panamik**, 140 km north of Leh. Camel caravans once transported Chinese goods along this route for exchanging with Indian produce. The relatively gentle climate here allows crops, fruit and nuts to grow, so some call it 'Ldumra' (orchard). There are guesthouses in villages throughout the valley, and temporary tented camps are occasionally set up by tour companies during the season, but it's still a good idea to take a sleeping bag.

It is possible to visit the Nubra-Shyok valleys over two days, but it's much preferable (and the same cost) to make the journey over three. After crossing the Khardung La, the first village is **Khardung**, 42 km later, boasting a magnificent setting. The road continues down the Shyok Valley to **Deskit**, which has an old and a new (less appealing) town centre and several places to stay. On a hill above the old village is a Gelugpa sect **monastery** (the largest in Nubra) built by the Ladakhi king Sohrab Zangpo in the early 1700s. There is large statue of Tsongkhapa, and the Rimpoche of Thikse monastery south of Leh oversees this monastery also. A further 10 km past Deskit is the village of **Hunder**, probably the most popular place to overnight, with several garden-guesthouses to chose from. Highly prized double-humped camels can occasionally be seen on the sand dunes near Hunder, allegedly descendents of the caravan-camels that used to ply the Silk Route, and it is possible to take a 15- to 30-minute camel ride (on a tame beast). Past Hunder the road continues to **Turtuk**, open to tourists since 2010. The scenery is impressive and the tiny settlements here are culturally Balti and practise Islam.

The second biggest monastery in Nubra is near **Tiger** village along the road to Panamik in the Nubra Valley. Called the **Samtanling** *gompa*, it was founded in 1842 and belongs to the Gelugpa sect. **Panamik** has several guesthouses and reddish, sulphurous hot springs nearby. The ILP allows travel only up **Ensa Gompa**, included on some itineraries, and approached by foot for the last 30 minutes.

Should you need medical help, there is a health centre at Deskit and a dispensary at Panamik. Traffic into and out of the Nubra Valley is controlled by the army at Pulu. From Leh there are two buses per week from June to September; a few have tried by bike, which can be put on the roof of the bus for the outward journey.

→ TREKKING IN LADAKH

Make sure your trekking guide is experienced and competent. A detailed book, although dated, is the Trailblazer guide *Trekking in Ladakh*, which can be bought in bookshops in Leh. Some treks, eg Spituk to Hemis and Hemis High Altitude National Park, charge a fee of Rs 25 per person per day or Rs 10 for Indians. For trekking, July and August are pleasant months. Go earlier and you will be trudging through snow much of the time. September and October are also good months, though colder at night.

HEMIS HIGH ALTITUDE NATIONAL PARK
Established in 1981, the park adjoining the monastery comprising the catchments of Markha, Rumbak and Sumda *nalas*. The reserve area has been expanded a couple of times, and now covers 4400 sq km making it the largest national park in South Asia. The rugged terrain with valleys often littered with rocks and rimmed by high peaks (some over 6000 m), supports limited alpine vegetation but contains some rare species of flora and fauna, including the ibex, Pallas' cat, *bharal* and *shapu*. It is the habitat of the endangered

and elusive snow leopard, now numbering around 200 (mainly in the Rumbak area, best spotted in winter). It is hoped that the activities of local villagers, who graze livestock within the park, can be restricted to a buffer zone so that their animals can be kept safe from attack by wolves and snow leopards. Villages used to trap the leopard, but now they are reimbursed for any livestock lost to snow leopard attacks.

There are camping sites within the park, which can be reserved through the Wildlife Warden in Leh. There are also homestays, see www.himalayan-homestays.com, run in conjunction with the Snow Leopard Conservancy India Trust (SNC-IT), www.snowleopard conservancy.org. SNC-IT also run 10-day winter expeditions, 'Quest of the Snow Leopard'. Since most of the park lies within 'restricted' areas, you need a special permit for entry, also issued in Leh.

There are a couple of short treks within Hemis National Park. An easy choice, good for when you are acclimatizing, goes through **Zingchen** gorge (where you camp) to the beautiful village of **Rumbak** (five hours) and then **Stok**. This can be done over two days/three nights, and takes in Stok La (pass) for amazing views on the third day. **Zingchen** to **Chilling**, three nights/four days, is a tougher option as it also crosses the bleak windswept **Gandha La** from where you get views to the Zanskar Valley.

RIPCHAR VALLEY TREK

This is a trek of four hard days; the average daily walking time is seven hours so don't underestimate it. A guide is recommended. The first stage involves transport from Leh (five or six hours), then an hour's walk to **Hinju** (3750 m); camp or homestay overnight at the village. Stage two continues up through the Ripchar Valley to cross the **Konze La** (4570 m), from where you will see the Zanskar River and gorge and the Stok range. Then descend to **Sumdo Chenmo**, quite a treacherous route as it involves river crossings. There is a monastery here with an impressive statue of the Buddha and some attractive wall paintings. A campsite lies just beyond the village. The next day takes you from Sumdo Chenmo to **Lanak** (4000 m), a walk of five or six hours. The final stage, about seven hours, from Lanak to **Chilling** is over the **Dungduchan La** (4700 m) with excellent views. The path continues down the valley following a stream to Chilling. Overnight in Chilling or make the two-hour drive back to Leh. Some agents also offer the option of rafting back to Leh from Chilling along the Zanskar River.

SHAM REGION

A relatively easy trek can be made from **Likir** to **Ang** and **Temisgang** over two nights/three days, passing through interesting villages and taking in the monasteries at Likir and **Rizong**.

LADAKH LISTINGS

WHERE TO STAY

Leh

$$$$-$$$ Grand Dragon, Old Leh Rd, Sheynam, T01982-257 786, www.thegrand dragonladakh.com. Big hotel with all mod cons, Wi-Fi and great views. Stunning dining room and a nod to eco-tourism with double-glazing, under-floor heating and solar panels. Open all year round.

$$$ Lha-Ri-Sa, Skara, T01982-252 000, www.ladakh-lharisa.com. With a boutique vibe, they offer stylish rooms and the outside of the building is simply beautiful. In the restaurant they serve up flavours from all over India as well as traditional Ladakhi food. Recommended, although it's on the outskirts of town.

$$ Lharimo, Fort Rd, T01982-252101, lharimo@yahoo.com. Attractive central hotel with scarlet window-frames and whitewashed exterior, large comfortable rooms have traditional bamboo ceilings and inoffensive aging wooden furniture, TV, clean tiled bathrooms. The big grassy lawn is perfect for relaxing.

$$ Yak-Tail, Fort Rd, T01982-252118, www.hotelyaktail.com. Open May-Oct. One of Leh's oldest hotels, comfortable and cosy (decent heating), some of the 30 rooms are 'houseboat style', others have balconies, some have lots of patterns. Restaurant nicely decorated with murals serves good Indian food, courtyard has been astro-turfed but swinging vines create a pleasing greenhouse effect.

$$-$ Oriental, below Shanti Stupa, T01982-253153, www.orientalguesthouse. com. 35 very clean rooms in traditional family home, good home cooking in the dining hall, great views across the valley, friendly, treks and travel arrangements reliable. Open all year. Recommended.

$$-$ Padma Guesthouse & Hotel, off Fort Rd down an alley, T01982-252630, (0)9906-982171, www.padmaladakh.net. Clean, charming rooms with common bath in guesthouse in the old family home, upstairs has mountain views (rooftop restaurant), plus hotel-style rooms in newer block, beautiful and peaceful garden, Buddhist chapel/meditation room, solar panels, good library, but most known for their outstanding hospitality. Highly recommended.

$ Saser, 500-800, Karzoo Lane, T01982-257162, nam_gyal@rediff.com. A good clean choice with large freshly painted rooms arranged around a grassy garden. Pay more for new laminate floors, cheerful bed-covers and better bathrooms. There's a generator and breakfast is available.

$ Silver Cloud, by Sankar Gompa, 15 mins' walk from centre, T01982-253128, (0)9622-175988, silvercloudpsd@hotmail.com. Ladakhi guesthouse with very clean rooms, friendly helpful family, rural-homestay atmosphere, excellent food, large garden, open during the winter months. Recommended.

RESTAURANTS

Leh

$$ Chopsticks Noodle Bar, Fort Rd. Great East Asian, Tibetan and regional food in a clean and attractive restaurant. Deservedly popular and worth at least 1 visit when in Leh.

$$-$ La Pizzeria, Changspa Rd, Changspa. Pretty authentic pizza, very pleasant ambiance, some mattress seating, and soft lantern light at night.

$$-$ Nirvana Café. Live music after 2100. Indoor and outdoor seating under lanterns and fairy lights, some Sinai-style slouching areas. Laid-back vibe and varied menu of South Asian, Asian and lots of Italian, prices slightly higher than average. No alcohol.

$$-$ Open Hand Espresso Bar & Bistro, off Fort Rd, www.openhand.in. A chic retreat, with loungers and seating on decking by an active vegetable garden, chunky wood furniture inside, great cakes, cappuccinos and home-cooked meals, healthy smoothies and more. Ethical shopping – clothes, silks, cushions, gifts, etc – plus Wi-Fi connection.

$ Chansa Traditional Ladakhi Kitchen, next to Chokhang Vihara, off Main Bazar. A chance to try traditional Ladakhi cuisine (vegetarian); simple indoor seating, or outside under the shade of a parachute. Whiteboard shows the day's dishes, such as *sku* (a delicious chunky wholewheat pasta and veg broth), plus limited offerings of Chinese, Indian (great mushroom masala) and Western food. Cheap and tasty.

$ High Life Tibetan Restaurant, Fort Rd. Exceptional range of high-quality Tibetan food, plus good salads and Western dishes, inviting indoor seating with gingham tablecloths or big outdoor area.

$ Lala's Art Cafe, off Main Bazar, Old Town. Quaint restored Ladakhi house in the Old Town with a roof terrace, and shrine on the ground floor. Coffee and cakes are the order of the day.

$ Tenzin Dickey, Fort Rd. Delicious *kothay* (fried *momos*), soups, and other Tibetan/Chinese dishes, some Western food, all vegetarian, and the Tibetan herbal tea is pretty good. Simple and neat little place with checked tablecloths.

WHAT TO DO

Trekking agents
K2, Hill Top Building, Main Bazar, T01982-253 980 532, www.k2adventureleh.com. Good rates for treks (Markha Valley), very friendly, environment conscious.

Rimo Expeditions, Kang-lha Chen Hotel, T01982-253348, www.rimoexpeditions.com. Insightful and informative about the local area, running a whole host of treks, as well as mountain biking, mountaineering, river rafting, cultural tours and family holidays. The best of the lot. Highly recommended.

GOING FURTHER
Manali and Kully Valley

The Kullu Valley was the gateway to Lahaul for the Central Asian trade in wool and borax. It is enclosed to the north by the Pir Panjal range, to the west by the Bara Bangahal and to the east by the Parvati range, with the Beas River running through its centre. The approach is through a narrow funnel or gorge but in the upper part it extends outwards. The name Kullu is derived from Kulantapith 'the end of the habitable world'. It is steeped in Hindu religious tradition; every stream, rock and blade of grass seemingly imbued with some religious significance. Today, the main tourist centre is Manali, a hive of adventurous activity and honeymooning in the summer months, a quiet and peaceful place to relax in the winter snow. There are several interesting places to stay; we recommend **Baikunth Magnolia** (Circuit House Road, The Mall Road, www.baikunth.com) and **Neeralaya** (Village Raison, Kullu Valley, www.neeralaya.com). And don't miss eating at **La Plage** (behind Club House, Old Manali).

BACKGROUND

Manali occupies the valley of the Beas, now much depleted by hydroelectric projects, with the once-unspoilt Old Village to the north and Vashisht up on the opposite hillside across the river. Set amidst picturesque apple orchards, Manali is packed with Pahari-speaking Kullus, Lahaulis, Nepali labourers and enterprising Tibetan refugees who have opened guesthouses, restaurants and craft shops. The town has become increasingly built-up with dozens of new hotel blocks. It is a major tourist destination for Indian holidaymakers and adventure-seeking foreigners, attracted by the culturally different hill people and the scenic treks this part of the Himalaya offers. In summer months Manali can be the end (or start) of an exciting two-day road route from Leh.

ARRIVING IN MANALI

Getting there The road from Leh to Manali, 530 km, goes via Keylong, crossing some very high passes. It is open mid-June or early July, until the end of September (depending on the weather). It takes two days by bus; **Himachal Tourism** (book at HPTDC Office, Fort Rd, T(0)9622-374300) run deluxe buses, leaving alternate days at 0500, overnight in Keylong (Rs 1500). **J&K SRTC** also run ordinary/deluxe buses (book at the bus stand). You can make the journey in one day by shared jeep or minibus (leaving around 2400 taking 22-24 hours, about Rs 1500 per seat). Private jeeps are expensive but recommended if you want to stop en route for photos or to visit monasteries near Leh (see page 175) on the way. Many travellers find the mountain roads extremely frightening; parts are very rough and landslides can cause severe delays. The spectacular scenery is the pay-back.

Moving on From Manali and the Kullu Valley back to Delhi it's an arduous 15-hour bus ride – all travel agents and many hotels can arrange the bus for you and there are many bus companies, most leave around 1600 so they arrive around 0700 in Delhi, usually stopping at Manju Ki Tilla first and then close to the main bus station in Delhi. A taxi will cost around Rs 9000. Alternatively, Bhuntar airport is just outside Kullu town (about 50 km from Manali) and there are daily flights to Delhi.

PLACES IN MANALI

The **Tibetan Monastery**, built by refugees, is not old but it's attractive and is the centre of a small carpet-making industry. Rugs and other handicrafts are for sale. The colourful **bazar** sells Kullu shawls, caps and Tibetan souvenirs.

Old Manali is 3 km away, across Manalsu Nala. Once a charming village of attractive old farmsteads with wooden balconies and thick stone-tiled roofs, Old Manali is rapidly acquiring the trappings of a tourist economy: building work continues unchecked in the lower reaches of the village, as ever more guesthouses come up to thwart those seeking an escape from the crowds of modern Manali. The main road continues through some unspoilt villages to the modern **Manu Mandir**, dedicated to Manu, the Law Giver from whom Manali took its name and who, legend tells, arrived here by boat when fleeing from a great flood centuries ago. Aged rickshaws may not make it up the hill, so visitors might have to get off and walk.

Vashisht is a small hillside village that can be reached by road or a footpath, a 30- to 40-minute walk from the tourist office. The temple hot spring baths are beautiful – a real experience. A two-hour walk past the village up the hillside leads to a **waterfall**.

Hadimba Devi Temple, the Dhungri temple (1553), in a clearing among ancient deodars, is an enjoyable 2-km walk from the tourist office. Built by Maharaja Bahadur Singh, the 27-m-high pagoda temple has a three-tier roof and some fine naturalistic woodcarving of animals and plants, especially around the doorway. The structure itself is relatively crude, and the pagoda is far from perfectly perpendicular. Massive deodar planks form the roof but in contrast to the scale of the structure the brass image of the goddess Hadimba inside, is tiny. A legend tells how the God Bhima fell in love with Hadimba, the sister of the demon Tandi. Bhima killed Tandi in battle and married Hadimba, whose spirituality, coupled with her marriage to a god, led to her being worshipped as a goddess. Today, she is seen as an incarnation of Kali. The small doorway, less than 1 m high, is surrounded by woodcarved panels of animals, mythical beasts, scrolls, a row of foot soldiers and deities, while inside against a natural rock is the small black image of the Devi. To prevent the master craftsman producing another temple to equal this elsewhere, the king ordered his right hand to be cut off. The artist is believed to have mastered the technique with his left hand and reproduced a similar work of excellence at Trilokinath in the Pattan Valley. Unfortunately, his new master became equally jealous and had his head cut off.

A **feast and sacrifice** is held in mid-July when the image from the new temple in Old Manali is carried to the Hadimba Temple where 18 ritual blood sacrifices are performed. Sacrifices include a fish and a vegetable, and culminate with the beheading of an ox in front of a frenzied crowd. This ceremony is not for the faint-hearted.

Naggar is an hour's drive south of Manali and has an interesting castle. Built in the early 16th century, it withstood the earthquake of 1905 and is a fine example of the timber-bonded building of West Himalaya. It was built around a courtyard with verandas, from where there are enchanting views over the valley. Now a hotel, it has a pleasant, unhurried atmosphere and it is a good place to stop a while. It is also an entry for treks to Malana. At Naggar, you will also find the fascinating **Roerich Gallery** ① *Tue-Sun 0900-1300 (winter from 1000), 1400-1700, Rs 30*, a 2-km climb from the castle. Russian artist Nicholas Roerich lived here and the excellent views inspired his artwork. The small museum downstairs has a collection of photos and his distinctive stylized paintings of the Himalaya using striking colours. Nicholas Roerich created the Roerich Pact in the 1930s in order to preserve culture and the arts in the wake of the First World War. It was originally signed by 21 countries.

GOING FURTHER
Corbett National Park

Corbett is India's first national park and one of its few successfully managed tiger reserves. As well as rich and varied wildlife and birdlife it is also extremely picturesque. The park is named after Jim Corbett who turned from hunting to photographing tigers in the 1920s and developed a great respect for the animals. In the 2011 Tiger Census, Corbett National Park had 164 tigers, with the highest density of 20 tigers per hundred square kilometres. The census showed a 15% increase on numbers. Even for a state like Uttarakhand, which promises safe habitat for these big cats, poaching is a cause of concern. It's a beautiful place to go on safari whether you catch sight of a big cat or not. You can also visit Jim Corbett's house/museum at Kaladhungi. There are a choice of interesting properties to stay; we recommend **Infinity Resorts** (8 km north of Ramnagar, www.infinityresorts.com), which was established by the Corbett Foundation and has done pioneering work in compensating local farmers for lost livestock to prevent revenge killings of big cats. Many people enjoy staying inside the park itself as then you can spend longer on safari. Rates for foreigners are double that of Indians for staying inside the park but you can get dorm rooms for as little as Rs 500 while other rooms are Rs 5000. You will need to book ahead at Uttarkhand Tourism in Delhi, www.kmvn.gov.in.

→ ARRIVING IN CORBETT NATIONAL PARK

GETTING THERE
Trains from Delhi take between 5½ and six hours, or you can drive to Corbett in around five hours, depeding on what time you leave Delhi.

ENTRY FEES
ⓘ *Corbett Tiger Reserve Reception Centre, T05947-251489, www.corbettnationalpark.in.* Current fees and opening hours are available from the website and it's good to check as this information does change frequently. At **Dhikala Gate**: foreigners Rs 1000, Indians Rs 200, valid for three days (two nights); each additional day costs Rs 450, Indians Rs 100. At **Bijrani**, **Sonanadi**, **Jhirna** and **Doumunda** gates: Rs 450, Indians Rs 100 per visit (four hours). Entrance permits are not transferable between gates (eg a morning visit to Bijrani and a night halt at Dhikala will require separate payment). **Vehicle fees**: Dhikala Rs 1500 per car/jeep, Indians Rs 500 (covers overnight stay). Bijrani, Sonanadi, Jhirna and Doumunda: Rs 500 per car/jeep, Indians Rs 250.

ACCESS
The main gate at Dhangarhi (for Dhikala) is approximately 16 km north of Ramnagar on the Ranikhet road. Only visitors who are staying overnight may enter Dhikala. A limit of 30 vehicles per day at each entrance is applied, half of which can be booked in advance – try to reserve at the time of booking your accommodation, with several months' notice. Prior reservation to enter is recommended for day visits, although not always necessary at dawn, when half the entry is determined on a first-come-first-served basis. This can mean queuing for hours in the dark in Ramnagar, being shuffled from one office to another, and still not getting in – you may be refused entry when the quota is filled. Travel agents cannot help as they are not allowed to apply for permits. A reservation at the Bijrani or Dhela **Forest Rest Houses** does not entitle visitors to

enter by the Dhangari Gate. From 1 March until the monsoon all roads around Dhikala, except the main approach road, are closed between 1100 and 1500 when visitors are not allowed to move about the forest. Most of the park is closed 30 June to 15 October; the Dhikala section is closed 15 June to 15 November.

VIEWING
Elephant rides are available from Dhikala, Khinanauli, Bijrani, Gairal and Jhirna. Each elephant can carry four people. This is a great way to see the jungle and the wildlife. Morning and evening, two hours, Rs 3000 from government operators, more with private operators; book at Dhikala or Bijrani reception (whichever is relevant). Book as early as possible on arrival since these rides are very popular. **Cars** and **jeeps** may drive round part of the park. A seat in a **cantor** (large open-topped truck) costs Rs 1500 for foreigners, Rs 620 Indians for a full-day tour (0800-1800). Apart from the immediate area within the complex at Dhikala, **don't go walking in the park**. Tiger and elephant attacks are not unknown. The two watch towers are good vantage points for spotting wildlife. Night driving is not allowed in the park.

→ WILDLIFE
The park has always been noted for its tigers; there are now 164 but they are not easily spotted. About 10% of visitors see one – usually entering at the Bijrani Gate. There are leopards too but they are seldom seen. Sambar, chital, para (hog deer) and muntjac (barking deer) are the main prey of the big cats and their population fluctuates around 20,000. Some, like the chital, are highly gregarious whilst the large sambar, visually very impressive with its antlers, is usually solitary. The two commonly seen monkeys of North India are the rhesus (a macaque – reddish face and brownish body) and the common langur (black face and silvery coat). Elephants are now permanent inhabitants since the Ramganga Dam has flooded their old trekking routes. There are a few hundred of them and they are seen quite often. Other animals include porcupine and wild boar (often seen around Dhikala – some can be quite dangerous, attacking unsuspecting visitors who have food with them). In total there are more than 50 species of mammal, though the dam appears to have caused significant losses. The last swamp deer was seen in March 1978, and the loss of habitat has been keenly felt by the cheetal, hog deer and porcupine, all of which appear to be declining.

There are 26 species of reptile and seven of amphibian in the park. Certain stretches of the river and in the Ramganga Lake are inhabited by the common mugger crocodile: notices prohibiting swimming warn "Survivors will be prosecuted"! The fish-eating gharial can also be found, as can soft-shelled tortoises, otters and river fish. The python is quite common.

The birdlife is especially impressive with over 600 species including a wide range of water birds, birds of prey such as the crested serpent eagle, harriers, Pallas' fishing eagle, osprey, buzzards and vultures. Woodland birds include: Indian and great pied hornbills, parakeets, laughing thrushes, babblers and cuckoos. Doves, bee-eaters, rollers, bulbuls, warblers, finches, robins and chats are to be seen in the open scrub from the viewing towers. The rarer ibisbill is one of the main attractions for serious twitchers.

DREAM TRIP 3
Delhi→Agra→Varanasi→Lucknow→Delhi 21 days

Delhi 2 nights, page 35

Agra 2 nights, page 67
Bus/train from Delhi (5-6 hrs/2½ hrs);
with a driver on Yamuna Expressway (3 hrs)

Gwalior 1-2 nights, page 189
Bus/train from Agra (2½ hrs/1¾ hrs)

Orchha 2 nights, page 194
Bus/train/driver from Gwalior (3 hrs/2 hrs);
train/taxi combo via Jhansi (2 hrs)

Khajuraho 2 nights, page 198
Bus/driver from Orchha (5 hrs/3½-4 hrs)

Bandhavgarh National Park 2 nights,
page 206
Driver from Khajuraho (4-5 hrs)
Public transport challenging

Varanasi 3 nights, page 210
Train from Katni or Umaria/driver
from Bandhavgarh (8-12 hrs/6-7 hrs)

Bodhgaya 2 nights, page 221
Train from Varanasi (or better from
Mughal Serai) to Gaya (2½-4 hrs)

Lucknow 1-2 nights, page 225
Overnight train from Gaya

Delhi 1 night, page 35
Overnight train or flight from Lucknow
(8-10 hrs/1 hr) for international flight home

GOING FURTHER

Allahabad page 208
Train from Katni (5-7 hrs) to Allahabad
then bus/train to Varanasi (3½-4 hrs)

DREAM TRIP 3
Delhi→Agra→Varanasi→Lucknow→Delhi

This trip takes you into the heart of India – the central plains and its rich cultural and spiritual history. Starting off in Delhi, you find a city on the rise. From the tomb of Sufi saint Nizamuddin to the malls of Saket, you'll see history in the making. You head south from Delhi to the fine Mughal architecture and romance of the Taj Mahal at Agra and the stunning Gwalior fort. And then, further east, you time travel to Orchha with its beautiful palace and fading glamour – a mix of Hindu and Islamic architecture.

Head east again to the well-preserved temples at Khajuraho, one of India's most famous sites. Most people come here to see the erotic sculptures but you will also see the most intricate carvings and ornate temple work here. There is one beautiful temple outside of the main site which is still a working temple dedicated to Lord Shiva. Join a *puja* there and hear the chants that have rung out for over a thousand years in this building.

Chance your luck at seeing a tiger in the beautiful national park of Bandhavgarh, southeast from Khajuraho. There are huge campaigns to preserve the tigers, to battle against the poachers and retain this living symbol of India.

Then it's time to head north to the ancient city of Varanasi – which seems older than time itself. You can see the traditions, bathing rituals and funeral rites that have gone on for thousands of years on the banks of the River Ganges. Further east, in Bodhgaya, you can meet Buddhist monks who have come from all over the world to make their own quest to the place where Buddha gained enlightenment. And finally, make a pit-stop in Lucknow to admire the intricate fusion architecture of the *imambaras* and indulge in the rich cuisine of the Nawabs.

NORTHERN MADHYA PRADESH

Having spent the first four nights in Delhi and Agra (see pages 35 and 67), Dream Trip 3 heads southeast to Madhya Pradesh and some of its key sites, including the proud forts of Gwalior and Orchha, to the sacred temples of Khajuraho and the jungles of Bandhavgarh; the state contains many of the tribal groups least touched by modernization and most of India's remaining genuine forest. The magnificent palaces of Orchha and temples of Khajuraho testify to the power of Rajput dynasties for over a thousand years. Further afield in Sanchi you'll find 2000-year-old stupas testament to India's Buddhist past.

Flowing westwards along the southern edge of the great Vindhyan ranges runs the Narmada, the site of one of the largest – and most controversial – dam development programmes in the world. Yet Madhya Pradesh remains largely unindustrialized and little visited, allowing the dense forests and grasslands of the east to house two of India's best national parks at Kanha and Bandhavgarh.

→ GWALIOR

Surrounded by attractive open plateau country immediately to the north of the Vindhyas, Gwalior is set in one of the state's driest regions. The majestic hill fort, formerly the key to control of the Central Provinces, dominates a ridge overlooking the town spread out below. It contains awe-inspiring Jain sculptures, Jain and Hindu temples and the charming sandstone palace. The Jai Vilas Palace, within its walls, bears testimony to the idiosyncratic tastes of the Scindia Maharajas. Much of the town, which sees few tourists, is very busy, noisy and crowded.

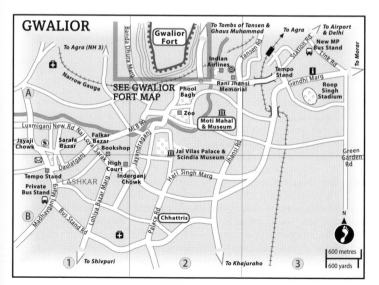

ARRIVING IN GWALIOR

Getting there There are daily flights from Delhi, but the *Shatabdi Express* gives Gwalior excellent train connections with both Agra and Delhi. The railway station and Madhya Pradesh State Bus Stand are southeast of the fort. From there, it is 6 km along the dusty MLB Road to the Jayaji Chowk area of Lashkar, the New Town.

Moving on From Gwalior it is a short jump to **Orchha** (see page 194) either by train or car and bus. The *Bhopal Shtbdi (12002)* leaves at 0930 arriving at Jhansi 1045, and the *Taj Express (12280)* takes two hours leaving Gwalior at 1200. From Jhansi it's 20 minutes in a taxi to Orchha (Rs 200).

Getting around In addition to a *tempo* stand near the station, there are unmetered autos and taxis. Gwalior is quite spread out and it's a stiff climb up to the fort.

Tourist information Tourist office ① *Platform 1, railway station, T0751-504 0777 and at MPTC hotel Tansen Residency, T0751-234 0370.*

HISTORY

In legend, Gwalior's history goes back to AD 8 when the chieftain **Suraj Sen** was cured of leprosy by a hermit saint, Gwalipa. In gratitude he founded and named the city after him. An inscription in the fort records that during the fifth-century reign of Mihiragula the Hun, a temple of the sun was erected here. Later, Rajput clans took and held the fort. Muslim invaders like **Qutb-ud-din-Aibak** (12th century) ruled Gwalior before it passed through a succession of Tomar Rajput, Mughal, Afghan and Maratha hands. During the 1857 **Mutiny**, the Maharaja remained loyal to the British but 6500 of his troops mutinied on 14 June. The next year, there was fierce fighting round Gwalior, the rebels being led by Tantia Topi and the **Rani of Jhansi**. When the fort was taken by the British, the Rani was found, dressed in men's clothes, among the slain.

THE FORT

① *Sunrise-sunset, foreigners Rs 100, Indians Rs 5, allow at least 2-3 hrs. Palaces open 0930-1700. English-speaking guides here expect Rs 200 (hotel guides charge more).*

The fort stands 91 m above the surrounding plain on a sandstone precipice, 2.8 km long and 200-850 m wide. In places the cliff overhangs, elsewhere it has been steepened to make it unscaleable. The main entrance to the north comprised a twisting, easily defended approach. On the west is the **Urwahi Gorge** and another well-guarded entrance. The fort's size is impressive but the eye cannot capture all of it at once. Apart from its natural defences, Gwalior had the advantage of an unlimited water supply with many tanks on the plateau.

Approach The fort is a long walk from the town. You may enter from the northeast by the Gwalior or Alamgiri Gate but it is quite a steep climb. Mineral water is sold at the ticket counter; decline the booklet. Alternatively, take a taxi or an auto-rickshaw and enter from the west by the Urwahi Gate, where there are interesting Jain sculptures. After visiting the temples and palaces, you can descend to the Gujari Mahal in the northeast and pick up an auto from the Gwalior Gate. Visitors to the fort, particularly young women, should be prepared and aware that they may receive some unwanted attention from bored local teenage boys who often hang around inside the fort. Dressing modestly is definitely recommended.

Western entrance Above the **Urwahi Gate** there are 21 Jain sculptures dating from the seventh to 15th centuries, some up to 20 m tall. An offended Babur ordered their faces and genitalia to be destroyed. Modern restorers have only repaired the faces. There is a paved terrace along one side (ask to be dropped near the steps to view the sculptures since vehicles may not park along the road).

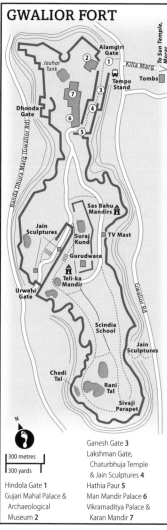

GWALIOR FORT

300 metres
300 yards

Hindola Gate **1**
Gujari Mahal Palace &
  Archaeological
  Museum **2**
Ganesh Gate **3**
Lakshman Gate,
  Chaturbhuja Temple
  & Jain Sculptures **4**
Hathia Paur **5**
Man Mandir Palace **6**
Vikramaditya Palace &
  Karan Mandir **7**

Northeast entrance A 1-km steep, rough ramp, with good views, leads to the main palace buildings. You pass through the **Gwalior Gate** (1660), the first of several gates, mostly built between 1486 and 1516. Next is the Badalgarh or **Hindola Gate (1)**, named because of the swing which was once here. It is (unusually) a true structural arch, flanked by two circular towers. Note the use of material from older buildings.

At the base of the ramp the **Gujari Mahal Palace** (circa 1510) containing the **Gujari Mahal Archaeological Museum (2)** ⓘ *Tue-Sun 1000-1700, Rs 30*. The pretty palace has an interesting collection including sculptures and archaeological pieces (second and first century BC), terracottas (Vidisha, Ujjain), coins and paintings and copies of frescoes from the Bagh caves. Ask the curator to show you the beautiful 10th-century Shalbhanjika (Tree Goddess) miniature. Some museums and palaces are closed on Monday. Some distance from the fort above, this palace was built by Raja Man Singh for his Gujar queen Mrignayani. The exterior is well preserved. The 'Bhairon' Gate no longer exists and the fourth is the simple **Ganesh Gate (3)** with a *kabutar khana* (pigeon house) and a small tank nearby. The mosque beyond stands on the site of an old shrine to the hermit Gwalipa, the present temple having been built later with some of the original material. Before the **Lakshman Gate** (circa 14th century) is the ninth-century Vishnu **Chaturbhuja Temple (4)**, with later additions, in a deep gap. A Muslim tomb and the northeast group of Jain sculptures are nearby. **Hathia Paur (5)**

(Elephant Gate, 1516), the last, is the entrance to the main Man Mandir palace which also had a Hawa gate, now demolished.

Man Mandir Palace (6) (1486-1516)   Built by Raja Man Singh, this is the most impressive building in the fort. The 30-m-high eastern retaining wall is a vast rock face on the cliff-side interrupted by large rounded bastions. The palace had ornamental parapets and cupolas, once brightly gilded, while blue, green and yellow tile-work with patterns of elephants, human figures, ducks, parrots, banana plants and flowers covered the exterior walls. The remarkable tiles, and the style of their inlay, are probably derived from Chanderi (200 km south) or Mandu. The beautifully decorated little rooms arranged round two inner courts have small entrances, suggesting they were built for the royal ladies. The iron rings here were used for swings and decorative wall hangings.

Interestingly, in addition to the two storeys above ground there are two underground floors which provided refuge from hot weather and acted as circular dungeons when required; these should not be missed. Guru Har Gobind who was once detained here was freed at the behest of Nur Jahan – he was permitted to take out any others who could touch his shawl so he attached eight tassels which enabled 56 prisoners to be freed with him. On 24 June 1658 Emperor Aurangzeb took his elder brother Murad captive en route to Delhi and then transferred him to Gwalior fort to be imprisoned. In December of the same year Aurangzeb ordered his execution.

Angled ventilation ducts allowed in fresh air while pipes in the walls were used as 'speaking tubes'. You will find an octagonal bath which would have been filled with perfumed water – the water welled up through inlet holes in the floor which have now been blocked. The south wall which incorporates the arched Hathia Paur with its guardroom above is particularly ornate with moulded and colourfully tiled friezes. A small **museum** ① *Sat-Sun 0800-1800, guides available, worthwhile for the underground floors if you don't have a torch; give a small tip*, opposite the façade, has interesting archaeological pieces of Hindu deities. **Note** A torch is essential to explore the lower floors: there are holes in the floor, some of which are quite deep. Underground levels are infested with bats (easily disturbed) and so there is a revolting smell.

The nightly **Son et Lumière** ① *Hindi at 1830, English at 1930 (1 hr later in summer), 45 mins, foreigners Rs 150, Indians Rs 40*, is well worth attending for stunning illumination of Man Mandir. The colourful spectacle traces the history of Gwalior fort through interesting anecdotes. Winter evenings can be chilly, so bring warm clothes; a torch is useful at any time of year. There is unlikely to be any transport available at the end of the show, so hire a taxi (Rs 250-300 return including wait), or make the fort your last stop when hiring a car for the day in the summer (day hire covers only a single fort visit).

Vikramaditya Palace (7) (1516) ① *Tue-Sun 0800-1700 (1 Apr-30 Sep, 0700-1000, 1500-1800), free.* Located between Man Mandir and Karan Mandir, the palace is connected with them by narrow galleries. Inside is a *baradari* (open hall) with a domed roof. Opposite the Dhonda Gate is the **Karan Mandir** (7) (1454-1479), more properly called the Kirtti Mandir after its builder Raja Kirtti Singh. It is a long, two-storeyed building with a large, pillared hall and fine plaster moulding on ceilings of adjacent rooms. Just northwest is the **Jauhar Tank** where the Rajput women performed *jauhar* (mass suicide) just before the fort was taken by Iltutmish in 1232, and also at Chittaurgarh. The two unremarkable Muslim palaces, Jahangiri and Shah Jahan Mahals are further north. Moving south from Hathia Paur, towards the east wall, are the **Sas Bahu Mandirs**. Dedicated to Vishnu, the 11th-century 'Mother and Daughter-in-law' pair of temples built by Mahipala Kachhawaha (1093) still preserve fine carvings in places. The larger 12-sided temple is more interesting although only the *Mahamandapa* (Assembly Hall) remains. The smaller temple has an ornately carved base with a frieze of elephants, and a vaulted ceiling under the pyramidal roof. The wide ridged stone 'awning' is well preserved. An impressive modern marble **gurudwara** (1970) in memory of Sikh Guru Har Gobind (1595-1644), who had been imprisoned in the fort, is to its south, providing a haven of cool respite for visitors; the Guru Granth Sahib is read throughout the day. West of the *gurudwara* is **Suraj Kund**, a large tank, first referred to in the fifth century, where Suraj Sen's leprosy was cured. The water is now green and stagnant.

Teli-ka Mandir Teli-ka Mandir probably means 'oil man's temple'. It is the earliest temple in Gwalior, and architecturally has more in common with some early Orissan temples than those in the south (though sometimes guides suggest a link with Telangana in modern Andhra Pradesh indicating the fusion of Dravidian and North Indian architectural styles). This unique 25-m-high Pratihara (mid-eighth century) Vishnu Temple is essentially a sanctuary with a *Garuda* at the entrance. The oblong vaulted roof rather resembles a Buddhist *chaitya* and the Vaital Deul (Bhubaneswar). Tillotson records how after the 'Mutiny' "this great medieval temple, for example, was put to service as a soda-water factory and coffee shop. By such acts of desecration the British showed Indian rulers how the ancient Hindu heritage was then regarded by those who laid claim to power and authority". It was reconstructed in 1881-1883. The Katora Tal behind was excavated when the fort was built, like many others here. The Ek-khamba Tal has a single stone column standing in it.

   Rani Tal (12), further south, was supposedly intended for the royal ladies; it is connected underground to the neighbouring **Chedi Tal**. Jain sculptures in the southeast corner can be seen from a path below the wall.

THE TOWN
After Daulat Rao Scindia acquired Gwalior in 1809 he pitched camp to the south of the fort. The new city that arose was **Lashkar** (The Camp) with palaces, King George Park (now Gandhi Park) and the *chhattris* of the Maharajas. **Jayaji Chowk**, once an elegant square, dominated by late 19th- and early 20th-century buildings, notably the Regal Cinema, and the Chowk Bazar can still be a pleasant place to watch people going about their business from one of the good little restaurants.

   Jai Vilas Palace (1872-1874) ① *Tue-Sun 1000-1730, tickets at gate: foreigners Rs 300, Indians Rs 40, guided tours (1 hr) sometimes compulsory*, designed by Lieutenant-Colonel Sir Michael Filose, resembles an Italian palazzo in places, using painted sandstone to imitate marble. Part of the palace is the present maharaja's residence but 35 rooms house the **Scindia Museum**, an idiosyncratic collection of royal possessions, curiosities (eg 3-D mirror portraits), carpets (note the Persian rug with royal portraits) and interesting memorabilia.

   In a separate building opposite (show ticket) is the extraordinary **Durbar Hall**. It is approached by a crystal staircase, gilded in 56 kg of gold, and in it hang two of the world's largest chandeliers each weighing 3.5 tonnes; before they were hung the ceiling was tested by getting 10 elephants to climb on to it via a 2-km ramp. Underneath is the dining room. The battery-operated silver train set transported cigars, dry fruit and drinks round the table, after dinner. The lifting of a container or bottle would automatically reduce pressure on the track, and so stop the train. Southeast of the fort is the spot where **Rani Lakshmi Bai** of Jhansi was cremated, marked by a stirring statue.

The **Royal Chhattris**, south of town, are each dedicated to a Gwalior Maharaja. These ghostly pavilions are in various stages of neglect. The lighted images are still clothed and 'fed' daily. Be there at 1600 when they are shown again by the guardians after their afternoon nap.

In the crowded Hazira in the **Old Town**, northeast of the fort, is the **Tomb of Ghaus Muhammad**, a 16th-century Afghan prince who helped Babur to win the fort. It is in an early Mughal style with finely carved *jali* screens. Hindus and Muslims both make pilgrimage to the tomb. Nearby, in an attractive garden setting, is the **Tomb of Tansen**, the most famous musician of Akbar's court. It is the venue for the annual music festival (November/December). The present tamarind tree replaces the old one which was believed to have magical properties. Tansen was an exponent of the *dhrupad* style, and laid the foundations for what in the 19th century became the Gwalior *ghurana* style, noted for its stress on composition and forceful performance. One of the best-known contemporary exponents is Amjad Ali Khan, a renowned sarod player. A recently built **Sun Temple** similar in style to Konark is at Morar, a few kilometres east of the tombs.

→ ORCHHA

Highly picturesque, in the middle of nowhere, abandoned and somewhat neglected, Orchha is an ideal stop between Gwalior and Khajuraho. Set on an island on a bend in the Betwa River, the fort palace from a bygone era is raised on a rocky promontory above the surrounding wooded countryside. This largely untouched island of peace and calm is approached from the congested, increasingly touristy village centre by a remarkable early 17th-century granite bridge built by Bir Singh Deo, while all around, the forest encroaches on the tombs and monuments.

ARRIVING IN ORCHHA
Getting there Orchha is quite easily reached by road from Gwalior via Jhansi (major trains stop here). After travelling 9 km southeast along the Khajuraho Road, a minor road turns south for the remaining 7 km to Orchha. There are taxis, *tempos* or buses from Jhansi station, but it is best to travel during daylight hours, and book and enquire about onward buses well ahead. See also Moving on, page 190.

Moving on After a couple of nights in Orchha, it's a five-hour bus journey to **Khajuraho** (see page 198). However, this road is particularly bumpy despite the popularity of this area, so if you can splash out on a taxi this is a good time to do it. It is around Rs 2400. There is also a crowded train option from Jhansi Junction to Khajuraho.

Getting around The fort palace complex and the village are all easily seen on foot. The riverside is a 10-minute stroll away. If you are laden with luggage you can get a rickshaw from the village centre to your hotel. Women are advised not to wander around the site alone.

HISTORY
The Bundela chief **Raja Rudra Pratap** (1501-1531) chose an easily defended and beautiful site for his capital. In the 11th century, a Rajput prince is said to have offered himself as a

sacrifice to the mountain goddess Vrindavasini; she prevented his death and named him *'Bundela'* (one who offered blood). The dynasty ruled over the area between the Yamuna and Narmada rivers, having stepped into the vacuum left by the Tughlaqs and extended their power, moving their base to Orchha (meaning hidden). Raja Rudra Pratap threw a wall around the existing settlement and began work on the palace building (circa 1525-1531) and an arched bridge to it. This was completed by his successor Bharti Chand (1531-1554) who was installed in the Raj Mahal with great ceremony.

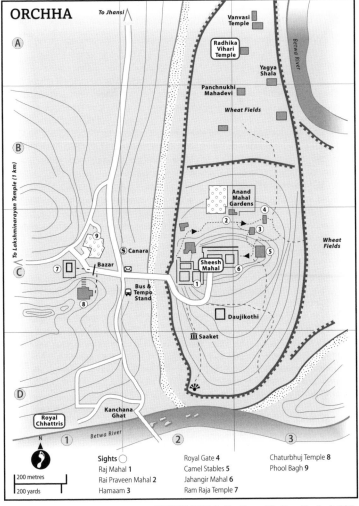

ORCHHA

To Jhansi

Vanvasi Temple

Radhika Vihari Temple

Yagya Shala

Betwa River

Panchnukhi Mahadevi

Wheat Fields

To Lakshminarayan Temple (1 km)

Anand Mahal Gardens

Wheat Fields

Canara

Bazar

Sheesh Mahal

Bus & Tempo Stand

Daujikothi

Saaket

Royal Chhattris

Kanchana Ghat

Betwa River

N

200 metres
200 yards

Sights ○	Royal Gate 4	Chaturbhuj Temple 8
Raj Mahal 1	Camel Stables 5	Phool Bagh 9
Rai Praveen Mahal 2	Jahangir Mahal 6	
Hamaam 3	Ram Raja Temple 7	

The continuing fortunes of the dynasty may have stemmed from the rulers' diplomatic skills. Though the third ruler, the religious **Madhukar Shah**, was defeated in battle by Akbar and was exiled in 1578 (died 1592), he nevertheless won the Mughal emperor's friendship. Later **Bir Singh Deo** (1605-1627), while opposing Akbar, aligned himself with Prince Salim (Jahangir), who later rewarded him with the throne of Orchha, thus ensuring its ongoing prosperity. The Jahangir Mahal was built to commemorate the emperor's visit to Orchha. However, Bir Singh's first son, Jhujan, ran foul of Shah Jahan and, ignoring orders, treacherously killed the neighbouring chief of Chauragarh. The imperial army routed Jhujan and Orchha was pillaged. In 1783 the Bundela capital was moved to Tikamgarh, leaving Orchha to the *dhak* forests, the Betwa River and its guardian eagles.

THE SITE

ⓘ *Foreigners Rs 250, Indians Rs 5, camera (no flash) Rs 20, video Rs 50; ticket office at palace, 0800-1800. Allow 2 hrs. Audio tour from Sheesh Mahal hotel, Rs 50. Highly recommended. The buildings are in a bad state of repair. If you go to the top take extra care and carry a torch.*

Orchha is a wonderful example of a medieval fort palace. Within the turreted walls are gardens, gateways, pavilions and temples, near the Betwa and Jamni rivers. On a moonlit night, the view across the palaces with their *chhattris* and ornamented battlements is enchanting. A suggested route is to visit the Raj Mahal with its Hall of Private Audience then go through the doorway to the Hall of Public Audience. From here go down the ramp and follow the path to the Rai Praveen Mahal. Continue along the path to the Jahangir Mahal, arriving back at the courtyard of the Sheesh Mahal.

The **Raj Mahal (1)**, to the right of the quadrangle, exemplifies Bundela Rajput architecture. There are two rectangular courtyards around which the floors rise in tiers (inspired by the Koshak Mahal in Chanderi, which was built a century earlier); typically there are cool chambers below ground and a fountain. Some of the original blue tile decoration remains on the upper outer walls. To the left of the first courtyard is the Hall of Private Audience which would have been covered with rich carpets and cushions (note floor-level windows). The Hall of the Public Audience has two quarter-size plaster elephants. Despite the neglected appearance of the royal chambers off the second courtyard, some have beautiful murals on the ceilings and walls. Representing both religious and secular themes, one series is devoted to the *Ramayana*, another to Vishnu's incarnations, others to scenes of court life – musicians, hunters, river excursions, fairground. Normally locked, but the caretaker will unlock some ground floor rooms. Don't miss Rooms 5 and 6 which have the best paintings, but you will need a torch. There is a Sheesh Mahal upstairs as well as good views of other palaces and temples from the very top; watch your step though, especially in strong winds.

Rai Praveen Mahal (2) was probably named after the musician-courtesan who was a favourite at the princely court of Indrajit, brother of Ram Shah (1592-1604). The low two-storey brick palace with cool underground chambers and beautifully carved stone niches is built to scale with surrounding trees and the Anand Mandal gardens. To get to the underground rooms, turn left down steps on exiting the main rooms.

The octagonal flowerbeds are ingeniously watered from two wells. A new path takes you via the **hamaam (3)**, bypassing the **Royal Gate (4)**, and past the **Camel Stables (5)** to the most impressive of the three palaces.

Jahangir Mahal (6), built in the 17th century by Raja Bir Singh Deo to commemorate the Emperor's visit, synthesizes Hindu and Muslim styles as a tribute to his benefactor. The

70-m-sq palace, which is best entered from the east, the original main entrance flanked by elephants, can also be entered from the south. It has a large square interior courtyard, around which are the apartments in three storeys. The guided tour goes to the top of these up narrow and dark stairways. Each corner bastion and the northern projection in the middle of each side is topped by a dome. These contain apartments with intervening terraces – hanging balconies with balustrades and wide eaves create strong lines set off by attractive arches and brackets, decorative cobalt and turquoise blue tiles, *chhattris* and *jali* screens giving this huge palace a delicate and airy feel. There is a small **museum** ① *Sat-Thu 1000-1700*, with a run-down assortment of photos, sculptures and *sati* stones; labels are in Hindi.

A few minutes' walk south of the main palace complex is **Saaket** ① *1000-1700, Rs 40*, an excellent new museum displaying Ramayana paintings in traditional folk styles from Orissa, Bihar, Maharashtra, Andhra Pradesh and Bengal. The paintings, on palm leaves, silk and organically dyed cotton, are of the highest quality, and the stories behind them fascinating.

THE VILLAGE

Just south of the crossroads is the **Ram Raja Temple (7)** ① *0800-1230, 1900-2130 (1 hr later on summer evenings), cameras and leather articles must be left outside*, which forms a focus for village life. The temple courtyard and the narrow lane leading to it have stalls selling souvenirs and the area occasionally swells with pilgrims and *sanyasis*. The pink and cream paint is not in keeping with the other temples. It is interesting to visit during *arati*; otherwise there is little to see inside. Following the appearance of Rama in a dream, the pious Madhukar Shah brought an image of the god from Ayodhya and placed it in this palace prior to its installation in a temple. However, when the temple was ready it proved impossible to shift the image and the king remembered, only too late, the divine instruction that the deity must remain in the place where it was first installed. It is the only palace-turned-temple in the country where Rama is worshipped as king.

Chaturbhuj Temple (8) ① *usually open 0800-1700*, up the steps from the Ram Raja Temple courtyard, was built by King Madhukar Shah for his Queen Kunwari to house the image of Rama brought from Ayodhya. Laid out in the form of a cross, a symbolic representation of the four-armed god Krishna, there is a triple-arched gate with attractive *jharokas* on the exterior. The tallest *sikhara* is over the Garbagriha shrine, to the left of which you will see a Ganesh and a set of kettle drums. The high arches and ceilings with vaulting and lotus domes painted in a rich red in places, are particularly striking. You can climb up any of the corner staircases, which lead up, by stages, to the very top of the temple. The second level gives access to tiny decorated balconies which provided privileged seating. There are good views of the nine palaces from the top, reached by the mini labyrinth of narrow corridors and steps. On the roof are langurs, wild bee hives and vultures nesting in corner towers.

A 1-km paved path links the Ram Raja with Bir Singh Deo's early 17th-century **Lakshminarayan Temple** ① *0900-1700, 15-min walk*, on a low hill, which incorporates elements of fort architecture. The ticket attendant gives a 'tour', naming the characters illustrated; go up the tower, the steps are steep but there are very good views of the entire area. The typical village houses along the path are freshly whitewashed for **Diwali**. The diagonal plan enclosing the central square temple structure is most unusual. The excellent murals (religious and secular), on the interior walls and ceilings of the four cool galleries around the temple here, are well-preserved examples of the Bundela school. The paintings in red, black, yellow, grey and turquoise portray Hindu deities, scenes from the epics, historical events including the early British period (note the interesting details of Lakshmi Bai's battle against the British), as well as giving an insight into the domestic pleasures of royalty.

Phool Bagh (9) is a formal garden and an eight-pillared pavilion which has a cool underground apartment. Well worth a visit.

Of the 15 **Royal Chhattris** to former rulers grouped by the Kanchana Ghat by the river, about half are neglected and overgrown but pleasant for walking around in the late afternoon. A few are well preserved; ask the watchman if you want to look inside. He will take you to the upper levels by some very narrow, dark stairs: good fun but take a torch and be careful. He will expect a small tip. The chhattris are best photographed from the opposite bank: take a stick as dogs can be a problem.

The small but busy **village bazar**, with some interesting temples nearby, is about 10 minutes' walk from the riverside where a series of royal *chhattris* still stand as sentinels. The riverside is ideal for lazing under a shady tree. Cross the bridge and head upstream for better spots for swimming (watch out for currents).

→ KHAJURAHO

Khajuraho, home to what are now perhaps the most famous of India's temples on account of their remarkable erotic sculptures, lies in a rich, well-watered plain. Set miles from the nearest town in an open forested and cultivated landscape with the striking Vindhyan ranges as a backdrop, it is listed as a World Heritage Site. Sadly, Khajuraho's drastically defined rich and lean seasons have bred a particular culture, and you may find yourself subjected to a barrage of sleazy salesmen, touts and junior con artists capable of sweet-talking you in three different languages. Nevertheless, the village away from the tourist areas maintains a pleasant laid-back feel, and early mornings even at the main temples can be wonderfully calm and peaceful. The best time to visit is between October and March. From April to June it becomes very hot, dry and dusty.

ARRIVING IN
Khajuraho is well connected by buses and trains, although both are busy and the roads are poor. Buses travel to Jhansi and Satna, both with good railway connections, but they become horrifically packed: if you can afford only one taxi ride in India, let it be here. We hope that MP Tourism and the local governments get around to doing something about the roads.

Moving on Really your best bet getting from Khajuraho to **Bandhavgarh National Park** (see page 206) is with a driver (five hours). You can take a bus with many changes but it will take a lot longer. The railway station is around 7 km north of town, with daily trains to Jhansi and Varanasi. There is also an airport at Khajuraho for a quick getaway to Varanasi or Delhi.

Getting around Khajuraho is still a small village though the temples are scattered over 8 sq km. Although some are within walking distance, hiring a bike is a good alternative to getting a cycle-rickshaw to visit the temples to the east and south.

Tourist information Government of India Tourist Office ① *T07686-274051, Mon-Fri 0930-1800*. Madhya Pradesh Tourism ① *at airport T07686-274648 and railway station T07686-288880*.

BACKGROUND

Khajuraho was formerly the capital of the old kingdom of Jajhauti, the region now known as **Bundelkhand**. The name Khajuraho may be derived from *khajura* (date palm), which grows freely in the area and perhaps because there were two golden *khajura* trees on a carved gate here. The old name was Kharjuravahaka (scorpion bearer), the scorpion symbolizing poisonous lust.

Khajuraho's temples were built under later Chandela kings between AD 950 and 1050 in a truly inspired burst of creativity, but were 'lost' for centuries until they were accidentally 'discovered' by a British army engineer in 1839. Of the original 85 temples, the 20 surviving are among the finest in India.

Basham suggested that India's art came from secular craftsmen who, although they worked to instructions, loved the world they knew, their inspiration not so much a ceaseless quest for the absolute as a delight in the world as they saw it.

The gods and demi-gods in temples all over India are young and handsome, their bodies rounded, often richly jewelled. They are often smiling and sorrow is rarely portrayed. Temple sculpture makes full use of the female form as a decorative motif. Goddesses and

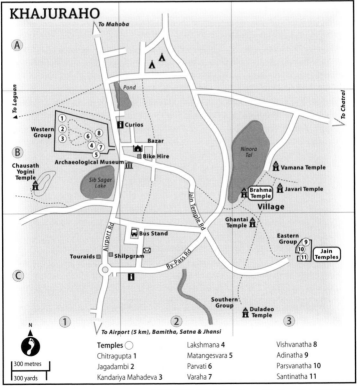

KHAJURAHO

To Mahoba
To Laguan
To Chatral
Pond
Western Group
Curios
Bazar
Archaeological Museum
Bike Hire
Chausath Yogini Temple
Sib Sagar Lake
Ninora Tal
Vamana Temple
Brahma Temple
Javari Temple
Village
Ghantai Temple
Jain Temple Rd
Airport Rd
Bus Stand
Shilpgram
Touraids
By-Pass Rd
Eastern Group
Jain Temples
Southern Group
Duladeo Temple
N
300 metres
300 yards
To Airport (5 km), Bamitha, Satna & Jhansi

Temples ○
Chitragupta 1
Jagadambi 2
Kandariya Mahadeva 3

Lakshmana 4
Matangesvara 5
Parvati 6
Varaha 7

Vishvanatha 8
Adinatha 9
Parsvanatha 10
Santinatha 11

female attendants are often shown naked from the waist up, with tiny waists and large, rounded breasts, posing languidly – a picture of well-being and relaxation.

Shakti worship and erotic sculptures Although each temple here is dedicated to a different deity, each expresses its own nature through the creative energy of Shakti. Tantric beliefs within Hinduism led to the development of Shakti cults which stressed that the male could be activated only by being united with the female in which sexual expression and spiritual desire were intermingled. Since this could not be suppressed it was given a priestly blessing and incorporated into the regular ritual. Romila Thapar traces its origin to the persisting worship of the Mother Goddess (from the Indus Valley civilization, third millennium BC), which has remained a feature of religion in India. Until last century, many temples kept *devadasis* (literally, servants of God), women whose duty included being the female partner in these rituals.

The presence of erotic temple sculptures, even though they account for less than 10% of the total carvings, have sometimes been viewed as the work of a degenerate society obsessed with sex. Some believe they illustrate the Kama Sutra, the sensuality outside the temple contrasting with the serenity within. Yet others argue that they illustrate ritual symbolism of sexual intercourse in **Tantric belief**. The Chandelas were followers of the Tantric cult which believes that gratification of earthly desires is a step towards attaining the ultimate liberation or *moksha*.

Whatever the explanation, the sculptures are remarkable and show great sensitivity and warmth, reflecting society in an age free from inhibitions. They express the celebration of all human activity, displaying one aspect of the nature of Hinduism itself, a genuine love of life.

Chandela Rajputs The Chandela Rajputs claimed descent from the moon. **Hemwati**, the lovely young daughter of a Brahmin priest, was seduced by the Moon God while bathing in a forest pool. The child born of this union was **Chandravarman**, the founder of the dynasty. Brought up in the forests by his mother who sought refuge from a censorious society, Chandravarman, when established as ruler of the local area, had a dream visitation from his mother. She implored him to build temples that would reveal human passions and in doing so bring about a realization of the emptiness of desire.

The Chandelas, whose symbol recalls the 16-year-old king who slayed a lion barehanded, developed into a strong regional power in the early 10th century. Under their patronage Jajhauti became prosperous, and the rulers decorated their kingdom with forts, palaces, tanks and temples, mainly concentrated in their strongholds of Mahoba, Kalinjar, Ajaigarh and also Dudhai, Chandpur, Madanpur and Deogarh (Jhansi District).

With the fading of Chandela fortunes, the importance of Khajuraho waned but temple building continued, at a much reduced pace, until the 12th century. Far removed from the political centres of the kingdom, the location of Khajuraho minimized the danger of external attack and symbolized its role as a celestial refuge.

THE TEMPLES
ⓘ *Sunrise to sunset. Foreigners Rs 250, camera Rs 25. Guides charge around Rs 400 for a small group (enquire at the India Tourism Office). Choose carefully as some push the new Cultural Centre, souvenir shop and puppet show (overpriced at Rs 250) and others can be a little leary around the sculptures. Audio tours Rs 50 plus Rs 500 deposit. Avoid the toilets. Son et lumière*

every evening at the Western group of temples, in English at 1900, Hindi at 2000, foreigners Rs 350, Indians Rs 120.

The temples, built mostly of a fine sandstone from Panna and Ajaigarh – although granite was used in a few – can be conveniently divided into three groups: the **Western** (opposite bazar), **Eastern** (30 minutes away on foot) and **Southern**. The Western Group, which dominates the village, is the most impressive and the gardens the best kept. The temples in the other two groups are remarkable and pleasing in their own right but if you feel that temple fatigue is likely to set in, then the Western Group is the one to see, especially the Lakshmana Temple. Allow a day (minimum five hours) for sightseeing. Naturally early morning offers the best light – grab a chai in the square opposite the entrance and get in the temples before the crowds.

The temples here are compact and tall, raised on a high platform with an ambulatory path around, but with no enclosure wall. Each follows an east-west axis and has the essential *garbha-griha* (sanctum) containing the chief image, joined to the hall for *mandapa* (worshippers) by a *antarala* (vestibule). The hall is approached through an *ardha mandapa* (porch); both have pyramidal towers. Larger temples have lateral transepts and balconied windows, an internal ambulatory and subsidiary shrines. The sanctuary is surmounted by a tall *sikhara* (tower), while smaller towers rise from other parts of the temple, imitating mountain peaks culminating in the highest. The sanctum is usually *sapta-ratha* (seven projections in plan and elevation), while the cubical section below the *sikhara* repeats the number, having seven bands, *sapta-bada*. The whole, studded with sculptured statues with clear lines of projections and recesses, makes most effective use of light and shade. The sculptures themselves are in the round or in high or medium relief depicting cult images, deities, celestial nymphs, secular figures and animals or mythical beasts.

In India's medieval period of temple building, simple stonework techniques replaced previous wooden and brick work. Temples were heavily and ornately decorated. Heavy cornices, strong, broad pillars and the wide base of the *sikhara* (tower) give them the feeling of strength and solidity, only partly counteracted by the ornate friezes.

Western Group **Varaha Temple** (circa AD 900-925), a shrine dedicated to Vishnu in his third incarnation as Varaha, the boar. Vishnu, the preserver, is usually depicted resting on a bed of serpents, until summoned to save the world from disaster. The rat-demon Hiranyaksha stole the earth and dragged it down to his underwater home. The gods begged for Vishnu's help. The demon created 1000 replicas of himself to confuse any pursuer, but Vishnu incarnated himself as a boar and was able to dig deep and seek out the real demon. Thus, Hiranyaksha was destroyed and the world saved. The 2.6-m-long Varaha is of highly polished sandstone covered with 674 deities. He is the Lord of the Three Worlds – water, earth and heaven, and under him is the serpent *Sesha* and the feet of the broken figure of *Prithvi*, the earth goddess. The lotus ceiling shows superb relief carving.

Lakshmana Temple (circa AD 950) best preserves the architectural features that typify the larger temples here. The **platform** has friezes of hunting and battle scenes with soldiers, elephants and horses as well as scenes from daily life including the erotic. The **basement** again has bands of carvings – processional friezes showing animals, soldiers, acrobats, musicians, dancers, domestic scenes, festivities, ceremonies, loving couples and deities. The details differentiate between an **officer** (beard), **general** (beard and belly) and **priest**

(beard, belly and stick). An ordinary soldier has none of these. You might spot the occasional error – a camel with legs jointed like a horse, for example. Note the beautifully carved elephants at shoulder height, each one different. On the **walls** are the major sculptures of gods and goddesses in two rows, with *sura-sundaris* or *apsaras* in attendance on the raised sections and loving couples discreetly placed in the recesses. All the figures are relaxed, resting their weight on one leg, thus accentuating their curves. The bands are broken by ornate balconied windows with carved pillars and overhanging eaves. The nymphs shown attending to their toilet, bearing offerings, dancing, playing musical instruments or as sensual lovers, are executed with great skill. They are graceful and fluid (note the taut muscle or creased skin), with expressive faces and gestures. The best examples are seen in the recesses below the main tower. The **façades** are covered in superb sculpture. On the south façade are a couple of minstrels, their faces expressing devotional ecstasy, a dancing Ganesh, ladies attending to their toilet, and groups of lovers. Moving to the southwest, a *sura-sundari* applies vermilion while another plays with a ball. In the northwest corner is a nymph after her bath in her wet clothes. The south face of the northwest shrine has a fine Ganesh panel. On the north face, returning towards the porch, there is a group of *apsaras* accomplished in art and music (one plays the flute, another paints, yet another writes a letter). The east face of the subsidiary shrine in the southeast corner has a master architect with his apprentices. Leave shoes at the entrance and enter the **interior** through a simple *makara-torana* flanked by gladiators. The circular ceiling of the porch (*ardha mandapa*) is a superbly carved open lotus blossom. In the hall (*mandapa*) is a raised platform possibly used for dancing and tantric rituals. At each corner of the platform are pillars with carved brackets with *apsaras* which are among the finest sculptures at Khajuraho. There are eight figures on each column, representing the eight sects of Tantra. The sanctum (*garba-griha*) doorway has a panel showing incarnations of Vishnu while the lintel has Lakshmi with Brahma and Siva on either side. A frieze above depicts the nine planets including *Rahu*, while Krishna legends and innumerable carvings of animals, birds and humans, appear on the wall. The *pancha-ratha* sanctum has a three-headed Vishnu as Vaikuntha, and around it are 10 incarnations and 14 forms of Vishnu.

Kandariya Mahadeva Temple (circa 1025-1050) is the most developed, the largest and tallest of the Khajuraho temples. Dedicated to Siva, the elaborately carved *makara torana* doorway leads to a porch with an ornate ceiling and a dark inner sanctum with a marble linga. The temple roof rises in a series of seven bands of peaks to the summit of the central, 31-m-high *sikhara*. There are 84 smaller, subsidiary towers which are replicas. The architectural and sculptural genius of Khajuraho reaches its peak in this temple where every element is richly endowed. The platform is unique in the way it projects to the sides and rear, reflecting the plan of the transepts. It also has the highest and most ornamental basement with intricately carved processional friezes. Leaving the temple, walk to the rear of the delightful gardens to the other two temples.

Along the same platform, to Kandariya's north is the **Jagadambi Temple** (early 11th century), which is similar in layout and predates the next temple, the Chitragupta. It has a standing Parvati image in the sanctum but was originally dedicated to Vishnu. The outer walls have no projecting balconies but the lavish decorations include some of the best carvings of deities – several of Vishnu, a particularly fine *Yama*, numerous nymphs and amorous couples. In between is the ruined **Mahadeva Shrine** (11th century). Little remains except a porch, under which Sardula, a mythical lion, towers over a half-kneeling woman.

Chitragupta Temple (early 11th century) is the only one here dedicated to Surya, the Sun God. Longer and lower than its companions, it has been much restored (platform, steps, entrance porch, northeast façade). Unlike the simple basement mouldings of the Jagadambi, here there are processional friezes; the *maha-mandapa* ceiling too has progressed from the simple square in the former to an ornate octagonal ceiling. The *garbha griha* has Surya driving his chariot of seven horses, while on the south façade is a statue of Vishnu with 11 heads signifying his 10 incarnations.

Vishvanatha Temple (1002) is dedicated to Siva. According to the longer inscription on the wall, it originally had an emerald linga in addition to the stone one present today. Built before the Kandariya Mahadeva, they are similar in design and plan. The high, moulded basement has fine scrollwork and carvings of processions of men and animals as well as loving couples. On the nine principal basement niches of both are the *Sapta-matrikas* (seven 'Mothers') with Ganesha and Virabhadra. The excellent carvings include a fine musician with a flute and amorous couples inside the temple, and divinities attended by enchanting nymphs in innumerable poses (one removing a thorn from her foot), on the south façade. Only two subsidiary shrines of the original four remain. Sharing the same raised platform and facing the temple is the **Nandi Pavilion** with a fine elephant frieze on the basement. It houses a 2.2-m polished sandstone Nandi bull (Siva's vehicle). Before coming down the steps note the sleeping *mahout* on an elephant!

Outside this garden complex of temples and next to the Lakshmana temple is the **Matangesvara Temple** (AD 900-925), simpler in form and decoration than its neighbour and unlike all the others, still in everyday use. It has an interesting circular interior which contains a large Siva linga dating back 1000 years. You do not need to pay to get into this temple and morning or evening *puja* is very beautiful and very welcoming.

Chausath Yogini (late ninth century) is a ruined Jain temple in coarse granite on a platform. It stands apart from the rest of the Western Group beyond the tank. Only 35 of the original *chausath* (64) shrines to the *yoginis* (attendants of Kali), of the 'open-air' temple, remain.

Eastern Group South of the village is the ruined **'Ghantai' Temple** (late 10th century). The fine carvings of *ghanta* (chains-and-bells) on the pillars, the richly ornamented doorway and ceiling of the entrance porch can only be seen from the road. Walk through Khajuraho village to the small **Javari Temple** (late 11th century), with its tall, slender *sikhara*. It has a highly decorative doorway and finely sculpted figures on the walls. About 200 m north is the **Vamana Temple** (late 11th century), with a four-armed Vamana incarnation of Vishnu in the sanctum. This is in the fully developed Chandela style and has a single tower and no ambulatory. The walls are adorned with sensuous *sura-sundaris*. Returning to the modern part of Khajuraho, you pass the early 10th-century so-called **Brahma Temple** on the bank of Ninora-tal. A Vishnu temple, wrongly attributed to Brahma, it has a sandstone *sikhara* on a granite structure.

Three Jain temples stand within an enclosure about 500 m southeast of the Ghantai Temple; others are scattered around the village. The **Parsvanatha Temple** (mid-10th century), is the largest and one of the finest. The curvilinear tower dominates the structure and is beautifully carved. There are no balconies but light enters through fretted windows. Although a Jain temple, there are numerous Vaishnav deities, many of them excellently carved on the three wall panels. Some of the best known non-erotic sculptures too are found here, particularly the graceful *sura-sundaris* (one applying kohl and another removing a thorn, on the south façade; one tying ankle-bells on the north façade), as well as the fine *Dikpalas* in the corners. The interior is richly carved with elephants, lions, sea goddesses and Jain figures. The temple was originally dedicated to Adinatha, but the modern black marble image of Parsvanatha was placed in the sanctum in 1860. Next, is the smaller and simpler **Adinatha Temple** (late 11th century), where only the sanctum (containing a modern image) and vestibule have survived – the porch is modern. The sculptures on three bands again depict attractive *sura-sundaris*, the niches have *yakshis*, the corners, *Dikpalas*. **Santinatha Temple** with its 4.5-m statue of Adinatha is the main place of Jain worship. An inscription dating it at AD 1027-1028 is covered with plaster – the thoroughly renovated temple retains its ancient heart and medieval sculptures. The small sand-coloured structures around the temples are reconstructions around remains of old shrines. There is also a small Jain museum and picture gallery here.

Southern Group The two temples stand on open land. The setting, attractive at sunset, lacks the overall ambience of the Western Group but the backdrop of the Vindhyas is impressive. **Duladeo Temple**, 800 m southwest of the Jain temples down a path off the road, is the last the Chandelas built here, when temple building was already in decline. There are 20 *apsara* brackets but the figures are often repetitive and appear to lack the quality of carving found in earlier temples. The shrine door and *mandapa* ceiling have some fine carving while the linga has 11 rows of 100 lingas. **Chaturbhuja Temple** (circa 1100), 3 km south of the village, anticipates the Duladeo but lacks erotic sculptures. The sanctum contains an exceptional 2.7-m four-armed *Dakshina-murti* Vishnu image while outside there are some fine *Dikpalas*, nymphs and mythical beasts in niches.

EXCURSIONS FROM KHAJURAHO

At **Rajgarh**, 5 km south, is the imposing ruined 19th-century hilltop fort-palace of the Maharaja which the Oberoi Group will convert to a heritage hotel. It is particularly interesting when villagers congregate for the Tuesday Market. Get there by auto-rickshaw or car. **Panna National Park** ① *Nov-May, and the entrance fee is Rs 2000 for foreigners, Rs 1000 for Indians and elephant safari is Rs 1500 for foreigners and Rs 500 for Indians. Panna*, is accessed along the Satna Road with attractive waterfalls (Rs 100) on the way. Ken River, parts of which have been declared a sanctuary for fish eating gharials, flows across the Panna National Park, which is a Project Tiger Reserve. The park, rich in biodiversity, covers dense forest, open meadows, plateaus and gorge with waterfalls, and supports chinkara, sambar, nilgai and the big cats. Although tiger sightings are rare, it is pleasant to visit in winter. There is little wildlife to be seen in the dry season (when the gharials are removed for their own protection). There are some beautiful places to stay. Access is easiest from Madla, 27 km from Khajuraho. Jeep or motorbike hire from Khajuraho, or bus; tour of park can be arranged in Madla.

NORTHERN MADHYA PRADESH LISTINGS

WHERE TO STAY

Gwalior

$$$$ Usha Kiran Palace, Jayendraganj Lashkar, T0751-244 4000, www.tajhotels.com. 40 very atmospheric rooms (and vast suites) in 120-year-old maharaja's palace. Beautiful spa (musicians play live behind jali screens) and gardens, swimming pool, good restaurant, billiards and bar. It retains character of charming royal guesthouse.

$$ Tansen, 6A Gandhi Rd, T0751-234 0370, www.mptourism.com. 36 rooms, good restaurant, bar, tourist information and quiet location.

Orchha

$$$$-$$$ Amar Mahal, T07680-252102, www.amarmahal.com. Beautiful Maharajah's palace decorated in traditional Bundelkhand style, with luxurious, attractively decorated rooms arranged around 2 courtyards, one with pool. Excellent buffet-style restaurant with 24-carat gold-painted ceiling.

$$$-$$ Orchha Resort, Kanchanghat, on riverside, T07680-252222, www.orchharesort.com. 32 immaculate although characterless a/c rooms and 12 musty tents arranged around parched tennis court with the redeeming feature of an extraordinary backdrop of the royal *chhatris*. Excellent vegetarian restaurant.

$$$-$$ Sheesh Mahal (MP Tourism). In a breathtakingly stunning location inside the fort, T07680-252624 (book in advance). 8 beautiful ornate rooms and 2 magnificent suites with terrace, antique fittings and furniture, huge marble tub, panoramic view from toilet. Full of character and atmospheric charm, restaurant has great views, friendly staff.

$$-$ Ganpati, just north of main crossroads, T07680-252765. www.orchhahotelganpatipalaceview.com. A wide range of clean rooms. Best are the large, amusingly named 'sweet rooms' with a/c, murals and great views of the fort. Hot showers, small courtyard and gardens, great views of palace and very friendly owner.

Khajuraho

$$$$ The Lalit, opposite Circuit House, T0786-272111, www.thelalit.com. Beautiful, top-notch hotel with all the trimmings including sparkling new rooms and extravagant suites. Luxury spa and excellent restaurant.

$$-$ Zen, Jain Temple Rd, T07686-274228, www.hotelzenkhajuraho.co.in. Large, bright ramshackle rooms with clean attached bath, nice garden. Italian restaurant in the garden and owner now promises 10% discount for all Footprint readers!

$$-$ Casa di William, opposite western group of temples, T07686-274244. Very conveniently located, 15 pleasant and clean rooms with bath, some a/c. Absolutely stunning sunset views of temples from roof restaurant, massage, internet, bike rental. Very friendly and helpful staff, Italian management. Good value.

RESTAURANTS

Khajuraho

$$ Mediterraneo, Jain Temple Rd. Good bruschetta, fresh pasta dishes, tasty pizza, good desserts, Indian chefs. Beware of imitators – a 'branch' has opened in Orchha but has nothing to do with this great place.

$$ Raja's Café, Main Rd, near Western Temples entrance. Probably the best food you will get in Khajuraho and great coffee too – all with the backdrop of the temples. There's a nicely designed a/c room downstairs on days that swelter or head up the spiral staircase for great views.

BANDHAVGARH

Bandhavgarh and neighbouring Kanha national parks protect the landscapes that inspired Kipling's Jungle Book *and, despite the continued predations of poachers, Bandhavgarh still offers the possibility of tracking a tiger. Facilities for wildlife viewing in the parks are improving and a number of new safari resorts have opened: some massively luxurious, others working to involve local communities in the conservation effort. The park is set in extremely rugged terrain with many hills. The marshes which used to be perennial now support a vast grassland savannah. Though it involves quite a journey you may be rewarded with sighting one of the few tigers; a three-day stay gives you a 90% chance of seeing one. There are also interesting cave shrines scattered around the park, with Brahmi inscriptions dating from the first century BC. You can visit the remains of a fort believed to be 2000 years old where you may spot crag martins and brown rock thrush.*

Bandhavgarh (pronounced Bandogarh) is not very far from Rewa, famous as the original home of the white tiger, now only found in zoos. Before becoming a national park in 1968, it was the game reserve of the Maharajas of Rewa. The conservation programme helps to protect wildlife from disease, fire, grazing and poaching.

→ ARRIVING IN BANDHAVGARH

GETTING THERE AND AROUND

For information, contact Field Director, Bandhavgarh Tiger Reserve, Umaria, T07653-222214. This compact park is in the Vindhya hills with a core area of 105 sq km and a buffer zone of 437 sq km. The main entrance and park office is at Tala to the north of the park. The park is open 1 October-30 June. The temperature ranges from 42-42°C and average annual rainfall is 1500 mm.

MOVING ON

Umaria station, 30 minutes from Bandhavgarh National Park, has a few trains to **Varanasi** (see page 210); alas, on the current schedule they leave excruciatingly early in the morning – opt for the *Sarnath Express (15061)* which leaves at 0427, taking 12 hours to reach Varanasi. Expected driving time is nine hours. If time is not an issue, you may want to extend the itinerary and spend a couple of nights in Allahabad (see Going further, page 208), a five- to seven-hour journey from nearby Katni. From Allahabad there are buses and trains to Varanasi where you can continue the Dream Trip 3 itinerary.

WILDLIFE

Bandhavgarh park has a wide variety of game and has a longer 'season' than Kanha. Its main wild beasts are tiger, leopard, sloth bear, gaur, sambar, chital, muntjac, *nilgai*, chinkara and wild pigs. There are over 60 tigers, but they remain very elusive. The flowering and fruit trees attract woodland birds which include green pigeon, Jerdon's leaf bird, crested serpent eagle and variable hawk eagle.

VIEWING

You need to plan a long way ahead. As a way of restricting visitors and conserving the wildlife, the daily quota of safaris is very limited, and in Tala zone (the best place to visit) game drives book out six months in advance. Unfortunately, at the time of writing the online booking system refuses payment from non-Indian credit cards, so the only way you can ensure your safari is to book it well in advance through your hotel. Annoyingly, park fees and regulations change regularly, again best to check with your hotel. Currently the fees are Game safari in Tala zone is Rs 6500 per trip for foreigners. Six people are allowed in one vehicle. Other zone are Rs 4500 per trip for foreigners.

BANDHAVGARH LISTINGS

WHERE TO STAY

$$$$ Samode Safari Lodge, www.samode.com. This stunning addition to the **Samode** chain in Rajasthan is the ultimate in luxury, while still leaving a light footprint on the earth. Designed to blend with the surroundings, no trees were cut down in this new build and there is a good nod to eco-tourism with rainwater harvesting, solar energy and villas made from local materials with local craftsmen.
$$$$ Treehouse Hideaway, Village Vijarhia, T(0)8800-637711, www.treehouse hideaway.com. Worlds apart from any treehouse you might have had as a kid, these are boutique treehouses are made of regularized dark wood with beautiful decor and stunning views. They also have a hide overlooking the water hole and a 2-tiered restaurant in a large *mahua* tree. All meals are included in the price. Very special.
$$$ Skays Camp, T(0)9425-331209, www.skayscamp.in. This is a great-value place with a beautiful garden and delicious food. What makes this place so special is the passion of the owners. Satyendra Tiwari is an acclaimed wildlife photographer and knowledgeable birder, guide and naturalist. His British wife Kay is a wildlife artist. Together they gather information on flora and fauna of the area as well as producing tourist guides to the butterflies, snakes and birds and creating tiger identification papers. Satyendra is working on a book on tigers.

GOING FURTHER
Allahabad

The narrow spit of land at the confluence of the Ganga and Yamuna rivers, normally an almost deserted river beach of fine sand, becomes home for two weeks once every 12 years to the **Kumbh Mela**, when more than 70 million pilgrims converge to bathe in the holy waters. Allahabad has grown around this spot and is today a rapidly expanding commercial and administrative city. It is particularly sacred for Hindus because it is at the confluence of three rivers, the Ganga, Yamuna and the mythological underground Saraswati. For the Muslims and the British too, this became a strategically vital centre; they have left their imprint on the landmarks of the city, making it an interesting city to explore, particularly the Civil Lines area to the north.

ARRIVING IN ALLAHABAD
Getting there and around Bamrauli airport is 18 km west of town. The Civil Lines (MG Marg) Bus Stand is used by buses arriving from the north and west, while Zero Road Bus Stand, halfway between the Junction and City railway stations, serves local and southern routes, including Khajuraho. Just south of the Civil Lines, Allahabad Junction Station is the main stop for Delhi and Kolkata trains. Many of the city's hotels are in Civil Lines, within easy reach of the Junction station (rear exit) and the bus stands. Although this centre is quite compact you need an auto-rickshaw to get to some of the main sights, including the fort and the *sangam*. Taxis and cycle-rickshaws are also easily available.

Tourist information Ilawart Tourist Bungalow ① *35 MG Marg, T0532-2440 8873, Mon-Sat 1000-1700 (closed 2nd Sat in month); also at the railway station, daily 0800-1800*, has competent staff and can provide city maps and numerous leaflets. Car hire can be arranged here (Rs 6.5 per km, minimum 200 km).

PLACES IN ALLAHABAD
Prayag (the confluence) The purifying power of a sacred river is strongest at a confluence. In addition, the mythical underground **Sarasvati River** is also said to surface here. Bathing here is auspicious at all times of the year, more so at **Magh Mela** which occurs every year for 15 days (January/February) and longer at the **Kumbh Mela** when pilgrims bathe at *prayag* to wash away a lifetime's sins. In legend, Hindu gods and demons vied for the *kumbha* (pot) that held the *amrit* (nectar of immortality). During the 12-day fight for possession, Vishnu spilt four drops of *amrit* which fell to earth, making four sacred places: Allahabad, Haridwar (Uttarakhand), Ujjain (Madhya Pradesh) and Nasik (Maharashtra). Holiest of all is Allahabad, the site of the **Maha** (great) **Kumbh Mela**. This festival moves every three years, returning to Allahabad every 12th year. There are still rows of tents at the *prayag*, which give a good indication of the sheer size of the Kumbh Mela, when the area becomes a canvas city, home to over a million people. Boats leave from nearby ghats, the nearest being the one by the fort.

Mughal Period Allahabad has few monuments pre-dating the Muslim period. The **fort**, begun in 1583, was the largest of Akbar's forts. It has three massive gateways and 7-m-high walls, seen to advantage from across the river. The Marathas held it from 1739 to 1750, then the Pathans, and finally the British from 1801. Most of the fort is closed to visitors. Under the fort's east wall is the **Undying Banyan Tree** (*Akshaivata*), an underground temple from which pilgrims threw themselves to achieve salvation in death. To see, ask for a permit at the tourist office.

Khusrau Bagh This typical Mughal garden enclosure makes a peaceful retreat from the city, and houses the handsome tomb of Prince Khusrau. After staging an unsuccessful rebellion against his father Jahangir in 1607, Khusrau spent the next year in chains. When freed, he encouraged a plot to assassinate his father but was discovered. Partially blinded and kept a captive, he was murdered in 1615 by his own brother, who became the Emperor Shah Jahan (ruled 1627-1658). Of the three impressive mausoleums, Khusrau's is the furthest east with decorative plasterwork, stone lattice windows and his burial chamber underground. The central tomb is thought to be his sister's and is beautifully painted inside. Furthest west is the tomb of his Rajput mother, whose cenotaph of white marble is located at the top of the building; she committed suicide in 1603 by over-dosing on opium. On arrival someone will appear with the keys to the mausoleums, and expect a bit of baksheesh. The southern gate to the gardens remains impressively intact, the large wood door covered with horseshoes.

Buildings from the British Period Canning Town, opposite Junction Railway Station, was laid out on a grid in the 1860s. Within it are the Old High Court and Public Offices, classical-style buildings from the late 19th century including the Gothic-style **All Saints' Cathedral**. At the east end of the Civil Lines is Alfred Park (now Chandra Sekhar Azad Park), north of which stands **Muir College**, a fine example of 'Indo-Saracenic' architecture. It was later established as the University of Allahabad. West of this is the extraordinary **Mayo Hall** with **St Joseph's Roman Catholic Cathedral** (1879) to its south. **Holy Trinity Church** (early 19th century) on J Nehru Marg, contains memorials from the Gwalior Campaign (1843) and the 'Uprising' (1857).

Allahabad Museum ① *Chandra Sekhar Azad Park, Kamla Nehru Rd, T0532-260 1200, closed Mon and 2nd Sun of month, 1000-1700, foreigners Rs 100, Indians Rs 5, 18 galleries,* contains a wide range of stone sculptures (second century BC from Bharhut and Kaushambi; first century AD Kushana from Mathura; fourth to sixth century Gupta and 11th-century carvings from Khajuraho). It also has a fine collection of Rajasthani miniatures, terracotta figurines, coins and paintings by Nicholas Roerich. **Anand Bhavan** ① *T0532-246 7071, Tue-Sun 1000-1700, Rs 50,* the former Nehru family home, contains many interesting items. These relate to: Motilal Nehru (1861-1931), active in the Independence Movement; Jawaharlal Nehru (1889-1964), Independent India's first prime minister; Indira Gandhi (1917-1984; prime minister 1966-1977, 1980-1984); and her sons Sanjay Gandhi who died 1980 and Rajiv Gandhi (prime minister 1984-1989) who was assassinated in 1991. The **garden** ① *free,* is pleasant to relax in. Next to it stands **Swaraj Bhawan** ① *Tue-Sun 1000-1700, Rs 50,* where Indira Gandhi was born.

Recommended hotels (both **$$**) in Allahabad include: **Allahabad Regency** (16 Tashkent Marg, Civil Lines, T0532-240 7835, www.hotelallahabadregency.com), a red-and-white heritage bungalow with arched portico dating from 1866, delightful manicured gardens and salubrious bar as well as a nice pool and health club; and **Yatrik** (33 Sardar Patel Marg, Civil Lines, T0532-226 0921-6, www.hotelyatrik.com), which has a stark modernist façade that hides a lovely back garden with sizable pool (closed in winter), 38 smart and homely air-conditioned rooms and a restaurant but no bar. It's well-priced for what you get.

VARANASI AND AROUND

Perhaps the holiest of India's cities, Varanasi defies easy description. A highly congested maze of narrow alleys winds behind its waterfront ghats, at once highly sacred yet physically often far from clean. As an image, an idea and a symbol of Hinduism's central realities, the city draws pilgrims from around the world, to worship, to meditate, and above all to bathe. It is a place to be born and a place to die. In the cold mists of a winter's dawn, you can see life and death laid bare. For an outside observer it can be an uncomfortable, albeit unmissable experience, juxtaposing the inner philosophical mysteries of Hinduism with the practical complications of living literally and metaphorically on the edge.

More holy places surround Varanasi: Sarnath, one of Buddhism's major centres, Jaunpur, a city with a strong Islamic history, and Allahabad, a sacred place for Hindus due to its position at the confluence of the Ganja and Yamuna rivers.

→ VARANASI

The riverside city, and the focus for most tourists and pilgrims, extends from Raj Ghat in the north to Assi Ghat in the south. At dawn the riverbank's stone steps begin to hum with activity. Early risers immerse themselves in the water as they face the rising sun, boatmen wait expectantly on the waterside, pilgrims flock to the temples, flower sellers do brisk business, astrologers prepare to read palms and horoscopes while families carry the dead to their last rites by the holy river. A few steps away from the ghats, motorbikers speed through the lanes past wandering *sadhus*, hopeful beggars, curious visitors and wandering cows, while packs of stray dogs scavenge among the piles of rubbish.

ARRIVING IN VARANASI

Getting there Airlines link Varanasi with Delhi, Kolkata and other cities. From Babatpur airport, 22 km away, take a taxi from the prepaid booth. Most trains stop at Junction Station near the Cantonment, about 5 km northwest of the Old City and the budget hotels. Some trains do not pass through Varanasi itself but stop at Mughal Sarai, 17 km away, which is accessible by road from Varanasi. Shared jeeps cost Rs 25 between the two stations, or a taxi is Rs 300. Most long-distance buses arrive at the bus stands near Junction Station.

Note On arrival at Junction Station, you will be accosted by rickshaw-wallahs who are desperate to get you to a hotel which pays them commission. It can be stressful; don't believe touts who say your chosen hotel is closed or full – such things rarely change in Varanasi. Several budget hotels offer free pick-up from the station (call on arrival), or try to get at least 50 m outside of the station area before bargaining for an auto (Rs 80) or cycle-rickshaw (Rs 50). Note that autos are not permitted into the narrow lanes near the main ghats, and you will have to walk the last stretch (15-25 minutes to hotels). However, autos can get close to Assi Ghat, from where it's a two-minute walk to hotels.

Moving on Frequent trains go to Gaya (3½ to four hours), from where you take a rickshaw on to **Bodhgaya** (see page 221), the next stop on this trip. The train is much preferable to the bus.

Getting around The only way to see the heart of the Old City is on foot, though no visit is complete without an early-morning boat trip along the ghats. Varanasi is quite spread out: the university to the south is nearly 7 km from the spacious Cantonment area and the Junction Station to the north. Around town, cycle-rickshaws and autos are plentiful. Shared autos run along main routes, though it is difficult (as a tourist) to avoid being

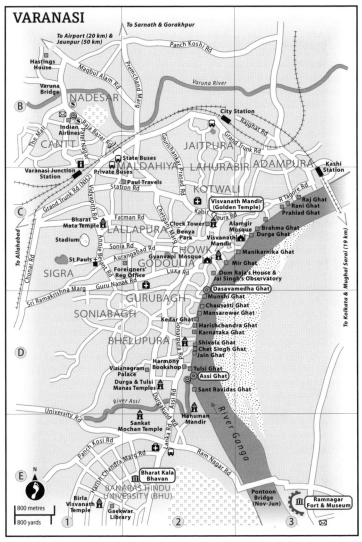

VARANASI

To Sarnath & Gorakhpur

To Airport (20 km) &
Jaunpur (50 km)

Panch Koshi Rd

Hastings
House

Magbul Alam Rd

Premchand Marg

Varuna River

Varuna
Bridge

NADESAR

City Station

B

Rajghat Rd

Raja Bazar Rd

Indian
Airlines

Grand Trunk Rd

Gaurishankar Prasad Rd

JAITPURA

LAHURABIR

ADAMPURA

Kashi
Station

The Mall

CANTT

State Buses

MALDAHIYA

Private Buses

KOTWALI

R Tagore Rd

Raj Ghat

Varanasi Junction
Station

Paul Travels

Station Rd

Rani Ghat

Visvanath Mandir
(Golden Temple)

Prahlad Ghat

C

Grand Trunk Rd (NH2)

Vidyapith Rd

Kabir

Chaura Rd

Brahma Ghat

To Allahabad

Fatman Rd

Chetganj Marg

Clock Tower

Alamgir
Mosque

Durga Ghat

Bharat
Mata Temple

LALLAPURA

Benya
Park

Visvanath
Mandir

Manikarnika Ghat

Sonia Rd

Mir Ghat

Chunar Rd

Stadium

Aurangabad Rd

Gyanvapi Mosque

St Pauls

Annie Besant Rd

GODOULIA

Dom Raja's House &
Jai Singh's Observatory

SIGRA

Foreigners'
Reg Office

Luxa Rd

Dasavamedha Ghat

Guru Nanak Rd

Munshi Ghat

Sri Ramakrishna Marg

GURUBAGH

Chausatti Ghat

SONIABAGH

Mansarower Ghat

Kedar Ghat

Harishchandra Ghat

Sonapura Rd

Karnataka Ghat

BHELUPURA

Shivala Ghat

Chet Singh Ghat

Jain Ghat

D

Harmony
Bookshop

Tulsi Ghat

Vizianagram
Palace

Durgakund Rd

Pu Issy

Assi Ghat

River Ganga

Durga & Tulsi
Manas Temples

Sant Ravidas Ghat

River Assi

University Rd

Hanuman
Mandir

Sankat
Mochan Temple

Panch Kosi Rd

Harish Chandra Marg Rd

Ram Nagar Rd

E

N

Bharat Kala
Bhavan

BANARAS HINDU
UNIVERSITY (BHU)

800 metres

Pontoon
Bridge
(Nov-Jun)

Ramnagar
Fort & Museum

800 yards

Birla
Visvanath
Temple

Gaekwar
Library

1

2

3

To Kolkata & Mughal Sarai (19 km)

pressured into private hire. Unmetered taxis are best for longer sightseeing trips. The city has some of the disadvantages of pilgrimage centres, notably rickshaw drivers who seem determined to extort as much as possible from unsuspecting visitors.

Tourist information Tourist Information Counter ⓘ *Junction Railway Station, near 'Enquiry', T0542-250 6670, open 0600-2000*, provides helpful maps and information. Government of India Tourist Office ⓘ *The Mall, Cantt, T0542-2501784, Mon-Sat 0900-1630*, is well run, with helpful manager and staff; **guides** are available at set rates. Also at Babatpur Airport.

HISTORY

Varanasi derives its name from two streams, the Varuna to the north and the Assi, a small trickle, on the south. **Banaras** is a corruption of Varanasi but it is also called **Kashi** (Siva's 'City of Light') by Hindus. As one of the seven sacred cities of Hinduism, it attracts well over one million pilgrims while about 50,000 Brahmins are permanent residents. The Jains too consider it holy because three *tirthankars* (seventh Suarsvanath, 11th Shyeyanshnath, 23rd Parsvanath) were born here.

Varanasi is said to combine the virtues of all other places of pilgrimage, and anyone dying within the area marked by the **Panch Kosi Road** is transported straight to heaven. Some devout Hindus move to Varanasi to end their days and have their ashes scattered in the holy Ganga. Every pilgrim, in addition to visiting the holy sites, must make a circuit of the Panch Kosi Road which runs outside and round the sacred territory of Varanasi. This starts at Manikarnika Ghat, runs along the waterfront to Assi Ghat, then round the outskirts in a large semi-circle to Barna Ghat. The 58-km route is lined with trees and shrines and the pilgrimage is supposed to take six days, each day's walk finishing in a small village, equipped with temples and *dharamshalas*.

Varanasi was probably an important town by the seventh century BC when Babylon and Nineveh were at the peak of their power. The Buddha visited in 500 BC and it was mentioned in both the *Mahabharata* and the *Ramayana*. It became a centre of culture, education, commerce and craftsmanship but was raided by **Mahmud of Ghazni's** army in 1033 and by Qutb-ud-din Ghuri in 1194. **Ala-ud-din Khalji**, the King of Delhi (1294-1316), destroyed temples and built mosques on their sites. The Muslim influence was strong so even in the 18th century the city was known briefly as Mohammadabad. Despite its early foundation hardly any building dates before the 17th century, and few are more than 200 years old.

The city stands as the chief centre of Sanskrit learning in North India. Sanskrit, the oldest of the Indo-European languages, used for Hindu ritual has been sustained here long after it ceased to be a living language elsewhere. The **Banaras Hindu University** has over 150,000 rare manuscripts. Hindu devotional movements flourished here, especially in the 15th century under Ramananda, and **Kabir**, one of India's greatest poets, lived in the city. It was here that **Tulsi Das** translated the Ramayana from Sanskrit into Hindi.

OLD CENTRE

Visvanath Temple (1777) has been the main Siva temple in Varanasi for over 1000 years. Tourists have to enter by Gate 2, but can exit from any gate, and there is stiff security by the entrances (take passport ID, bags not permitted). The original temple, destroyed in the 12th century, was replaced by a mosque. It was rebuilt in the 16th, and again destroyed within a century. The present **'Golden' Temple** was built in 1777 by Ahilya Bai of Indore. The gold plating on the roof was provided by Maharaja Ranjit Singh in 1835. Its pointed spires are typically North Indian in style and the exterior is finely carved. The 18th-century **Annapurna Temple** (*anna* food; *purna* filled) nearby, built by Baji Rao I, has shrines dedicated to Siva, Ganesh, Hanuman and Surya. Ask for directions as you make your way through the maze of alleys around the temples.

The **Gyan Kup** (Well of Knowledge) next door is said to contain the Siva lingam from the original temple – the well is protected by a stone screen and canopy. The nearby **Gyanvapi Mosque** (Great Mosque of Aurangzeb), with 71-m-high minarets, shows evidence of the original Hindu temple, in the foundations, the columns and at the rear.

The 17th-century **Alamgir Mosque** (Beni Madhav ka Darera), impressively situated on Panchganga Ghat, was Aurangzeb's smaller mosque. It was built on the original Vishnu temple of the Marathas, parts of which were used in its construction. Two minarets are missing – one fell and killed some people and the other was taken down by the government as a precaution. You can climb to the top of the mosque for fantastic views (donation expected); again, bags are prohibited and you may be searched.

BACK LANES

The maze of narrow lanes, or *galis*, along the ghats through the old quarters exude the smells and sounds of this holy city. They are fascinating to stroll through though easy to get lost in. Some find it too over-powering. Near the Town Hall (1845) built by the Maharaja of Vizianagram, is the **Kotwali** (Police Station) with the Temple of **Bhaironath**, built by Baji Rao II in 1825. The image inside is believed to be of the Kotwal (Superintendent) who rides on a ghostly dog. Stalls sell sugar dogs to be offered to the image. In the temple garden of **Gopal Mandir** near the Kotwali is a small hut in which Tulsi Das is said to have composed the *Binaya Patrika* poem.

The **Bhelupura Temple** with a museum marks the birthplace of the 23rd Jain Tirthankar **Parsvanath** who preached non-violence. The **Durga Temple** (18th-century) to the south along Durga Kund Road, was built in the Nagara style. It is painted red with ochre and has the typical five spires (symbolizing the elements) merging into one (Brahma). Non-Hindus may view from the rooftop nearby. Next door in a peaceful garden, the **Tulsi Manas Temple** (1964) in white marble commemorates the medieval poet Tulsi Das. It has walls engraved with verses and scenes from the *Ramcharitmanas*, composed in a Hindi dialect, instead of the conventional Sanskrit, and is open to all (closed 1130-1530). Good views from the second floor of 'Disneyland-style' animated show. **Bharat Mata Temple**, south of Varanasi Junction Station, has a relief map of 'Mother India' in marble.

RIVERFRONT

The hundred and more **ghats** on the river are the main attraction for visitors to Varanasi. Visit them at first light before sunrise (0430 in summer, 0600 in winter) when Hindu pilgrims come to bathe in the sacred Ganga, facing the rising sun, or at dusk when synchronized *pujas* are performed, culminating in leaf-boat lamps being floated down the river, usually from 1800 (later in summer). Large crowds gather at Dasasvamedha (Main) Ghat and Mir Ghat every night, or there's a more low-key affair at Assi Ghat. Start the river trip at Dasasvamedha Ghat where you can hire a boat quite cheaply especially if you can share (bargain to about Rs 150-200 per hour for two to eight people, at dawn). You may go either upstream (south) towards Harishchandra Ghat or downstream to Manikarnika Ghat. You may prefer to have a boat on the river at sunset and watch the lamps floated on the river, or go in the afternoon at a fraction of the price quoted at dawn. For photographs, visit the riverside between 0700 and 0900. The foggy sunshine early in the morning often clears to produce a beautiful light.

Kite flying is a popular pastime, as elsewhere in India, especially all along the riverbank. The serious competitors endeavour to bring down other flyers' kites and so fortify their twine by coating it with a mix of crushed light bulbs and flour paste to make it razor sharp. The quieter ghats, eg Panchganga, are good for watching the fun: boys in their boats on the river scramble to retrieve downed kites as trophies that can be re-used even though the kites themselves are very cheap. Cricket is also played on the ghats, particularly those to the north which are more spacious and less crowded.

Dasasvamedha Ghat Commonly called 'Main Ghat', Dasasvamedha means the 'Place of Ten Horse Sacrifices' performed here by Brahma, God of Creation. Some believe that in the age of the gods when the world was in chaos, Divodasa was appointed King of Kashi by Brahma. He accepted, on condition that all the gods would leave Varanasi. Even Siva was forced to leave but Brahma set the test for Divodasa, confident that he would get the complex ceremony wrong, allowing the gods back into the city. However, the ritual was performed flawlessly, and the ghat has thus become one of the holiest, especially at eclipses. Bathing here is regarded as being almost as meritorious as making the sacrifice.

Moving south You will pass **Munshi Ghat**, where some of the city's sizeable Muslim population (25%) come to bathe. The river has no religious significance for them. Close by is **Darbhanga Ghat** where the mansion had a hand-operated cable lift. Professional washermen work at the **Dhobi Ghat**; there is religious merit in having your clothes washed in the Ganga. Brahmins have their own washermen to avoid caste pollution. The municipality has built separate washing facilities away from the ghat.

Narad Ghat and **Chauki Ghat** are held sacred since the Buddha received enlightenment here under a *peepul* tree. Those who bathe together at Narad, supposedly go home and quarrel! The pink water tower here is for storing Ganga water. High water levels are recorded at **Raj Ghat**. The flood levels are difficult to imagine when the river is at its lowest in January and February. **Mansarovar Ghat** leads to ruins of several temples around a lake. **Kedar Ghat** is named after Kedarnath, a pilgrimage site in the Uttarakhand, with a Bengali temple nearby.

The **Harishchandra Ghat** is particularly holy and is dedicated to King Harishchandra. It is now the most sacred *smashan* or cremation ghat although Manikarnika is more popular. Behind the ghat is a *gopuram* of a Dravidian-style temple. The **Karnataka Ghat** is one of many regional ghats which are attended by priests who know the local languages, castes, customs and festivals.

The **Hanuman Ghat** is where Vallabha, the leader of a revivalist Krishna bhakti cult was born in the late 15th century. **Shivala Ghat** (Kali Ghat) is privately owned by the ex-ruler of Varanasi. **Chet Singh's Fort**, Shivala, stands behind the ghat. The fort, the old palace of the Maharajas, is where the British imprisoned him but he escaped by climbing down to the river and swimming away. **Anandamayi Ghat** is named after the Bengali saint Anandamayi Ma (died 1982) who received 'enlightenment' at 17 and spent her life teaching and in charitable work. **Jain Ghat** is near the birthplace of Tirthankar Shyeyanshnath. **Tulsi Ghat** commemorates the great saint-poet Tulsi Das who lived here (see Tulsi Manas Temple, page 213). Furthest upstream is the **Assi Ghat**, where the River Assi meets the Ganga, one of the five that pilgrims should bathe from in a day. The order is Assi, Dasasvamedha, Barnasangam, Panchganga and Manikarnika. Upstream on the east bank is the Ramnagar Fort, the Maharaja of Varanasi's residence (see page 216). Here the boat will turn to take you back to Dasasvamedha Ghat.

Moving north Leaving Dasasvamedha Ghat, you come to **Man Mandir Ghat** ① *open dawn till dusk, Rs100 foreigners, Rs 5 Indians*, which is dominated by a Rajput palace and was built by Maharajah Man Singh of Amber in 1600; it is one of the oldest in Varanasi. The palace was restored in the last century with brick and plaster. The beautiful stone balcony on the northeast corner gives an indication of how the original looked. Maharaja Jai Singh of Jaipur converted the palace into an **observatory** in 1710 (see also Jaipur, page 89). Like its counterparts in Delhi, Jaipur and Ujjain, the rooftop observatory comprises a collection of instruments built of brick, cement and stone. At the entrance is the Bhittiyantra, or wall quadrant, over 3 m high and in the same plane as the line of longitude. Similarly placed is the Samratyantra which is designed to slope upwards pointing at the Pole Star. From the top of the Chakra Yantra there is a superb view of the ghats and the town. Near the entrance to the palace is a small **Siva Temple** whose shrine is a lingam immersed in water. During droughts, water is added to the cistern to make it overflow for good luck.

The **Dom Raja's House** is next door, flanked by painted tigers. The *doms* are the 'Untouchables' of Varanasi and are integral to the cremation ceremony. As Untouchables they can handle the corpse, a ritually polluting act for Hindus. They also supply the flame from the temple for the funeral pyre. Their presence is essential and also lucrative since there are fees for the various services they provide. The Dom Raja is the hereditary title of the leader of these Untouchables.

Mir Ghat leads to a sacred well; widows who dedicate themselves to prayer, are fed and clothed here. Then comes **Lalita Ghat** with the distinctive Nepalese-style temple with a golden roof above ① *entrance Rs 30*, and wood carvings decorating the exterior. Above **Manikarnika Ghat** is a well into which Siva's dead wife Sati's earring is supposed to have fallen when Siva was carrying her after she committed suicide. The Brahmins managed to find the jewel from the earring (*manikarnika*) and returned it to Siva who blessed the place. Offerings of *bilva* flowers, milk, sandalwood and sweetmeats are thrown into the tank where pilgrims come to bathe. Between the well and the ghat is *Charanpaduka*, a stone slab with Vishnu's footprint. Boatmen may try to persuade you to leave a 'private' offering to perform a *puja* (a ploy to increase their earnings).

The adjoining **Jalasayin Ghat** is the principal burning ghat of the city. The expensive scented sandalwood which the rich alone can afford is used sparingly; usually not more than 2 kg. You may see floating bundles covered with white cloth; children, and those dying of 'high fever', or smallpox in the past, are not cremated but put into the river. This avoids injuring Sitala the goddess of smallpox. **Note** Photography is not permitted at the burning ghats, though travellers might be told that it is allowed and then a large fine demanded. Other scams involve conmen collecting 'donations' to provide wood for burning the poor. Beware of pestering individuals declaring they are "not a guide"; they have the potential to ruin your experience.

Tourists are few and far between after the burning ghat. **Scindia Ghat**, originally built in 1830, was so large that it collapsed. **Ram Ghat** was built by the Maharaja of Jaipur. Five rivers are supposed to meet at the magnificent **Panchganga Ghat** – the Ganga, Sarasvati, Gyana, Kirana and Dhutpapa. The stone column can hold around 1000 lamps at festivals. The impressive flights of stone steps run up to the Alamgir Mosque (see page 213). At **Gai Ghat** there is a statue of a Nandi bull whilst at **Trilochana Ghat** there is a temple to Siva in his form as the 'Three-eyed' (*Trilochana*); two turrets stand out of the water. A beautiful little palace is found at **Rani Ghat**, then **Raj Ghat** is the last ghat you can reach before the path peters out. Excavations have revealed a site of a city from the eighth century BC on a grassy mound nearby. Raj Ghat was where the river was forded until bridges were built.

OTHER INTERESTING SIGHTS

Varanasi is famous for ornamental brasswork, silk weaving and for its glass beads, exported all over the world. *Zari* work, whether embroidered or woven, once used silver or gold thread but is now done with gilded copper or brass. You can watch weavers at work in Piti Kothi, the Muslim area inland from Raj Ghat. The significance of **silk** in India's traditional life is deep-rooted. Silk was considered a pure fabric, most appropriate for use on ceremonial and religious occasions. Its lustre, softness and richness of natural colour gave it precedence over all other fabrics. White or natural coloured silk was worn by the Brahmins and others who were 'twice born'. Women wore bright colours and the darker hues were reserved for the lowest caste in the formal hierarchy, few of whom could afford it. Silk garments were worn for ceremonials like births and marriages, and offerings of finely woven silks were made to deities in temples. This concept of purity may have given impetus to the growth of silk-weaving centres around ancient temple towns like Kanchipuram, Varanasi, Bhubaneswar and Ujjain, a tradition that is kept alive today.

Banaras Hindu University (**BHU**), to the south of the city, is one of the largest campus universities in India and enjoys a pleasant, relaxed atmosphere. Founded at the turn of the 19th century, it was originally intended for the study of Sanskrit, Indian art, music and culture. The **New Visvanath Temple** (1966), one of the tallest in India, is in the university semicircle and was financed by the Birla family. It was planned by Madan Mohan Malaviya (1862-1942), chancellor of the university, who believed in Hinduism without caste distinctions. The marble Siva temple modelled on the old Visvanath Temple, is open to all.

Bharat Kala Bhavan ① *BHU, Mon-Sat 1030-1630 (Jul-Apr), 0730-1300 (May-Jun) closed holidays, foreigners Rs 100, camera Rs 50 (lockers at entrance).*This peaceful museum contains a wealth of sculptures from Mathura and Sarnath, and an excellent gallery of miniature paintings including Mughal and Company works. Don't miss the Nidhi Gallery (limited hours, 1200-1300 and 1500-1600) containing treasures such as Jahangir's opium cup and priceless pieces of jewellery. Upstairs is an interesting exhibition on Benares containing old prints and photos, and also the Alice Boner gallery showing the life and work of this Swiss painter/sculptor who immigrated to India in 1935.

Across the river in a dramatic setting on the edge of narrow crowded streets is the run-down 17th-century **Ramnagar Fort**, the former home of the Maharaja of Varanasi. The ferry costs Rs 10 return, or there are rickshaws from the main gate of BHU which cross a bone-jarring pontoon bridge to the fort (under water June to October), Rs 10 each way, or take a boat back or else walk over the pontoon bridge. The **museum** ① *T0542-233 9322, 1000-1700, Rs 16,* has palanquins, elephant *howdahs* and headdresses, costumes, arms and furniture gathering dust. Look out for the amazing locally made astrological clock and peer inside the impressive Durbar Hall, cunning designed to remain cool in the summer heat, with lifesize portraits lining one wall. Nearby Ramnagar village has *Ramlila* performances during Dasara (October to November) and has some quieter backalleys which make for a relaxing hours wandering.

→ SARNATH

Sarnath, 10 km northeast of Varanasi, is one of Buddhism's major centres in India. The museum houses some superb pieces, including the famed four-lion capital that is the symbol of the Indian Union. The *stupas*, monasteries and Buddha statues make an interesting contrast to nearby Hindu Varanasi.

Tourist information Modern Reception Centre ① *T0542-259 5965, T(0)9580-574420, Mon-Sat 1000-1700*, provides a map and information.

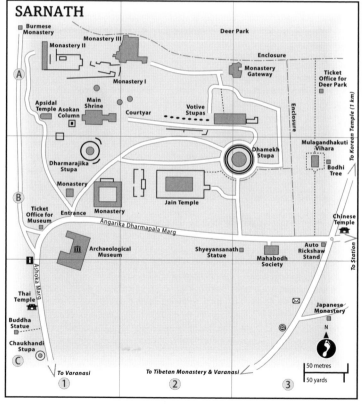

BACKGROUND

When he had gained enlightenment at Bodhgaya, the Buddha came to the deer park at Sarnath and delivered his first sermon (circa 528 BC), usually referred to as *Dharmachakra* (The Wheel of Law). Since then, the site has been revered. The Chinese traveller Hiuen Tsang described the *sangharama* (monastery) in AD 640 as having 1500 monks, a 65-m-high *vihara*, a figure of the Buddha represented by a wheel, a 22-m-high stone *stupa* built by Ashoka, a larger 90-m-high *stupa* and three lakes. The remains here and the sculptures now at the Indian Museum, Kolkata and the National Museum, Delhi, reveal that Sarnath was a centre of religious activity, learning and art, continuously from the fourth century BC until its abandonment in the ninth century AD and ultimate destruction by Muslim armies in 1197.

ARCHAEOLOGICAL MUSEUM

ⓘ *Sat-Thu 0900-1700, entrance Rs 5, cameras and bags must be left outside.*

The Archaeological Museum has a well-displayed collection of pieces from the site, including the famous lion capital from the Ashokan Column. The four lions sitting back to back are of highly polished sandstone and show Mauryan sculpture at its best. Also on display are a Sunga period (first century BC) stone railing, Kushana period (second century AD) Boddhisattvas and Gupta period (fifth century AD) figures including a magnificent seated Buddha.

ENCLOSURE

ⓘ *Open sunrise-sunset, foreigners Rs 100, video Rs 25.*

The **Dhamekh Stupa** (Dharma Chakra) dating to fifth to sixth century AD, is the most imposing monument at Sarnath, built where the Buddha delivered his first sermon to his five disciples. Along with his birth, enlightenment and death, this incident is one of the four most significant. The *stupa* consists of a 28-m-diameter stone plinth which rises to a height of 13 m. Each of the eight faces has an arched recess for an image. Above this base rises a 31-m-high cylindrical tower. The upper part was probably unfinished. The central section has elaborate Gupta designs, eg luxuriant foliation, geometric patterns, birds and flowers. The Brahmi script dates from the sixth to ninth centuries. The *stupa* was enlarged six times and the well-known figures of a standing Boddhisattva and the Buddha teaching were found nearby.

The **Dharmarajika Stupa** was built by the Emperor Ashoka to contain relics of the Buddha. It was enlarged on several occasions but was destroyed by Jagat Singh, Dewan of the Maharaja of Benares, in 1794, when a green marble casket containing human bones and pearls was found. The British Resident at the maharaja's court published an account of the discovery thereby drawing the attention of scholars to the site.

The **main shrine**, marking the place of the Buddha's meditation, is attributed to Ashoka and the later Guptas. To the rear is the 5-m lower portion of a polished sandstone **Ashokan Column** (third century BC). The original was about 15 m high and was topped by the lion capital which is now in the Archaeological Museum (see above). The column was one of many erected by Ashoka to promulgate the faith and this contained a message to the monks and nuns not to create any schisms and to spread the word. The monastery (fifth century onwards) in the southwest corner is one of four (the others are along the north edge of the enclosure). All are of brick, with cells off a central courtyard that are in ruins.

OTHER PLACES OF INTEREST

The site is also holy to Jains because **Shyeyanshnath**, the 11th Tirthankar, was born near the Dhamekh *stupa*. The word 'Sarnath' may be derived from his name. A large temple and (on the opposite side of the road) a statue have been built to commemorate him. The modern **Mulagandhakuti Vihara** ① *open 0400-1130, 1330-2000*, (1929-1931) contains frescoes by the Japanese artist Kosetsu Nosu depicting scenes from the Buddha's life. An urn in the ground is supposed to hold a Buddha relic obtained from Taxila (Pakistan). The wall around the **Bodhi tree** (*Tpipal, Ficus religiosa*) is thick with prayer flags. The tree, planted in 1931, is a sapling of the one in Sri Lanka that was grown from a cutting taken there circa 236 BC by Mahinda's sister Princess Sanghamitta. Past the Mulagandhakuti temple is the **deer park/zoo** ① *open 0800-dusk, Rs 20*, where you can see birds, deer and crocodiles.

The colourful and peaceful **Burmese monastery** is worth the detour from the road. The **Chinese monastery** has a map showing Hiuen Tsang's route to India during AD 629-644, as well as old photos on display. Tibetan, Japanese, Cambodian, Korean and Thai monasteries have also been built around the old complex. The 24-m-high **standing statue** of Lord Buddha, next to the Thai monastery, was completed in March 2011.

Chaukhandi, 500 m south, has a fifth-century *stupa*. On top of this is an octagonal brick tower built by Akbar in 1588 to commemorate the visit his father Humayun made to the site. The inscription above the doorway reads "As Humayun, king of the Seven Climes, now residing in paradise, deigned to come and sit here one day, thereby increasing the splendour of the sun, so Akbar, his son and humble servant, resolved to build on this spot a lofty tower reaching to the blue sky".

VARANASI AND AROUND LISTINGS

WHERE TO STAY

$$$$ Jukaso Ganges, Guleria Ghat, near Manikarnika Ghat, T0542-240 6666, www.welcomeheritagehotels.in. Beautiful newly renovated palace with 15 comfortable rooms (mostly river-facing, some with delightful private balconies), great bathrooms, around an inner courtyard. Roof terrace for dining, lovely seating out the front on the ghats, and charming public spaces in an amazingly elegant building. Breakfast included. Located on the northern ghats by among stunning ancient buildings – the less touristed part.

$$$$ Suryauday Haveli, Shivala Ghat, Nepali Kothi, T0542-654 0390, www. suryaudayhaveli.com. Newly opened hotel directly on the ghats in a renovated century-old stone edifice built by the Nepali kings. Some rooms river-facing, there's a fabulous roof deck, lovely courtyard, and yoga in mornings/sunset boat ride (free). Candlelit dinner accompanied by live Indian music in evenings should be special, although the quality of food isn't up to scratch (yet). Rooms are spacious with traditional elements of decor. An excellent location, and a characterful and swish place to stay right on the Ganga, but don't expect 5 stars. Rates drop by almost 50% May-Sep, breakfast included.

$$$ Ganges View, Assi Ghat, T0542-231 3218, www.hotelgangesview.com. Old patrician home converted into a welcoming guesthouse with a tastefully decorated range of small rooms, more expensive on the upper level with the better views, very pleasant atmosphere, interesting clientele, lovely riverside verandas, beautiful artwork adorns the public spaces, vegetarian restaurant (guests only), Wi-Fi Rs 25 per hr. Deservedly popular so book ahead.

$$$-$$ Shiva Ganges View, Mansarovar Ghat, T0542-245 0063, www.varanasiguest house.com. In a British-built old family house, 8 large spotless rooms have high ceilings, multiple windows, mosquito nets and coolers – but somewhat strange furniture and clashing decor. Great views from the front upstairs rooms, which share a balcony and have a/c; lower rooms have air-coolers and are cheaper. Very chatty owner.

$$-$ Ganpati, next to **Alka** on Mir Ghat, T0542-239 0059, www.ganpatiguest house.com. Atmospheric old building, 20 rooms range from cubby holes sharing bathrooms to spacious doubles with TV and river-fronting private balconies, some rooms have a/c. Great views from rooftop, good restaurant, but the booking system can be hit-and-miss.

RESTAURANTS

$$-$ Lotus Lounge, Mansarovar Ghat, T(0)9838-567717. Top spot for Ganga views from chilled-out terrace, prices are reasonable for inventive Asian and Western dishes, interesting salads and decent breakfasts. A perfect place if you need to get away from the bustle, plus a clean toilet. Closed in summer.

$$-$ Open Hand Cafe, Dumraun Bagh Colony, nr Assi Ghat, www.openhand.in. Excellent coffee, great pastries and food, and a relaxing cosy place to hang out with

free Wi-Fi. Fair-trade. The shop is worth checking out.

$$-$ Pizzeria Café Vaatika, Assi Ghat. Wonderful shady terrace on the Ganga, friendly staff, Italian and Indian food, excellent cold coffee. A perfect place to relax.

$ Megu, Kalika Lane near Golden Temple. Lunchtimes only, 1000-1600, closed Sun. This tiny restaurant specializes in Japanese food and is popular with those in the know. Fantastic ginger chicken, and the Korean *bibimbap* is a winner.

BODHGAYA AND AROUND

Bodhgaya, a quiet sprawling village near the River Niranjana (Phalgu), is one of the holiest Buddhist pilgrimage centres in India. It was under the Bo tree here that Gautama, the prince, attained Enlightenment to become the Buddha. During the winter months, monks from the Himalayans head down to sultry Bodhgaya to escape the cold.

→ ARRIVING IN BODHGAYA

GETTING THERE AND MOVING ON

Trains from Varanasi take about three hours, and from Mughal Serai 2½ hours or less. Aim to travel between Gaya and Bodhgaya in daylight only, for your own safety. Rickshaws to Bodhgaya are available from outside Gaya station. Overnight trains to **Lucknow** (see page 225) usually take between 10 and 13 hours; there are two trains per week taking only eight hours.

TOURIST INFORMATION

Bihar Tourism ① *in the BSTCD complex on Dumahan Rd, T0631-220 0445, Mon-Fri 1000-1700*, is not very useful.

→ THE SITE

Declared a World Heritage Site in 2002, Bodhgaya was 'lost' for centuries until rediscovered by Burmese Buddhists in 1877, which led to restoration work by the British. Lamas, Rimpoches and Buddhists from all over the world assemble here during the week-long *monlam* (December-January) when the area north of the bus station resembles a medieval encampment with tents serving as informal restaurants and accommodation. The food is smoky and there are long waits, but it is atmospheric and full of colour. The 'tourist season' draws to a close at the end of February when many restaurants close and most meditation courses stop running.

MAHABODHI TEMPLE

① *0400-2100, entrance free.*

Asoka's original shrine near the Bodhi tree was replaced a temple in the second century, which in turn has been through several alterations. The temple on a high and broad plinth, with a soaring 52-m-high pyramidal spire with a square cross-section and four smaller spires, houses a gilded image of the Enlightened Buddha. The smaller spires may have been added when Burmese Buddhists attempted extensive rebuilding in the 14th century. An ornately carved stone railing in bas relief surrounds the temple on three sides and several carved Buddhist *stupas* depict tales from the Buddha's early life. The lotus pond where the Buddha may have bathed is to the south, with a seated Buddha statue at its centre. Adjacent to the north side of the temple is the *Chankramana*, a raised platform (first century) with lotus flowers carved on it, which marks the consecrated promenade used by the Buddha while meditating. Further north, the **Animeshlochana** is another sacred spot where the Buddha stood to gaze in gratitude at the Bodhi tree for a week, after his Enlightenment.

The original Bodhi tree (pipal or *Ficus religiosa*) was supposedly destroyed by Asoka before he was converted, and others which replaced it also died. The present tree behind the temple is believed to come from the original stock – Prince Mahinda carried a sapling from the sacred Bo tree to Sri Lanka when he went to spread Buddhism there. This in turn produced a sapling which was brought back to Bodhgaya. The red sandstone slab, the **Vajrasila**, under the tree marks the place where Gautama sat in meditation.

The temple also attracts Hindu pilgrims since the Buddha is considered to be one of the *avatars* or incarnations of Vishnu. The candlelit ceremony at dusk is a particularly atmospheric time to visit, when pilgrims circle the outskirts of the temple among thousands of fairy lights.

MUSEUMS

Near the entrance to the Mahabodhi Temple is a **Multi-media Museum** ① *daily 0800-2000, Rs 100*, which gives a 3D history of Bodhgaya lasting one hour. More worthwhile is the **Archaeological Museum** ① *T0631-220 0739, Sat-Thu 0900-1700, Rs 10, photography not permitted*, which houses the original 2-m sculptured railings and pillars from the Mahabodhi Temple. The lighter proportions and the quality of the carving date the sandstone railings to the Sunga period (first century BC), while the less-weathered granite railings are from the Gupta period (sixth to seventh century AD). There are also many fine statues of the Buddha and Hindu deities, dating from the eighth-12th centuries, on display.

OTHER TEMPLES

Pilgrims from many lands have built their own temples. You can start at the giant 20-m stone **Buddha statue** which was built in 1989. Next door, the modern two-storey, spotless **Japanese Temple** ① *0700-1200, 1400-1800*, has beautiful polished marble floors and gold images of the Buddha. The **Tibetan Temple** and **Monastery** next to this (1938) is ornately painted and has a *Dharma Chakra* (Wheel of Law) which must be turned three times when praying for forgiveness of sins. A large 2-m metal ceremonial drum in red and gold is also on display. Opposite is the **Nipponji Temple** complex with a free clinic, monastery and a

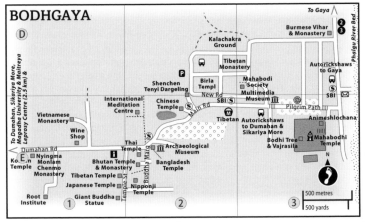

Peace Bell (rung from 0600-1200 and at 1700). Returning to the Mahabodhi Temple you will pass the colourful **Bhutan Temple** protected by carved Himalayan deities, a glittering pagoda-style **Thai Temple** and a **Bangladesh Temple**. The **Chinese Temple** houses an enormous, revolving ceremonial prayer drum.

TEACHING CENTRES

Meditation courses varying from a week to a month are available (most only during the October-March season), following both the Mahayana and Hinanyana traditions; enquire at the Burmese, Tibetan and Thai monasteries. The **Root Institute** ① *off Dumahan Rd, office hrs 0830-1130 and 1330-1630, T0631-220 0714, www.rootinstitute.com*, offers popular Vipassana courses from October to March (dates listed on the website, usually bi-monthly), rooms for personal retreats (year round) and is involved in community self-help schemes; the accommodation and setting is lovely and payment is by donation. **Insight Meditation** ① *www.bodhgayaretreats.org*, has been running 10-day retreats since 1975, during January and February in the Thai monastery. The **International Meditation Centre** ① *T0631-220 0707*, holds a variety of courses throughout the year.

→SASARAM

① *This Muslim site, between Gaya and Varanasi, is well worth a visit. The tombs are a short rickshaw ride from the railway station, which has left luggage (Rs 10).*

Sher Shah Suri, who was responsible for the tombs, asked the master-builder Aliwal Khan to build a tomb for his father Hasan Khan around 1535. This later inspired the building of the impressive second tomb for Sher Shah himself. The first imitated the octagonal structure and walled enclosure of the earlier Lodi tombs but was rather plain. What followed, however, was extraordinary not only in scale, but also in its conception. **Sher Shah's mausoleum** ① *Mar-Jul 0700-1800, Aug-Feb 0800-1700, Rs 100*, was set in a large artificial lake so it appears to float. A modern redbrick gateway opposite the Dak Bungalow leads down to the tombs. You enter it by a causeway after going through a guard room on the north bank (originally visitors approached by barge from the ghat on the east side). The grounds and lake provide a relaxing break, though travellers report a certain amount of hassle from local youth.

BODHGAYA AND AROUND LISTINGS

WHERE TO STAY

$$$ The Royal Residency, Dumahan Rd, T0631-220 0181, www.theroyalresidency. net/bodhgaya. The most attractive rooms of the higher end hotels, though the exterior is typically blank and it's at least 1 km from the centre. Flatscreen TVs, a/c, quality furniture, wide inviting beds and large marble bathrooms with walk-in showers and tubs. Restaurant is featureless, as is the bar (1000-2200, beer Rs 250). Some suites.

$ Rahul Guest House, behind Kalachakra Ground, T0631-220 0709, T(0)9934-463849, rahul_bodhgaya@yahoo.com. Bright and cheery rooms (some with attached bath), spotless sheets, fans, clean paintwork, towels, plus great front terraces with views to paddies. Although new buildings are fast encroaching, it remains a more peaceful location and is the best value choice among the small cluster of guesthouses here.

$ Siddartha Vihar, Bodhgaya Rd, T0631-220 0445. The state tourism department runs 3 adjacent lodgings, by far the best is the Siddartha with decent and reasonably priced a/c and non-a/c rooms with balconies and TVs in a quirky circular building; next door **Buddha Vihar** and **Sujata Vihar** have dorm beds.

$ Kundan Bazar Guest House, Bhagalpur village, T0631-220 0049, www.kundan bazar.com. This guesthouse with bright super-clean rooms fulfils all travellers' needs, with free Wi-Fi in the rooms, a community kitchen, free bicycles, use of the washing machine, bookshop, clothes for sale and rooftop café with amazing views. 20 mins' walk from the Mahabodhi temple. Great value.

RESTAURANTS

$ Lotus, next to Fujiya Green, near Kalachakra. Delicious food, covers all bases from *thukpa* to Mexican, relaxing and friendly place.

LUCKNOW

In Kipling's **Kim** *"no city – except Bombay, the queen of all – was more beautiful in her garish style than Lucknow". The capital of the state sprawls along the banks of the Gomti River in the heart of Uttar Pradesh. The ordered Cantonment area contrasts with the cream-washed buildings of the congested city centre, dotted with an incredible variety of decaying mansions and historic monuments, the best of which are breathtaking. In the heart of the old city traditional craftsmen continue to produce the rich gold zari work, delicate* chikan *embroidery and strong attar perfume. The arts still flourish and the bookshops do brisk trade in serious reading. Veils have largely disappeared as progressive college girls speed along on their scooters weaving between cows, cars and rickshaws.*

→ ARRIVING IN LUCKNOW

GETTING THERE AND MOVING ON
The modern airport, connected by direct flights to Delhi, Kolkata and Patna, is 14 km south of the city, about half an hour by taxi (prepaid Rs 320) or auto (available outside for about Rs 180). The Junction Railway Station, where trains from Gaya arrive, is in the southeast corner of the Hussainabad area, close to the historic sights. From Lucknow, it's an overnight train journey back to **Delhi** (see page 35) for your international flight home.

GETTING AROUND
The main sites are close enough to the centre to visit by cycle-rickshaw, or by hopping on a cheap shared *tempo* which run on fixed routes. However, the city is quite spread out and for extended sightseeing it is worth hiring a taxi.

TOURIST INFORMATION
Tourist office ① *Charbagh Railway Station, Main Hall, daily 0600-2200, also at the airport*, has brochures and enthusiastic staff. **UP Tours** ① *Gomti Hotel, Mon-Sat 0900-1800.*

→ BACKGROUND

Today Lucknow is a major administrative centre and market city, growing rapidly on both sides of the Gomti River from its historic core along the river's right bank. Although the discovery of **Painted Grey Ware** and **Northern Black** pottery demonstrates the long period over which the site has been occupied, its main claim to fame is as the capital of the cultured Nawabs of **Oudh** (*Avadh*), and later the scene of one of the most remarkable episodes in the 'Uprising' of 1857. Lucknow developed rapidly under the Mughal Emperor Akbar's patronage in the 16th century. In the early 18th century, Nawab Saadat Khan Burhan-ul-Mulk, a Persian courtier, founded the Oudh Dynasty. The city's growing reputation as a cultural centre attracted many others from Persia, leaving an indelible Shi'a imprint on the city's life. The builder of 'modern' Lucknow was Nawab Asaf-ud-Daula who shifted his capital here from Faizabad in 1775. In the attempt to build a wonderful city he emptied the regal coffers.

In the mid-1850s under **Lord Dalhousie**, the British annexed a number of Indian states. He evolved a policy of lapse whereby the states of Indian princes without direct heirs could be taken over on the ruler's death. Chronic mismanagement was also deemed just cause for takeover, the justification given for the annexation of Oudh. The novelist Premchand in *The Chess Players* attributes the fall of Oudh to the fact that "small and big, rich and poor, were dedicated alike to sensual joys ... song, dance and opium". History suggests that Nawab Wajid Ali Shah continued with his game of chess even as British soldiers occupied his capital. A strong British presence was established in the city as it became a key administrative and military centre. **Satyajit Ray**'s film *'Satranj Ki Khilari (The Chess Players)'* is an excellent portrayal of these times.

When the '**Uprising**' (previously referred to as the Mutiny) broke in 1857, Sir Henry Lawrence gathered the British community into the Residency which rapidly became a fortress. The ensuing siege lasted for 87 days. When the relieving force under Sir Colin Campbell finally broke through, the once splendid Residency was a blackened ruin, its walls pockmarked and gaping with cannonball holes. Today it is a mute witness to a desperate struggle.

Under the **Nawabs**, Lucknow evolved specialized styles of dance, poetry, music and calligraphy. The Lucknowi *gharana* (house) of music and the exquisite crafts are reminders of its splendid past as it remains the regional cultural capital. Today, of the vintage modes

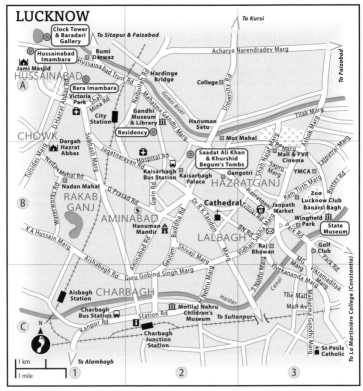

of travel, only the *ekka* (one-horse carriage) has survived. To trace its Muslim heritage, visit the Bara and Chhota Imambaras, Shah Najaf Imambara and take a look at the Rumi Darwaza, Clock Tower and Chattar Manzil. Among the colonial monuments, the Residency and Constantia are the most rewarding.

Parivartan Chowk and the black **Mayawati monument**, which faces **Clarks Avadh Hotel**, symbolize *parivartan* (the spirit of 'change') which the 1997-1998 government of the fiery Chief Minister Mayawati hoped to encourage by giving increasing power to the scheduled castes. Recently Lucknow has been through periods of violent communal tension which is partly explained by the important BJP presence here.

→ PLACES IN LUCKNOW

The original city centre is believed to be the high ground crowned by the Mosque of Aurangzeb on the right bank of the Gomti. Tillotson, an architectural historian, suggests that the major buildings of Asaf-ud-Daula, built after 1775 – the **Bara Imambara**, the **Rumi Darwaza** (Turkish Gate) and the **mosque** – between them dramatically illustrate the 'debased Mughal' style of 'Indo-European' architecture in decline. The monuments have been divided into three main groups. They usually open between 0600 and 1700.

NORTH WEST AND HUSSAINABAD
Just south of the Hardinge Bridge was the **Machhi Bhavan** (Fish House) enclosure. Safdarjang, Governor of Oudh (1719-1748), was permitted to use the fish insignia (a royal/imperial symbol/crest) by the Mughal Emperor Akbar. The Machhi Bhavan itself, once a fort, was blown up by the British in 1857, the only surviving part being the *baoli* which escaped because it was sunk into the hillside. Allow two to three hours for the Hussainabad tour.

The **Bara Imambara** ① *foreigners Rs 350, ticket also allows access to the Chhota Imambara and the Baradari, guide fees are posted outside, foreigners not permitted in the Asifi Mosque,* is a huge vaulted hall which, like all *imambaras*, serves as the starting point for the Muharram procession (see page 296). The vast hall (50 m long and 15 m high), built by Asaf-ud-Daula to provide employment during a famine, is one of the largest in the world, unsupported by pillars. Look out for the notice: "Spiting (sic), smoking and call of nature strictly prohibited"! The remarkable *bhul-bhulaya*, a maze of interconnecting passages above, is reached by stairs; a delightful diversion. One visitor spent over an hour trying to find his way out. The five-storeyed *baoli* is connected directly with the River Gomti. Legends suggest that secret tunnels connect the lower steps, which are always under water, with a treasure stored beneath the *imambara* itself.

At the end of the avenue leading up to the *imambara* from the river is the **Rumi Darwaza** (1784), a spectacular gate that resembles a conch-shell, built in the Byzantine style. Further along is the 19th-century Gothic 67-m-high Hussainabad **clock tower** (1880s) designed by Roskell Payne, which contains the largest clock in India though three of the four faces have been smashed. Next to it is the attractive octagonal Hussainabad Tank (1837-1842), around which is the Taluqdar's Hall and the incomplete Satkhanda (1840) seven-storeyed watchtower. There are excellent views of Lucknow from the top. Also worth a look is the restored **Baradari** ① *Tue-Sun 0800-1800, entrance included in the Bara Imambara ticket,* housing a picture gallery with portraits of the Nawabs of Oudh.

Hussainabad Imambara (Chhota Imambara) ① *sunrise-sunset, entrance included in the Bara Imambara ticket*, with its golden dome and elaborate calligraphy and containing beautiful chandeliers, gilt-edged mirrors and a silver throne (1837), is illuminated during Muharram. Further west is the extensively renovated **Jami Masjid** begun by Muhammad Shah and finished by his wife in the mid-1840s. **Victoria Park** (1890) with several British tombs is nearby. South of the park is the Chowk, the Old City bazar, where there are some interesting old buildings including the **Dargah of Hazrat Abbas** which contains a relic, a metal crest from the battle at Kerbala. Nearby is **Nadan Mahal** (c 1600), with the tomb of Shaikh Abdur Rahim, Akbar's Governor of Oudh, and son of Ibrahim Chishti. This is a fine building, built in the Mughal style and faced with red sandstone.

RESIDENCY AND HAZRATGANJ AREA

The Residency's 3000 mostly European occupants, hastily brought there by **Sir Henry Lawrence**, came under siege on 30 June 1857. Two days later Lawrence was fatally injured. After 90 days, General Sir Henry Havelock and General Sir James Outram appeared through the battered walls with a column of Highlanders. However, the siege was intensified and sepoy engineers began tunnelling to lay mines to blow the place up. From quite early on, there was a shortage of food and eventually smallpox, cholera and scurvy set in. Havelock was slowly dying of dysentery. The heroic Irishman, Henry Kavanagh, had sat in the tunnels and shot mutineers as they wriggled forward to lay more mines. He then volunteered to run the gauntlet through the enemy lines to find Sir Colin Campbell's relieving force, which he did by swimming the Gomti. On 17 November, Lucknow was finally relieved. Of the 2994 men, women and children who had taken refuge in the Residency, only 1000 marched out.

The **Residency Compound** is now a historic monument. You enter through the Bailey Guard gate. The **Treasury** on your right served as an arsenal while the grand Banquet Hall next door housed the wounded during the 'Uprising'. On the lawn of **Doctor Fayrer's House**, to your left, stands a marble cross to Sir Henry Lawrence. **Begum Kothi**, which belonged to Mrs Walters who married the Nawab of Oudh, can be reached through the long grass, but the old officers' mess has made way for flats and apartments.

The **Residency** (1800) ① *foreigners Rs 100, cameras Rs 25*, to the northeast, built by Saadat Ali Khan, has *tykhanas* (cool underground rooms) where there is a museum, the highlight of which is an 1873 model of the complex, which gives you a good idea of how extensive and self-sufficient the original settlement was. At the time of the 'Uprising' the Residency was overlooked by high houses, now all destroyed, which gave cover to snipers firing into the compound. There are many etchings and records including Tennyson's *Relief of Lucknow*. Suggestions of a wooden staircase for officers, an underground passage to the palace, a secret room hidden in the wall behind false doors, all conjure up images of the past. The graves of Lawrence, Neill and others are in the church **cemetery**. Women visitors should not visit the cemetery alone. Just outside the Residency on the banks of the Gomti is a white obelisk commemorating the 'Nationalist Insurgents' who lost their lives in 1857.

Southeast of the Residency, near the Hanuman Setu, is the **Chattar Manzil** (Umbrella Palace) now the Central Drug Research Institute, where the submerged basement provided natural air conditioning. There are also the sad remains of the **Kaisarbagh Palace** (1850) conceived as a grand chateau. Better preserved are the almost twin **tombs** of Saadat Ali Khan (1814) and Khurshid Begum. To its east again are **Nur Bakhsh Kothi** and Tarawali

Kothi (circa 1832), the observatory of the royal astronomer Colonel Wilcox, which is now the **State Bank of India**.

EASTERN GROUP

Shah Najaf Imambara (1814-1827) ⓘ *free entry*, near the Gomti, has the tombs of Nawab Ghazi-ud-Din Haidar and his three wives, with its white dome and elaborate interior decorations, including a huge array of chandeliers, mirrors and paintings. It was used by sepoy mutineers as a stronghold in 1857. Wajid Ali Shah's (ruled 1847-1856) pleasure garden **Sikander Bagh**, created for his favourite wife, retains the original gateway and mosque.

To the south of these are **Wingfield Park**, laid out in the 1860s, which contains a marble pavilion and some statues. Within the **Zoo** ⓘ *Tue-Sun 0830-1730, foreigners Rs 100*, off Park Rd, is the **State Museum** ⓘ *Banarsi Bagh, T0522-220 6158, Tue-Sun 1000-1700 (last entrance at 1600), foreigners Rs 50*, the oldest in Uttar Pradesh and one of the richest in India, exhibits Hindu, Buddhist and Jain works including stone sculptures from Mathura, and busts and friezes from Allahabad and Garhwal, dating from the first to 11th centuries. Also marble sculptures, paintings, natural history and anthropology. Marvellous relics of the British Raj, removed at the time of Independence, languish in the backyard. **Christchurch** (1860), a memorial to the British killed during the 'Uprising' is nearby, along with the imposing Legislative Council Chamber (1928) and **Raj Bhawan** (Government House), enlarged in 1907.

To the east is Constantia, now **La Martinière College**, planned as the country residence of Major-General Claude Martin (1735-1800), a French soldier of fortune who is buried in the crypt. He ran highly successful indigo and money-lending businesses. The curious wedding cake of a building was completed after Martin's death from the endowment set aside by him for a school here and at Kolkata for 'Anglo-Indians' (Kipling's *Kim* being one of them). For the students' bravery during the siege of the Residency, the school was unique in being awarded Battle Honours. The chapel, historical photos and the crypt are interesting. You may ask to look around both outside and within. The office is at the east end.

Further south is **Dilkusha** (Heart's Delight), once a royal shooting lodge in what was a large deer park. There are graves of soldiers who died here during the 'Uprising', including that of General Havelock; his grave obelisk is in Alam Bagh, 100 m northeast of the garden's main gateway.

MOVING ON
To Delhi

After a night or two in Lucknow, it's an overnight train journey back to Delhi (see page 35) for your international flight home.

LUCKNOW LISTINGS

WHERE TO STAY

$$$$ Vivanta by Taj, Vipin Khand, Gomti Nagar, 5 km east of railway station, T0522-671 1000, www.vivantabytaj.com. 110 rooms in elegant colonial-style modern building, excellent restaurants, good pool, attractive gardens (transplanted mature palms), city's most luxurious hotel and the only really quiet one.

$$$-$$ Le Place Sarovar Portico, 6 Shahnajaf Rd, T0522-400 4040, www.sarovarhotels.com. 50 large contemporary-styled rooms in a modern, friendly chain hotel, very well maintained, attractive grill resto-bar on the roof, 24-hr coffee shop, breakfast included. Good location and atmosphere.

$ Lucknow Homestay, 10 Mall Av, T0522-223 5460, naheed2k@gmail.com. 7 modest rooms a couple of kilometres southeast of the city centre (and expect train noise), but homely and clean, attracts any backpackers passing through. Use of fridge/kettle, free Wi-Fi, breakfast included, cheap lunch/dinner available, good library. Recommended.

RESTAURANTS

$$$ Falaknuma, on rooftop of **Clarks Avadh**. Serves tasty, spicy Nawabi cuisine by candlelight, good views, beer available, attentive service and live *ghazals* of exceptionally high quality. Recommended.

$$$ Oudhyana, at Vivanta by Taj (see above). Special Avadhi food, lovely surroundings, the finest dining in town. Book in advance.

$$ Royal Inn/Royal Café, 9/7 Shahnajaf Rd, T0522-409 5555. Open 1100-2300.

Excellent and huge menu of mainly Indian and Chinese dishes, veg and non-veg. Large hygienic modern surrounds, attracts families, deservedly popular. It's not cheap but expect quality.

$ Moti Mahal, 75 Hazratgang, T0522-262 33375. Open 0800-2330. Huge menu, mainly North Indian but some Chinese and South Indian, good ice creams, family-friendly split-level surroundings.

DREAM TRIP 4
Kolkata→Darjeeling→Sikkim→Kaziranga→Kolkata
21 days

Kolkata 3 nights (or 2, then 1 on train), page 233

Kurseong 1 night, page 251
Train from Kolkata to NJP (overnight, 10 hrs), or flight to Bagdogra (1 hr)
Onward jeep from Siliguri (1½ hrs)

Darjeeling 3 nights, page 252
Jeep from Kurseong (1 hr) or toy train (3 hrs)

Pelling and Pemayantse 2 nights, pages 261 and 262
Jeep from Darjeeling (5 hrs)

Yuksom and Tashiding 2 nights, page 263
Jeep from Pelling via Khecheopalri Lake (2 hrs)

Guwahati 1 night, page 265
Jeep from Yuksom, either to Bagdogra (6 hrs) for flight to Guwahati (1 hr) or to NJP for overnight train

Shillong 1 night, page 269
Jeep/bus from Guwahati (4 hrs/5 hrs)

Cherrapunji 2 nights, page 271
Bus/jeep from Shillong (1½ hrs)

Guwahati 1 night, page 265
Bus/jeep from Cherrapunji (5-6 hrs)

Kaziranga 2 nights, page 272
Bus from Guwahati (4½ hrs)

Tea tourism in Northeast Assam 2 nights, page 276
Bus or private vehicle from Kaziranga to Jorhat (2½ hrs); to Dibrugarh (6 hrs) via Sibsagar

Kolkata 1 night, page 233
Fly back from Jorhat/Dibrugarh to connect with your international flight home

GOING FURTHER

Murshidabad page 248
Train from Kolkata (5 hrs, inconvenient times)

Singalila National Park page 257
Jeep from Darjeeling to the checkpoint at Manebhanjang (1 hr)

Tezpur to Tawang page 273
Frequent buses from Guwahati to Tezpur (4 hrs)

DREAM TRIP 4
Kolkata → Darjeeling → Sikkim → Kaziranga → Kolkata

This trip starts in Kolkata, the cultural and sporting capital of India. Still lagging behind the other metro-cities, the city retains a peppering of colonial buildings and a unique atmosphere that captivates and fascinates, from the old mansions of North Kolkata to the hazy expanse of the Maidan. A few hours north of Kolkata, discover the peace and beauty of rural Bengal in the sultry town of Murshidabad on the Bagirathi River.

Further north still, in the foothills of the Himalaya, lie Kurseong and Darjeeling, where you'll find fresh air and mountainscapes that invigorate the soul. The cooler climate is perfect for easily accessible walks to tea estates and villages, as well as for the challenging trek through Singalila National Park.

Next stop is gorgeous little Sikkim, where forested mountains are interspersed with curious Buddhist monasteries and sacred lakes. Especially memorable is the vast complex of Pemayangste Monastery near Pelling, while the sweet village of Yuksom is ideal for pottering and relaxing, as well as being the place to start the classic trek to Gocha La.

You'll experience a marked change in altitude and landscape as you travel southeast to Guwahati, the capital of Assam, which lies on the River Brahmaputra. Close to the city is Kamakhya Temple: a holy and hectic place of Sakti worship. A different atmosphere is found in Meghalaya to the south, a mountainous tribal area that is known as the wettest place on earth. Fascinating markets are a highlight here, as are the extraordinary living root bridges in the forests around Cherrapunji. Further east into Assam is Kaziranga National Park, most famed for its large population of one-horned rhinoceros. Assam is also renowned for its tea, and a stay in a remote plantation bungalow is the perfect conclusion to this eastern journey.

KOLKATA (CALCUTTA)

To Bengalis Kolkata is the proud intellectual capital of India, with an outstanding contribution to the arts, services, medicine and social reform in its past, and a rich contemporary cultural life. As the former imperial capital, Kolkata retains some of the country's most striking colonial buildings, yet at the same time it is truly an Indian city. Unique in India in retaining trams, and the only place in the world to still have hand-pulled rickshaws, you take your life in your hands each time you cross Kolkata's streets. Kolkata's Maidan, the parkland, provides an essential breathing space in a city packed with some of the most densely populated slums, or bustees, anywhere in the world.

→ ARRIVING IN KOLKATA

GETTING THERE

Netaji Subhas Chandra Bose International Airport at Dum Dum serves international and domestic flights with a new 'integrated terminal' (opened 2013). Taxis to the city centre take 45-60 minutes and there is a prepaid taxi booth before exiting the airport (to get to Sudder Street, the backpacker hub, costs Rs 270). There are also a/c buses which leave from outside Terminal 1, some of which go to Howrah and Esplanade (for Sudder Street), and cost about Rs 40. Arrival at **Howrah station**, on the west bank of the Hooghly (Hugli), can be daunting, and the taxi rank outside is often chaotic; the prepaid taxi booth is to the right as you exit – check the price chart near the booth and note that Sudder Street is less than 5 km away. Trains to/from the north use the slightly less chaotic **Sealdah terminal**, east of the centre, which also has prepaid taxis. Long-distance buses arrive at **Esplanade**, 15 minutes' walk from most budget hotels.

MOVING ON

If flying, it's easiest to take a taxi to the airport in Kolkata; factor in an hour for the journey and expect to pay around Rs 400 (more if your hotel arranges the taxi). Flights leave daily from Kolkata to the Indian metro-cities, and to other cities in northeast India, including Bagdogra Airport, near Siliguri in North Bengal. From Bagdogra Airport you can get pre-paid taxis for onward travel into the hills (see page 251). Overnight trains go from Sealdah Station in Kolkata to NJP station in North Bengal, taking about 10 hours. It's not advisable to take a bus all the way to North Bengal, as the road is very bad and the journey too gruelling.

GETTING AROUND

You can cover much of Central Kolkata on foot. For the rest you need transport. You may not fancy using hand-pulled **rickshaws**, but they become indispensable when the streets are flooded. **Buses** and minibuses are often jam packed, but routes comprehensively cover the city – conductors and bystanders will help you find the correct bus. The electric **trams** can be slightly better outside peak periods. The **metro**, though on a limited route and very crowded, is the easiest way of getting from north to south. **Taxis** are relatively cheap (note that the meter reading is not the true fare – they have conversion charts which work out at about double the meter) but allow plenty of time to get through very congested traffic. Despite the footpath, it is not permitted to walk across the Vidyasagar Bridge (taxi drivers expect passengers to pay the Rs 10 toll).

KOLKATA

To Belur Math

To Kumartuli & Dakshineshwar Kali Temple

Rabindra Setu

Howrah Bridge

Rabindra Bharat Univers Museu

JORASANKO

Armenian Ghat

M M Burman St

Mahatma Gandhi Rd

Roman Catholi Cathedr

Howrah Station

Motiseal Ghat

BARA BAZAR

Sikh Gurudwara

Armenian Church

Kolutola St

GT Rd

Church Rd

Rishi Ban Kim Ch Rd

HOWRAH

Moghan David Synagogue

Bourne Rd

Parsi Temple

Nakhod Mosqu

Telkal Ghat

Strand Rd

N Subhas St

Beth El Synagogue

TIRETA BAZAR

Ramkrishnapur Ghat

Old Court House St

BBD BAGH

W Bengal Tourist Office

BOW BAZAR

Chandpal Ghat

St John's Church

Chandni Chowk

Babu Ghat

Govt Place West

Govt Place East

Raj Bhavan

Tipu Sultan's Mosque

To Botanical Gardens & Shalimar Railway Station

Torgeshore Rd

GT Rd

Sibpur Rd

Outram Ghat

Hugli River

Ranji Stadium

Eden Gardens

Eden Gardens Rd

Esplanade

Esplanade

Len

GT Rd

Strand Rd

G Nanak Sarani

New Market

Lindsay St

Sudder St

Red Rd

Dufferin Rd

Nehru Rd

Indian Museum

Princep Ghat

Vidyasagar Setu

SEE CENTRAL KOLKATA MAP

MAIDAN

Fort William

Park St

Asiatic Society

Park St

Russell St

Napier Rd

St George's Gate

Casuarina Av

Chowringhee

Maidan

HASTINGS

Kidderpore Rd

Race Course

Queens Way

Cathedral Rd

Ho Chi Minh Sarani

Planetarium

US Consulate

Shakespeare Sarani

Monapa

Hospital Rd

Munshigani Rd

Entrance to Racecourse

Polo Ground

Victoria Memorial & Museum

St Paul's Cathedral

Pretoria St

Camac St

Gallerie 88

La Martiniere School

Kidderpore Docks (for Andamans Ferry)

Academy of Fine Arts

AJC Bose Rd

AJC Bose Rd

Rabindra Sadan

Foreigners' Registration Office

Bengal Home Industries

Central Plaza

Woodlands Nursing Home

KIDDERPORE

Bhawanipur Rd

Harish Mukharji Rd

Netaji Bhavan

Elgin Rd

Heysham Rd

Tivol Cour

Max Muller Bhavan

Zoo

Belvedere Rd

Tolly's Nullah

BHAWANIPUR

Ashutosh Mukherjee Rd

Sarat Bose Rd

National Library

Bhawanipur

Paddopukur Rd

P Baria Sarani

Nepal Consulate

Diamond Harbour Rd

Horticultural Gardens

Kalighat Rd

To Tolly Club, Rabindra Sarobar, Seagull Media & Bookshop, Help Tourism, South City Mall

Calcutta Hospital

To IIM, Behala & State Archaeological Museum

To Kali Temple

To Birla Academy of Art & Culture

A
B
C
D
E
F

1
2
3
4

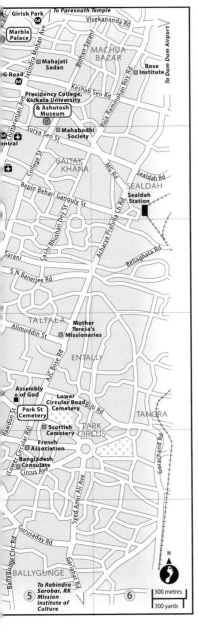

TOURIST INFORMATION

India Tourism ⓘ *4 Shakespeare Sarani, T033-2282 5813, Mon-Fri 0930-1800, Sat 0900-1300,* can provide a city map and information for all India. More useful is **West Bengal Tourism Development Corporation** ⓘ *BBD Bagh, T033-2248 8271, www.west bengaltourism.gov.in, Mon-Fri 1030-1630, Sat 1030-1300;* also a counter at the station in Howrah.

→ BACKGROUND

Calcutta, as it came to be named, was founded by the remarkable English merchant trader **Job Charnock** in 1690. He was in charge of the East India Company factory (ie warehouse) in Hooghly, then the centre of British trade from eastern India. Attacks from the local Muslim ruler forced him to flee – first down river to Sutanuti and then 1500 km south to Chennai. However, in 1690 he selected three villages – Kalikata, Sutanuti and Govindpur – where Armenian and Portuguese traders had already settled, leased them from Emperor Aurangzeb and returned to what became the capital of British India.

The first fort here, named after King William III (completed 1707), was on the site of the present BBD Bagh. A deep defensive moat was dug in 1742 to strengthen the fort – the Maratha ditch. The Maratha threat never materialized, but the city was captured easily by the 20-year-old **Siraj-ud-Daula**, the new Nawab of Bengal, in 1756. The 146 British residents who failed to escape by the fort's river gate were imprisoned for a night in a small guard room about 6 m by 5 m with only one window – the infamous '**Black Hole of Calcutta**'. Some records suggest 64 people were imprisoned and only 23 survived.

The following year **Robert Clive** re-took the city. The new Fort William was built and, in 1772, Calcutta became the capital of

British administration in India with Warren Hastings as the first Governor of Bengal. Some of Calcutta's most impressive colonial buildings were built in the years that followed, when it became the first city of British India. It was also a time of Hindu and Muslim resurgence.

Colonial Calcutta grew as new traders, soldiers and administrators arrived, establishing their exclusive social and sports clubs. Trade in cloth, silk, lac, indigo, rice, areca nut and tobacco had originally attracted the Portuguese and British to Bengal. Later Calcutta's hinterland producing jute, iron ore, tea and coal led to large British firms setting up headquarters in the city. Calcutta prospered as the commercial and political capital of British India up to 1911, when the capital was transferred to Delhi.

Calcutta had to absorb huge numbers of migrants immediately after Partition in 1947. When Pakistan ceased trading with India in 1949, Calcutta's economy suffered a massive blow as it lost its supplies of raw jute; its failure to attract new investment created critical economic problems. In the late 1960s the Communist Party of India Marxist, the CPI(M), was elected – and their dominance was to last over 30 years. From 2000, the CPI(M) were committed to a mixed economy and sought foreign private investment, and the city's economy has experienced a much needed upturn. In the 2011 state assembly election the communist government was defeated after 34 years in power by the Trinamool Congress. Controversial politician Mamata Bannerjee, known as "Didi", is the current Chief Minister and is the first woman to hold this position. The city officially changed its name to Kolkata in 2001.

→ CENTRAL KOLKATA

BBD BAGH (DALHOUSIE SQUARE) AND AROUND

Many historic Raj buildings surround the square, which is quietest before 0900. Renamed Benoy Badal Dinesh (BBD) Bagh after three Bengali martyrs, the square has an artificial lake (tank) fed by natural springs that used to supply water to Kolkata's first residents. On Strand Road North is the dilapidated **Silver Mint** (1824-1831). The **Writers' Building** (1780), designed by Thomas Lyon as the trading headquarters of the East India Company, was refaced in 1880. It is now the state Government Secretariat. The classical block with 57 sets of identical windows was built like a barracks inside. The white domed **General Post Office** (1866) was built on the site of the first Fort William. Around the corner, there is a quaint little **Postal Museum** ① *Mon-Sat 1100-1600, entrance free*, which displays shabby maps, original post boxes and has a philatelic library. Facing the Hooghly on Strand Road is colonnaded **Metcalfe Hall** ① *Mon-Sat 1000-1700, entrance from rear* modelled on the Palace of Winds in Athens. This was once the home of the Imperial Library, and still contains the journals of the Asiatic Society in the ground floor **library** ① *Mon-Fri 0945-1815, allegedly*, plus a small exhibition on the first floor including glazed tiles from Gaur and Pandua, and a gallery of bricks. Unsurprisingly, the visitors' book shows an average of two tourists per month. Elegant **St Andrew's Kirk** (1814) ① *0900-1400*, like the earlier St John's Church (1787), was modelled partially on St Martin-in-the-Fields, London. **Mission Row** (now RN Mukherjee Road) is Kolkata's oldest street, and contains the **Old Mission Church** (consecrated 1770), built by the Swedish missionary Johann Kiernander. The **Great Eastern Hotel** (1841) was in Mark Twain's day "the best hotel East of the Suez", but from the 1970s it steadily declined. It is now undergoing major restoration by the Lalit group of hotels and was due to open in 2013 (though that looks unlikely from the present state of the building).

ON THE ROAD
Train touts

Many railway stations – and some bus stations and major tourist sites – are heavily populated with touts. Self-styled 'agents' will board trains before they enter the station and seek out tourists, often picking up their luggage and setting off with words such as "Madam!/Sir! Come with me madam/sir! You need top-class hotel …". They will even select porters to take your luggage without giving you any say.

For a first-time visitor such touts can be more than a nuisance. You need to keep calm and firm. Decide in advance where you want to stay. If you need a porter on trains, select one yourself and agree a price (Rs 40 should be more than sufficient) before the porter sets off with your baggage. If travelling with a companion, one can stay guarding the luggage while the other gets hold of a taxi and negotiates the price to the hotel. It sounds complicated and sometimes it feels it. The most important thing is to behave as if you know what you are doing!

Directly south of BBD Bagh is the imposing **Raj Bhavan** (1799-1802), the residence of the Governor of West Bengal, formerly Government House. It was modelled on Kedleston Hall in Derbyshire, England (later Lord Curzon's home), and designed by Charles Wyatt, one of many Bengal engineers who based their designs on famous British buildings (entrance not permitted). The beautiful old **Town Hall** (1813) has been converted into the **Kolkata Museum** ① *Mon-Sat 1100-1800 (ticket counter closes 1700), foreigners Rs 10 (Rs 15 on Sat), bag deposit*, telling the story of the independence movement in Bengal through a panoramic, cinematic display, starring an animatronic Rabindranath Tagore. Visitors are sped through in grouped tours, however, and some of the videos drag on rather. There's a good life-size diorama of a Bengali street and some great film posters. The bright-red gothic **High Court** (1872) was modelled on the medieval cloth merchants' hall at Ypres in Flanders. It is possible to enter through Gate F: a fascinating glimpse into rooms crammed floor-to-ceiling with books, and bustling with black-robed lawyers (no cameras allowed). The **State Bank Archives & Museum** ① *11th Fl, SBI, 1 Strand Rd, Tue-Fri 1430-1700, free*, in a recent building designed to look period, is a grand marble-floored repository of information; it also contains paintings of Raj India, furniture and memorabilia related to the early days of banking.

Esplanade Mansions is a stunning art nouveau building on Esplanade Row East, built in 1910 by Jewish millionaire David Ezra. At the other end of the street, the minarets and domes of **Tipu Sultan's Mosque**, built by Tipu's son in 1842, poke out above market stalls selling stationery and little kebab restaurants. The **Ochterlony Monument** (1828), renamed Shahid Minar (Martyrs' Memorial) in 1969, was built as a memorial to Sir David Ochterlony, who led East India Company troops against the Nepalese in 1814-1816. The 46-m-tall Greek Doric column has an Egyptian base and is topped by a Turkish cupola.

St John's Church ① *0800-1700, entrance Rs 10*, was built on soft subsoil that did not allow it to have a tall spire and architecturally it was thought to be 'full of blunders'. Verandas were added to the north and south in 1811 to reduce the glare of the sun. Inside the vestry are Warren Hastings's table and chair, plus Raj-era paintings and prints. *The Last Supper*, by Johann Zoffany was restored in 2010 and shows the city's residents dressed as the apostles. Job Charnock is buried in the grounds. His octagonal mausoleum, the oldest piece of masonry in the city, is of Pallavaram granite (from Madras Presidency), which is named charnockite after him. The monument built by Lord Curzon to commemorate the **Black Hole of Calcutta** was brought here from Dalhousie Square (BBD Bagh) in 1940.

Eden Gardens ① *daily 1200-1700*, which are situated in the northwest corner of the Maidan, were laid out in 1834 and named after Lord Auckland's sisters Emily and Fanny Eden. There are pleasant walks, a lake and a small Burmese pagoda (typical of this type of Pyatthat). The gardens encompass the **Ranji Stadium** ① *usually open for matches only, a small tip at Gate 14 gains entry on other days*, where the first cricket match was played

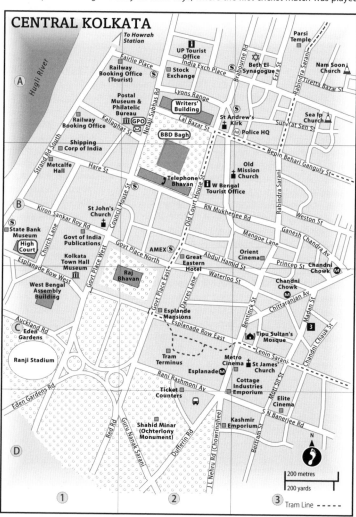

CENTRAL KOLKATA

in 1864. Re-vamped in 2011 for the Cricket World Cup, it attracts massive crowds for IPL and Test matches.

SUDDER STREET

Conveniently close to Chowringhee and Esplanade, Sudder Street is the focus for Kolkata's backpackers and attracts touts, beggars and drug pushers aplenty. Beggars on Chowringhee and Park Street often belong to organized syndicates who have to pay a large percentage of their 'earnings' for the privilege of working the area. A popular ploy is for a woman to ask for milk or rice for her baby. Nearby is the vast and archaic shopping hub of **New Market**, opened in 1874 (largely rebuilt since a fire in 1985 and recently revamped), and originally called Sir Stuart Hogg Market. The clock tower outside, which strikes every 15 minutes, was imported from England. It used to be said that you could buy anything from a needle to an elephant (on order) in one of its stalls. Today it's still worth a visit; come early morning to watch it come alive (closed Sundays).

Around the corner from Sudder Street is the **Indian Museum** ① *27 Chowringhee (JL Nehru Rd), T033-2286 1679, www.indianmuseumkolkata.org, Mar-Nov Tue-Sun 1000-1700, Dec-Feb 1000-1630, foreigners Rs 150, Indians Rs 10, cameras Rs 50/100 with tripod; no bags allowed (there is a cloakroom)*, possibly Asia's largest. The Jadu Ghar (House of Magic) was founded in 1814 and has an enormous collection. The colonnaded Italianate building around a central courtyard has 36 galleries (though large sections are often closed off for restoration). Parts are poorly lit and gathering dust so it is best to be selective. Highlights include: the stone statutory with outstanding exhibits from the Harappa and Moenjodaro periods; the Cultural Anthropology room with information on India's tribes; and the excellent new Mask Gallery (hidden on the fourth floor, up the stairs past the ground floor coin collection and library). There are some lovely miniature paintings, the Egyptian room has a popular mummy and the Plant Gallery is curiously beautiful, with jars, prints and samples filling every inch of space. The animals in the Natural History Gallery have been there since 1878 while the birds are so dirty they are all uniformly black in colour. The geological collection with Siwalik fossils is mind-bogglingly huge. Allow a couple of hours.

PARK STREET

Park Street Cemetery ① *daily 0800-1630, free, information booklet Rs 100, security guard opens gate and will expect you to sign the visitors' book*, was opened in 1767 to accommodate the large number of British who died 'serving' their country. The cemetery is a peaceful paradise and a step into history, located on the south side of one of Kolkata's busiest streets, with a maze of soaring obelisks shaded by tropical trees. The heavily inscribed decaying headstones, rotundas, pyramids and urns have been restored, and gardeners are actively trying to beautify the grounds. Several of the inscriptions make interesting reading. Death, often untimely, came from tropical diseases or other hazards such as battles, childbirth and even melancholia. More uncommonly, it was an excess of alcohol, or as for Sir Thomas D'Oyly, through "an inordinate use of the hokkah". Rose Aylmer died after eating too many pineapples! Tombs include those of Colonel Kyd, founder of the Botanical Gardens, the great oriental scholar Sir William Jones, and the fanciful mausoleum of the Irish Major-General 'Hindoo' Stuart. Across AJC Bose Road, on Karaya Road, is the smaller and far more derelict **Scottish Cemetery** ① *daily 0700-1730, free, pamphlet by donation to the caretaker*, established in 1820. The Kolkata Scottish Heritage Trust began work in

2008 to restore some of the 1600 tumbledown graves but the undergrowth is rampant and jungle prevails. It is also known as the 'dissenters' graveyard', as this was where non-Anglicans were buried. Also nearby, on AJC Bose Road, is the enormous **Lower Circular Road Cemetery** created in 1840 when Park Street Cemetery became full.

The **Asiatic Society** ① *1 Park St, T033-2229 0779, www.asiaticsocietycal.com, Mon-Fri 1000-1800, free*, the oldest institution of Oriental studies in the world, was founded in 1784 by the great Orientalist, Sir William Jones. It is a treasure house of 150,000 books and 60,000 ancient manuscripts in most Asian languages, although permission is required to see specific pieces. The museum includes an Ashokan edict, rare coins and paintings. The library is worth a visit for its dusty travelogues and titles on the history of Kolkata. The original 1804 building is to the rear; you can ask to view the impressive staircase adorned with statues and paintings. Here also is the manuscript restoration department, where staff are pleased to explain the work they undertake. Bring a passport, as the signing-in process to visit the building is (at least) a triplicate process.

THE MAIDAN

This area, 200 years ago, was covered in dense jungle. Often called the 'lungs of the city', it is a unique green, covering over 400 ha along Chowringhee (JL Nehru Road). Larger than New York's Central Park, it is perhaps the largest urban park in the world. In it stands Fort William and several clubhouses providing tennis, football, rugby, cricket and even crown green bowls. Thousands each day pursue a hundred different interests – from early-morning yogis, model plane enthusiasts, weekend cricketers and performers earning their living, to vast political gatherings.

The massive **Fort William** was built by the British after their defeat in 1756, on the site of the village of Govindapur. Designed to be impregnable, it was roughly octagonal and large enough to house all the Europeans in the city in case of an attack. Water from the Hooghly was channelled to fill the wide moat and the surrounding jungle was cleared to give a clear field of fire; this later became the Maidan. The barracks, stables, arsenal, prison and St Peter's Church are still there, but the fort now forms the Eastern Region's Military Headquarters and entry is forbidden.

At the southern end of the Maidan is **Kolkata Race Course**, run by the Royal Calcutta Turf Club. The history of racing goes back to the time of Warren Hastings and the 1820s grandstand is especially handsome.

CHOWRINGHEE AND AROUND

You can still see some of the old imposing structures with pillared verandas (designed by Italian architects as residences for prominent Englishmen), though modern high-rise buildings and a flyover have transformed the skyline of what was the ancient pilgrim route to Kalighat.

St Paul's Cathedral ① *0900-1200, 1500-1800, 5 services on Sun*, is the original metropolitan church of British India. Completed in 1847, its Gothic tower (dedicated in 1938) was designed to replace the earlier steeples which were destroyed by earthquakes. The cathedral has a fine altar piece, three 'Gothic' stained-glass windows, two Florentine frescoes and the great West window by Burne-Jones. The original stained-glass East window, intended for St George's Windsor, was destroyed by a cyclone in 1964 and was replaced by the present one four years later.

Academy of Fine Arts ① *2 Cathedral Rd, Tue-Sun 1500-2000 (ground floor galleries), 1200-1900 (museum) entrance free*, was founded in 1933. The first floor museum has a newly restored gallery showing 33 pictures by Rabindranath Tagore, plus his writings and some personal effects. The textiles gallery and other sections have been closed for years, but may reopen soon. The ground floor galleries show changing exhibitions, contemporary paintings and sculptures by Indian artists.

Victoria Memorial (1906-1921) ① *T033-2223 1889-91, www.victoriamemorial-cal. org. Gardens open 0530-1815 (ticket counter closes at 1745), Rs 4; museum open Tue-Sun 1000-1700 (ticket counter closes at 1630, very crowded on Sun), foreigners Rs 150, cameras not permitted inside; son et lumière show, summer 1945, winter 1915, 45 mins, Rs 20 front seats, Rs 10 elsewhere*, was the brain-child of Lord Curzon. The white marble monument to Queen Victoria and the Raj, designed in Italian Renaissance/Indo-Saracenic style, stands in large, well-kept grounds with ornamental pools. A seated bronze Queen Victoria dominates the approach from the north, while a marble statue stands in the main hall where visitors sometimes leave flowers at her feet. The building is illuminated in the evening; the musical fountain is a special draw. The statues over the entrance porches (including Motherhood, Prudence and Learning), and around the central dome (of Art, Architecture, Justice, Charity) came from Italy. The impressive weather vane, a 5-m-tall bronze winged Angel of Victory weighing three tonnes, looks tiny from below. The principal gallery, covering the history of the city, is well-presented and makes interesting reading. It includes some fascinating lithographs and illustrations of the city during the Raj period. The painting gallery has magnificent works by European artists in India from 1770-1835, including Zoffany, the two Daniells and Samuel Davis. Recently, the upper gallery of the Queen's Hall was reopened after more than a decade, and visitors can now walk around the inside of rotunda again.

→ NORTH KOLKATA

COLLEGE STREET

This is the heart of intellectual Kolkata with the **university** and several academic institutions, including the old **Sanskrit College** and the elite **Presidency College**. Europeans and Indian benefactors established the Hindu College (1817) to provide a liberal education. In 1855, this became the Presidency College. A centre for 19th-century Bengali writers, artists and reformers, it spawned the early 20th-century Swadeshi Movement. The famous **Indian Coffee House** (opened in 1944), cavernous haunt of the city's intelligentsia, has tonnes of atmosphere and is always packed despite the average coffee and food. Along the pavements are interesting second-hand book stalls. The **Ashutosh Museum of Indian Art** ① *University Centenary Building, Mon-Fri 1100-1630, closed university holidays, entrance Rs 10*, is well maintained and worth a visit. The ground floor is packed with eastern Indian pieces of sculpture and terracotta tiles depicting figures. The first floor has colourful Bengali and Orissan folk art, faded textiles, and a hoard of paintings including 14th- to 19th-century miniatures, Kalighat paintings, Nepalese art and Tibetan *thankas*. Also look out for the model of the Senate Hall (1873-1960) which was pulled down to make way for the concrete monster of the present Centenary block, in the days before heritage buildings were accorded any value.

MARBLE PALACE

ⓘ *46 Muktaram Babu St, closed Mon and Thu, 1000-1600. Free pass from WBTDC (see page 252), 24 hrs ahead, or baksheesh (Rs 20 pp) to the security man at the gate and a further tip to the attendant who will accompany you around, shoes must be removed, no photography allowed.*

Located in *Chor Bagan* ('Thieves' Garden'), the one-man collection of Raja Rajendra Mullick is housed in his ornate home (1835) with an Italianate courtyard, classical columns and Egyptian sphinxes. Family members still inhabit a portion of the house while servants' descendants live in the huts that encircle the grounds. Six sleeping marble lions and statuary grace the lawns and there is a veritable menagerie at the back of the garden. The galleries are crammed with statues, porcelain, clocks, mirrors, chandeliers and English (Reynolds), Dutch (Reubens) and Italian paintings, disorganized and gathering dust. The pink, grey and white Italian marble floors are remarkable, as is the solid rosewood statue of Queen Victoria. Allow one hour, or take a book and relax in the garden. The rambling museum on two floors has more than just curiosity appeal – it is one of Kolkata's gems.

HOWRAH BRIDGE AREA

Howrah Bridge (Haora), or Rabindra Setu, was opened in 1943. This single-span cantilever bridge, the quintessential image of Kolkata, replaced the old pontoon (floating) bridge that first joined the city of Kolkata with Howrah and the railway station. To avoid affecting river currents and silting, the two 80-m-high piers rise from road level; the 450-m span expands by a metre on a hot day. It is the busiest bridge in the world in terms of foot passengers, with over 3.5 million pedestrians per day (many with improbable loads on their heads). Wrestlers can be seen underneath and there is a daily **flower market** beneath the eastern end at Mullik Ghat, with piles of marigolds glowing against the mud. At night the bridge is illuminated, which makes a fine sight – if waiting for a night train at Howrah station go to the first floor waiting rooms for a good aspect. The pedestrian-free **Vidyasagar Setu Bridge**, further south, has eased the traffic burden slightly.

Southeast of Howrah Bridge, the gorgeously well-kept **Armenian Church** of **Holy Nazareth** (1724) is a reminder of the important trading role the small Armenian community, who mostly came from Iran, played from the 17th century. The church is open 0600-1200 on weekdays or you can ask someone to open up in order to view the beautifully maintained interior. A gravestone in the compound is inscribed with the date 1630. The 150 or so Armenians in the city still hold a service in Armenian in one of their two churches in the city every Sunday. Their college on Mirza Ghalib Street (also the birthplace of William Makepeace Thackeray in 1811) has boarding pupils from Armenia who are usually orphans. To the east of the Church of Holy Nazareth is the **Roman Catholic Cathedral** (1797), built by the Portuguese. The Jewish community, mostly Sephardic, of Baghdadi origin, was also once very prominent in commerce. Their two synagogues are well maintained with stained-glass windows. The grander of the two is the church-like and cavernous **Moghan David Synagogue** (1884) ⓘ *Canning St, daily 0900-1700*, while the nearby **Beth El Synagogue** ⓘ *26/1 Pollock St, Sun-Fri 1000-1700*, is smaller. Just around the corner from the Moghan David Synagogue, on Brabourne Road hidden behind market stalls, is the older and derelict **Neveh Shalome Synagogue** (now inaccessible). There are only around 30 to 40 elderly Jews left in the city (the community numbered about 6000 before WWII) who continue to congregate at Nahoum & Son's bakery in the New

ON THE ROAD
Worship of the clay goddess

Durga Puja, the 17th-century festival in honour of the clay goddess, precedes the full moon in late September/early October, when all offices and institutions close down and the Metro only operates from the late afternoon.

Images of the 10-armed, three-eyed goddess, a form of Shakti or Kali astride her 'vehicle' the lion, portray Durga slaying Mahisasura, the evil buffalo demon. Durga, shown with her four children, Lakshmi, Sarasvati, Ganesh and Kartik, is worshipped in thousands of brightly illuminated and beautifully decorated *pandals* (marquees). Traditionally these are made of bamboo and coloured cloth, but often modern *pandals* are veritable works of art constructed to complex designs and tapping into current themes or re-creating popular Indian landmarks. The priests perform prayers at appointed times in the morning and evening. On the fourth and last day of festivities, huge and often emotionally charged processions follow devotees who carry the clay figures to be immersed in the river at many points along the banks. The potters return to collect clay from the river bank once again for the following year.

You can see the image makers in Kumartuli (see page 244) a few days earlier and visit the *pandals* early in the day, before they become intensely crowded. Local communities are immensely proud of their *pandals* and no effort is spared to put on the most impressive display. The images are decorated with intricate silver, golden or *shola* (white pith) ornaments; there are moving electric light displays, and huge structures are built (sometimes resembling a temple) in order to win competitions.

Market; the Jewish Girls School in Park Street no longer has Jewish pupils, in fact the vast majority of the girls are Muslims from a nearby neighbourhood. To view the interior of the synagogues, it is necessary to get signed permission either from **Nahoum's Bakery** (easiest) or from the office at 1 Hartford Lane.

A few reminders that there was once a Chinatown in Kolkata remain in the form of Chinese 'churches'. Seek out the **Sea Ip Church** (1905), which has an intricately carved wooden altar and the **Nam Soon Church**, with a school at the rear. The latter is gorgeously maintained with bright paint, a huge bell and drum, and a little courtyard with trees. Both are willingly opened by the custodians. At the top of Bentinck Street, where it meets BB Ganguly Street, are several tiny old-fashioned shoe shops run by aging members of the Chinese community.

RABINDRA BHARATI MUSEUM

Trams run along Rabindra Sarani, previously known as the Chitpur Road and one of the oldest streets in the city. Rising above street-level are the three green domes, 27 minarets and multiple archways of **Nakhoda Mosque** (1926), Kolkata's principal mosque holding 10,000 worshippers. A large brick gateway leads to **Rabindra Bharati Museum** ⓘ *6/4 Dwarakanath Tagore Lane (red walls visible down lane opposite 263 Rabindra Sarani), Mon-Fri 1000-1700, Sat 1000-1330, Sun and holidays 1100-1400, www.museum.rbu.ac.in/about_rb/*, in a peaceful enclave away from the teeming chaos of Rabindra Sarani. It occupies the family home of Rabindranath Tagore, who won the Nobel Prize for Literature in 1913. It showcases Tagore's life and works, as well as the 19th-century Renaissance movement in Bengal. Be sure to explore along all the corridors, as it's easy to miss the galleries of Indian and European art, and the Japanese exhibition rooms.

KUMARTULI

South of the Dakshineshwar Temple (see below) is Kumartuli. Off Chitpur Road, the *kumars* or potters work all year, preparing clay images around cores of bamboo and straw. For generations they have been making life-size idols for the *pujas* or festivals, particularly of goddess Durga on a lion, slaying the demon. The images are usually unbaked since they are immersed in the holy river at the end of the festival. As the time of the *pujas* approaches, you will see thousands of images, often very brightly painted and gaudily dressed, awaiting the final finishing touch by the master painter. There are also *shola* artists who make decorations for festivals and weddings. The potters' area of Kumartuli is being slowly rebuilt, and concrete structures are replacing the towering bamboo workshops that were so very photogenic.

NORTHEAST OF THE CITY CENTRE

Just north of the Belgachia Metro station is a cluster of three Digambar Jain temples, one of the most tranquil spots in the city. The meticulously maintained and ornate **Paresnath Temple** ① *0700-1200, 1500-2000, no leather*, is dedicated to the 10th Tirthankara. Consecrated around 1867, it is richly decorated with mirrors, Victorian tiles and Venetian glass mosaics.

Difficult to find (and perhaps not worth the effort unless you are a true aficionado of Raj history) is **Clive's House**, off Jessore Road in Nagarbajar, Dum Dum. This was the country home of the first governor-general of the East India Company and is the oldest colonial monument in Kolkata. For years, Bangladeshi immigrants lived in and around the derelict property until it was restored in 2008. The brick walls are being re-consumed by plant life and it requires some imagination to envisage its former glory.

BELUR MATH AND THE DAKSHINESHWAR KALI TEMPLE

Some 16 km north of the city is **Belur Math** ① *0600-1200, 1600-1900*, the international headquarters of the **Ramakrishna Mission**, founded in 1899 by Swami Vivekananda, a disciple of the 19th-century Hindu saint Ramakrishna. He preached the unity of all religions and to symbolize this the Math ('monastery') synthesizes Hindu, Christian and Islamic architectural styles in a peaceful and meditative atmosphere.

On the opposite side of the river from Belur Math is the **Dakshineshwar Kali Temple** ① *0600-1200, 1500-1800, 1830-2100, no photography allowed inside*. This huge Kali temple was built in 1847 by Rani Rashmoni. The 12 smaller temples in the courtyard are dedicated to Siva and there are also temples to Radha and Krishna. Because of the Rani's low caste, no priest would serve there until Ramakrishna's elder brother agreed and was succeeded by Ramakrishna himself. Here, Ramakrishna achieved his spiritual vision of the unity of all religions. The temple is crowded with colourfully clad devotees, particularly on Sundays when there are lengthy queues, and is open to all faiths. A boat (Rs 8) takes 20 minutes to/from to Belur Math across the Hooghly. Buses from BBD Bagh go to Dunlop Intersection, from where it's a short ride to the temple; trains run from Sealdah to Dakshineshwar.

NETAJI MUSEUM

ⓘ *Netaji Bhavan, 38/1 Elgin Rd, daily (except Mon) 1100-1430 (last entry 1615), Rs 5, no photography.*

This museum remembers the mission of Subhas Chandra Bose, the leader of the INA (Indian National Army), and is in the house where he lived before he had to flee the British oppressors. On the first floor, you can view his bedroom and study (where walls are painted with the tricolours of the Congress flag), although panes of glass prevent close inspection of his possessions. A detailed video is played in the second floor rooms showing old footage and giving a detailed explanation of his life's work. Interesting is the German Room, with a photo of Netaji meeting Hitler and information on Azad Hind and the Indo-German Friendship Society.

KALI TEMPLE

ⓘ *Off Ashok Mukherjee Rd, 0500-1500, 1700-2200.*

This is the temple to Kali (1809), the patron goddess of Kolkata, usually seen in her bloodthirsty form garlanded with skulls. There was an older temple here, where the goddess's little toe is said to have fallen when Siva carried her charred corpse in a frenzied dance of mourning, and she was cut into pieces by Vishnu's *chakra*. Where once human sacrifices were made (up until 1835, a boy was beheaded every Friday), the lives of goats are offered daily on two wooden blocks to the south of the temple. When visiting the temple, priests will attempt to snare foreigners for the obligatory *puja*. A barrage may start as far away as 500 m from the temple. Don't be fooled in to handing over your shoes and succumbing to any priests until you are clearly inside the temple, despite being shown 'priest ID' cards. An acceptable minimum donation is Rs 50. Books showing previous donations of Rs 3000 are doubtless faked. Having done the *puja*, you'll probably be left alone to soak up the atmosphere.

MOTHER TERESA'S HOMES

Mother Teresa, an Albanian by birth, came to India to teach as a Loreto nun in 1931. She started her Order of the Missionaries of Charity in Kalighat to serve the destitute and dying 19 years later. **Nirmal Hriday** ('Pure Heart'), near the Kali Temple, the first home for the dying, was opened in 1952. Mother Teresa died on 5 September 1997 but her work continues. You may see nuns in their white cotton saris with blue borders busy working in the many homes, clinics and orphanages in the city.

GARIAHAT AND RABINDRA SAROBAR

The southern neighbourhoods around Gariahat are more middle-class and greener than Central Kolkata, but no less interesting, with plenty of good restaurants and small hotels. On Gariahat Road, the shiny white edifice of **Birla Mandir** ⓘ *0600-1100 and 1630-2030,* pulls in a lot of devotees and it is particularly impressive when lit up at night. Taking 22 years to complete, another gift of the Birla family, it is modelled on the Lingaraj Temple at Bhubaneshwar and is covered with carvings both inside and out. No photos are permitted inside. Just north of the temple is the **CIMA Gallery**, which is worth a look. South of the Birla Mandir, beyond the southeast corner of Gariahat Crossing, is Gariahat market which specializes in fish and is a fascinating hive of activity, especially in the early morning. Running west from the crossing is Rash Behari Avenue, one of the city's liveliest streets, a 2-km stretch lined with sari stalls, *menhdi* (henna) artists, momo vendors and vegetable sellers. A couple of blocks south, housed in a modern high-rise, the **Birla Academy of Art and Culture** ① *108/109 Southern Av, T033-2466 2843, Tue-Sun 1600-2000*, concentrates on medieval and contemporary paintings and sculpture. The ground-floor sculpture gallery has been recently remodelled and displays some beautiful pieces including Buddhist and Hindu statues. It is well lit and worth visiting. The upper levels host changing art exhibitions.

The large and pleasant lake of **Rabindra Sarobar** is shaded by ancient trees and surrounded by a pathway perfect for joggers and walkers. There are several rowing clubs (the oldest dates from 1858), and Laughing Clubs meet in the mornings (around 0600) to mix yoga and group laughing. A road from the southwest corner of the lake leads to the trim little **Japanese Buddhist temple** on Lake Road (1935), the oldest temple of the Nichiren sect in India. Visitors are welcomed and can join in the hypnotic prayers by beating handheld drums (at dawn and dusk). A slim congregation of ex-Ghurkhas, Nepali ladies and bemused Bengalis are drawn in. The interior is restful with an elaborate golden shrine, gaudy flowers, ornamental lanterns and origami birds which somehow come together to pleasing effect. It's possible to walk from the temple south, via Dhakuria Bridge, to the Dakshinapan shopping complex (handicrafts and handloom) and refresh at Dolly's Tea Shop.

ALIPORE

South of the Maidan, the elite address of Alipore is home to a couple of sights. On Belvedere Road the **National Library** was once the winter residence of the Lieutenant Governors of Bengal. Built in the Renaissance Italian style, with a double row of classical columns, it is approached through a triple arched gateway and a drive between mahogany and mango trees. The library itself, the largest in the country with over eight million books, is now mainly housed in an adjacent newer building (sadly the old building can no longer be entered). Opposite is the **zoo** ① *Fri-Wed 0900-1700, Rs 10*. Opened in 1876, the grounds house a wide variety of animal and bird life. The white tigers from Rewa and the tigon, a cross between a tiger and a lion are the rarest animals. A reptile house and aquarium are across the road. There are restaurants, and picnics are permitted, however it's often terrifyingly busy (particularly at the weekend). Nearby, on Alipore Road, the expansive **Agri Horticultural Gardens** ① *0600-1300 and 1400-1830, Rs 10*, are the most peaceful green space in the city. The Horticultural Society was started in 1820 by the Baptist missionary William Carey. Bring a book; you'll be the only visitor during the week.

STATE ARCHAEOLOGICAL MUSEUM

① *1 Satyen Roy Rd, off Diamond Harbour Rd, Behala (next to Behala tram depot), Wed-Sun 1000-1630 (last entry 1600), entrance Rs 5.*
This little-visited yet well-presented museum has seven galleries over two floors, housed in a modern structure adjacent to the original colonial building. Galleries are devoted to West Bengal sites, such as the Buddhist remains of Nandadirghi Vihara near Malda, and the terracotta Hindu temples in Purulia. There's a meagre selection of local stone sculpture, intricate metal work, and a selection of Bengali paintings including Kalighat Pat (mostly religious in nature, but the famous 'Two Women and a Rose' is a notable secular

exception), and Murshidabad-style painting. Shared autos run from Kalighat metro to Behala, terminating close to the museum entrance.

BOTANICAL GARDENS

ⓘ 20 km south from BBD Bagh, 0700-1700, Rs 50, avoid Sun and public holidays when it is very crowded.

Kolkata's Botanical Gardens, on the west bank of the Hooghly, were founded in 1787 by the East India Company. The flourishing 250-year-old banyan tree, with a circumference of almost 400 m, is perhaps the largest in the world. The original trunk was destroyed by lightning in 1919 but over 2800 offshoots form an impressive sight. The avenues of Royal Cuban palms and mahogany trees are worth seeing, and there are interesting and exotic specimens in the herbarium and collections of ferns and cactii. The gardens are peaceful and deserted during the week and make a welcome change from the city. To reach the Botanical Gardens catch a bus from Esplanade; minibuses and CTC buses (No C-12) ply the route.

GOING FURTHER
Murshidabad

Named after Nawab Murshid Kuli Khan, a Diwan under Emperor Aurangzeb, Murshidabad became the capital of Bengal in 1705 and remained so up to the time of the battle of Plassey. The town lies on the east bank of the Bhagirathi, a picturesque tributary of the Ganga, with imposing ruins scattered around and an enchanting time-warp feel. A vibrant **vegetable bazar** takes place each morning beneath decaying columns left over from the days of the Nawabs, and the town comes to life for the famed Muslim festival of **Muhurram** at the end of January. Come during the week to avoid the crowds.

Nizamat Kila on the river bank was the site of the old fort and encloses the Nawabs' Italianate **Hazarduari** ('1000 doors') **Palace** ① *Sat-Thu 1000-1500, Rs 100, no photography*, built in 1837. It is now a splendid museum with a portrait gallery, library and circular durbar hall and contains a rare collection of old arms, curios, china and paintings. The large newer **Imambara** (1847) opposite, also Italianate in style, is under a continuous process of renovation and is worth exploring. The domed, square **Madina** (pavillion) with a veranda that stands nearby may be what remains of the original Imambara. There are numerous 18th-century monuments in the city which are best visited by cycle-rickshaw ① *Rs 100-150 for 3 hrs*. Mir Jafar and his son Miran lived at **Jafaragunj Deorhi**, known as the traitor's gate. **Kat-gola** ① *Rs 50*, the atmospheric garden palace of a rich Jain merchant, houses a collection of curios including Belgian glass mirror-balls and has an old Jain temple and boating 'lake' in the grounds. The **Palace of Jagat Sett**, one of the richest financiers of the 18th century, is 2 km from the Jafargung Cemetery to the north of the palace. The brick ruins of **Katra Masjid** (1723), modelled on the great mosque at Mecca and an important centre of learning, are outside the city to the east. It was built by Murshid Kuli Khan who lies buried under the staircase. **Moti Jheel** (Pearl Lake) and the ruins of **Begum Ghaseti's Palace** are 2 km south of the city. Only a mosque and a room remain. **Khosbagh** (Garden of Delight) ① *across the river, easily accessible by bamboo ferries, Rs 1, 24-hr*, has three walled enclosures. It is recommended to hire a boat (Rs 250 from **Hotel Manjusha**, see below) to journey upstream to **Baranagar**, three well-preserved terracotta temples in the Bangla style; drift back down and stop off at the Jain town of **Azimganj**.

Recommended places to stay and eat in Murshidabad are **Indrajit** (near railway station, T03482-271858, www.hotelindrajit.com) and **Manjusha** (by Hazarduari Palace, T03482-270321). The former has a wide choice of rooms, friendly staff and an excellent multi-cuisine restaurant and bar, while the latter has simple clean rooms, with serene riverside setting for spotting dolphins and lush garden of flowers and fruit trees. The charming manager can help with bike, rickshaw and boat hire.

KOLKATA LISTINGS

WHERE TO STAY

Discounts are often available online.

$$$$ Chrome, 226 AJC Bose, South Kolkata, T033-3096 3096, www.chrome hotel.in. Space-age hotel with slick modern rooms dense with gadgetry, 'adrenalin' showers and trendy colour schemes. 6 categories, The 'Edge' suites being the zenith, but all are supremely comfortable. Good city-scapes from the higher levels. **Khana Sutra** restaurant, rooftop bar/club **Inferno** on the 7th floor and **Nosh** café in the lobby. Swimming pool is planned.

$$$$ Oberoi Grand, 15 Chowringhee (JL Nehru), Central Kolkata, T033-2249 2323, www.oberoi hotels.com. Atmospheric Victorian building opposite the Maidan, exquisitely restored, range of rooms and suites with giant 4-posters, all are spacious, those with balconies overlooking the raised garden and pool are charming, bathrooms a tad old-fashioned but in keeping with the colonial style, excellent Thai restaurant, billiards in the bar, lovely pool for guests, wonderful spa.

$$$$ The Park, 17 Park St, T033-2249 9000, www.theparkhotels.com. Trendy designer hotel, one of Kolkata's most reputable, good restaurants, nightclubs, health club, 24-hr café, service can be disappointing.

$$$$ Taj Bengal, 34B Belvedere Rd, Alipore, T033-2223 3939, www.tajhotels. com. Opulent and modern, restaurants are plush, imaginative, intimate, with good food (ground-floor Indian cheaper than 5th floor), leisurely service, unusual Bengali breakfast, **Khazana** shop is excellent.

$$$ Tollygunge Club, 120 Deshapran Sasmal Rd, T033-2473 4539, www.thetolly gungeclub.org. On the south side of the city in 100 acres of grounds with an 18-hole golf course, swimming pool, tennis and other activities. Good bar and restaurants. The place has charm and atmosphere that helps you overlook worn-out towels and

casual service, ask for a renovated room, and enjoy the colonial feel.

$$$-$$ The Bodhi Tree, 48/44 Swiss Park (near Rabindra Sarovar metro, exit Swiss Park), T033-2424 6534, www.bodhitree kolkata.com. Simply beautiful little boutique hotel with just 6 rooms, each furnished in a distinct regional style (eg rural Bengal, with mud-plastered walls), flatscreen TVs, 1 penthouse. The in-house café is a delight, dinner is available, business centre, free Wi-Fi, small library, serves alcohol. Prices are entirely reasonable for the special experience. Discounts for single women travellers/ social workers. A real oasis; recommended.

$$ Fairlawn, 13A Sudder St, T033-2252 1510/ 8766, www.fairlawnhotel.com. A Calcutta institution, the old-fashioned but characterful rooms have a/c, TV, hot water, and are comfortable. Semi-formal meals at set times aren't the best, but breakfast and afternoon tea are included. It's a throwback to the Raj, bric-a-brac everywhere, photos cover all the communal spaces, quite a place and the garden terrace is great for a beer. Wi-Fi Rs 250 per day.

$ Broadway, 27A Ganesh Chandra Av, T033-2236 3930, www.broadwayhotel.in. Amazingly good-value hotel in a characterful building that hasn't changed much since it opened in 1937. Very clean rooms are non-a/c but airy with powerful fans, antique furniture and Bengali-red floors, towels, some with common bath, plus 24-hr checkout. Noisy on the lower levels at the front. The bar is very appealing (see page 250). Highly recommended.

$ Sunflower Guest House, 7 Royd St, near Sudder St, T033-2229 9401, www.sunflower guesthouse.com. An airy 1950s building with clean well-maintained rooms, TV, hot water, more costly with a/c and newer bathrooms. Spacious lounge area, the staff are kindly. Good location. No single room rates.

RESTAURANTS

$$$ Baan Thai, Oberoi Grand (see Where to stay), T033-2249 2323. Excellent selection, imaginative decor, Thai-style seating on floor or chairs and tables.

$$$ Oh! Calcutta, in the Forum Mall, 10/3 Elgin Rd, South Kolkata, T033-2283 7161. Fantastic fish and seafood, plus many vegetarian options, this award-winning restaurant (branches across India, another in Kolkata on EM Bypass) re-creates Bengali specialities. It's an attractive venue; the only minor oddity is the location inside a mall.

$$ Kewpie's, 2 Elgin Lane (just off Elgin Rd), South Kolkata, T033-2486 1600/9929. Tue-Sun 1200-1500, 1700-2245. Authentic Bengali home cooking at its best, add on special dishes to basic *thali*, unusual fish and vegetarian. Just a few tables in rooms inside the owners' residence, a/c, sells recipe book. Highly recommended, book in advance.

$$ Mirch Masala, 49/2 Gariahat Rd, Gariahat, T033-2461 8900. Lunch 1200-1500, dinner 1900-2230. This popular restaurant-bar has walls decorated with *pukkah* murals depicting Bollywood stars. Food can be a bit heavy (mainly Indian, non-veg) but the atmosphere is lively and staff competent.

$$ Fire and Ice, Kanak Building, Middleton St, T033-2288 4073, www.fireandice pizza.com. Open 1100-2330. Pizzas here are the real deal, service is excellent, and the ambience relaxing. Decor is very much what you would expect from a pizza-place at home. Definitely worth it.

$$-$ Anand, 19 Chittaranjan Av, Central Kolkata, T033-2212 9757. Open 0900-2130, Sun from 0700, closed Wed. Great South Indian food. Mammoth *dosas*, stuffed *idly*, all-vegetarian, family atmosphere and warmly decorated. Barefoot waiters are efficient. Queues at weekends.

$$-$ Bhojohori Manna, Esplanade, Central Kolkata. Open 1130-2130 (closed for cleaning 1630-1800). The newest branch of the Bengali chain, with budget prices for veg dishes and pricier fish items. Ticks on the whiteboard indicate availability, choice can be limited in the evenings as they sell out.

BARS AND CLUBS

Bars

The larger hotels have pleasant bars and upmarket restaurants serve alcohol. The top hotels are well stocked, luxurious but pricey. In Sudder St, **Fairlawn**'s pleasant garden terrace is popular at dusk attracting anyone seeking a chilled beer. The clientele is quite mixed, fairy lights set the greenery glowing and it's perfect for a first night drink to acclimatize – but beware the below-average food and stiff charges for snacks. **Blue & Beyond** at the Lindsay Hotel, is a rooftop bar/restaurant with great views over New Market and Kolkata. Women are welcome in the **Broadway Bar** at the Broadway Hotel (last orders 2230), where marble floors, polished art deco seating, soft lighting, whirring fans and windows open to the street make it probably the best choice in the city. Lone women will feel comfortable as it's a busy and respectable place.

Discos and nightclubs

Someplace Else (Park Hotel). Pub, live bands play loud music to the same crowd each week. **Tantra** (Park Hotel). Taped music, large floor, young crowd, no shorts or flip-flops, cover charge. Next door **Roxy** is less popular, but has free entry and is more relaxed, with slouchy sofas upstairs.

Shisha Reincarnated, Block D, 6th floor, 22 Camac St, T033-2281 1313, www.shisha reincarnated.com. Open 1800-2400, Wed, Fri and Sat 1800-0200. Dark and stylish with a chilled atmosphere and low red lights, huge bar lined with spirits, and DJs every night (varying music styles). Hookahs cost Rs 300, the roof-deck is the best place to hang out.

NORTH BENGAL HILLS

The Himalayan foothills of northern West Bengal contain a wealth of trekking opportunities and hill stations in stunning locations, including the region's prime tourist destination, Darjeeling. The old colonial summer retreat is surrounded by spectacular views and still draws plenty of visitors to enjoy cooler climes, outstanding trekking and a good cuppa.

→ KURSEONG

Kurseong (1450 m) or 'Place of the White Orchid' is a small town worthy of a nights' pause on the way to Darjeeling. There is pleasant walking to be done in the surrounding tea gardens and orange orchards, and locals will sincerely tell you that they call Kurseong 'paradise'.

ARRIVING IN KURSEONG

Getting there Flights from Kolkata arrive at Bagdogra Airport, near Siliguri, from where prepaid taxis travel into the hills. Overnight trains go from Sealdah Station in Kolkata to NJP station, also near Siliguri, taking about 10 hours. From outside NJP, you can either take private transport or wait for a shared jeep to fill up (which can sometimes take a while) to travel on to Kurseong/Darjeeling. There are also public jeep stands in Siliguri itself, with more frequent departures to all hill station destinations (1½ hours to Kurseong). Cycle- or auto-rickshaws make the trip between NJP and the jeep stands. The Darjeeling Himalayan Railway from Siliguri to Kurseong is currently not operational, due to landslides in 2011 and 2012 (see www.dhrs.org for updates and box, page 254).

Moving on Two trains a day leave Kurseong for **Darjeeling** (see page 252) along the narrow-gauge DHR line, at 0700 and 1500, taking almost three hours. Jeeps leave for Darjeeling from near the train station, taking one hour. Private jeeps/taxis can also be hired.

PLACES IN KURSEONG

There are no grand sights in the town, but it is an interesting hike up to the ridge, via St Mary's hamlet (north of the market along Hill Cart Road). Shortcuts past quaint houses and the eerie Forestry College lead up to **St Mary's Well and Grotto**, which has fine views and a shrine with candles. Tracks through a young forest reach imposing Dow Hill School, established 1904, and either continue up and over the ridge to tiny Chetri Bustee, or bear right to the little **Forest Museum** at Dow Hill. Head back down via scenically located **Ani Gompa**, housing a small community of nuns belonging to the Red Hat sect, and past pretty cottages using footpaths. It's around a five-hour walk with stops; ask locals for directions, but double any time frame they give to destinations. Useful sketch maps can be provided by **Cochrane Place** (see listings, page 259), where it is also possible to arrange guided hikes tailored to match walkers' interests and stamina. In the town itself there's the narrow and crowded *chowk* market to explore, while a half-hour walk from the railway station brings you to **Eagle's Crag** (shadowed by the TV tower), an awesome vantage point in clear weather.

The **Makaibari Tea Estate**, 4 km from town, makes an interesting excursion. Dating from 1859, it is India's oldest tea garden, responsibly managed by charismatic Rajah Banerjee who has done much to support the community and initiate environmental and organic development on the estate. The highest price ever fetched at a tea auction was for Makaibari leaves when Rs 18,000 was paid for a kilogram in 2003. Nearby **Ambootia Tea Estate** also conducts factory visits, and from here there's a walk to an ancient Siva temple amid massive Rudraksh and Banyan trees. Kurseong is famed for its plethora of boarding schools. At **Tung** nearby, the St Alphonsus Social and Agricultural Centre, run by a Canadian Jesuit, is working with the local community through education, housing, agricultural, forestry and marketing projects. They welcome volunteers; contact **SASAC** ⓘ *Tung, Darjeeling, West Bengal, T0354-234 2059, sasac@satyam.net.in.*

→ DARJEELING

For tens of thousands of visitors from Kolkata and the steamy plains, Darjeeling is a place to escape the summer heat. Built on a crescent-shaped ridge, the town is surrounded by hills, which are thickly covered with coniferous forests and terraced tea gardens. The idyllic setting, the exhilarating air outside town and the stunning views of the Kanchenjunga (Kangchendzonga) range (when you can see through the clouds) attract plenty of trekkers too. Nevertheless, Darjeeling's modern reality is a crowded, noisy and in places shockingly dirty and polluted town. Between June and September the monsoons bring heavy downpours, sometimes causing landslides, but the air clears after mid-September. Winter evenings are cold enough to demand log fires and lots of warm clothing.

ARRIVING IN DARJEELING
Getting there You can reach Darjeeling by jeep from Kurseong in one hour, arriving at the motor stand in the lower town or at **Clubside** on the Mall, which is more convenient for most accommodation. The DHR train service from Kurseong (see www.dhrs.org and box, page 254) is picturesque but very slow (three hours). Bagdogra, near Siliguri, is Darjeeling's nearest airport. NJP, also near Siliguri, is the nearest mainline train station (see Arriving in Kurseong, for further details).

Moving on Jeeps leave Darjeeling for **Jorethang** (see page 261) on the border of Sikkim state 0800-1500 (it's best to book a front seat, a day in advance) and take two hours. You will need to get a permit for Sikkim when in Darjeeling (see box, page 262), as they are not available in Jorethang. In Jorethang, change to a jeep for Pelling. For private hire, enquire with a travel agent, your hotel, or at the tourist information office.

Getting around Most of Darjeeling's roads slope quite gently so it is easy to walk around the town. The lower and upper roads are linked by a series of connecting roads and steep steps. For sights away from the centre you need to hire a taxi. Note that roads can get washed away during the monsoon and may remain in poor condition till October. Be prepared for seasonal water shortages and frequent power cuts. After dark a torch is essential.

Tourist information WBTDC ⓘ *Bellevue Hotel, 1st floor, 1 Nehru Rd, T0354-225 4102, 1000-1700, off-season 1030-1600,* not much information available. DGHC ⓘ *Maple Tourist Lodge, Old Kutchery Rd (below Natural History Museum), T0354-225 5351, Mon-Sat 1030-1600 (closed 2nd and 4th Sat in month).* Recently relocated, since the old office on the Mall was burnt down in February 2011. There's also a DGHC kiosk at **Clubside** ⓘ *daily 1000-1600.*

BACKGROUND

Darjeeling means region of the *dorje* (thunderbolt) and its official but rarely used spelling is Darjiling. The surrounding area once belonged to Sikkim, although parts were annexed from time to time by the Bhutanese and Nepalese. The East India Company returned the territory's sovereignty to the Rajas of Sikkim, which led to the British obtaining permission to gain the site of the hill station called Darjeeling in 1835, in return for an annual payment. It was practically uninhabited and thickly forested but soon grew into a popular health resort after a road and several houses were built and tea growing was introduced. The Bengal government escaped from the Kolkata heat to take up its official summer residence here. The upper reaches were originally occupied by the Europeans, who built houses with commanding views. Down the hillside on terraces sprawled the humbler huts and bazars of the Indian town.

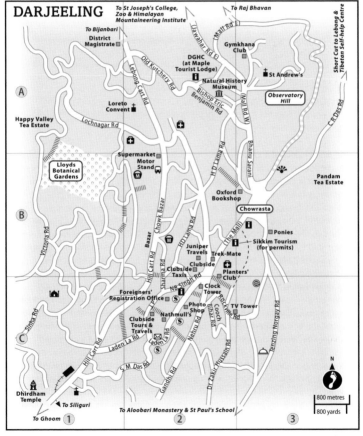

DARJEELING

ON THE ROAD
Darjeeling Himalayan Railway – a mini miracle

For many people, the journey on the somewhat erratic narrow-gauge 'toy train' between Siliguri and Darjeeling is a rewarding experience and is now recognized as a World Heritage Site. The brainchild of East Bengal Railway agent Franklyn Prestage, the train promised to improve access to the hills from the sweltering humidity of the Kolkata plains in the summer, following the line of an earlier steam tramway; the name was changed to the Darjeeling Himalayan Railway Company (DHR) in 1881. It is a stunning achievement, winding its way along 82 km of 0.6 m gauge track, with gradients of up to 1:19, often with brilliant views over the plains. From Siliguri, it ascends to Kurseong, continuing to Ghoom, the highest railway station in India at 2438 m, before descending 305 m to Darjeeling.

Following numerous landslips in recent years, the service between Siliguri and Kurseong is currently suspended. However, there is a twice daily diesel service between Kurseong and Darjeeling (see www.dhrs.org for details and updates) and a special tourist steam service, with newly refurbished carriages, between Darjeeling and Ghoom in summer (departing 1040, returning 1200, and again at 1320, returning 1440; but check times at the station, Rs 240). Bookings must be made 90 days in advance, although it is possible to buy spare seats on the day from agents who have private counters set up at Darjeeling station. This is a must for steam buffs – despite derailments which are "swiftly dealt with and you are lifted back on the tracks within 20 minutes." All trains pass through Batasia Loop, 5 km from Darjeeling, which allows the narrow-gauge rail to do a figure-of-eight loop. The tourist train stops for photos here; there's a war memorial in a pleasant park with good mountain views.

PLACES IN DARJEELING

In the pedestrianized centre of town, on the ridge, **Chowrasta** is the natural heart of Darjeeling and particularly atmospheric at dawn and dusk. The **Mahakal Mandir** atop **Observatory Hill**, dedicated to Siva, is a pleasant walk though the views of the mountains are obscured by tall trees. Sacred to both Hindus and Buddhists, the temple is active and colourful, with prayer flags tied to every tree and pole in the vicinity. Beware of the monkeys as they bite. Further along Jawahar Road West is **Shrubbery (Nightingale) Park**, a pleasant detour if it's still too early to visit the zoo. Views to the north are excellent from the renovated park, and evening cultural shows take place here (information from the DGHC tourist office).

Padmaja Naidu Himalayan Zoological Park ① *daily 0830-1630 (summer), 0830-1600 (winter) except Thu, Rs 100*, houses high-altitude wildlife including Himalayan black bears, Siberian tigers, Tibetan wolves and plenty of red pandas, as well as deer, a multitude of birds and the gorgeously marked rare clouded leopard. There are large enclosures over a section of the hillside, though at feeding time and during wet weather they retreat into their small cement enclosures giving the impression that they are restricted to their cells. There is a reasonably successful snow leopard breeding programme, with over 40 births since 1983, and it is the only Asian zoo to have successfully introduced red pandas into the wild. Entrance fees to the zoo also include the **Himalayan Mountaineering Institute** ① *T0354-227 0158, no photography, entrance is through the zoo on Jawahar Rd West*. Previously headed by the late Tenzing Norgay who shared the first climb of Everest in

ON THE ROAD
Darjeeling tea gardens

An ancient Chinese legend suggests that 'tay', or tea, originated in India, although tea was known to have been grown in China around 2700 BC. It is a species of Camellia, Camellia thea. After 1833, when its monopoly on importing tea from China was abolished, the East India Company made attempts to grow tea in Assam using wild chai plants found growing there and later introduced it in Darjeeling and in the Nilgiri hills in the south. Today India is the largest producer of tea in the world. Assam grows over half and Darjeeling about a quarter of the nation's output. Once drunk only by the tribal people, it has now become India's national drink.

The orthodox method of tea processing produces the aromatic lighter coloured liquor of the Golden Flowery Orange Pekoe in its most superior grade. The fresh leaves are dried by fans on withering troughs to reduce the moisture content and then rolled and pressed to express the juices which coat the leaves. These are left to ferment in a controlled environment to produce the desired aroma. Finally the leaves are dried by passing them through a heated drying chamber and then graded – the unbroken being the best quality, down to the fannings and dust. The more common crushing, tearing, curling (CTC) method produces tea which gives a much darker liquor.

Most of Darjeeling's tea is sold through auction houses, the largest centre being in Kolkata. Tea tasting and blending are skills that have developed over a long period of time and are highly prized. The industry provides vital employment in the hill areas and is an assured foreign exchange earner.

1953, the Institute has trained up many a mountaineer and runs training courses during dry months of the year. Within the complex, the Everest Museum traces the history of attempted climbs from 1857 and the Mountaineering Museum displays old equipment including that used on the historic Tenzing-Hillary climb.

The decaying **Natural History Museum** ① *Bishop Eric Benjamin Rd, 0900-1630, Rs 10*, was set up in 1903 and has a large collection of fauna of the region and a certain charm; the basement has a curious diorama and specimen jars. The **Tibetan Refugee Self-help Centre** ① *T0354-225 5938, thondup@cal.vsnl.net.in, Mon-Sat 0800-1700, closed for lunch*, with its temple, school and hospital is north of town. From Chowrasta, take the lane to the right towards the viewpoint, and then walk down for about 30 minutes (ask around). After the Chinese invasion, thousands of Tibetan refugees settled in Darjeeling (many having accompanied the Dalai Lama) and the rehabilitation centre was set up in 1959 to enable them to continue to practise their skills and provide a sales outlet. You can watch them at work (carpet weaving, spinning, dyeing, woodwork, etc) during the season, when it is well worth a visit. The shop sells fabulous woollen carpets (orders taken and posted), textiles, curios and jewellery, though these are not cheap to buy.

On the way to the refugee centre is the lovely **Bhutia Bustee Monastery**, which was built on Observatory Hill in 1765 but was moved to its present position in 1861. Someone will show you around and point out gold-flecked murals that have been gorgeously restored. South of town, the **Aloobari Monastery**, on Tenzing Norgay Road, is open to visitors. Tibetan and Sikkimese handicrafts made by the monks are for sale.

Near the market are **Lloyd Botanical Gardens** ① *Mon-Sat 0600-1700*. These were laid out in 1878 on land given by Mr W Lloyd, owner of the Lloyd's Bank. They have a modest collection of Himalayan and Alpine flora including banks of azaleas and rhododendrons, magnolias, a good hothouse (with over 50 species of orchid) and a herbarium. It is a pleasant and quiet spot. **Victoria Falls**, which is only impressive in the monsoons, provides added interest to a three-hour nature trail. There are several tea gardens close to Darjeeling, but not all welcome visitors. One that does is the **Pattabong Estate** on the road towards Sikkim.

AROUND DARJEELING

The 11-km, 45-minute journey from Darjeeling to Ghoom (Ghum) on the tourist steam train is highly recommended (see box, page 254). The little **Railway Museum** ① *daily 1000-1300 and 1400-1600, Rs 20, ticket from station and staff will unlock the gate*, outlines the history of the Darjeeling Himalayan Railway and has some interesting old photos. Also, at at **Ghoom** (**Ghum**), altitude 2257 m, is the important **Yiga Choeling Gompa**, a Yellow Hat Buddhist Monastery. Built in 1875 by a Mongolian monk, it houses famous Buddhist scriptures (beautifully displayed) in an interior the colour of the surrounding forests. The austere monastery is a nice walk from the end of Ghoom's main market street. Also worth visiting is the **Sakyaguru Monastery**, closer to the Darjeeling road, which has 95 monks.

The disused **Lebong Race Course**, 8 km from Darjeeling, was once the smallest and highest in the world and makes a pleasant walk, heading down from Chowrasta. It was started as a parade ground in 1885, and there is now talk of it becoming a race course once more.

If the weather is clear, it is worth rising at 0400 to make the hour's journey for a breathtaking view of the sunrise on Kanchenjunga at **Tiger Hill** ① *shared jeep from Darjeeling Rs 80-100 return, just go to Clubside motor stand for 0430 to pick one up*. Mount Everest (8846 m), 225 km away, is visible on a good day. The mass of jeeps and the crowds at sunrise disappear by mid-morning; it's a nice walk back from Tiger Hill (about two hours, 11 km) via Ghoom and the **Japanese Peace Pagoda**, where drumming between 1630-1900 is worth seeing.

GOING FURTHER
Trekking around Darjeeling

The trekking routes around Darjeeling are well established, having been popular for over 100 years. Walks lead in stages along safe tracks and through wooded hills up to altitudes of 3660 m. Trails are lined with rhododendrons, magnolias, orchids and wild flowers, and pass through forests, meadows and small villages, with a stunning backdrop of mountains stretching from Mount Everest to the Bhutan hills, including the third highest mountain in the world, Kanchenjunga. The best trekking seasons are April to May, when the magnolias and rhododendrons are in full bloom, and October to November when air clarity is best. In winter the lower-altitude trails that link Rimbick with Jhepi (18 km) can be very attractive for birdwatchers.

Agents in Darjeeling can organize four- to seven-day treks, providing guide, equipment and accommodation, though it is perfectly possible to go it alone. The West Bengal Forest and Wildlife Departmentis is strongly encouraging visitors to take a guide/porter when entering the **Singalila National Park**. If you haven't arranged a trek through an agent in Darjeeling, local guides can be hired in Manebhanjang for Rs 300-500 per day (although paying more secures someone who speaks good English and has a better knowledge of local flora and fauna); porters are Rs 200-250. Entry fees for the park are also paid at the checkpoint in Manebhanjang (foreigners Rs 200, still camera Rs 50, video camera Rs 100).

DARJEELING TREKS

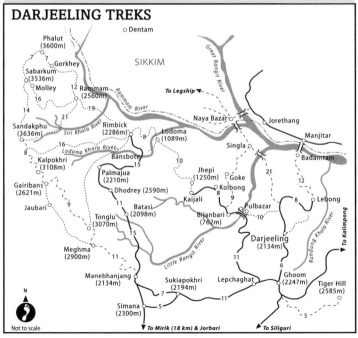

SINGALILA TREK

The 160-km Singalila trek starts from the small town of **Manebhanjang**, 26 km from Darjeeling. The journey to and from Darjeeling can be done by shared or private jeep in one hour. Other possible starting points are: **Dhotrey** (a further hour by jeep, north of Manebhanjang), which cuts out a large chunk of the steep ascent to Tonglu; or **Rimbick**, via Gurdum. If you have not arranged for transport to meet you at a particular point, then it is entirely possible to travel back to Darjeeling from any roadhead by jeep, with services at least once daily.

From Manebhanjang, the route heads to **Tonglu** or **Tumling**, **Jaubari** and **Gairibans**, ascending to **Sandakphu** on the third day. This small collection of lodges and government buildings is the highest point in West Bengal and the prime destination for most trekkers. Located 57 km from Darjeeling, it is accessible by jeep (the same narrow bumpy track used by hikers), which is how many Indian tourists make the journey during the season. Sandakphu offers fantastic views, including the eastern face of Everest (8846 m, 140 km away as the crow flies), Kanchenjunga (8586 m), Chomolhari (the highest peak in Bhutan), Lluhe and Makchu (the fourth and fifth highest peaks in the world, respectively) and numerous peaks, such as Pandim, that lie in Sikkim. A five-minute walk past the towering Sherpa lodge brings you to three hillocks on the left side of the path; the middle one of these is the very highest point at 3636 m. The drive back to Manebhanjang by prearranged 4WD can take four hours along the very rough track, if you finish the trek here. Otherwise, the route continues to **Phalut** and **Rimbick**, from where there are around three jeeps a day to take you back to Darjeeling (Rs 100, four hours). Although the last stages of the route pass just south of the border with Sikkim, entering Sikkim is not permitted here; agents say this may change in future, so ask in Darjeeling about the current situation.

There are government Trekkers' Huts and private lodges of varying standards and prices (on an organized trek these will have been booked for you) at Tonglu, Sandakphu, Phalut, Gorkhey, Molley, Rammam, Rimbick, Siri Khola and other villages. Although room is usually available, it's wise to book in advance during May/June and October when trails can be very busy. Any trekking agent in Darjeeling can arrange bookings for a small fee. Private lodges are generally friendly, flexible and provide reasonable basic accommodation. Some places can prepare yak curry on request; you should also be sure to sample hot *chhang*, the local millet brew, served in a wooden keg and sipped through a bamboo straw.

Note Singalila is not an easy trek: several parts are very steep and tough; temperatures at night are freezing, even in May, and it is essential to take plenty of warm clothes.

NORTH BENGAL HILLS LISTINGS

WHERE TO STAY

Kurseong

$$-$ Cochrane Place, 132 Pankhabari Rd, Fatak (2 km from Kurseong on the road to Mirik), T0354-233 0703, www.imperial chai.com. Rebuilt and recreated colonial home with de luxe rooms crammed with antiques and atmosphere, the personal touch of the owner in evidence throughout. Passion fruits grow by balconies, the tiered garden is delightful (organic veg), spa/ yoga/meditation and 'stick' massage are reasonably priced, superlative meals and tea menu (see Restaurants). Views of Kanchenjunga from some rooms. Newer annex is cheaper and simpler, still very comfortable with a chalet air. Dorm beds for backpackers Rs 736. Lovely walking through tea gardens and villages nearby. Management are informative and interesting. Wheelchair access. Highly recommended.

$$-$ Tourist Lodge, Hill Cart Rd (1 km from station), T0354-234 4409. Gloomy corridors but some lovely wooden rooms (check a couple), good views, 24-hr hot water, heaters in winter, snack bar, decent bar and restaurant. Car hire. Recommended.

Darjeeling

$$$$ The Elgin, HD Lama Rd, T0354-225 7226, www.elginhotels.com. Beautifully renovated 120-year-old colonial hotel, rooms are full of atmosphere with polished floors, fireplaces, nooks and crannies while being plush and well-appointed, marble bathrooms. Photos, brass fittings and carpets give warmth to public spaces, lounge and bar area pleasantly like a country sitting room, tiered garden is small and flower-filled but looks onto a high fence. Annoyingly, there is no option but to take a package including all meals, and high tea is grossly overpriced for outside guests.

$$$$ Windamere, Observatory Hill, T0354-225 4041/2, www.windamere hotel.com. Enviable location, good views when clear, a true relic of the Raj. Spacious rooms and cottages (no phone or TV in some), beware those with dated bathrooms (limited hot water), terraces, chintzy and cluttered with memorabilia, coal fires (can be smoky), hotties in bed, pre-war piano favourites accompany tea. Lounge/bar is a characterful place for a drink, outside guests welcome for high tea (disappointing) or beer (Rs 180). Full-board only.

$$$$-$$$ Cedar Inn, Dr Zakir Hussain Rd, T0354-225 4446, www.cedarinndarjeeling. com. Slightly out of town, but with great views and free shuttle service to town throughout the day. Family friendly, health club, sauna, lovely garden with wrought iron furniture. Wood-panelled rooms are stylish and thoughtfully laid out (bathrooms a bit 1980s), fireplaces in some, public areas filled with enormous plants, bar and restaurant are welcoming and informal. Extension in same style as the original building, essential to book in advance.

$$-$ Dekeling Resort, 51 Gandhi Rd (The Mall), T0354-225 4159, www.dekeling.com. Homely rooms are noticeably warm, most have private bath (24-hr hot water), delightful lounge areas with stoves. Range of room tariffs, some attic front rooms with views, 2 doubles with shared bath are a bargain (No 11 is best). Good restaurant, brilliant hosts, reserve ahead (1 month in advance in high season). Noisy when jeeps depart at 0400 for Tiger Hill with lots of hooting.

RESTAURANTS

Kurseong

$$ Chai Country, at **Cochrane Place**
(see Where to stay). A meal at **Cochrane**
is not to be missed when in Kurseong.
Food is gourmet and inventive, best are
the Anglo-Indian dishes with a twist (dhal
with mint, oyster mushrooms smoked
with tea) otherwise African curry, veggie
shepherd's pie and more; puddings are
exquisite (baked mango). No liquor licence.

Darjeeling

$$ Glenary's, Nehru Rd (The Mall), T0354-
225 7554, glens_getaways@sancharnet.in.
Tearoom with excellent confectionery
and pastries, friendly, first-class breakfast,
Kalimpong cheese and wholemeal bread
sold. Licensed restaurant upstairs is pricier
but lively and with a good atmosphere,
bar downstairs has local band on Sat
(supposedly 1900-2200 but often finishes
early). Speedy internet café.
$$-$ Lunar, 51 Gandhi Rd, T0354-225 4194.
Open from 0730. Thoroughly delicious
pure veg Indian dishes, and some decent
sandwiches, pizzas and Chinese. Modern
and informal, family environment, big
windows for the view. *Lassis* are fragrant
and creamy, service competent and kindly.
$ Dekeva's, Dekling Hotel, 52 Gandhi Rd,
Clubside. Nice little place with Tibetan
specialities, plus Chinese and Continental,
cosy, very popular.

ENTERTAINMENT

Darjeeling

The bar at the **Windamere** (see Where
to stay) has a cosy lounge-feel among
knick-knacks. **Joey's Pub**, though housed
in an unlikely looking heritage cottage,
gathers a rowdy crowd every night
for drinks in a true pub ambiance.
Surprisingly good typical British bar
snacks, very social, open 0930-2300.

SIKKIM

Khangchendzonga (Kanchenjunga), the third highest mountain in the world, dominates the skyline of Sikkim. The state is renowned as much for its wonderful wildlife and rich variety of plants and flowers as for its ethnically varied population. Sikkim's original inhabitants, the Lepchas, call the region Nye-mae-el, meaning 'Paradise'. To the later Bhutias it is Beymul Denjong, or the 'Hidden Valley of Rice'. The name Sikkim itself is commonly attributed to the Tsong word Su-khim, meaning 'New' or 'Happy House'. The monasteries of Rumtek and Pemayangtse are just two among a wealth of fascinating centres of Buddhism in the state.

Sikkim is an orchid-lover's paradise, with 660 species found at altitudes as high as 3000 m. Organic farming and ecotourism are officially enshrined in government policy, and although trekking is less developed than in other parts of the Himalaya, the state attracts ramblers and trekkers in serious numbers.

From Kalimpong or Darjeeling, head by jeep via Jorethang to Pelling to visit Pemayangtse Monastery. Then continue, via Khecheopalri Lake, to Yuksom and Tashiding. Road journeys within Sikkim are very scenic, but numerous hairpin bends and unsealed sections can also make them extremely slow, so expect to travel at 10-40 kph. Conditions deteriorate considerably during the monsoon, which can sometimes make travel impossible.

→ SOUTHWEST SIKKIM

This enchanting region contains the essence of Sikkim: plunging rice terraces, thundering rivers, Buddhist monasteries etched against the sky, and the ever-brooding presence of Mount Khangchendzonga.

ARRIVING IN SOUTHWEST SIKKIM
Getting there Jeeps leave Darjeeling for Jorethang on the border of Sikkim state 0800-1500 (it's best to book a front seat, a day in advance) and take two hours. You will need to get a permit for Sikkim when in Darjeeling (see page 262), as they are not available in Jorethang. In Jorethang, change to a jeep for Pelling. For private hire, enquire with a travel agent, your hotel, or at the tourist information office.

Moving on There are jeeps from Pelling and Yuksom either to **Bagdogra** (six hours) for flights to **Guwahati** (one hour, see page 265) or to NJP for overnight train services.

PELLING
Pelling sits on a ridge with good views of the mountains. The rather bleak little town has three areas linked by a winding road, Upper and Middle with views and hotels, and Lower Pelling with banks and other services. Upper Pelling is expanding rapidly with new hotels springing up to accommodate honeymooners from Kolkata, and makes the most convenient base for visits to Pemayangtse. You can also visit the **Sanga Choelling Monastery** (circa 1697), possibly the oldest in Sikkim, which has some colourful mural paintings. The hilltop monastery is about 3 km along a fairly steep track through thick woods (about 30 minutes). The area is excellent for walking. The **Sikkim Tourist Centre** ⓘ *Upper Pelling, near Garuda, T03595-250855*, is helpful.

Inner Line Permits (ILPs) are issued to foreigners to enter Sikkim for up to 30 days, with a possible extension of a further 30 days. You can contact an Indian mission abroad when applying for an Indian visa (enclosing two extra photos), but it's easier to apply in India at any **FRO** (Foreigners' Registration Office) or the **Sikkim Tourism Office** in New Delhi, Kolkata, Siliguri or Darjeeling (check www.sikkim.gov.in for office details). The checkpoint at Rangpo, on the border with West Bengal, issues a 30-day permit for foreigners in just 10 minutes, but, if you're entering via Jorethang (for Pelling, Pemayangtse and Yuksom), you'll need to arrange your ILP in advance. The easiest place to do this is at the **Sikkim Tourist Office** in Darjeeling (Main Old Bellevue Hotel, opposite Glenaries, Nehru Road, Mon-Sat 1000-1600) where the processing time is 10 minutes; take one copy of your passport and visa, and one passport photo. The FRO in Darjeeling also issue ILPs but the process is longer and more complicated.

ILPs are extendable at the FRO in Gangtok (Yangthang Building, Kazi Rd, Gangtok, T03592-203041, open daily 1000-1600) or by the Superintendent of Police in Namchi (south) and Geyzing (west). On exiting Sikkim, it is not permitted to return for three months.

Certain areas in north and west Sikkim (Chungthang, Yumthang, Lachen, Chhangu, Dzongri) have been opened to groups of two to 20 travellers, on condition that travel is with a registered agency. The required **Restricted Areas Permits (RAP)** can be arranged by most local travel agents and are valid for five days; apply with photocopies of your passport (Indian visa and personal details pages), ILP and two photos.

PEMAYANGTSE

Just 2 km east of Pelling, the awe-inspiring **monastery of Pemayangtse** (perfect Sublime Lotus) ① *0700-1600, Rs 10, good guided tours, 0700-1000 and 1400-1600 (if closed, ask for key), no photography inside*, was built during the reign of the third Chogyal Chador Namgyal in 1705, making it the second oldest in Sikkim.

For many, the monastery is the highlight of their visit to Sikkim; it certainly has an aura about it. Take an early morning walk to the rear of the monastery to see a breathtaking sunrise in perfect peace. The walls and ceiling of the large *Dukhang* (prayer hall) have numerous *thangkas* and wall paintings, and there is an exceptional collection of religious artworks including an exquisite wooden sculpture on the top floor depicting the heavenly palace of Guru Rimpoche, the *Santhokpalri*, which was believed to have been revealed in a dream. The old stone and wood buildings to the side are the monks' quarters. According to tradition the monks have been recruited from Sikkim's leading families as this is the headquarters of the Nyingmapa sect. Annual *chaam* dances are held in late February and in September.

The **Denjong Padma Choeling Academy** (DPCA), set up to educate needy children, runs several projects, such as crafts and dairy, and welcomes volunteers, who can also learn about Buddhism and local culture. The meditation centre offers courses and can accommodate visitors for a small charge and volunteers for free at the new hostel (see below); a rewarding experience. Volunteer teachers can spend up to six weeks here between March and December. **Rabdanste**, the ruined palace of the 17th- to 18th-century capital of Sikkim, is along the Gezing-bound track from the monastery, 3 km from Pelling. From the main road, turn left just before the white sign 'Gezing 6 km', cross the archery field and turn right behind the hill (road branches off just below Pemanyangtse). Follow the narrow rocky track for 500 m to reach the palace.

KHECHEOPALRI LAKE AND YUKSOM

A road west of the Pelling–Yuksom road leads to this tranquil lake where the clear waters reflect the surrounding densely wooded slopes of the hills with a monastery above; Lepchas believe that birds remove any leaf that floats down. Prayer flags flutter around the lake and it is particularly moving when leaflamps are floated with special prayers at dusk. The sanctity of the lake may be attributed to its shape in the form of a foot (symbolizing the Buddha's footprint), which can be seen from the surrounding hills. The lake itself is not visually astonishing, but walks in the surrounding hills are rewarding and a night or two can easily be spent here. There are staggering views from the tiny hamlet by the *gompa* on the ridge (accessed by the footpath in the car park, just ask for the *gompa*) where homestays are available. The lake can be visited in passing, but, if you are not on a tight schedule, you can trek from Pelling to Yuksom via the lake (without a permit) in two days, a beautiful journey. Or, after spending a night near the lake, put your bags on a public jeep to either Yuksom (to be dropped off at a hotel) and make a one-day trek to catch them up; locals will advise you on the way.

Delightfully scenic little **Yuksom** (Yuksam), 42 km north from Pelling by jeepable road, is where the first Chogyal was crowned in 1641, thus establishing the kingdom of Sikkim. The wooden altar and stone throne stand beside Nabrugang *chorten*, with lovely wall paintings and an enormous prayer wheel, in a beautifully peaceful pine forest. During **Buddha Purnima** (the Buddha's birthday) in late April and May, women from the local community gather mid-morning to sing and pray in a low-key yet moving ceremony. Below Nabrugang, past pretty houses, **Kathok Lake** is a small green pool and the reflection of the prayer flags that surround it are photogenic, and the monastery of the same name nearby is worth the short uphill walk.

Although most people are in Yuksom because it is the starting point for the Gocha La trek, the village makes a quiet and relaxing base for a few days' stay, with several day walks leading out from the centre. It's a 45-minute climb to the attractive **hermit's retreat** at **Dhubdi** (circa 1700) above the village. A rewarding three-hour hike leads to **Hongri Monastery**, about halfway to Tashiding, mainly following a stone trail. Descending the path between the Yangri Gang and Panathang hotels, it is 45 minutes to a wooden bridge over the Phamrong Khola which has deliciously icy pools (accessed from the other side). The trail continues to Tsong village, with a sweet homestay in the first cottage in Lower Tsong (Rs 150 per night, three beds, contact Tara Chetri T(0)9775-816745) and onwards up the steep hill to the plain stone-slab monastery. It's a perfect picnic spot, with stone tables among the mossy *chortens* and glorious views. From here, it is another three to four hours' walk to Tashiding.

SIKKIM LISTINGS

WHERE TO STAY

Pelling
$$$-$$ Norbu Ghang Resort, Main Rd, Upper Pelling, T03595-250566, www.norbughanghotels.com. Cottage rooms with a pretty garden, views from the terrace are superb. Restaurant and bar. The **Norbu Ghang Retreat and Spa**, opened 2012, is adjacent (meals inclusive).

Pemayangtse
$$$$ Elgin Mount Pandim, 15-min walk below monastery, T03593-250756, www. elginhotels.com. Sparkling bright rooms, some with beautiful mountain views, in freshly renovated and upmarket building that once belonged to the Sikkimese royal family. Large grounds, breakfast included.

Yuksom
$$$ Yuksum Residency, Main Rd, T03595-241277, www.yuksumresidency.com. Huge construction rather out of keeping with the village around, white marble predominates and terrace lit-up at night. Rooms are massive and well appointed

(especially the suite with parquet flooring), furnishings high quality rather than rustic, flatscreen TVs, lots of light and some with good views. Giftshop has some nice jewellery, the restaurant is a bit stiff.
$$ Tashigang, T03595-241202, hoteltashigang@rediffmail.com. Intimate rooms with lovely views (some with balcony), wooden floors, striped bedspreads and simple tasteful furnishings. Aging in a good way. Marble and tile bathrooms, some suites, everything clean and polished. Own vegetable patch and restaurant, peaceful garden. Very welcoming and staff are on the ball.
$ Hotel Yangrigang, Main Rd, T03595-241217, yan13jan@yahoo.com. The main backpacker hub, with an acceptable restaurant and internet facilities (Rs 60 per hr) as well as good-standard rooms (doubles Rs 400-500) mostly with twin beds, bigger and better views upstairs (Rs 700-800) with comfy beds. Manager is informative and pleasant. Treks easily arranged from here.

NORTHEAST STATES

The Northeast is a true frontier region. It has more than 2000 km of border with Bhutan, China, Myanmar (Burma) and Bangladesh, and is connected to the rest of India by a narrow 20-km-wide corridor of land, aptly known as the 'chicken neck' by locals. One of the most ethnically and linguistically diverse regions in Asia, the Northeast is made up of seven states, each with its own distinct culture and traditions. Assam, the most densely populated and largest of the states, occupies the scenic lowlands of the Brahmaputra Valley and attracts visitors to some of India's best national parks. Meghalaya's beautiful hills have the dubious distinction of being the wettest region in the world, as well as one of the friendliest. To the north, Arunachal Pradesh, only recently opened to visitors, is home to fascinating tribal culture and the Buddhist enclave of the majestic Tawang Valley – more like Tibet than India. The little-visited southeastern states of the region – Nagaland, Manipur, Mizoram and Tripura – are not included in this guide but make up a remote tribal area that is fascinating to explore if you have sufficient time.

→GUWAHATI AND SOUTHWEST ASSAM

The lush valley of the Brahmaputra, one of the world's great rivers, provides the setting for Assam's culturally rich and diverse communities. Although it is tea that has put the state on the world map, the fertile river valley is home to generations of rice farmers, and tribal populations continue to have a significant presence. Despite its commanding position on the south bank of the mighty Brahmaputra, it is easy to forget that Guwahati is a riverside town, the waterside having little impact on people's lives. The main entrance point for visitors to the northeastern states, the city retains a relaxed and friendly atmosphere. Paltan Bazar, where most visitors arrive, is very busy and crowded as are the narrower streets and markets of Fancy Bazar to the west.

ARRIVING IN GUWAHATI

Getting there **LBG International Airport** (23 km from the city) has flights from Kolkata, Delhi, Bagdogra (one hour) and airports throughout the northeast, plus flights from Bangkok and Bhutan. **Assam State Transport** (**ASTC**) runs an air-conditioned coach to the city for Rs 100 (ticket office near Arrivals); prepaid taxis cost Rs 400 or shared taxis Rs 120. Trains, including the overnight service from NJP, arrive at the **railway station** in the central Paltan Bazar, while long-distance private buses arrive at the **ISBT** (Interstate Bus Terminal), 8 km from the centre, connected to the city centre by canter (red minibus; Rs 10).

Moving on Guwahati is at the junction of NH31, 37 and 40, and is well connected by road to all major centres in the northeast. Frequent buses/jeeps for **Shillong** (see page 269) leave from the bus stand at Paltan Bazar, close to the train station, and take about four hours. You can also hire a private jeep from the bus stand. For information on river cruises, see box, page 268.

Getting around It is easy to walk around the two main commercial areas of Paltan and Pan (pronounced *Paan*) Bazars, which have most of the hotels and restaurants. Citybuses or (red) canters are cheap and very efficient around the city (conductors call out the stops), whereas auto-rickshaws need hard bargaining. Political incidents in the city mean

ON THE ROAD
Permits for travel to the Northeast

Since 1 January 2011, foreigners no longer require a **Restricted Area Permit (RAP)** to visit Nagaland, Manipur and Mizoram, although they will still need to register themselves at the Foreigners Registration Office (FRO) within 24 hours of arrival. Visitors to Assam, Meghalaya and Tripura do not need permits either, but may be asked to register on arrival/departure at the airport. (Indians still require Inner Line Permits (ILPs) from the Ministry of Home Affairs.) A RAP is still required for **Arunachal Pradesh**, as it is a sensitive border region, and for certain parts of **Sikkim** (see page 261). If you're planning to travel into Arunachal Pradesh (on the Tezpur to Tawang route, for example, see page 273), or if the regulations change, you can apply for a RAP in advance from the **Ministry of Home Affairs** (Foreigners' Division, Lok Nayak Bhavan, Khan Market, New Delhi 110003, T011-2461 1430); send two photos and allow up to six weeks. Groups of four and married couples stand a better chance. In Kolkata, RAPs are issued at the **Foreigners Regional Registration Office** (FRRO, 237A AJC Bose Road, T033-2283 7034, Monday-Friday 1100-1630); come between 1100 and 1400 and ask for the Officer in Charge; bring one photo and a copy of your passport and visa. It takes a minimum of 24 hours for permits to be issued, and the cost is at the discretion of the FRRO, which at the time of writing was Rs 1395 per person for each state. If you don't fancy the bureaucratic hassle of applying in person, local travel agents can help. They can obtain permits within a few days and even supply them by fax or email. For Arunachal Pradesh agents can obtain permits for individual travellers at a cost of around US$100 plus commission, valid for up to 30 days.

there is a visible military presence. Carry a torch when walking at night; large holes in the pavement lie in wait to plunge unwary travellers straight down into the sewers.

Tourist information Information booths for Assam, Nagaland and Meghalaya are at the airport, with useful maps; also a counter for Assam at the railway station. **Assam Tourism** ① *Tourist Lodge, Station Rd, T0361-254 7102, www.assamtourism.org, daily 1000-1630.* **Assam Tourism Development Corporation (ASTDC)** ① *AK Azad Rd, Paryatan Bhavan, T0361-263 3654.*

HISTORY

Guwahati, on the site of the ancient capital of a succession of local chieftains, was once known as Pragjyotishpur ('City of Astrology'). The **Navagrah** ('nine planets') **Temple** on a hill here was the ancient centre of astronomy and astrology. It was also a centre of learning and a place of Hindu pilgrimage. In the seventh century, Hiuen Tsang described its beautiful mountains, forests and wildlife. Today it is the business capital of Assam, while **Dispur**, the 'Capital Area', is just to the south.

PLACES IN GUWAHATI

The 10th-century **Janardhan Temple**, on the bank of the Brahmaputra, was rebuilt in the 17th century and has been modernized since. The Buddha image here uniquely blends Hindu and Buddhist features. The **Umananda (Siva) Temple** ① *Peacock Island in the Brahmaputra, reached by 10-min ferry ride, Rs 10, 0930-1630,* was built by an Ahom king in 1594, in the belief that Uma, Siva's consort, had stayed there. Enter the candlelit rear shrine with other pilgrims to receive a blessing. The wooded island can be circled by the footpath and gives pleasant views of the banks. **Assam State Museum** ① *Tue-Sun 1000-1630 (Mar-Sep), 1000-1545 (Oct-Feb), ticket counter closes 1300-1330, closed 2nd and 4th Sat of the month, Rs 5*, has an extensive and beautiful sculpture collection, and covers epigraphy and textiles in recently refurbished galleries. It is also informative on the neighbouring cultures, with sections on village life, crafts and ethnography – a reconstruction of a mud-brick thatched house can be explored. **Assam State Zoo and Botanical Gardens** ① *off Zoo Rd, 6 km southwest of the city, Rs 50, cameras Rs 70*, is a cheap way to get up close to one-horned rhinos, snow leopards, tigers and snakes for those who don't want to take their chances at Kaziranga or other national parks.

Excursions from Guwahati Kamakhya Temple, 7 km west, is believed to be an old Khasi sacrificial site on Nilachal Hill. A centre for Tantric Hinduism and Sakti worship, rebuilt in 1665 after the 10th-century temple was destroyed by a Brahmin convert to Islam. It typifies Assamese temple architecture with its distinctive beehive-shape *sikhara* (spire), the nymph motifs and the long turtleback hall. The dark sanctum contains the creative

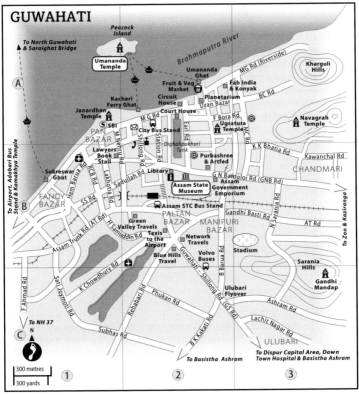

ON THE RIVER
Brahmaputra cruises

Assam is dominated by the mighty and unpredictable Brahmaputra, one of the world's great rivers, and taking a cruise along it is a once-in-a-lifetime experience. There are a couple of companies that have regular trips, but the most well-established is **Assam Bengal Navigation** (www.assambengalnavigation.com), based in Guwahati, who run four-, seven-, 10- and 14-day cruises aboard the charming *RV Charaidew* and *RV Sukapha*, both with 12 en suite cabins, nostalgic saloon bar and quintessential sundeck; *Sukapha* also has a small Ayurvedic spa. Land excursions visit the national parks (including Kaziranga), villages and historical sites and provide opportunities to barbecue on the islands of the mighty river. Cruises along the Hooghly are also available (all year round) for seven or eight nights, between Kolkata and Jangipur. These stop at lesser-visited towns and sights along the river, which are especially atmospheric and perfectly unstressful. The company also runs **Diphlu River Lodge**, a beautiful resort on the edge of Kaziranga National Park (see Where to stay, page 281). Other river cruise companies include **Brahmaputra River Cruises** (www.brahmaputrarivercruises.com).

part of the goddess which is said to have fallen here and pilgrims enter to touch the wet *yoni* of Kamakhya (Sakti). Apart from the carved stone symbol of Sakti's genitals, there are (unusually) no other images of the goddess inside the sanctum. Western visitors are allowed into the sanctum but should be prepared for the highly charged atmosphere and to walk barefoot on a floor awash with the sacrificial blood of a goat. No Bengali would leave Assam without visiting this temple, hence queues can be immense (a donation to the priests of Rs 500 will grant instant access, or go at dawn to be first in line).

Further up the hill is a smaller temple and a viewpoint with panoramic views of the Brahmaputra. It can be visited by bus from MG Road (towards Adabari Bus Stand); ask to be dropped near Kamakhya. From here take a canter from AT Road to the temple or walk up the steep and slippery rocky path at the back of the hill. An intense and memorable outing.

→MEGHALAYA

Meghalaya ('abode of the clouds'), with its pine-clad hills, beautiful lakes, high waterfalls and huge caverns, has been tagged the 'Scotland of the East' because of the similarity of climate, terrain and scenery. This is the wettest region in the world: between May and September the rain comes down like waterfalls as the warm monsoon air is forced up over the hills. Home to the Garo, Khasi and Jaintia tribes, the hill state retains an untouched feel. There are traditional Khasi villages near Shillong with views into Bangladesh.

People Meghalaya is divided into three distinct areas, the Garo, Khasi and Jaintia Hills, each with its own language, culture and particular customs. All three tribes are matrilineal, passing down wealth and property through the female line, with the youngest daughter taking responsibility for caring for the parents. The greeting 'kublei' covers 'hello' and 'goodbye', while 'kublei shibun' means 'thank you very much'. The Khasi, Jaintia and Garo tribes each had their own small kingdoms until the 19th century when the British annexed them. The Garos, originally from Tibet, were animists. The Khasis are believed to be Austro-Asiatic. Jaintias are Mongolian and similar to the Shans of Burma. They believed in the universal presence of god and so built no temples. The dead were commemorated by erecting monoliths and groups of these can be seen in Khasi villages in central Meghalaya between Shillong and Cherrapunji. In the 19th century many Jaintias and Khasi were converted to Christianity by missionaries, although they continued many of their old traditions.

→SHILLONG

Situated among pine-clad hills and lakes, Shillong retains a measure of its colonial past particularly around Ward's Lake and in the quieter suburbs. Elsewhere in town, unattractive newer buildings have encroached upon open spaces, and Shillong's trade-mark mists are being replaced by smog. Since the days of the British, Shillong has been an educational hub and school children (often boarders from other northeastern states) are ever-present. A major attraction is the biggest market in the Northeast, while the daily betting on the archery competition (see box, page 271) is a unique feature.

ARRIVING IN SHILLONG

Getting there Buses or jeeps from Guwahati (four hours) drop off in the centre of Shillong, from where it's walkable to budget hotels, or you can get private transport to more distant hotels.

Moving on Private taxis can take you to **Cherrapunji** (see page 271), or shared jeeps leave from Mowlang Hat jeep stand when full. The journey takes 1½ hours to Cherrapunji (Sohra) town from where a taxi can take you on to your hotel.

Tourist information Information and a free map is available from **India Tourism** ① *GS Rd, Police Bazar, T0364-222 5632, Mon-Fri 0930-1730, Sat 0930-1400.* **Meghalaya Tourism** ① *opposite Meghalaya Bus Stand, Jail Rd, T0364-222 6220, www.meghalayatourism. com, daily 0700-1900,* have cheap day-tours around Shillong and further afield. **Directorate of Tourism** ① *Nokrek Building, 3rd Meghalaya Secretariat, Lower Lachaumiere, T0364-250 0736, www.megtourism.gov.in, 0700-1800.*

PLACES IN SHILLONG

The horseshoe-shaped **Ward's Lake** ① *Rs 5, camera Rs 10, Wed-Mon 0830-1800 (winter 0830-1630),* is pretty and popular for boating. Behind it is the **Botanical Garden** ① *0900-1700.* Other colonial remnants include the immaculate little Presbyterian and All Saints churches.

The Northeast's largest market, **Bara Bazar** ('BB' or *lewduh*) is well worth a visit to see authentic local colour. It attracts tribal people, mainly women, who come to buy and sell produce – mountains of vegetables, spices, giant fish, pots, chickens in baskets and even bows and arrows. Porters scurry up and down the tiny alleys with crazy loads on their backs; look out *jadoh* stalls where you can sample Khasi food.

The **Wankhar Museum of Entomology** ① *T0364-254 4473, Rs 100, Mon-Sat 1100-1600, photos Rs 10 per shot,* is in a private house between Police Bazar and Wahingdoh, where beautiful butterflies, moths, beetles, spiders and stick insects are pinned out in a colourful one-room display. The seven-storeyed **Don Bosco Museum** ① *T0364-255 0260, www.dbcic.org, Mon-Sat 0900-1730 (summer), 0900-1630 (winter), Rs 150, photos Rs 100 per shot, leave bags in the cloakroom,* showcases the history and culture of the seven sister states of the Northeast. Computers in each room give in-depth information, as do display boards. A 'sky-walk' up the pointed roof gives 360-degree views of Shillong. It is an excellently presented museum, and even the two galleries on Christianity and religion are surprisingly interesting. The museum is in Mawlai, a pleasant 20-minute walk from the Butterfly Museum or accessible by shared taxi. The **Rhino Memorial Museum** ① *Hospital Rd, 0900-1300 and 1400-1800, entrance free*, in a striking building, has a tribal collection with a bizarre mix of military paraphernalia.

Just over 1 km away from Police Bazar is Lady Hydari Park ① *0800-1630, Rs 5, camera Rs 10, video Rs 1000*, designed like a Japanese garden, where the pine native to the area – *Pinus khasiana* – thrives amongst English flowerbeds. It is well laid out with a tiny **Forest Wildlife Museum** (displaying the world's most threadbare clouded leopard) and a **Mini Zoo** with living leopards, bears, deer, monkeys and birds.

On the north side of town is the 18-hole golf course, amid pines, dating from 1898 and ideal for an early-morning walk. To the south, the **Crinoline Waterfalls** has a swimming pool surrounded by orchids, potted bonsais and a rock pool with reeds and water lilies. Further south at Lumparing, Laban, the Buddhist **Lamasery** is interesting, but be prepared for a steep climb.

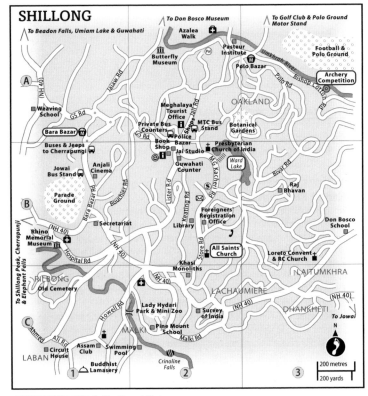

ON THE ROAD
The Archery Stakes

The Archery Stakes, unique to Shillong, take place Monday to Saturday. Members of different clubs shoot more than 500 arrows at a tiny cylindrical bamboo target for four minutes. The punters predict the number that will stay in the target, and anyone who has guessed the last two digits of the total of arrows stuck is rewarded with an 80:1 win. A second shoot takes place an hour later when the odds are 6:1 but if you correctly forecast both results the odds are as high as 4500:1. Naturally, the bookies are the best-dressed men in town. Start times of the event vary but it's usually around 1530-1600 (ask locally in the morning), and to find the (inconspicuous) field, go to Polo Bazar (just past the Polo Towers Hotel) and ask someone. Shared taxis go from the bazar for Rs 5, or you can walk the 1.5 km along the south side of the river to the archery ground. There are bookies' shops all over town and elsewhere in the state; bets are even placed as far off as Kolkata and Mumbai. The Stakes were legalized in 1983 when the state government realized that it could raise a hefty 40% tax on the daily money-spinner.

AROUND SHILLONG

Shillong Peak (10 km, 1960 m) is 3 km off the Cherrapunji Road (motorable, save for the last short walk), commanding spectacular views. **Elephant Falls** (12 km), off the Cherrapunji Road, is a picturesque spot with two high waterfalls. You can walk down to the lowest pool and get a good view, though the falls themselves are less impressive between November and May. The artificial **Umiam Lake** (Barapani), 20 km, offers fishing, boating and watersports from the Orchid Lake Resort.

→CHERRAPUNJI

The old administrative headquarters of the Khasis, picturesque Cherrapunji (also known as Shora, the official government name) is a pleasant, quiet town spread out along a ridge with gravestones dotting the surrounding hillocks. The best time to visit for spectacular views is during the drier months of November to February. The heat and humidity can be oppressive in the summer. By mid-March it is hazy most days and you should expect the odd torrential downpour. It holds the record as the wettest place on earth, with an average of 11,900 mm rainfall annually.

The colourful **Ka Iewbah Sohrarim** (market) is held every eight days in Cherra Bazar and attracts hordes of Khasi tribespeople. There is also a smaller *Iewrit* (market) every fourth day. Khasi women all wear a checked apron tied over one shoulder, and both sexes wrap up in Welsh plaid blankets against the cold. The local orange flower honey is sold during the winter season, along with sacks of betel nuts (*kwai*), gruesome chunks of meat, and anything else you care to imagine. Little food stalls are a good place to sample Khasi food. If possible, time your visit to Cherrapunji to coincide with a market day (see www. cherrapunji.com for dates). If the market is due to fall on a Sunday, the date is moved to the preceding Saturday as most people observe the Christian day of rest.

Nohkalikai Falls, reputedly the world's fourth highest, is 5 km west of Cherrapunji, near Sohrarim. There is always a significant flow of water, while multiple torrents are seen during the rainy season. Limestone caves nearby include Krem Mawmluh (4503 m) with a five river passage and Krem Phyllut (1003 m) at **Mawsmai**, with a large fossil passage and two stream ways. Mawsmai also has high waterfalls in the wet season.

The most astonishing sight around Cherrapunji – and a must-see of the Northeast region – is the series of **living root bridges** found near Mawshamok. Here, Khasi tribespeople have trained the roots of the *ficus elastica* rubber tree into robust bridges, spanning streams that become raging torrents in the monsoon. It takes 15 to 20 years for the bridges to become strong enough to support the crossing of people and goods between the villages, but they last for several centuries (possibly up to 800 years) – getting sturdier as they age. There is an excellent eco-friendly resort (see Where to stay, page 281) that can provide sketch maps for the challenging treks to the bridges. From the resort, there is a very steep 45-minute descent to the tangled mass of **Ummunoi** 'single' root-bridge, which is well worth the effort and pain of the ascent back up. Or it is possible to make a day-trek to the extraordinary **Umshiang 'double-decker'** model ⓘ *camera Rs 10, video Rs 50*, in Nongriat village, from where it is a short walk to icy turquoise pools. This trek involves descending 3000 steps through the dense jungle, past pretty hamlets and several other root-bridges, with plenty of ups and well as downs. An overnight stay at **Nongriat** is highly recommended if you don't mind roughing it.

→KAZIRANGA NATIONAL PARK

Kaziranga was declared a game sanctuary in 1916 to save the Indian greater one-horned rhino and became a national park in 1974. It is now a World Heritage Site. In a beautiful setting on the banks of the Brahmaputra, and with the Karbi Anglong Hills to the south, the 430-sq-km park combines elephant grass mixed with thorny rattan cane, areas of semi-evergreen forest and shallow swamps.

ARRIVING IN KAZIRANGA NATIONAL PARK
Getting there To get here from Cherrapunji, you'll have to return to Guwahati (five to six hours), then catch a bus to Kohora (215 km, four hours), near the main entrance for the park on the NH37. It's preferable (budget permitting) to get a private vehicle to collect you in Guwahati and take you directly to your park hotel.

Moving on Buses from Guwahati pick up at Kohora on the edge of Kaziranga National Park en route to **Jorhat** (two hours, see page 277) and Dibrugarh (five to six hours, via Sibsagar, see pages 279 and 277), although they may be crowded. A private vehicle can be arranged through most hotels and may be the better option.

Getting around Entry into the park is by private vehicle, hired jeep or trained elephants. Although elephants cover less ground than motor vehicles, they can get a lot closer to the wildlife, particularly rhinos and buffalo. **Elephant rides** ⓘ *book the night before through the Forest Range Officer, foreigners Rs 1000, Indians Rs 120, plus jeep transfer from town, Rs 150*, carry four people and get mixed reports; the consensus seems to be that they are less enjoyable when demand is heavy. The viewing posts just inside the park may offer quieter viewing. **Jeeps** for five or six people can be hired from the **Department of Tourism** in Kaziranga or private agents. Government jeeps cost Rs 700 (Rs 120 per person in a shared vehicle) for three hours; private ones Rs 1000-1200 for 50 km or 2½ hours. A car or jeep

GOING FURTHER
Tezpur to Tawang

Before heading east to Kaziranga, those who are not tied to a limited schedule could head north from Guwahati to **Tezpur** to make the memorable journey to **Tawang** in Arunachal Pradesh. The whole route is spectacular, passing waterfalls, terraced paddy fields, alpine forest and mountain streams. The road north crosses the border at Bhalukpon and continues towards Bomdila and Dirang, before entering the Tawang Valley. Note that for travel to Arunachal Pradesh, visitors must obtain a Restricted Area Permit (RAP); see box, page 266, for details.

ARRIVING IN TEZPUR
Getting there **Saloni Airport**, just to the north of Tezpur, has flights to/from Kolkata. Tezpur is served by frequent buses from Guwahati (180 km; five hours) and other cities in Assam.

Moving on For those not travelling with a hired jeep, **ASTC** and several private companies with offices near the bus stand run buses and Sumos to Tawang and destinations in between. Sumos are the preferable option (though more expensive) as they are significantly quicker and better suited to the narrow, terrifying roads. The whole journey takes a gruelling 12-14 hours (better to do this on the way back!). On the way to Tawang, break the journey at Bomdila or Dirang, and try to book onward Sumo tickets in advance; ask for 'number 1 seat' for the best views and comfort. Returning from Tawang, again, the best seats are reserved days in advance, so do some forward planning. Check travel conditions locally (Sela Pass is frequently closed by snow), and, if you're in a private vehicle, don't travel after dark as visibility is very poor. Once you have returned to Tezpur, you can rejoin the main itinerary by catching one of the frequent buses to Kaziranga (two hours; see opposite).

Tourist information The Tourist Lodge ① *Jenkins Rd, Tezpur, T03712-221016, Mon-Sat 1000-1615; closed every 2nd and 4th Sat of the month*, has a brochure and can sketch out a map of town.

PLACES IN TEZPUR
Tezpur, on the north bank of the Brahmaputra, 180 km northeast of Guwahati, is the site of Assam's first tea plantations. The town's ancient origins can be seen at **Da Parbatia**, 5 km west, which has the entrance gate of an early Gupta-style temple. In Tezpur's centre, **Chitralekha Udyan** (Cole Park) ① *Rs 10, camera Rs 20, boat Rs 10, 0900-2000*, was created after an earthquake revealed ancient remains and is now a pleasant park around a lake; some of the slabs of friezes and sculpture unearthed are on display outside the **museum** ① *at the Dak Bungalow, near the Tourist Lodge*. The **Station Club**, opposite the District Commissioner's office, is one of Assam's oldest planters' clubs dating from 1875, with period furniture and a bar worthy of a drink if you can find a member to invite you. Otherwise they are happy to let you look around. A nice spot for sunset is **Agrigarh** ① *Rs 10, 0800-1930*, a 1-km stroll past Ganesh Ghat, with hilltop views over the Brahmaputra and the town; climb the lookout tower to catch the breeze. Possibly the largest Siva linga in India is found inside **Mahabhairab Mandir**, a Rs 15 rickshaw ride from the centre, which has a nightly *puja* at around 1830.

An interesting excursion is to take a Guwahati-bound bus, get off at the bridge over the Brahmaputra, then negotiate with a boatman to take you to the river's confluence with the Bhoreli for some river **dolphin watching**. Some hotels offer such trips.

TEZPUR TO BHALUKPONG

Nameri National Park ① *35 km north of Tezpur, on the Arunachal border, entry and camera fees are similar to Kaziranga*, is on the river Jia Bhoroli and covers 210 sq km. It is home to tigers (26 in 2006), elephants, Indian bison, barking and hog deer, Himalayan black bears as well as 300 bird species, including the shy and endangered white-winged wood ducks. Flora includes evergreens, bamboo and some open grassland. Buses/Sumos travelling between Tezpur and Tawang can drop travellers off at Hatigate on the main road. From here, it is 2.5 km down a track to the **Eco Camp**, a wonderful overnight stop and good place to arrange visits to the park.

Bhalukpong, 20 km west of Nameri, is on the Assam-Arunachal border; be prepared to show your RAP here (see above). This nondescript village is surrounded by the forests of **Pakhui Game Sanctuary**, a mass of ferns, moss and orchids, with a hot spring, orchid garden and good fishing. You can camp (take your own tent) on the picturesque bank of the River Jia Bhoreli or stay in the government tourist cottages overlooking the river. Jeeps and buses from Tezpur all pass through Bhalukpong en route to Tawang.

BOMDILA

Between Bhalukpong and Bomdila is the Orchid Research Centre at Tipi, with 500 species of orchid in its glasshouse. On a clear day, Bomdila has marvellous views of the snow-capped mountains. There's a craft centre, apple and cherry orchards, three Buddhist *gompas* and a museum. Transport links are good, there is internet connection and hotels are generally more comfortable than those in Dirang, but it is a sprawling rather unattractive place. Buses leave from the bus stand in the lower part of town and Sumos from the main bazar, 2 km up the hill and therefore more convenient for hotels. **Himalayan Holiday** in the market has some basic tourist information.

DIRANG

About an hour's drive after Bomdila, the road cuts through the miniature village of Old Dirang and continues another 5 km to larger (newer) Dirang, which has a few guesthouses and simple places to eat. It is a more appealing stop than Bomdila when breaking the journey to Tawang, though make sure you book an onward ticket in advance. The obvious attraction is the old village, huddled around the confluence of two rivers, where a population of some 1200 Monpa tribespeople inhabit traditional stone dwellings with slatted wooden upper levels and woven roofs. One of the morning Sumos to Bomdila can drop you off at the ancient three-storey **Khatsikpa Gompa** atop a small ridge, from where it's a steep walk past *stupas* and *mani* walls down to the village. It's an easy walk back to New Dirang following the road along the river, criss-crossing a couple of bridges on the way.

TO TAWANG

After passing through the pretty Dirang Valley shrouded in pine woods, the route snakes past lonely army camps and teetering villages to the **Sela Pass** which at 4215 m presents a far starker view. Stop a while here above the clouds, along one of the highest motorable roads in the world, with views of a high-altitude lake and graphite peaks streaked with snow. **Jaswantpur**, 13 km from the pass, has the a memorial to the brave Jawan (soldier),

Jaswant Singh, his fiancé and her friend, who valiantly held up the advancing Chinese army in 1962 for three days before laying down their lives.

The road then descends alongside a river before emerging on the edge of Tawang Valley, where the folded foothills are of an unimaginable scale, plunging and twisting towards Tibet. Numerous tiny hamlets and golden *gompas* speckle the near-vertical slopes opposite the improbably large village of **Jang**, 42 km before Tawang. Houses here are checkerboard Assamese-style or Monpa cubes, and many older Monpa wear a densely woven black yak-wool skullcap, the tentacles of which channel rainwater away from the wearer's face. After crossing the river, the old village of **Lhou** is especially atmospheric (worth a visit if using private transport) before the final 18 km to Tawang township.

TAWANG

Although set in breathtakingly dramatic scenery at 3500 m, the town of Tawang itself is not immediately attractive. The prayer wheels in the Old Market square, overlooked by a mini *gompa* and flower-laden balconies, have charm and two Tibetan-style gates are beautifully maintained. Most people are here to see the **monastery**, birthplace of the sixth Dalai Lama, and the second largest Buddhist monastery in the world (after Lhasa). Dating originally from 1681, it houses around 450 *lamas* belonging to the Gelugpa (Reformed) Sect of Mahayana Buddhist monks. Buddhism arrived in the area with Padmasambhava in the eighth century but the local Monpas were converted to the Tantric Buddhist cult only after the establishment of the monastery here by Merag Lama in the 17th century. During renovations in the 1990s, the main building was completely rebuilt. The lofty prayer hall, containing a 5.5-m-high golden Buddha heaped with silky prayer scarves, sees monks gather at 0500 and again at 0715 for worship (observers welcome) after which the young trainees go to the monastic school next door. It generally takes 15-20 years for the *lamas* to complete their doctorates in Buddhist philosophy, though the current Dalai Lama was just 25 when he finished. The **museum** ① *opened on request, Rs 20, cameras Rs 20*, contains a wealth of treasures, including 700-year-old sculptures, numerous *thangkas* and priceless manuscripts.

Exiting via the south gate of the monastery complex takes you down a grassy ridge, strung with small *chortens* and *mani* walls, for some excellent views. Visible on a ridge northeast from the monastery is the **Gyangong Ani Gompa**, home to some three dozen nuns who are studying there, a 1½-hour (5-km) walk down and up a steep ravine (only advisable in dry weather).

AROUND TAWANG

Just above Tawang monastery is the **Lake District**, an exceptionally beautiful area with many high-altitude lakes, including the tranquil Sangeshar Lake where a dance sequence from the film *Koyla* was shot. After a fork and an army outpost, the road continues towards **Klemta**, just a few kilometres from the border. There are a few scattered monasteries and a shrine to all faiths at the spot where Guru Nanak rested as he trekked into Tibet, 500 years ago. To explore this area you'll have to hire a jeep and guide, carry snacks and drinks, and be prepared for steep, treacherous mountain roads. It is all worth it for the breathtaking mountain scenery.

Gorsam Chorten, an immense 12th century stupa is 100 km from Tawang, near Jimithang, where there are some simple places to stay. The setting is amazing, and the road little travelled by foreigners. A few public Sumos run to the village each week, taking two to three hours; book ahead with an agent in Tawang or hire a vehicle.

must be accompanied by a Forest Department Guard (Rs 50), who can give directions as well as spot wildlife. Cars and jeeps pay a road toll, Rs 150.

There are four road routes for visiting the park: the **Central Range** (Kohora, Daflang, Foliomari) is the most visited as it is full of big mammals; the **Western Range** (Baguri, Monabeel, Bimoli, Kanchanjuri) has the highest rhinoceros density but tall elephant grass makes visibility difficult; the **Eastern Range** (Agortoli, Sohola, Rangamatia) has good possibilities for seeing wildlife, but at a distance; the **Burhapahar Range**, furthest west, only became accessible relatively recently, and jeep safaris here are more expensive. Keep receipts as fees are valid for several trips in one day.

Tourist information Park roads are open 0730-1100, 1400-1630. Foreigners Rs 250. Camera fees change regularly: currently Rs 50, video, Rs 500. There's a 25% discount on fees after three consecutive days.

Best time to visit The best months to visit are November, and February-March before it gets too hot (December and January are best for birds, but is also peak tourist season). The park is closed from 30 April to 1 November each year, during monsoons. Wear cotton clothing but take a jacket. Summer maximum: 35°C, minimum: 18°C; winter maximum: 24°C, minimum: 7°C; annual rainfall 2300 mm, heavy in summer.

WILDLIFE

The **rhino** population is over 2000 here, and they are easily seen in the marshes and grasslands. Despite Kaziranga's status as a national park, poachers still manage to kill the animal for its horn, which is used in Chinese and Tibetan medicine. The park also has over 1000 wild buffalo, sambar, swamp deer (over 500), hog deer, wild pig, hoolock gibbon, elephant (1246 in 2004), python and tiger (89 at last count in 2000), the only predator of the one-horned rhino. There is a rich variety of shallow-water fowl, including egrets, pond herons, river terns, black-necked stork, fishing eagles and adjutant storks, pelicans and the rare Bengal florican. There are otters and dolphins in the river.

Panbari Forest Reserve, 12 km from Kaziranga, has hoolock gibbons and a good variety of birdlife. Contact the Forest Office in Guwahati, for permission to visit.

→NORTHEAST ASSAM

ARRIVING IN NORTHEAST ASSAM

Getting there Jorhat airport (7 km outside town) and Dibrugarh airport (16 km outside town) both have flights to/from Kolkata and Guwahati daily. Buses from Guwahati pick up at Kohora on the edge of Kaziranga National Park en route to Jorhat (two hours) and Dibrugarh (five or six hours, via Sibsagar), although they may be crowded. A private vehicle can be arranged through most hotels and is the better option.

Moving on ASTC buses run frequently between Jorhat, **Sibsagar** and **Dibrugarh** (see pages 277 and 279). To return to Kolkata, take one of the regular flights from Jorhat or Dibrugarh airports.

ON THE ROAD
Plantation labour

Today Assam produces about 55% of India's tea. With small tea growers on the rise as well as traditional large plantations, there are now around 800 tea estates. Old colonial tea planters' bungalows surrounded by neat rows of emerald green tea bushes are sprinkled throughout the landscape, particularly in Upper Assam. After an early experiment using imported Chinese labourers ended in near mutiny, the British began the mass recruitment of Adivasis from the Chota Nagpur Plateau, Andhra Pradesh and Orissa. They have been assimilated into Assamese society but are recognized as a separate 'tea tribe', with a language, customs and dances that remain unique. One of the largest groups of organized labour in India today, they enjoy benefits undreamed of by other workers, including free health care, education and subsidized food. The lifestyle of the plantation, hardly changed since the Raj, has been tarnished by the rise of insurgency, with isolated tea companies being targeted for extortion to fund militant groups, and by labour disputes between workers and managers.

JORHAT

Jorhat is one of Assam's major tea centres with a **Tea Festival** held in November. It's a relatively orderly town with good facilities but there are no historical sites nearby – most people only stop here because it is convenient for visiting **Majuli Island** to the north (one of the largest river islands in the world, accessed by ferry from Jorhat), or en route to a tea plantation bungalow (see Where to stay, page 281). The main commercial street, Gar-Ali, runs south for about 1 km from the railway station, down to AT Road where the bus stands are located to the west. Parallel to Gar-Ali (one block west) is MG Road, where you will find the helpful **Assam Tourism Office** ① *T0376-232 1579, Mon-Sat 1000-1700 in summer, 1000-1615 in winter*, some cheap lodges and a miniature one-room **museum** ① *inside the Post Graduate Training College, Mon-Sat 0930-1700, free*, displaying Ahom artefacts and curvaceous Krishnas minus his flute. During February (check dates with tourist office), horse races are held at the 1876 **Gymkhana Club** ① *Club Rd North, T0376-221 1303, office open 0800-1600*, where there is also an 18-hole golf course, tennis, billiards and a bar with ancient staff, piano and pictures of England.

SIBSAGAR AND AROUND

District headquarters of the largest tea and oil producing area in the Northeast, **Sibsagar** was the Ahom capital for two centuries. The Ahoms arrived from southern China in 1228 and set up their first capital at Charaideo, 28 km from present-day Sibsagar, in 1253. Initially they were Buddhists, though Hinduism came to prevail. Daupadi (the Ahom King's wife) built the huge tank in the centre of town and the three temples on its bank in 1734. The central tower of the Siva Dol is one of the tallest in India, while the interior has an inverted lingum. It is a fascinating place to witness **Sivaratri** (celebrated in early March). On the east bank there is a small Buddhist Temple and a birdwatching tower, while on the west bank is the square red-brick **Tai Museum** ① *Fri-Wed 1000-1600, Rs 5*. Ahom artefacts are displayed, including two wooden dragons found at Charaideo, brass pots and plates, silks, combs, basketry, ancient manuscripts and two *dolas* with wooden basins in which the women sat to be carried around.

All the sites around Sibsagar are open sunrise-sunset and charge foreigners a Rs 100 entrance fee. The **Joysagar Tank** at **Rangpur**, 5 km away, and the three temples on its bank date from 1697. The main Joydol (Vishnu temple) sits in pretty gardens; its exterior still has the original decorative terracotta tiles. The Shivadol and Devidol temples are less impressive, but free to enter. **Talatal Ghar**, 4 km from Sibsagar, is a large two-storey palace which is being restored. Nearby, the two-storeyed oval **Rang Ghar** was the royal sports pavilion where elephant fights and games took place – said to be the oldest amphitheatre in Asia. Take a Tata Magic from AT or BG Rd (Rs 10, 20 minutes) to Joysagar, from where you can walk back in the direction of Sibsagar to visit Talatal Ghar and Rang Ghar (1.5 km away).

Gaurisagar, 12 km along the road to Jorhat, also has three temples and a tank dating from the time of Queen Phulesari (1722-1791). Striking **Karen Ghar**, 8 km east along the road to Sonari, was built in 1752 by King Rudra Singha and is a seven-storeyed palace, three floors of which are underground. Less impressive **Charaideo** 28 km east, was the original capital of the Ahoms, where the royals were buried in *maidams* (vaults covered by soil and bricks) along with their personal effects.

MAJULI ISLAND

Majuli Island is one of the largest river islands in the world, though constantly changing, and currently around 650 sq km. The flooding of the Brahmaputra River means that at times Majuli is reduced to a cluster of islands, some as small as a hut top. Roads keep shifting but villagers adapt to re-routing by building cost-effective bamboo bridges. Cut off from the mainland to the south about 400 years ago, it is served by ferries from Jorhat, but it can still be accessed from North Lakhimpur by road (with two ferry crossings, six hours) during summer. The island is essentially a flat expanse of paddy fields and sky with very little motorized traffic, making it a peaceful place for cycling or exploring **Mishing villages** (where homes are built on stilts, not only to avoid flood-risk but also because it is believed to be more hygienic).

On the first Wednesday of the month **Gimnur Polo** (in February-March), the colourful Mishing festival of Ali-Ai-Lvigang is celebrated. See www.majulitourism.com, or contact Majuli's tourism officer (Jyoti Narayan Sarma, T(0)9435-657282) for festival dates. Majuli is also a birdwatchers' paradise.

At the forefront of Assamese Vaishnava culture, the island is an important centre for arts, crafts and science. Work is in progress to declare it a World Heritage Site. The *satras* (monasteries) here, inspired by the 15th-century saint Sankardeva and his disciple Madhavdeva, are worth visiting – particularly those to the east of Kamalabari. They are essentially small, self-sufficient villages where Vishnu is worshipped through regular performances of dance dramas at the temples. Out of 64 *satras*, 22 remain, the others have fallen victim to erosion by the Brahmaputra. A useful sketch map showing the location of the *satras* is available from La Masion de Ananda.

Satras in and around **Kamalabari** and **Garamur** can be visited on foot, but others require a bicycle or rickshaw. **Auniati**, 5 km west of Kamalabari, is home to 450 monks and has a little museum with old manuscripts, utensils, jewellery and silver of the Ahom kings (entrance Rs 50). **Bengenatti**, east of Uttar Kamalabari, is a centre for performing arts and tribal dance forms. Others worth visiting are **Nauten Kamalabari** and **Dekhinpat**. Colourful traditional masks are still made at **Natun Chamaguri**, 12 km east of Kamalabari, and a visit is recommended.

DIBRUGARH

Much of the town of Dibrugarh was destroyed during the 1950 earthquake, only a few old buildings remain on the main streets. The new town on the Brahmaputra is surrounded by tea estates, where a couple of delightful old tea-planters bungalows are available for guests to soak up some Raj nostalgia (see Where to stay, page 281). Dibrugarh is a convenient stop when setting off for (or returning from) eastern and central Arunachal Pradesh as transport connections are good and hotels are comfortable.

NORTHEAST STATES LISTINGS

WHERE TO STAY

Guwahati

$$$ Brahmaputra Ashok, MG Rd, T0361-260 2281, www.hotelbrahmaputraashok.com. Standard rooms are old style but with wooden floors and decent shower rooms (riverside ones with nice views), central a/c, TV, bamboo and cane furniture, restaurant, travel agency, Wi-Fi. The **Kaziranga** bar, with its zebra print furniture, is fun and there's Silver Streak disco on Sat nights.

$$ Baruah Bhavan, T(0)9954-024165, www.heritagehomeassam.com. An Assamese mansion over 100 years old with 6 luxurious rooms, modern amenities and a charming roof terrace. Home-cooking (Assamese, Indian, Chinese, reasonably priced), breakfast included, internet, transport can be arranged. A short walk from the riverside.

$ Prashaanti Tourist Lodge (Assam Tourism), Station Rd, close to railway station, T0361-254 4475, astdcorpn@sancarnet.in. Decent-sized rooms with nets, bathroom and balcony, clean sheets and TV. Good restaurant and upstairs bar, tourist information (1000-1700). Great value for non-a/c doubles but single rooms cost almost as much. Book in advance, they are often full.

Shillong

$$$$-$$ Lakkhotaa Lodge, Mawpun, Polo Hills, T0364-259 0523/4, www.lakkhotaalodge.com. A modern palace with 9 handcrafted rooms that are truly sumptuous. Run by a Jaintia/American couple who have paid every attention to guests comfort, melding Feng Shui elements with art from all over the world: Italian marble floors, a Gujarati marriage 'mandap', Moghul tiles, Uzebek tables and Cherokee designs. Each room is unique with marble bathroom and views over pine trees or the golf course. Excellent and varied cuisine, gift shop, fitness room. A single starts from Rs 6000, doubles from Rs 8000, up to a presidential suite at Rs 16,000 (plus tax). A bunk-bed room sleeping 2, Rs 1500 per person plus tax, gives budget travellers the chance to enjoy billiards, a glorious bar and luxurious seating areas (inside and out). Golf can be arranged.

$$$ Tripura Castle, Cleve Colony, T0364-250 1111, www.tripuracastle.com. The first heritage hotel in the northeast, with 10 art deco-style rooms with brass fireplaces, polished wood and heaps of class. The tea lounge, billiards and atmospheric bar all add to its charm, and there's a good new restaurant/café. With 24 hrs' notice they can prepare top-notch Khasi food. It was once the summer residence of the maharajahs of Tripura.

$$ Ken & Twill's, Law-U-Sib, Lumbatngen, Madanriting, T(0)9856-030474, www.saimikapark.com. Well away from the city centre in amongst pine trees, this homely house with 5 rooms is named after the lovely owner's parents. Plenty of character with wooden floors, Cherrapunji stone walls, open-plan lounge/ dining room with fireplace, quilts in the bedrooms plus fridge and TV; it encourages a long stay. Mrs Phanbuh also has a place in Cherrapunji.

$$ Pinewood, Rita Rd, behind Ward's Lake, T0364-222 3146, www.meghalayatourism.org. An atmospheric Raj relic, however lurking behind the nostalgic colonial bungalow is a monstrous new plate-glass 'annex' with 75 rooms due to open soon. The 40 original rooms vary according to price, standard ones are old-fashioned (needing a coat of paint) but charming in their way with working fireplaces (single/double Rs 1600/2200), also **$$$** cottages, and dorm (Rs 150). Restaurant with good menu, nice bar, billiards, gym, free Wi-Fi.

$$-$ Earle Holiday Home, Oakland Rd, T0364-222 6614, T(0)9863-118214. Rooms in the old cottages are about the cheapest you'll find, spartan and faded but clean with squat loos and geysers, it's a good idea to book ahead. The original turreted bungalow has larger semi-delux rooms while the annex (being extended) has more comfortable rooms in a range of categories. The Dhaba restaurant is one of the nicest places to eat in Shillong.

Cherrapunji
$$-$ Cherrapunji Holiday Resort, Laitkynsew village, T03637-244 218/9, T(0)9436-115925, www.cherrapunji.com. Lovely hosts and an idyllic setting make this resort particularly enchanting. Double tents (only available in high season), or spacious rooms with comfy beds and nice bathrooms, plus an excellent restaurant. Plenty of help is given to lone trekkers, sketch maps of the area are provided, experienced guides lead river canyoning expeditions (best Oct-Feb), there's free Wi-Fi and good look-out points nearby. At a lower altitude than Cherrapunji town (920 m), it feels significantly warmer. Highly recommended.

Kaziranga National Park
$$$$ Diphlu River Lodge, 15 km west of Kohora, T0361-260 2223, www.diphlu riverlodge.com. Utterly chic luxury with a rustic slant, 12 Mishing-style huts, connected by bamboo walkway, surround rice paddies with a prime location on the edge of the national park. Rooms are furnished in a colonial theme from natural materials, bathrooms are inspired, 2 verandas for lounging, and the staff all faultless. Once inside the peaceful enclave everything is included in the price (apart from alcohol) – limitless visits to Kaziranga, walks with naturalists, picnics, meals, visits to Mishing villages. Come here for peace and serenity.

$$ Wild Grass, 1.5 km from NH37, 5.5 km from Kohora, ask for Kaziranga IB Bus Stop, 400 m north of resort, T03776-262085, T(0)9954-416945, www.oldassam.com. Unpretentious and relaxing, with a lovely location, 18 spotless rooms in 2 lofty chalets, wooden floors, cane furniture, can get very cold in winter. Great meals (Rs 450 for 2 people) and service, beautiful walks through forests and tea plantations, excellent guided tours, pickup from Guwahati for groups, cultural shows in the evenings by the campfire of Assamese dancing. Half price May-Oct.

Jorhat
$$$ Kaziranga Golf Resort, Sangsua & Gatoonga Tea Estates, T033-2229 9034, www.kazirangagolfresort.com. This charming golf resort has new cottages attached to the old clubhouse, and further accommodation in the **Banyan Grove** planter's bungalow 15 mins away (previously known as Mistry Sahib's Bungalow). Refurbishment has mingled gloriously period furniture with modern features, and the wide verandas and strolls through the plantations are nostalgic pleasures. The joy of these 2 places is in their location deep in the heart of tea country, with sweeping time-warp gardens. Guests can use the 18-hole golf course, and there's a pool.

Dibrugarh
$$$ Chowkidinghee Chang Bungalow (aka Jalannagar South Bungalow), off Mancotta Rd, 1.5 km from Dibrugarh. A truly charming indulgence in colonial history, this manager's bungalow on the edge of a tea estate has gloriously period rooms opening out onto enormous screened verandas with white cane furniture. Built on stilts to avoid floods and wild animals. Shiny wood floors throughout, there's a Victorian fireplace in the sitting-cum-dining room, both bedrooms are en suite and

have dressing rooms. An additional room downstairs is not nearly as attractive. The proximity of the road is the only thing to gripe about. Bring your own alcohol.

$$$-$$ Mancotta Chang Bungalow, off Mancotta Rd, Milan Nagar, 5 km from Dibrugarh. Another heritage planter's bungalow on stilts exudes the same ambiance but is larger, with 2 fabulous colonial bedrooms on the upper level, 2 modern rooms downstairs (walk through the patio doors in the morning to enjoy the garden) and a separate bungalow with a post-war feel that sleeps 2 singles. In the upstairs rooms chintzy curtains, brass fittings, Seypoy prints and plenty of tumblers and brandy glasses make drinks on the veranda more attractive than the satellite TV. Bathrooms have enamel claw-footed tubs. Horse riding, tea tours and more are arranged by **Purvi Discovery** who also take the bookings.

RESTAURANTS

Guwahati
$$$ Mainland China, 4th floor, Dona Planet, GS Rd, T0361 246 6222. Daily 1200-1530, 1900-2300. Fabulous Chinese food in tip-top surrounds, from the famous nationwide chain.

$$-$ Beatrix, MC Rd, T0361-266 7563. Open Mon-Sat 1030-2200, Sun from 1600. Good-quality family restaurant (a/c upstairs), cartoon decor and clean surrounds. Varied menu, with some interesting dishes, lone diners with appreciate the 'mini-meals' (which are still very generous). Recommended.

Shillong
$$ City Hut Family Dhaba, Earle Holiday Home, T0364-222 0886. Open 1100-2130, closed every last Tue of the month.

Probably the nicest restaurant in Shillong, with a huge choice including Mexican and Thai. Interesting Indian and Chinese dishes (paneer steak, tandoori duck, great thalis Rs 125-150), the cute gazebos are reserved for couples and families.

$$-$ Le Galerie, 1st floor at **Center Point Hotel**. Daily 1130-2130. Tempting Indian and Chinese food that is well-priced, good vegetarian selection, unfussy decor with old pictures of Meghalaya, windows all around, efficient staff, very popular with families.

$ Bread Cafe, 1st floor above Barbeque, GS Rd. Daily 1000-2000. Serves good pizzas and fast food, 'real' sandwiches on 'real' bread, pasta, good coffee, cheap and cheerful though the TV is sometimes rather loud. Recommended.

PRACTICALITIES

INS AND OUTS

→ BEST TIME TO VISIT NORTH INDIA

By far the best time to visit North India is from October to April. It is intensely hot, especially on the plains, during May and June and then humidity builds up as the monsoon approaches. The monsoon season lasts from between two and three months, from July to September, with the east seeing the strongest and longest rains when large parts of Kolkata can be knee-deep in water for hours at a time. If you are travelling during the monsoon you need to be prepared for extended periods of torrential rain and disruption to travel. Hot summers are followed by much cooler and clearer winters, and in Delhi the temperatures can plummet to near freezing in January. Some of the region's great festivals such as **Durga Puja** in West Bengal and **Diwali** take place in the autumn and winter.

→ GETTING TO NORTH INDIA

AIR

India is accessible by air from virtually every continent. Most international flights arrive in Delhi or Mumbai. Some carriers permit 'open-jaw' travel, arriving in, and departing from, different cities in India. Some (eg **Air India**, **Jet Airways** or **British Airways**) have convenient non-stop flights from Europe, eg from London to Delhi, takes only nine hours.

You can fly to numerous destinations across India with **Jet Airways**, **Indigo** or **Spicejet**. The prices are very competitive if domestic flights are booked in conjunction with Jet on the international legs. In 2013 the cheapest return flights to Delhi from London started from around £500, but leapt to £800+ as you approached the high season of Christmas, New Year and Easter.

From Europe Despite the increases to Air Passenger Duty, Britain remains the cheapest place in Europe for flights to India. From mainland Europe, major European flag carriers including **KLM** and **Lufthansa** fly to Delhi and/or Mumbai from their respective hub airports. In most cases the cheapest flights are with Middle Eastern or Central Asian airlines, transiting via airports in the Gulf. Several airlines from the Middle East (eg **Emirates**, **Gulf Air**, **Kuwait Airways**, **Qatar Airways** and **Oman Air**) offer good discounts to Indian regional capitals from London, but fly via their hub cities, adding to the journey time. Consolidators in the UK can quote some competitive fares, such as: www.skyscanner.net, www.ebookers.com; **North South Travel** ① *T01245-608291, www.northsouthtravel.co.uk (profits to charity)*.

From North America From the east coast, several airlines including **Air India**, **Jet Airways**, **Continental** and **Delta** fly direct from New York to Delhi and Mumbai. **American** flies to both cities from Chicago. Discounted tickets on **British Airways**, KLM, Lufthansa, Gulf Air and Kuwait Airways are sold through agents although they will invariably fly via their country's capital cities. From the west coast, **Air India** flies from Los Angeles to Delhi and Mumbai, and **Jet Airways** from San Francisco to Mumbai via Shanghai. Alternatively, fly via Hong Kong, Singapore or Bangkok using one of those countries' national carriers. **Air Canada** operates between Vancouver and Delhi.

Air Brokers International ℹ *www.airbrokers.com*, is competitive and reputable. STA ℹ *www.statravel.co.uk*, has offices in many US cities, Toronto and Ontario. Student fares are also available from Travel Cuts ℹ *www.travelcuts.com*, in Canada.

From Australasia Qantas, Singapore Airlines, Thai Airways, Malaysian Airlines, Cathay Pacific and Air India are the principal airlines connecting the continents, although Qantas is the only one that flies direct, with services from Sydney to Mumbai. STA and Flight Centre offer discounted tickets from their branches in major cities in Australia and New Zealand. Abercrombie & Kent ℹ *www.abercrombiekent.co.uk*, Adventure World ℹ *www.adventure world.net.au*, Peregrine ℹ *www.peregrineadventures.com*, and Travel Corporation of India ℹ *www.tcindia.com*, organize tours.

Airport information The formalities on arrival in India have been increasingly streamlined during the last few years and the facilities at the major international airports greatly improved. However, arrival can still be a slow process. Disembarkation cards, with an attached customs declaration, are handed out to passengers during the inward flight. The immigration form should be handed in at the immigration counter on arrival. The customs slip will be returned, for handing over to the customs on leaving the baggage collection hall. You may well find that there are delays of over an hour at immigration in processing passengers passing through immigration who need help with filling in forms.

    Departure tax Rs 500 is payable for all international departures other than those to neighbouring SAARC countries, when the tax is Rs 250 (not reciprocated by Sri Lanka). This is normally included in your international ticket; check when buying. (To save time 'Security Check' your baggage before checking in at departure.)

→ TRANSPORT IN NORTH INDIA

AIR

India has a comprehensive network linking the major cities of the different states. Deregulation of the airline industry has had a transformative effect on travel within India, with a host of low-budget private carriers offering sometimes unbelievably cheap fares on an ever-expanding network of routes in a bid to woo the train-travelling middle class. Promotional fares as low as Rs 9 (US$0.20) are not unknown, though such numbers are rendered somewhat meaningless by additional taxes and fuel charges – an extra US$30-50 on most flights. On any given day, booking a few days in advance, you can expect to fly between Delhi and Kolkata for around US$100 one way including taxes, while a month's notice and flying with a no-frills airline can reduce the price to US$70-80; regional routes, eg Lucknow to Kolkata, are often cheaper than routes between main cities.

    Competition from the efficiently run private sector has, in general, improved the quality of services provided by the nationalized airlines. It also seems to herald the end of the two-tier pricing structure, meaning that ticket prices are now usually the same for foreign and Indian travellers. The airport authorities too have made efforts to improve handling on the ground.

    Although flying is comparatively expensive, for covering vast distances or awkward links on a route it is an option worth considering, though delays and re-routing can be irritating. For short distances (eg Delhi–Agra), and on some routes where you can sleep during an overnight journey (eg Varanasi–Kolkata) it makes more sense to travel by train.

The best way to get an idea of the current routes, carriers and fares is to use a third-party booking website such as www.cheapairticketsindia.com (toll-free numbers: UK T0800-101 0928, USA T1-888 825 8680), www.cleartrip.com, www.makemytrip.co.in, or www.yatra.com. Booking with these is a different matter: some refuse foreign credit cards outright, while others have to be persuaded to give your card special clearance. Tickets booked on these sites are typically issued as an email ticket or an SMS text message – the simplest option if you have an Indian mobile phone, though it must be converted to a paper ticket at the relevant carrier's airport offices before you will be allowed into the terminal. Makemytrip.com and Travelocity.com both accept international credit cards.

RAIL

Trains can still be the cheapest and most comfortable means of travelling long distances saving you hotel expenses on overnight journeys. It gives access to booking station Retiring Rooms, which can be useful from time to time. Above all, you have an ideal opportunity to meet local travellers and catch a glimpse of life on the ground. Remember the dark glass on air-conditioned coaches does restrict vision. See also www.indianrail.gov.in and www.erail.in.

High-speed trains There are several air-conditioned 'high-speed' Shatabdi (or 'Century') Express for day travel, and Rajdhani Express ('Capital City') for overnight journeys. These cover large sections of the network but due to high demand you need to book them well in advance (up to 90 days). Meals and drinks are usually included.

Classes A/c First Class, available only on main routes, is very comfortable (bedding provided). It will also be possible for tourists to reserve special coaches (some air conditioning) which are normally allocated to senior railway officials only. A/c Sleeper, two and three-tier configurations (known as 2AC and 3AC), are clean and comfortable and popular with middle class families; these are the safest carriages for women travelling alone. A/c Executive Class, with wide reclining seats, are available on many Shatabdi trains at double the price of the ordinary a/c Chair Car which are equally comfortable. First Class (non-a/c) is gradually being phased out, and is now restricted to a handful of routes in the south, but the run-down old carriages still provide a pleasant experience if you like open windows. Second Class (non-a/c) two and three-tier (commonly called Sleeper), provides exceptionally cheap and atmospheric travel, with basic padded vinyl seats and open windows that allow the sights and sounds of India (not to mention dust, insects and flecks of spittle expelled by passengers up front) to drift into the carriage. On long journeys Sleeper can be crowded and uncomfortable, and toilet facilities can be unpleasant; it is nearly always better to use the Indian-style squat loos rather than the Western-style ones as they are better maintained. At the bottom rung is Unreserved Second Class, with hard wooden benches. You can travel long distances for a trivial amount of money, but unreserved carriages are often ridiculously crowded, and getting off at your station may involve a battle of will and strength against the hordes trying to shove their way on.

Indrail passes These allow travel across the network without having to pay extra reservation fees and sleeper charges but you have to spend a high proportion of your time on the train to make it worthwhile. However, the advantages of pre-arranged reservations and automatic access to 'Tourist Quotas' can tip the balance in favour of the pass for some travellers.

Tourists (foreigners and Indians resident abroad) may buy these passes from the tourist sections of principal railway booking offices and pay in foreign currency, major credit cards, traveller's cheques or rupees with encashment certificates. Fares range from US$57 to US$1060 for adults or half that for children. Rail-cum-air tickets are also to be made available.

Indrail passes can also conveniently be bought abroad from special agents. For people contemplating a single long journey soon after arriving in India, the Half- or One-day Pass with a confirmed reservation is worth the peace of mind; two- or four-day passes are also sold.

The UK agent is SDEL ⓘ *103 Wembley Park Dr, Wembley, Middlesex HA9 8HG, UK, T020-8903 3411, www.indiarail.co.uk*. They make all necessary reservations and offer excellent advice. They can also book Air India and Jet Airways internal flights.

Cost A/c first class costs about double the rate for two-tier shown below, and non a/c second class about half. Children (aged five to 12) travel at half the adult fare. The young (12-30 years) and senior citizens (65 years and over) are allowed a 30% discount on journeys over 500 km (just show your passport).

Period	US$ A/c 2-tier	Period	US$ A/c 2-tier
½ day	26	21 days	198
1 day	43	30 days	248
7 days	135	60 days	400
15 days	185	90 days	530

Fares for individual journeys are based on distance covered and reflect both the class and the type of train. Higher rates apply on the Mail and Express trains and the air-conditioned Shatabdi and Rajdhani Expresses.

Internet services Much information is available online via www.railtourismindia. com, www.indianrail.gov.in, www.erail.in and www.trainenquiry.com, where you can check timetables (which change frequently), numbers, seat availability and even the running status of your train. Internet e-tickets can be bought and printed on www.irctc. in – a great time-saver when the system works properly. Another best option is to use a third-party agent such as www.makemytrip.com or www.cleartrip.com, which provide an easily understood booking engine and accept foreign cards. An alternative is to seek a local agent who can sell e-tickets, which can cost as little as Rs 10 (plus Rs 20 reservation fee, some agents charge up to Rs 150 a ticket, however), and can save hours of hassle; simply present the printout to the ticket collector. However, it is tricky if you then want to cancel an e-ticket which an agent has bought for you on their account.

Note All train numbers changed to five-digit numbers in 2010-2011; in most cases, adding a '1' to the start of an old four-figure number will produce the new number. Otherwise, try your luck with the 'train number enquiry' search at www.indianrail.gov. in/ inet_trnno_enq.html.

Tickets and reservations It is now possible to reserve tickets for virtually any train on the network from one of the 1000 computerized reservation centres across India. It is always best to book as far in advance as possible (usually up to 60 days). To reserve a seat on a particular train, note down the train's name, number and departure time and fill in a reservation form while you line up at the ticket window; you can use one form for up to four passengers. At busy stations the wait can take an hour or more. You can save a lot of time and effort by asking a travel agent to get your tickets for a fee of Rs 50-100. If the class you want is full, ask if special 'quotas' are available (see above). If not, consider buying a 'wait list' ticket, as seats often become available close to the train's departure time; phone the station on the day of departure to check your ticket's status. If you don't have a reservation for a particular train but carry an Indrail Pass, you may get one by arriving three hours early. Be wary of touts at the station offering tickets, hotels or exchange.

Timetables Regional timetables are available cheaply from station bookstalls; the monthly *Indian Bradshaw* is sold in principal stations. The handy *Trains at a Glance* (Rs 40) lists popular trains likely to be used by most foreign travellers and is available at stalls at Indian railway stations and in the UK from SDEL (see page 287).

ROAD

Road travel is sometimes the only choice for reaching many of the places of outstanding interest, particularly national parks or isolated tourist sites. For the uninitiated, travel by road can also be a worrying experience because of the apparent absence of conventional traffic regulations. Vehicles drive on the left – in theory. Routes around the major cities are usually crowded with lorry traffic, especially at night, and the main roads are often poor and slow. There are a few motorway-style expressways, but most main roads are single track. Some district roads are quiet, and although they are not fast they can be a good way of seeing the country and village life if you have the time.

Bus Buses now reach virtually every part of India, offering a cheap, if often uncomfortable, means of visiting places off the rail network. Very few villages are now more than 2-3 km from a bus stop. Services are run by the State Corporation from the State Bus Stand (and private companies which often have offices nearby). The latter allow advance reservations, including booking printable e-tickets online (check www.redbus.in and www.viaworld.in) and, although tickets prices are a little higher, they have fewer stops and are a bit more comfortable.

Bus categories Though comfortable for sightseeing trips, apart from the very best 'sleeper coaches' even **air-conditioned luxury coaches** can be very uncomfortable for really long journeys. Often the air conditioning is very cold so wrap up. Journeys over 10 hours can be extremely tiring so it is better to go by train if there is a choice. If you must take a sleeper bus (a contradiction in terms), choose a lower berth near the front of the bus. The upper berths tend to be really uncomfortable on bumpy roads. **Express buses** run over long distances (frequently overnight), these are often called 'video coaches' and can be an appalling experience unless you appreciate loud film music blasting through the night. Ear plugs and eye masks may ease the pain. They rarely average more than 45 kph. **Local buses** are often very crowded, quite bumpy, slow and usually poorly maintained. However, over short distances, they can be a very cheap, friendly and easy way of getting about. Even where signboards are not in English someone will usually give you directions. Many larger towns have **minibus** services which charge a little more than the buses and pick up and drop passengers on request. Again very crowded, and with restricted headroom, they are the fastest way of getting about many of the larger towns.

Bus travel tips Some towns have different bus stations for different destinations. Booking on major long-distance routes is now computerized. Book in advance where possible and avoid the back of the bus where it can be very bumpy. If your destination is only served by a local bus you may do better to take the Express bus and 'persuade' the driver, with a tip in advance, to stop where you want to get off. You will have to pay the full fare to the first stop beyond your destination but you will get there faster and more comfortably. When an unreserved bus pulls into a bus station, there is usually an unholy scramble for seats, whilst those arriving have to struggle to get off! In many areas there is an unwritten 'rule of reservation' using handkerchiefs or bags thrust through the windows to reserve seats. Some visitors may feel a more justified right to a seat having fought their way through the crowd, but it is generally best to do as local people do and be prepared with a handkerchief or 'sarong'. As soon as it touches the seat, it is yours! Leave it on your seat when getting off to use the toilet at bus stations.

Car A car provides a chance to travel off the beaten track, and gives unrivalled opportunities for seeing something of India's great variety of villages and small towns. Until recently, the most widely used hire car was the Hindustan Ambassador. However, except for the newest model, they are often very unreliable, and although they still have their devotees, many find them uncomfortable for long journeys. For a similar price, Maruti cars and vans (Omni) are much more reliable and are now the preferred choice in many areas. Gypsy 4WDs and Jeeps are also available, especially in the hills, where larger Sumos have made an appearance. Maruti Esteems and Toyota Qualis are comfortable and have optional reliable air-conditioning. A specialist operator can be very helpful in arranging itineraries and car hire in advance.

Car hire With a driver, car hire is cheaper than in the West. A car shared by three or four can be very good value. Be sure to check carefully the mileage at the beginning and end of the trip. Two- or three-day trips from main towns can also give excellent opportunities for sightseeing off the beaten track in reasonable comfort. Local drivers often know their way much better than drivers from other states, so where possible it is a good idea to get a local driver who speaks the state language, in addition to being able to communicate with you. In the mountains, it is better to use a driver who knows the roads. Drivers may sleep in the car overnight although hotels (especially pricier ones) should provide a bed for them. They are responsible for their expenses, including meals. Car (and auto) drivers increase their earnings by taking you to hotels and shops where they get a handsome commission (which you will pay for). If you feel inclined, a tip at the end of the tour of Rs 100 per day in addition to their daily allowance is perfectly acceptable. Check beforehand if fuel and inter-state taxes are included in the hire charge.

Cars can be hired through private companies. International companies such as **Hertz**, **Europcar** and **Budget** operate in some major cities and offer reliable cars; their rates are generally higher than those of local firms (eg **Sai Service**, **Wheels**). The price of an imported car can be three times that of the Ambassador.

Car with driver	Economy Maruti 800 Ambassador	Regular a/c Maruti 800 Contessa	Premium a/c Maruti 1000 Opel	Luxury a/c Esteem Qualis
8 hrs/80 km	Rs 800	Rs 1000	Rs 1400	Rs 1800+
Extra km	Rs 4-7	Rs 9	Rs 13	Rs 18
Extra hour	Rs 40	Rs 50	Rs 70	Rs 100
Out of town				
Per km	Rs 7	Rs 9	Rs 13	Rs 18
Night halt	Rs 100	Rs 200	Rs 250	Rs 250

Taxi Yellow-top taxis in cities and large towns are metered, although tariffs change frequently. These changes are shown on a fare chart which should be read in conjunction with the meter reading. Increased night time rates apply in most cities, and there might be a small charge for luggage. Insist on the taxi meter being flagged in your presence. If the driver refuses, the official advice is to contact the police. This may not work, but it is worth trying. When a taxi doesn't have a meter, you will need to fix the fare before starting the journey. Ask at your hotel desk for a guide price. As a foreigner, it is rare to get a taxi in the big cities to use the meter – if they are eager to, watch out as sometimes the meter is rigged and they have a fake rate card. Also, watch out for the David Blaine-style note shuffle: you pay with a Rs 500 note, but they have a Rs 100 note in their hand. This happens frequently at the prepaid booth outside New Delhi train station too, no matter how small the transaction.

At stations and airports it is often possible to share taxis to a central point. It is worth looking for fellow passengers who may be travelling in your direction and get a prepaid taxi. At night, always have a clear idea of where you want to go and insist on being taken there. Taxi drivers may try to convince you that the hotel you have chosen 'closed three years ago' or is 'completely full'. Say that you have a reservation.

Rickshaw Auto-rickshaws (autos) are almost universally available in towns across North India and are the cheapest and most convenient way of getting about. It is best to walk a short distance away from a hotel gate before picking up an auto to avoid paying an inflated rate. In addition to using them for short journeys it is often possible to hire them by the hour, or for a half or full day's sightseeing. In some areas younger drivers who speak some English and know their local area well may want to show you around. However, rickshaw drivers are often paid a commission by hotels, restaurants and gift shops so advice is not always impartial. Drivers generally refuse to use a meter, often quote a ridiculous price or may sometimes stop short of your destination. If you have real problems it can help to note down the vehicle licence number and threaten to go to the police. Beware of some rickshaw drivers who show the fare chart for taxis.

Cycle-rickshaws and **horse-drawn tongas** are more common in the more rustic setting of a small town or the outskirts of a large one. You will need to fix a price by bargaining. The animal attached to a tonga usually looks too undernourished to have the strength to pull the driver, let alone passengers.

India has an enormous range of accommodation. You can stay safely and very cheaply by Western standards right across the country. In all the major cities there are also high-quality hotels, offering a full range of facilities; in small centres hotels are much more variable. In Madhya Pradesh, old Maharajas' palaces and forts have been privately converted into comfortable, unusual hotels. In the peak season (October to April) bookings can be extremely heavy in popular destinations. It is sometimes possible to book in advance by phone, fax or email, but double check your reservation, and always try to arrive as early as possible in the day.

HOTELS

Price categories The category codes used in this book are based on prices of double rooms excluding taxes. They are **not** star ratings and individual facilities vary considerably. The most expensive hotels charge in US dollars only. Modest hotels may not have their own restaurant but will often offer 'room service', bringing in food from outside. In temple towns, restaurants may only serve vegetarian food. Many hotels operate a 24-hour checkout system. Make sure that this means that you can stay 24 hours from the time of check-in. Expect to pay more in Delhi and, to a lesser extent, in Kolkata for all categories. Prices away from large cities tend to be lower for comparable hotels.
Off-season rates Large reductions are made by hotels in all categories out-of-season in many resorts. Always ask if any is available. You may also request the 10-15% agent's commission to be deducted from your bill if you book direct. Clarify whether the agreed figure includes all taxes.

Taxes In general most hotel rooms rated at Rs 3000 or above are subject to a tax of 10%. Many states levy an additional luxury tax of 10-25%, and some hotels add a service charge of 10% on top of this. Taxes are not necessarily payable on meals, so it is worth settling your meals bill separately. Most hotels in the **$$** category and above accept payment by credit card. Check your final bill carefully. Visitors have complained of incorrect bills, even in the most expensive hotels. The problem particularly afflicts groups, when last-minute extras appear mysteriously on some guests' bills. Check the evening before departure, and keep all receipts.

Hotel facilities You have to be prepared for difficulties which are uncommon in the West. It is best to inspect the room and check that all equipment (air conditioning, TV, water heater, flush) works before checking in at a modest hotel. Many hotels try to wring too many years' service out of their linen, and it's quite common to find sheets that are stained, frayed or riddled with holes. Don't expect any but the most expensive or tourist-savvy hotels to fit a top sheet to the bed.

In some states **power cuts** are common, or hot water may be restricted to certain times of day. The largest hotels have their own generators but it is best to carry a good torch.

In some regions **water supply** is rationed periodically. Keep a bucket filled to use for flushing the toilet during water cuts. Occasionally, tap water may be discoloured due to rusty tanks. During the cold weather and in hill stations, hot water will be available at certain times of the day, sometimes in buckets, but is usually very restricted in quantity.

PRICE CODES

WHERE TO STAY

$$$$	over US$150	**$$$**	US$66-150
$$	US$30-65	**$**	under US$30

Price for a double room in high season, excluding taxes.

RESTAURANTS

$$$ over US$12	**$$** US$6-12	**$** under US$6

Price for a two-course meal for one person, excluding drinks and service charge.

Electric water heaters may provide enough for a shower but not enough to fill a bath tub. For details on drinking water, see opposite.

Hotels close to temples can be very **noisy**, especially during festivals. Music blares from loudspeakers late at night and from very early in the morning, often making sleep impossible. Mosques call the faithful to prayers at dawn. Some find ear plugs helpful.

HOMESTAYS

At the upmarket end, increasing numbers of travellers are keen to stay in private homes and guesthouses, opting not to book large hotel chains that keep you at arm's length from a culture. Instead, travellers get home-cooked meals in heritage houses and learn about a country through conversation with often fascinating hosts. Delhi has many new and smart family-run B&Bs springing up. Tourist offices have lists of families with more modest homestays. Companies specializing in homestays include Home & Hospitality, www.homeandhospitality.co.uk, **MAHout**, www.mahoutuk.com and **Sundale Vacations**, www.sundale.com.

→ FOOD AND DRINK IN NORTH INDIA

FOOD

You find just as much variety in dishes crossing India as you would on an equivalent journey across Europe. Combinations of spices give each region its distinctive flavour.

The larger hotels, open to non-residents, often offer **buffet** lunches with Indian, Western and sometimes Chinese dishes. These can be good value (Rs 400-500; but Rs 850 in the top grades) and can provide a welcome, comfortable break in the cool. The health risks, however, of food kept warm for long periods in metal containers are considerable, especially if turnover at the buffet is slow. We have received several complaints of stomach trouble following a buffet meal, even in five-star hotels.

It is essential to be very careful since food hygiene may be poor, flies abound and refrigeration in the hot weather may be inadequate and intermittent because of power cuts. It is best to eat only freshly prepared food by ordering from the menu (especially meat and fish dishes). Avoid salads and cut fruit, unless the menu advertises that they have been washed in mineral water.

If you are unused to spicy food, go slow. Food is often spicier when you eat with families or at local places. Popular local restaurants are obvious from the number of people eating in them. Try a traditional *thali*, which is a complete meal served on a large stainless steel plate. Several preparations, placed in small bowls, surround the central serving of wholewheat chapati and rice. A vegetarian *thali* would include dhal (lentils), two or three curries (which can be quite hot) and crisp poppadums. A variety of pickles are offered – mango and lime are two of the most popular. These can be exceptionally hot, and are designed to be taken in minute quantities alongside the main dishes. Plain *dahi* (yoghurt), or *raita*, usually acts as a bland 'cooler'. Simple *dhabas* (rustic roadside eateries) are an alternative experience for sampling authentic local dishes.

Many city restaurants and backpacker eateries offer a choice of so-called **European options** such as toasted sandwiches, stuffed pancakes, apple pies, fruit crumbles and cheesecakes. Italian favourites (pizzas, pastas) can be very different from what you are used to. **Ice creams**, on the other hand, can be exceptionally good; there are excellent Indian ones as well as some international brands.

India has many delicious tropical **fruits**. Some are seasonal (eg mangoes, pineapples and lychees), while others (eg bananas, grapes and oranges) are available throughout the year. It is safe to eat the ones you can wash and peel.

In cities and larger towns, you will see all types of regional Indian food on the menus, with some restaurants specializing in South Indian food such as *dosas*, *uttapams idlis*. North Indian kebabs and the richer flavoursome cuisine of Lucknow are also worth seeking out. In Bengal, there is an emphasis on fish and seafood, especially river fish, the most popular being *hilsa* and *bekti*. *Bekti* is grilled or fried and is tastier than the fried fish of the west as it has often been marinated in mild spices first. Bengali *mishti* (sweetmeats) are another distinctive feature. Many are milk based and the famous *sandesh*, *roshogolla*, *roshomalai* and *pantua*. Pale pinkish brown, *mishti doi*, is an excellent sweet yoghurt eaten as a dessert, typically sold in hand-thrown clay pots.

DRINK
Drinking water used to be regarded as one of India's biggest hazards. It is still true that water from the tap or a well should never be considered safe to drink since public water supplies are often polluted. Bottled water is now widely available although not all bottled water is mineral water; most are simply purified water from an urban supply. Buy from a shop or stall, check the seal carefully and avoid street hawkers; when disposing bottles puncture the neck which prevents misuse but allows recycling.

There is growing concern over the mountains of plastic bottles that are collecting and the waste of resources needed to produce them, so travellers are being encouraged to carry their own bottles and take a portable water filter. It is important to use pure water for cleaning teeth.

Tea and **coffee** are safe and widely available. Both are normally served sweet, and with milk. If you wish, say 'no sugar' (*chini nahin*), 'no milk' (*dudh nahin*) when ordering. Alternatively, ask for a pot of tea and milk and sugar to be brought separately. Freshly brewed coffee is a common drink in South India, but in the North, ordinary city restaurants will usually serve the instant variety. Even in aspiring smart cafés, espresso or cappuccino may not turn out quite as you'd expect in the West.

Bottled **soft drinks** such as Coke, Pepsi, Teem, Limca and Thums Up are universally available but always check the seal when you buy from a street stall. There are also several brands of fruit juice sold in cartons, including mango, pineapple and apple – Indian brands are very sweet. Don't add ice cubes as the water source may be contaminated. Take care with fresh fruit juices or *lassis* as ice is often added.

Indians rarely drink **alcohol** with a meal. In the past wines and spirits were generally either imported and extremely expensive, or local and of poor quality. Now, the best Indian whisky, rum and brandy (IMFL or 'Indian Made Foreign Liquor') are widely accepted, as are good Champagnoise and other wines from Maharashtra. If you hanker after a bottle of imported wine, you will only find it in the top restaurants or specialist liquor stores for at least Rs 1000.

For the urban elite, refreshing Indian beers are popular when eating out and so are widely available. 'Pubs' have sprung up in the major cities. Elsewhere, seedy, all-male drinking dens in the larger cities are best avoided for women travellers, but can make quite an experience otherwise – you will sometimes be locked into cubicles for clandestine drinking. If that sounds unsavoury then head for the better hotel bars instead; prices aren't that steep. In rural India, local rice, palm, cashew or date juice *toddy* and *arak* is deceptively potent.

Most states have alcohol-free dry days or enforce degrees of Prohibition. Some upmarket restaurants may serve beer even if it's not listed, so it's worth asking. In some states there are government approved wine shops where you buy your alcohol through a metal grille. For dry states and liquor permits, see page 306.

→ FESTIVALS IN NORTH INDIA

India has a wealth of festivals with many celebrated nationwide, while others are specific to a particular state or community or even a particular temple. Many fall on different dates each year depending on the Hindu lunar calendar so check with the tourist office.

THE HINDU CALENDAR

Hindus follow two distinct eras: The *Vikrama Samvat* which began in 57 BC and the *Salivahan Saka* which dates from AD 78 and has been the official Indian calendar since 1957. The *Saka* new year starts on 22 March and has the same length as the Gregorian calendar. The 29½-day lunar month with its 'dark' and 'bright' halves based on the new and full moons, are named after 12 constellations, and total a 354-day year. The calendar cleverly has an extra month (*adhik maas*) every 2½ to three years, to bring it in line with the solar year of 365 days coinciding with the Gregorian calendar of the West.

Some major national and regional festivals are listed below. A few count as national holidays: **26 January**: Republic Day; **15 August**: Independence Day; **2 October**: Mahatma Gandhi's Birthday; **25 December**: Christmas Day.

Jan New Year's Day (1 Jan) is accepted officially when following the Gregorian calendar but there are regional variations which fall on different dates, often coinciding with spring/harvest time in Mar and Apr. 14 Jan, **Makar Sankranti**, marks the end of winter and is celebrated with kite flying.
Feb Vasant Panchami, the spring festival when people wear bright yellow clothes to mark the advent of the season with singing, dancing and feasting.
Feb-Mar Maha Sivaratri marks the night when Siva danced his celestial dance of destruction (*Tandava*), which is celebrated with feasting and fairs at Siva temples, but preceded by a night of devotional readings and hymn singing.

Mar **Holi**, the festival of colours, marks the climax of spring. The previous night bonfires are lit symbolizing the end of winter (and conquering of evil). People have fun throwing coloured powder and water at each other and in the evening some gamble with friends. If you don't mind getting covered in colours, you can risk going out but celebrations can sometimes get very rowdy (and unpleasant). Some worship Krishna who defeated the demon Putana.

Apr/May **Buddha Jayanti**, the 1st full moon night in Apr/May marks the birth of the Buddha.

Jul/Aug **Raksha (or Rakhi) Bandhan** symbolizes the bond between brother and sister, celebrated at full moon. A sister says special prayers for her brother and ties coloured threads around his wrist to remind him of the special bond. He in turn gives a gift and promises to protect and care for her. Sometimes *rakshas* are exchanged as a mark of friendship. **Narial Purnima** on the same full moon. Hindus make offerings of *narial* (coconuts) to the Vedic god Varuna (Lord of the waters) by throwing them into the sea. 15 Aug is **Independence Day**, a national secular holiday is marked by special events. **Ganesh Chaturthi** was established just over 100 years ago by the Indian nationalist leader Tilak. The elephant-headed God of good omen is shown special reverence. On the last of the 5-day festival after harvest, clay images of Ganesh are taken in procession with dancers and musicians, and are immersed in the sea, river or pond.

Aug/Sep **Janmashtami**, the birth of Krishna is celebrated at midnight at Krishna temples.

Sep/Oct **Dasara** has many local variations. Celebrations for the 9 nights (*navaratri*) are marked with **Ramlila**, various episodes of the Ramayana story are enacted with particular reference to the battle between the forces of good and evil. In some parts of India it celebrates *Rama*'s victory over the Demon king *Ravana* of Lanka with the help of loyal *Hanuman* (Monkey). Huge effigies of *Ravana* made of bamboo and paper are burnt on the 10th day (*Vijaya dasami*) of Dasara in public open spaces. In West Bengal the focus is on Durga's victory over the demon *Mahishasura*, and the festival is known as **Durga Puja** and is celebrated in Kolkata and surrounding towns, culminating with the submersion of the idols into the river on the final night.

Oct/Nov **Gandhi Jayanti** (2 Oct), Mahatma Gandhi's birthday, is remembered with prayer meetings and devotional singing.

Diwali/Deepavali (*Sanskrit ideepa* lamp), the festival of lights. Some Hindus celebrate Krishna's victory over the demon *Narakasura*, some Rama's return after his 14 years' exile in the forest when citizens lit his way with oil lamps. The festival falls on the dark *chaturdasi* (14th) night (the one preceding the new moon), when rows of lamps or candles are lit in remembrance, and *rangolis* are painted on the floor as a sign of welcome. Fireworks have become an integral part of the celebration which are often set off days before Diwali. Equally, Lakshmi, the Goddess of Wealth (as well as Ganesh) is worshipped by merchants and the business community who open the new financial year's account on the day. Most people wear new clothes; some play games of chance.

Guru Nanak Jayanti commemorates the birth of Guru Nanak. **Akhand Path** (unbroken reading of the holy book) takes place and the book itself (*Guru Granth Sahib*) is taken out in procession.

Dec **Christmas Day** (25 Dec) sees Indian Christians celebrate the birth of Christ in much the same way as in the West; many churches hold services/mass at midnight. There is an air of festivity in city markets which are specially decorated and illuminated. Over **New Year's Eve** (31 Dec) hotel prices peak and large supplements are added for meals and entertainment in the upper category hotels. Some churches mark the night with a Midnight Mass.

MUSLIM HOLY DAYS

These are fixed according to the lunar calendar. According to the Gregorian calendar, they tend to fall 11 days earlier each year, dependent on the sighting of the new moon.

Ramadan, known in India as 'Ramzan', is the start of the month of fasting when all Muslims (except young children, the very elderly, the sick, pregnant women and travellers) must abstain from food and drink, from sunrise to sunset.

Id ul Fitr is the 3-day festival that marks the end of Ramzan.

Id-ul-Zuha/Bakr-Id is when Muslims commemorate Ibrahim's sacrifice of his son according to God's commandment; the main time of pilgrimage to Mecca (the Hajj). It is marked by the sacrifice of a goat, feasting and alms giving.

Muharram is when the killing of the Prophet's grandson, Hussain, is commemorated by Shi'a Muslims. Decorated *tazias* (replicas of the martyr's tomb) are carried in procession by devout wailing followers who beat their chests to express their grief. Lucknow is famous for its grand *tazias*. Shi'as fast for the 10 days.

→ RESPONSIBLE TRAVEL

As well as respecting local cultural sensitivities, travellers can take a number of simple steps to reduce, or even improve, their impact on the local environment. Environmental concern is relatively new in India. Don't be afraid to pressurize businesses by asking about their policies.

Litter Many travellers think that there is little point in disposing of rubbish properly when the tossing of water bottles, plastic cups and other non-biodegradable items out of train windows is already so widespread. Don't follow an example you feel to be wrong. You can immediately reduce your impact by refusing plastic bags and other excess packaging when shopping – use a small backpack or cloth bag instead – and if you do collect a few, keep them with you to store other rubbish until you get to a litter bin.

Plastic mineral water bottles, an inevitable corollary to poor water hygiene standards, are a major contributor to India's litter mountain. However, many hotels, including nearly all of the upmarket ones, most restaurants and bus and train stations, provide drinking water purified using a combination of ceramic and carbon filters, chlorine and UV irradiation. Ask for '*filter paani*'; if the water tastes like a swimming pool it is probably quite safe to drink, though it's best to introduce your body gradually to the new water. If purifying water yourself, bringing it to a boil at sea level will make it safe, but at altitude you have to boil it for longer to ensure that all the microbes are killed. Various sterilizing methods can be used that contain chlorine (eg Puritabs) or iodine (eg Pota Aqua) and there are a number of mechanical or chemical water filters available on the market.

Bucket baths or showers The biggest issue relating to responsible and sustainable tourism is water. The traditional Indian 'bucket bath', in which you wet, soap then rinse off using a small hand-held plastic jug dipped into a large bucket, uses on average around 15 litres of water, as compared – to 30-45 for a shower. These are commonly offered except in four- and five-star hotels.

Support responsible tourism Spending your money carefully can have a positive impact. Sleeping, eating and shopping at small, locally owned businesses directly supports communities, while specific community tourism concerns, such as those operated by the Orchha Home-Stay in Orchha, www.orchha.org, and Skay's Camp, near Bandhavgarh National Park, www.skayscamp.in, both in Madhya Pradesh, provide an economic motivation for people to stay in remote communities, protect natural areas and revive traditional cultures, rather than exploit the environment or move to the cities for work.

Transport Choose walking, cycling or public transport over fuel-guzzling cars and motorbikes.

ESSENTIALS A-Z

Accident and emergency

Contact the relevant emergency service (police T100, fire T101, ambulance T102) and your embassy. Make sure you obtain police/medical reports required for insurance claims.

Customs and duty free
Duty free

Tourists are allowed to bring in all personal effects 'which may reasonably be required', without charge. The official customs allowance includes 200 cigarettes or 50 cigars, 0.95 litres of alcohol, a camera and a pair of binoculars. Valuable personal effects and professional equipment including jewellery, special camera equipment and lenses, laptop computers and sound and video recorders must be declared on a **Tourist Baggage Re-Export Form** (TBRE) in order for them to be taken out of the country. These forms require the equipment's serial numbers. It saves considerable frustration if you know the numbers in advance and are ready to show them on the equipment. In addition to the forms, details of imported equipment may be entered into your passport. Save time by completing the formalities while waiting for your baggage. It is essential to keep these forms for showing to the customs when leaving India, otherwise considerable delays are very likely at the time of departure.

Prohibited items

The import of live plants, gold coins, gold and silver bullion and silver coins not in current use are either banned or subject to strict regulation. Enquire at consular offices abroad for details.

Drugs

Be aware that the government takes the misuse of drugs very seriously. Anyone charged with the illegal possession of drugs risks facing a fine of Rs 100,000 and a minimum 10 years' imprisonment. Several foreigners have been imprisoned for drugs-related offences in the last decade.

Electricity

India's supply is 220-240 volts AC. Some top hotels have transformers. There may be pronounced variations in the voltage, and power cuts are common. Power back-up by generator or inverter is becoming more widespread, even in humble hotels, though it may not cover a/c. Socket sizes vary so take a universal adaptor; low-quality versions are available locally. Many hotels, even in the higher categories, don't have electric razor sockets. Invest in a stabilizer for a laptop.

Embassies and consulates

For information on visas and immigration, see page 306. For a comprehensive list of embassies (but not all consulates), see http://india.gov.in/overseas/indian_missions.php or http://embassy.goabroad.com. Many embassies around the world are now outsourcing the visa process which might affect how long the process takes.

Health

Local populations in India are exposed to a range of health risks not encountered in the Western world. Many of the diseases cause major problems for the local poor and destitute and, although the risks to travellers is more remote, they cannot be ignored. Obviously 5-star travel is going to carry less risk than backpacking on a budget.

Health care in the region is varied. There are many excellent private and government clinics/hospitals. As with all medical care, first impressions count. It's worth contacting your embassy or consulate on arrival and asking where the recommended clinics are (ie those used by diplomats). You can also ask about locally recommended medical dos and don'ts. If you do get ill, and you have the opportunity, you should also ask your medical insurer whether they are satisfied that the medical centre/hospital you have been referred to is of a suitable standard.

Before you go

Ideally, you should see your GP or travel clinic at least 6 weeks before your departure for general advice on travel risks, malaria and vaccinations. Make sure you have travel insurance, get a dental check (especially if you are going to be away for more than a month), know your own blood group and if you suffer a long-term condition such as diabetes or epilepsy make sure someone knows or that you have a Medic Alert bracelet/necklace with this information on it. Remember that it is risky to buy medicinal tablets abroad because the doses may differ and India has a huge trade in false drugs.

Vaccinations

If you need vaccinations, see your doctor well in advance of your travel. Most courses must be completed by a minimum of 4 weeks. Travel clinics may provide rapid courses of vaccination, but are likely to be more expensive. The following vaccinations are recommended: typhoid, polio, tetanus, infectious hepatitis and diptheria. For details of malaria prevention, contact your GP or local travel clinic.

The following vaccinations may also be considered: rabies, possibly BCG (since TB is still common in the region) and in some cases meningitis and diphtheria (if you're staying in the country for a long time). Yellow fever is not required in India but you may be asked to show a certificate if you have travelled from Africa or South America. Japanese encephalitis may be required for rural travel at certain times of the year (mainly rainy seasons). An effective oral cholera vaccine (Dukoral) is now available as 2 doses providing 3 months' protection.

Websites

Blood Care Foundation (UK), www.bloodcare.org.uk A Kent-based charity 'dedicated to the provision of screened blood and resuscitation fluids in countries where these are not readily available'. They will dispatch certified non-infected blood of the right type to your hospital/clinic. The blood is flown in from various centres around the world.
British Travel Health Association (UK), www.btha.org This is the official website of an organization of travel health professionals.
Fit for Travel, www.fitfortravel.scot. nhs.uk This site from Scotland provides a quick A-Z of vaccine and travel health advice requirements for each country.
Foreign and Commonwealth Office (FCO) (UK), www.fco.gov.uk This is a key travel advice site, with useful information on the country, people, climate and lists the UK embassies/consulates. The site also promotes the concept of 'know before you go' and encourages travel insurance and appropriate travel health advice. It has links to Department of Health travel advice site.
The Health Protection Agency, www.hpa.org.uk Up-to-date malaria advice guidelines for travel around the world. It gives specific advice about the right drugs for each location. It also has useful information for those who are pregnant, suffering from epilepsy or planning to travel with children.
Medic Alert (UK), www.medicalalert.com This is the website of the foundation that produces bracelets and necklaces for those with existing medical problems. Once you have ordered your bracelet/necklace you write your key medical details on paper inside it, so that if you collapse, a medic can identify you as having epilepsy or a nut allergy, etc.

**Travel Screening Services (UK),
www.travelscreening.co.uk** A private
clinic dedicated to integrated travel
health. The clinic gives vaccine, travel
health advice, email and SMS text
vaccine reminders and screens returned
travellers for tropical diseases.
**World Health Organisation,
www.who.int** The WHO site has links
to the *WHO Blue Book* on travel advice.
This lists the diseases in different regions
of the world. It describes vaccination
schedules and makes clear which countries
have yellow fever vaccination certificate
requirements and malarial risk.

Books

*International Travel and Health, World Health
Organization Geneva*, ISBN 92-4-15802-6-7.
Lankester, T, *The Travellers Good Health
Guide*, ISBN 0-85969-827-0.
Warrell, D and Anderson, A (eds),
*Expedition Medicine (The Royal Geographic
Society)*, ISBN 1-86197-040-4.
Young Pelton, R, Aral, C and Dulles, W,
The World's Most Dangerous Places, ISBN
1-566952-140-9.

Language

Hindi, spoken as a mother tongue
by over 400 million people, is India's
official language. The use of English is
also enshrined in the Constitution for a
wide range of official purposes, notably
communication between Hindi and non-
Hindi speaking states. The most widely
spoken Indo-Aryan languages are: Bengali
(8.3%), Marathi (8%), Urdu (5.7%), Gujarati
(5.4%), Oriya (3.7%) and Punjabi (3.2%).
Among the Dravidian languages Telugu
(8.2%), Tamil (7%), Kannada (4.2%) and
Malayalam (3.5%) are the most widely
used. In West Bengal more than 85% of the
population speak Bengali.

English now plays an important role
across India. It is widely spoken in towns
and cities and even in quite remote villages
it is usually not difficult to find someone
who speaks at least a little English. Outside
of major tourist sites, other European
languages are almost completely unknown.
The accent in which English is spoken
is often affected strongly by the mother
tongue of the speaker and there have
been changes in common grammar which
sometimes make it sound unusual. Many
of these changes have become standard
Indian English usage, as valid as any other
varieties of English used around the world.
It is possible to study a number of Indian
languages at language centres.

Money → *UK £1 = Rs 98, €1 = Rs 83,
US$1 = Rs 62 (Aug 2013)*
Indian currency is the Indian Rupee (Re/
Rs). It is **not** possible to purchase these
before you arrive. If you want cash on
arrival it is best to get it at the airport bank,
although see if an ATM is available as
airport rates are not very generous. Rupee
notes are printed in denominations of
Rs 1000, 500, 100, 50, 20, 10. The rupee is
divided into 100 paise. Coins are minted in
denominations of Rs 10, 5, Rs 2, Rs 1 and
(the increasingly uncommon) 50 paise.
Note Carry money, mostly as traveller's
cheques or currency card, in a money belt
worn under clothing. Have a small amount
in an easily accessible place.

Currency cards

If you don't want to carry lots of cash,
prepaid currency cards allow you to
preload money from your bank account,
fixed at the day's exchange rate. They look
like a credit or debit card and are issued
by specialist money changing companies,
such as Travelex and Caxton FX. You can
top up and check your balance by phone,
online and sometimes by text.

Traveller's cheques (TCs)

TCs issued by reputable companies
(eg **Thomas Cook**, **American Express**)
are widely accepted. They can be easily

exchanged at small local travel agents and tourist internet cafés but are rarely used directly for payment. Try to avoid changing at banks, where the process can be time consuming; opt for hotels and agents instead, take large denomination cheques and change enough to last for some days.

Credit cards

Major credit cards are increasingly acceptable in the main centres, though in smaller cities and towns it is still rare to be able to pay by credit card. Payment by credit card can sometimes be more expensive than payment by cash, whilst some credit card companies charge a premium on cash withdrawals. **Visa** and **MasterCard** have an ever-growing number of ATMs in major cities and several banks offer withdrawal facilities for Cirrus and Maestro cardholders. It is however easy to obtain a cash advance against a credit card. Railway reservation centres in major cities take payment for train tickets by Visa card which can be very quick as the queue is short, although they cannot be used for Tourist Quota tickets.

ATMs

By far the most convenient method of accessing money, ATMs are all over India, usually attended by security guards, with most banks offering some services to holders of overseas cards. Banks whose ATMs will issue cash against Cirrus and Maestro cards, as well as Visa and MasterCard, include **Bank of Baroda**, **Citibank**, **HDFC**, **HSBC**, **ICICI**, **IDBI**, **Punjab National Bank**, **State Bank of India** (SBI), **Standard Chartered** and **UTI**. A withdrawal fee is usually charged by the issuing bank on top of the conversion charges applied by your own bank. Fraud prevention measures quite often result in travellers having their cards blocked by the bank when unexpected overseas transactions occur; advise your bank of your travel plans before leaving.

Changing money

The **State Bank of India** and several others in major towns are authorized to deal in foreign exchange. Some give cash against Visa/MasterCard (eg **ANZ**). American Express cardholders can use their cards to get either cash or TCs in Delhi. The larger cities have licensed money changers with offices usually in the commercial sector. Changing money through unauthorized dealers is illegal. Premiums on the currency black market are very small and highly risky. Large hotels change money 24 hrs a day for guests, but banks often give a substantially better rate of exchange. It is best to exchange money on arrival at the airport bank or the Thomas Cook counter. Many international flights arrive during the night and it is generally far easier and less time consuming to change money at the airport than in the city. You should be given a foreign currency encashment certificate when you change money through a bank or authorized dealer; ask for one if it is not automatically given. It allows you to change Indian rupees back to your own currency on departure. It also enables you to use rupees to pay hotel bills or buy air tickets for which payment in foreign exchange may be required. The certificates are only valid for 3 months.

Cost of living

The cost of living in India remains well below that in the West. The average wage per capita is about Rs 68,700 per year (US$1200). Manual, unskilled labourers (women are often paid less than men), farmers and others in rural areas earn considerably less. However, thanks to booming global demand for workers who can provide cheaper IT and technology support functions and many Western firms transferring office functions or call centres to India, salaries in certain sectors have sky rocketed. An IT specialist can earn an average Rs 500,000 per year and upwards – a rate that is rising by around 15% a year.

Cost of travelling

Most food, accommodation and public transport, especially rail and bus, is exceptionally cheap, although the price of basic food items such as rice, lentils, tomatoes and onions have skyrocketed. There is a widening range of moderately priced but clean hotels and restaurants outside the big cities, making it possible to get a great deal for your money. Budget travellers sharing a room, taking public transport, avoiding souvenir stalls, and eating nothing but rice and dhal can get away with a budget of Rs 400-600 (about about US$7-11 or £6-7) a day. This sum leaps up if you drink alcohol (still cheap by European standards at about US$2, £1 or Rs 80 for a pint), smoke foreign-brand cigarettes or want to have your own wheels (you can expect to spend between Rs 150 and 200 to hire a Honda per day). Those planning to stay in fairly comfortable hotels and use taxis sightseeing should budget at US$50-80 (£30-50) a day. Then again you could always check into **Imperial Hotel** or the **Oberoi Amarvilas** for Christmas and notch up an impressive US$600 (£350) bill on your B&B alone. India can be a great place to pick and choose, save a little on basic accommodation and then treat yourself to the type of meal you could only dream of affording back home. Also, be prepared to spend a fair amount more in Delhi, where not only is the cost of living significantly higher but where it's worth coughing up extra for a half-decent room: penny-pinch in places like Varanasi where, you'll be spending precious little time indoors anyway. A newspaper costs Rs 5 and breakfast for 2 with coffee can come to as little as Rs 100 in a basic 'hotel', but if you intend to eat banana pancakes or pasta in a backpacker restaurant, you can expect to pay more like Rs 100-150 a plate.

Opening hours

Banks are open Mon-Fri 1030-1430, Sat 1030-1230. Top hotels sometimes have a 24-hr money changing service. **Post offices** open Mon-Fri 1000-1700, often shutting for lunch, and Sat mornings. **Government offices** open Mon-Fri 0930-1700, Sat 0930-1300 (some open on alternate Sat only). **Shops** open Mon-Sat 0930-1800. Bazars keep longer hours.

Safety
Personal security

In general the threats to personal security for travellers in India are remarkably small. However, incidents of petty theft and violence directed specifically at tourists have been on the increase so care is necessary in some places, and basic common sense needs to be used with respect to looking after valuables. Follow the same precautions you would when at home. There have been much-reported incidents of severe sexual assault in Delhi, Kolkata and some more rural areas in 2013. Avoid wandering alone outdoors late at night in these places. During daylight hours be careful in remote places, especially when alone. If you are under threat, scream loudly. Be very cautious before accepting food or drink from casual acquaintances, as it may be drugged.

The left-wing Maoist extremist Naxalites are active in east central India. They have a long history of conflict with state and national authorities, including attacks on police and government officials. The Naxalites have not specifically targeted Westerners, but have attacked symbolic targets including Western companies. As a general rule, travellers are advised to be vigilant in the lead up to and on days of national significance, such as Republic Day (26 Jan) and Independence Day (15 Aug) as militants have in the past used such occasions to mount attacks.

Following a major explosion on the Delhi to Lahore (Pakistan) train in Feb 2007 and the Mumbai attacks in Nov 2008, increased security has been implemented on many trains and stations. Similar measures at airports may cause delays for passengers so factor this into your timing. Also check your airline's website for up-to-date information on luggage restrictions.

That said, in the great majority of places visited by tourists, violent crime and personal attacks are extremely rare.

Travel advice

It is better to seek advice from your consulate than from travel agencies. Before you travel you can contact: **British Foreign & Commonwealth Office Travel Advice Unit**, T0845-850 2829 (Pakistan desk T020-7270 2385), www.fco.gov.uk. **US State Department's Bureau of Consular Affairs**, Overseas Citizens Services, Room 4800, Department of State, Washington, DC 20520-4818, USA, T202-647 1488, www.travel.state. gov. **Australian Department of Foreign Affairs Canberra**, Australia, T02-6261 3305, www.smartraveller.gov.au. Canadian official advice is on www.voyage.gc.ca.

Theft

Theft is not uncommon. It is best to keep TCs, passports and valuables with you at all times. Don't regard hotel rooms as being automatically safe; even hotel safes don't guarantee secure storage. Avoid leaving valuables near open windows even when you are in the room. Use your own padlock in a budget hotel when you go out. Pickpockets and other thieves operate in the big cities. Crowded areas are particularly high risk. Take special care of your belongings when getting on or off public transport.

If you have items stolen, they should be reported to the police as soon as possible. Keep a separate record of vital documents, including passport details and numbers of TCs. Larger hotels will be able to assist in contacting and dealing with the police. Dealings with the police can be very difficult and in the worst regions, such as Bihar, even dangerous. The paperwork involved in reporting losses can be time consuming and irritating and your own documentation (eg passport and visas) may be demanded.

In some states the police occasionally demand bribes, though you should not assume that if procedures move slowly you are automatically being expected to offer a bribe. The traffic police are tightening up on traffic offences in some places. They have the right to make on-the-spot fines for speeding and illegal parking. If you face a fine, insist on a receipt. If you have to go to a police station, try to take someone with you.

If you face really serious problems (eg in connection with a driving accident), contact your consular office as quickly as possible. You should ensure you always have your international driving licence and motorbike or car documentation with you.

Confidence tricksters are particularly common where people are on the move, notably around railway stations or places where budget tourists gather. A common plea is some sudden and desperate calamity; sometimes a letter will be produced in English to back up the claim. The demands are likely to increase sharply if sympathy is shown.

Telephone

The international code for India is +91. International Direct Dialling is widely available in privately run call booths, usually labelled on yellow boards with the letters 'PCO-STD-ISD'. You dial the call yourself, and the time and cost are displayed on a computer screen. Cheap rate (2100-0600) means long queues may form outside booths. Telephone calls from hotels are usually more expensive (check price before calling), though some will allow local calls free of charge. Internet phone booths, usually associated with cybercafés, are the cheapest way of calling overseas.

A double ring repeated regularly means it is ringing; equal tones with equal pauses means engaged (similar to the UK). If calling a mobile, rather than ringing, you might hear music while you wait for an answer.

One disadvantage of the tremendous pace of the telecommunications revolution is the fact that millions of telephone numbers go out of date every year. Current telephone directories themselves are often out of date and some of the numbers given in this book will have been changed even as we go to press. Our best advice is if the number in the text does not work, add a '2'. **Directory enquiries**, T197, can be helpful but works only for the local area code.

Mobile phones are for sale everywhere, as are local SIM cards that allow you to make calls within India and overseas at much lower rates than using a 'roaming'

service from your normal provider at home – sometimes for as little as Rs 0.5 per min. Arguably the best service is provided by the government carrier **BSNL/MTNL** but security provisions make connecting to the service virtually impossible for foreigners. Private companies such as **Airtel**, **Vodafone**, **Reliance** and **Tata Indicom** are easier to sign up with, but the deals they offer can be befuddling and are frequently changed. To connect you'll need to complete a form, have a local address or receipt showing the address of your hotel, and present photocopies of your passport and visa plus 2 passport photos to an authorized reseller – most phone dealers will be able to help, and can also sell top-up. **Univercell**, www.univercell.in, and **The Mobile Store**, www.themobilestore.in, are 2 widespread and efficient chains selling phones and sim cards.

India is divided into a number of 'calling circles' or regions, and if you travel outside

the region where your connection is based, eg from Delhi into Uttar Pradesh, you will pay higher 'roaming' charges for making and receiving calls, and any problems that may occur – with 'unverified' documents, for example – can be much harder to resolve.

Time

India doesn't change its clocks, so from the last Sun in Oct to the last Sun in Mar the time is GMT +5½ hrs, and the rest of the year it's +4½ hrs (USA, EST +10½ and +9½ hrs; Australia, EST -5½ and -4½ hrs).

Tipping

A tip of Rs 10 to a bellboy carrying luggage in a modest hotel (Rs 20 in a higher category) would be appropriate. In upmarket restaurants, a 10% tip is acceptable when service is not already included, while in places serving very cheap meals, round off the bill with small change.

Indians don't normally tip taxi drivers but a small extra is welcomed. Porters at airports and railway stations often have a fixed rate displayed but will usually press for more. Ask fellow passengers what a fair rate is.

Tourist information

There are **Government of India** tourist offices in the state capitals, as well as state tourist offices (sometimes **Tourism Development Corporations**) in the Delhi and some towns and places of tourist interest. They produce their own tourist literature, either free or sold at a nominal price, and some also have lists of city hotels and paying guest options. The quality of material is improving though maps are often poor. Many offer tours of the city, neighbouring sights and overnight and regional packages. Some run modest hotels and midway motels with restaurants and may also arrange car hire and guides. The

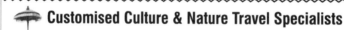

staff in the regional and local offices are usually helpful.

Visas and immigration

For embassies and consulates, see page 298. Virtually all foreign nationals, including children, require a visa to enter India. Nationals of Bhutan and Nepal only require a suitable means of identification. The rules regarding visas change frequently and arrangements for application and collection also vary from town to town so it is essential to check details and costs with the relevant embassy or consulate. These remain closed on Indian national holidays. Now many consulates and embassies are outsourcing the visa process, it's best to find out in advance how long it will take. For example, in London where you used to be able to get a visa in person in a morning if you were prepared to queue, it now takes 3-5 working days and involves 2 trips to the office.

At other offices, it can be much easier to apply in advance by post, to avoid queues and frustratingly low visa quotas. Postal applications take 10-15 working days to process.

Visitors from countries with no Indian representation may apply to the resident British representative, or enquire at the Air India office. An application on the prescribed form should be accompanied by 2 passport photographs and your passport which should be valid 6 months beyond the period of your visit. Note that visas are valid from the date granted, not from the date of entry.

Tourist visa Normally valid for 3-6 months from date of issue, though some nationalities may be granted visas for up to 5 years. Multiple entries permitted, and it is worth requesting this on the application form if you wish to visit neighbouring countries.

Liquor permits

Periodically some Indian states have tried to enforce prohibition. To some degree it is in force in Gujarat, Manipur, Mizoram and Nagaland. When applying for your visa you can ask for an All India Liquor Permit. Foreigners can also get the permit from any Government of India Tourist Office in Delhi or the state capitals. Instant permits are issued by some hotels.

Weights and measures

Metric is in universal use in the cities. In remote areas local measures are sometimes used. One lakh is 100,000 and 1 crore is 10 million.

INDEX